CCH BUSINESS OWNER'S TOOLKIT™

SAFE HARBORS

AN ASSET PROTECTION GUIDE FOR SMALL BUSINESS OWNERS

A *CCH Business Owner's Toolkit*™ Publication

by Nicholas C. Misenti, J.D.

edited by John L. Duoba

CCH INCORPORATED
Chicago

Cover designed by Tim Kaage, Laurel Graphx, Inc.

CCH BUSINESS OWNER'S TOOLKIT™ TEAM

Drew Snider, Publisher, Consumer Media Group (*dsnider@cch.com*) has over 25 years experience with business-information services (SRDS), consumer magazines (*Golfweek*), and home-based software applications (Parsons Technology).

Joel Handelsman (*jhandels@cch.com*) has almost 25 years of experience writing about business, tax, and financial topics. He has been involved in multiple new product and business ventures in the publishing industry, and has held a variety of management positions. Joel holds degrees from Northwestern University's Medill School of Journalism and DePaul University College of Law.

Alice H. Magos (*amagos@cch.com*) has over 35 years of experience running the operations of numerous small businesses. She is the author of the *CCH Business Owner's Toolkit*™ online advice column "Ask Alice." Alice is a popular instructor at small business seminars on accounting, financial planning, and using the Internet; is an accountant and a Certified Financial Planner; and holds degrees from Washington University in St. Louis and Northwestern University.

John L. Duoba (*jduoba@cch.com*) has more than 15 years of small business experience in book and magazine publishing, fulfilling various roles in editorial and production management. He has been involved in the publication of scores of titles, with multiple editions and issues raising the total well into the hundreds. John is a professional journalist and holds a degree from Northwestern University's Medill School of Journalism.

Paul N. Gada (*pgada@cch.com*) has over eight years of legal publishing experience, primarily in dealing with federal and state tax issues. He has helped create numerous editorial products, including newsletters, journals, books and electronic information systems. Paul is an attorney and holds degrees from the John Marshall Law School (LLM. - Tax and Employee Benefits), Southern Illinois University (JD), Northern Illinois University (MBA) and Loyola University of Chicago (BA).

Catherine Gordon (*cgordon@cch.com*) has over 15 years of experience in the tax, business, and financial publishing field and has worked as a tax consultant providing services to individuals as well as large and small companies. Catherine holds a juris doctorate degree from the State University of New York at Buffalo School of Law and a BA in sociology from the State University of New York at Stony Brook.

In addition, we would like to thank Susan M. Jacksack for her contributions to this book.

ABOUT THE AUTHOR

Nicholas C. Misenti is an attorney at law and certified public accountant. Attorney Misenti is of counsel to C.W. Briggs & Associates, P.C., 45 Glastonbury Boulevard, Glastonbury, CT, 06033, where he practices in the areas of estates & trusts, tax, business planning and asset protection law.

You can contact Attorney Misenti at (860) 652-6620 or by e-mail at nmisenti@briggslaw.com.

DEDICATION

I dedicate this book to my wife, Julie, and my children, Kali, Zack, Travis and Forrest. Julie, your love, support and encouragement made the writing of this book possible.

I would also like to thank John Duoba, Drew Snider, the entire CCH Consumer Media Group and, in particular, Susan M. Jacksack, who endorsed my ideas for this book and was instrumental in helping develop and organize the book.

FOREWORD

This book is intended for the small business owner. However, many of the strategies discussed are equally effective in larger businesses. In fact, many of America's wealthiest business owners have relied on these techniques to preserve their family's wealth. For example, when Rockefeller Center went bankrupt, the Rockefellers' protected *all* of their multi-million dollar real estate because they purposely structured and funded their business entities so that all of their business's assets were shielded from liability (this case is discussed in Chapter 8). Small business owners can and should adopt similar wealth-building strategies.

Taken together, all of these strategies can be termed a multi-layered approach to asset protection, offering redundant protection. One strategy alone may be sufficient to prevent loss. Taken together, however, they can present an insurmountable barrier to creditors. Today, it is entirely possible to protect *all* of the business owner's *personal and business assets*, even in the worst of financial circumstances.

Many of these strategies have been detailed in academic literature for some time, but have not become known to the public. In part, this is due to the fact that small business owners have relied on books that offer instructions on how to *create* a corporation or LLC, but offer virtually *no* guidance at all in what is perhaps the most important topic of all—how to protect personal and business assets from liability.

This failure is surprising given the fact that limiting liability is the very goal in creating a corporation or LLC. The result is that, today, most small business owners are not structuring or operating their businesses to avoid liability. Thus, owners are unknowingly exposing their personal and business assets to a high risk of loss, many times under the illusion that their corporation or LLC will afford them protection.

Typically, owners find out the truth only when financial troubles strike. At that point, usually it is too late, or extremely difficult, to preserve wealth, and the result is a significant loss of personal and business assets, and financial disaster. In many cases, the courts will thwart an attempt to implement asset protection strategies in the midst of a financial crisis. On the other hand, when everything is put into place in advance of financial difficulties, experience proves that the courts will uphold the validity of these strategies, even to the extent of preserving a business owner's entire fortune, and affording creditors no remedy at all. The time to act is now!

The strategies detailed in this book have been proven effective by actual court cases. Accordingly, readers will be guided by the factual situations taken from these cases. Some strategies are simple and low-cost to implement. For example, a million dollars of stock may be a total loss as a result of a major lawsuit or bankruptcy filing, but this *same million dollars of stock* invested in the *same exact companies* through an IRA would be *fully protected* from liability in most cases. As one court has said, the result seems grossly unfair to creditors, but it is the law. The courts have no power to change the law, but you have the power to use it to your advantage.

Other strategies are more complex, expensive and complicated to implement (e.g., an offshore trust or the operation of a business through two entities—an operating company with no vulnerable assets and a holding company with assets). As strategies are detailed in this guide, alternatives will be contrasted and compared in terms of costs, complexity and effectiveness, thus affording owners the opportunity of choosing a strategy based on their needs.

Many features in this book should make asset protection planning easier to understand and implement. Laws vary from state to state. Accordingly, chapters contain state-specific information and alternative strategies that can be used in different states. While multi-layered asset protection strategies are the most effective, they also can be quite complex. For that reason, we offer the information in this book to guide you, but urge that before attempting to implement these asset protection strategies, you always consult with the appropriate professionals that can make sure all is in order.

Drew Snider

Publisher, Consumer Media Group

Table of Contents

Table of Contents

Part I

Are Your Assets at Risk?

Every business owner needs a comprehensive asset protection plan because owning and operating a business can be risky. For example, businesses may default on open accounts with vendors, or default on mortgages or other secured loans from banks. Further, many of these debts may be personally guaranteed by the owners. Potentially, owners or employees may commit negligent acts while carrying out company activities.

Moreover, consumers may bring claims for injuries suffered due to the sale of defective products, or claims based on unfair and deceptive business practices, which (though unwarranted) could produce a financial settlement. Also, claims by employees, such as wrongful discharge and sexual harassment, are on the rise. These risks could bring about financial disaster for business owners, resulting in the loss of both business and personal assets.

A comprehensive asset protection plan, which can be designed based on the principles explained in this book, can prevent or significantly reduce these risks, and insulate business and personal assets from the claims of creditors. Unfortunately, many small business owners are unaware of these principles, or simply misunderstand them.

In order to limit exposure to events that could cost a company its assets or close it down completely, many small business owners form a corporation or limited liability company (LLC), hoping to protect the owners' personal assets outside of their businesses. However, many business owners are unaware that *significant exceptions* exist to this limited liability. And when an exception applies, *personal* liability is imposed on the owners, despite the fact that a corporation or LLC exists. Accordingly, owners' homes, cars, personal bank accounts, investment portfolios, etc., are all subject to the claims of business creditors. With knowledge and planning, however, these exceptions can be avoided, and thus limited liability preserved.

Beyond avoiding these exceptions, much more should be done to protect personal and business wealth. For example, most business owners mistakenly believe that assets within a corporation or LLC are automatically shielded from liability. However, most business owners face the greatest risk of liability from business transactions, and not personal dealings. Therefore, the business entity's assets, which can be significant in a successful operation, are exposed to the greatest risk of loss. Yet, a corporation or LLC can be *structured, funded and operated* so that the business's assets are not exposed to liability. And in the following chapters, we will show you how.

Further, personal and business assets can be placed in protected categories and thus out of the reach of creditors, so that, even in a worst-case scenario (e.g., a judgment in a major lawsuit or a bankruptcy filing), there will be *no* loss of assets in any event. This can be accomplished through state and federal exemption planning, and through the use of asset protection trusts.

Your exempt assets can usually include a residence; pension plans; wages; annuities; and various categories of personal property, including household goods, tools of the trade, and motor vehicles, among other things. Many categories of exempt assets have dollar caps. Moreover, the exemptions and the caps vary widely from state to state.

Exemption planning is a very important part of an asset protection plan. In fact, in some cases, it may shield the majority of your assets. However, once serious financial problems arise, it's often too late to transfer unprotected assets into exempt categories. The planning must be done beforehand, or you run the risk of having your transfers treated as ineffective or even fraudulent by the courts.

This multi-layered approach to asset protection offers redundant protection. One strategy alone may be sufficient to prevent loss. Taken together, however, they can present an insurmountable barrier to creditors. Today, it is entirely possible to protect *all* of the business owner's *personal and business assets*, even in the worst of financial circumstances.

Chapter 1: How Creditors Get Your Assets gives a summary of the types of liens, including judgment liens, that you may encounter as a small business owner and how they can cost you. Recognizing the dangers that certain liens pose for your business will allow you to prepare for such possibilities. We also offer strategies for battling those liens actually filed against you, as well as ways to avoid them in the first place.

Chapter 2: Bankruptcy—An Overview discusses the purpose of the bankruptcy code, for creditors and debtors, and the protections it offers under the law. Moreover, Congress is seriously considering bankruptcy reform for the first time in decades, and the implications of these potential changes are covered as well.

Chapter 3: Effective Asset Exemption Planning focuses on developing an overall understanding of how asset exemptions work. After reading this chapter, you will be able to decide whether an exemption will, or will not, protect an asset that you own, and how to most generously take advantage of it.

Chapter 4: Avoiding Challenges to Asset Transfers is an integral part of effective exemption planning. It covers strategies that can be used to make legal asset transfers, including the conversion of nonexempt assets into exempt assets.

Chapter 5: Using Asset Protection Trusts explains how you can, in effect, create another exemption by placing your assets in a sophisticated form of trust. Properly formed asset protection trusts will make your property unavailable to creditors even when no other exemptions apply.

After reading Part I, take an inventory of the assets you own, and how you own them. Then compare this list to the asset exemptions available in your state and, if applicable, under the federal bankruptcy code. In doing this, you will be able to gauge the degree of risk you face and make adjustments (conversions of assets) accordingly.

As detailed in Chapter 4, timing is critical in asset exemption planning. Ideally, then, you'll do this planning before your business is formed. Nevertheless, an owner of a thriving business also is an ideal candidate for effective exemption planning. Significant wealth can be protected before any serious problems develop.

The poorest candidate for exemption planning is the small business owner who is already in the midst of a financial crisis. Even here, however, steps can be taken, albeit cautiously, to protect assets. In this situation especially, you should seek the guidance of a professional advisor before undertaking any planning steps.

Chapter 1

How Creditors Get
Your Assets

Opening a business is a risky venture. However, a comprehensive asset protection plan can eliminate or significantly reduce these risks, and shield business and personal assets from the claims of creditors, should something go wrong. In this way, asset protection planning is just one aspect of business formation.

In order to best accomplish this goal, you need to be familiar with the nature of the debtor-creditor relationship, including the kinds of "liens" creditors can place against your assets. These liens have varying implications and significance in different types of proceedings between debtors and creditors.

Creditors with liens are termed "secured creditors." If they are not paid, secured creditors can, in effect, seize your assets to satisfy debts they are owed. Understanding the types of liens and how they work will allow you to effectively battle them in court, and possibly invalidate or eliminate them altogether.

THE DEBTOR-CREDITOR RELATIONSHIP

The world's economy is dependent on millions, perhaps billions, of debtor-creditor relationships. At every level, goods and services are provided in exchange for a promise, explicit or implicit, to pay for those goods and services. Almost every individual and business in America either owes money or is owed money, or both. It is these debtor-creditor relationships that make it essential to protect assets from creditors who would seize them to satisfy debts.

Debtor-creditor relationships are created in one of two ways:

- **Voluntarily** — Examples include loans of all types, credit lines and the use of credit cards. When a person purchases a car and finances the cost, the purchaser is voluntarily incurring debt. The same is true when a credit card is used to purchase goods or services; the purchaser is voluntarily creating a debt to the credit card company by using the card to make the purchase.

In fact, when a person goes into a restaurant and orders dinner, a debt is created because the food is prepared and served by the restaurant in exchange for the diner's implicit promise to pay for it. Both a dinner out and a mortgage on a house create a debt—but the debt to the restaurant is paid immediately. The mortgage, however, illustrates why asset protection is so important. If the payments aren't made, the creditor can often force the sale of the house to satisfy the mortgage debt.

- **Involuntarily** — If the employee of a small business is at fault in a traffic accident and injures someone, the business can be required to compensate the injured person. Similarly, if a house painter applies the wrong paint, or damages the carpets, a debt is created. The homeowner may insist that the painter correct the problem or provide compensation for the damage. Involuntary debt is the hidden risk to assets that can't be avoided. The impact of that risk, however, can be minimized.

TYPES OF LIENS

Creditors can be unsecured or secured. An unsecured, or general, creditor has a general claim against a debtor, which is not secured by any particular asset of the debtor. An unsecured creditor has the weakest claim, which may go unpaid. However, an unsecured creditor may become a secured creditor after a lawsuit and judgment. A secured creditor, who has a claim on a particular asset, can use the court system to seize the asset and to satisfy the debt. This clearly presents a significant risk for the business owner.

How does a creditor become a secured creditor and obtain an interest in a debtor's property? These interests are referred to as liens against the property in question. Certain liens can destroy asset protection planning, as illustrated in the explanations that follow. It is imperative that you have an understanding of the different types of liens you may encounter as a small business owner:

- Consensual

  — Purchase-Money Security Liens

  — Non-Purchase-Money Security Liens

- Statutory

    — Mechanic's Liens

    — Tax Liens

- Judgment

With this as a backdrop, we'll then examine how creditors might seek to get your assets through these types of liens, and what you can do, as an individual and as a small business owner, to maximize your protection against those creditors. The strategies outlined will address a broad spectrum of topics, from forms of property ownership to structuring debt to minimize exposure. The bankruptcy rules will play a large part in this, so be warned that Congress is currently considering legislation that would fundamentally change the rules relating to protecting assets by filing bankruptcy.

Consensual Liens

These are liens to which you voluntarily consent, as a result of a loan or other advance of credit. A homebuyer consents to a bank taking a security interest in the home when a mortgage is obtained. A security interest also is created when a car dealer arranges for financing for a car buyer. The property purchased secures the buyer's obligation to pay for the property. Consensual liens include:

- **Purchase-Money Security Interest Liens** — Here, the creditor extends credit to the debtor specifically for the purchase of the property that secures the debt. Examples include a first mortgage on a home, a car loan, and situations in which the seller finances the purchase of property, such as furniture, through a credit agreement.

- **Non-Purchase-Money Security Interest Liens** — Here, the debtor puts up property he or she already owns as collateral for a loan. The loan proceeds are then used to pay expenses (or perhaps to buy other property). Examples include a second mortgage (or refinancing of a mortgage) on a home or a loan used to pay operating expenses with previously owned office equipment put up as collateral.

Both types of consensual liens are usually non-possessory, meaning the debtor takes, or retains, possession of the property. However, it's possible for either type of consensual lien to be possessory. In that case, the creditor takes possession of the collateral. A loan from a pawnbroker, for example, usually would create a possessory, non-purchase-money security interest lien in the collateral.

While this seems very straightforward, the *type* of debt can have a large impact on the creditor's rights if a debtor defaults. The rules vary from state to state, but characteristics of a debt are critical to understand if assets are to be protected. Issues include:

Who is holding the property that secures the debt: the debtor or the creditor? In a car loan, the debtor has possession of the property. When a loan is obtained from a pawnshop, the creditor has possession of the property securing the loan.

Was the debt incurred to purchase property or not? For example, a mortgage loan is a purchase money loan since the proceeds were used to purchase a residence. In contrast, a refinancing loan is not a purchase money loan. The homeowner already owned the property.

What are the characteristics of the property purchased? This is often the essential inquiry when it comes to asset protection. The states, as well as the federal government, have a wide variety of laws relating to what assets are protected from creditors and how they are protected. The primary mechanism for protecting selected assets is a concept called "exemptions." In essence, the law may declare that certain property simply cannot be seized by a creditor.

For many people, the most important exemption is the homestead exemption. This protects part or all of the value of a residence from creditors other than lenders holding mortgages. Each state has its own rules. Some protect the residence fully; others provide little or no protection. Other types of property that might be protected are personal items and business tools of the trade (for more details, see our discussion in Chapter 3).

Statutory Liens

In certain circumstances, creditors obtain security interests by the operation of state (or federal) laws. These liens include:

- **Mechanic's Liens** — This type of lien arises when a contractor or mechanic performs work on property and is not paid. Examples include a contractor who installs a furnace in a home, or an auto mechanic who performs repairs to a car. This lien is a security interest in the property. If the owner tries to sell the property, the debtor will have a secured interest in the portion of the proceeds needed to pay the debt.

- **Tax Liens** — This type of lien is placed against property by the local, state or federal government, as authorized by statute, for delinquent taxes, including property, income and estate taxes.

Judgment Liens

This is the most dangerous form of lien, but one which the informed business owner may be able to eliminate. A judicial lien is created when a court grants a creditor an interest in the debtor's property, after a court judgment. These can arise in a wide variety of circumstances. For example, if a driver negligently injures someone in an accident, the injured person is likely to sue for damages. To the extent that insurance doesn't cover the judgment, a judicial lien may be placed against the negligent driver's property to secure payment of the claim to the injured party. A plaintiff who obtains a monetary judgment is termed a "judgment creditor." The defendant becomes a "judgment debtor." The judgment in the lawsuit provides the basis for the lien.

If the debt is not paid, the judgment creditor can then seek to enforce (or execute) the judgment. This can be accomplished by garnishing wages, seizing a bank account, or placing a lien against the debtor's property. The lien is the first step by the judgment creditor in a process that will culminate in a sale of the attached property, to satisfy the judgment debt.

Any lien placed on the defendant's assets as a result of a court judgment is known as a judgment lien. If a lien were placed on a home, the judgment creditor would then seek to foreclose on the property, in the same way a mortgage holder such as a bank would foreclose if it were not paid.

In this chapter, the term "judgment lien" is used in its strictest sense: a lien attributed to a court judgment, where *the court judgment* itself is the basis for the lien. An example would be a plaintiff who is awarded a monetary judgment against a defendant in a lawsuit based on negligence, and who is then granted an order of attachment against the debtor's property.

In contrast, this definition excludes a judgment based on a pre-existing debt or, more importantly, a pre-existing lien (i.e., a prior consensual lien or statutory lien). Thus, for example, this definition would exclude a judgment in a mortgage foreclosure. This distinction is critically important in discerning what types of liens against exempt property can be eliminated, as will become apparent later in this chapter.

BATTLING LIENS AGAINST YOU

When a creditor attempts to enforce a lien against your protected property, in a state court or bankruptcy proceeding, that lien may be invalidated or eliminated if it is a judgment lien, as that term is defined above. Or you may be able to bifurcate the lien, stripping away some of its value, in bankruptcy court.

As a general rule, consensual liens and statutory liens *cannot* be eliminated, even when they are attached to protected assets. So, these types of liens can destroy an asset exemption status granted to you under the law (see Chapter 3 for more on asset exemptions). The result is really no different than if the asset were not classified as exempt. Clearly, this understanding is important, as an examination of the asset exemption tables alone can lead to a conclusion that an asset is exempt and thus protected, when, in fact, it is fully subject to the claims of creditors.

This general rule is subject to a few exceptions involving non-purchase-money, non-possessory liens, which are discussed below and in Chapter 2. Further, the rules on lien elimination differ, to some degree, in state court proceedings and bankruptcy proceedings. These differences are also addressed below.

Eliminating Liens

The ability to eliminate judgment liens on exempt assets can be highly significant to the small business owner.

Example

John Smith, a Nevada resident, forms an LLC to operate his business. Smith's major supplier allows him to use an open account, but requires that he personally guarantee his LLC's contract on the account.

After two years, John experiences serious financial difficulties and defaults on the open account. At that time, the balance on the account is $80,000.

Let's say John's LLC, at this time, has no assets. His only personal asset is his residence, which has a value of $100,000 and a first mortgage with a balance of $40,000.

The supplier sues John personally based on his guarantee, receives a judgment of $80,000, and places a judgment lien on John's residence in this amount.

However, Nevada allows an asset exemption for a residence in the amount of $125,000. Thus, Smith's residence is an exempt asset (see Chapter 3). The judgment lien cannot be enforced.

Generally, a lien can be eliminated only if three conditions are met:

1. **The lien is against a class of assets known as exempt —** Determine whether the asset is exempt, under the state's post-judgment asset exemptions or under the federal bankruptcy exemptions, as the situation dictates (the state and federal governments allow debtors to keep certain property in such situations, so as not to completely ruin a person beyond financial repair, see Chapter 3). In a bankruptcy proceeding,

compare the federal and state exemptions, unless the state has opted out of the federal exemptions.

2. **The lien is a *type* of lien that can be eliminated** — If the asset is exempt, determine whether liens against the asset are of a type that can be eliminated. Remember, most judgment liens can be eliminated, while other liens, provided that they are valid, usually cannot be eliminated. In addition, as discussed later, the federal bankruptcy code allows for additional liens to be eliminated beyond what state laws allow.

3. **The amount of the lien impairs the exemption** — Calculate the amount of liens that *cannot* be eliminated. This amount is equal to the value of the asset less the amount of the exemption. Under this calculation, liens subject to elimination can always be discharged in their entirety if the asset is the object of an unlimited exemption, because the value of the asset equals the exemption amount. When the asset exemption is limited, or the value of the asset is much larger than the exemption, the amount of the liens that can not be eliminated will be significant, so that any new liens added to the property, such as judgment liens, cannot be eliminated. Detailed examples later in this chapter show how to calculate what portion, if any, of a lien can be eliminated.

These three conditions are discussed in detail below.

Lien Elimination on Exempt Assets

The first condition is really self-explanatory. Either an asset is exempt under the applicable state or federal law or it is not. It also follows that if the asset is not exempt, a lien against it can't be eliminated on the grounds that it impairs an exemption.

Each state enumerates asset exemptions in its laws. These exemptions are sometimes referred to as "post-judgment asset exemptions." In a state court proceeding, after a judgment is rendered against you, you will have to rely on your own state's exemptions. These asset exemptions are listed state-by-state in the Appendices of this book.

In a bankruptcy proceeding, certain assets are also exempt, and thus outside the reach of creditors. The federal bankruptcy law includes its own list of exemptions, which differ from the state lists. However, under the bankruptcy code, each state *may* allow its residents to choose between the federal bankruptcy asset exemptions and the state's post-judgment asset exemptions, when a federal bankruptcy action is filed.

Alternatively, a state may "opt out" of the federal exemptions and give its residents only the right to use the state's exemptions in a federal bankruptcy proceeding.

Plan Smart

As discussed in more detail in Chapter 3, exemptions vary widely from state to state. Some states have developed reputations for writing laws that favor either debtors or creditors.

For example, Florida, Texas and Iowa have generous exemptions that favor debtors. These states provide debtors with, among other things, basically an unlimited homestead exemption. Thus, in these states, it is possible for a debtor to protect a fully owned home worth millions of dollars in either a state court proceeding or a bankruptcy proceeding.

In contrast, Illinois has a reputation of having laws that favor creditors. It provides a debtor with only a $7,500 homestead exemption. Illinois has also opted out of the federal exemption system, so its residents don't have the option of using the more generous federal exemptions in bankruptcy.

Under current bankruptcy law, residency is determined as of 180 days (six months) before the date the proceeding is filed. However, be aware that Congress is considering changing this period.

So, changing your residence (e.g., from Illinois to Texas) can prove to be a very effective asset protection strategy. The move includes a conversion of assets that were not exempt in the old jurisdiction to a state where you can take advantage of an expansive list of exemptions. However, as discussed in Chapter 4, residence changes and asset conversions must be approached cautiously.

Liens Eligible for Elimination

The types of liens on exempt assets that can be eliminated depend, to some degree, on whether you are involved in a state court proceeding or a bankruptcy proceeding. The general rule is that, in either proceeding, only judgment liens against exempt property can be eliminated. However, even certain judgment liens cannot be eliminated.

More specifically, the following rules and exceptions tend to apply across the states and in bankruptcy proceedings:

- Judgment liens usually *cannot* be eliminated when these liens are for any of these situations:

  — alimony or child support

  — an order of restitution based on a criminal case

  — a judgment based on *a prior consensual lien* (e.g., a mortgage) *or a prior statutory lien* (e.g., a tax lien).

- Consensual liens and statutory liens on exempt property usually *cannot* be eliminated at all. This category includes purchase-money security interest liens, non-purchase-money security interest liens, mechanic's liens, and tax liens. Examples of liens from this category include first mortgages, second mortgages and home refinancings; car loans; loans for the purchase of supplies, office equipment, etc, where the assets purchased are put up as collateral for the loan; and delinquent property, income and estate taxes. Clearly, this category is very broad. Here, as a general rule, an asset exemption will be of no value, to the extent of these liens. However, there are exceptions that can invalidate a lien, and these are discussed later in this chapter.

State Laws. It is surprising that most states do *not* expressly describe, by statute, the types of liens that can be eliminated in state court when the liens impair an exemption, as this is obviously such an important issue.

North Carolina is one of the few states that do provide clear-cut rules by statute. Other states, which typically do not have such express provisions, usually rely on court decisions, coupled with limited statutory provisions, to define the types of liens that can be eliminated. The general rules we've outlined above are usually good guidelines.

However, in a few states, the courts may have developed narrow exceptions to the general rules. For example, Alabama courts have ruled that a judicial lien arising from a tort judgment cannot be eliminated. While an exception such as this will be rare, you should still be aware that, due to the vagaries of the law in each state, exceptions may exist in a few instances.

Bankruptcy Laws. Generally, the bankruptcy code follows the rules described above for eliminating liens that impair exempt assets. In addition, however, the code allows for the elimination of certain liens that impair exempt property that cannot be eliminated in a state court proceeding (see Chapter 2 for more on bankruptcy).

Warning

If you face any type of lien, don't automatically assume it can or cannot be eliminated. Always consult an attorney. In rare instances, an exception may exist to the rules discussed above that will not allow lien elimination in your particular state.

On the other hand, sometimes an argument can be made that will allow lien elimination when it first appeared that this was not possible.

Calculation of Lien Impairment

As previously described, only certain types of liens can be eliminated, and then only if the liens are attached to exempt assets.

The final step in lien elimination is to calculate whether the amount of a lien actually impairs an exemption. If all of the liens encumbering the property are of a type that cannot be eliminated (e.g., consensual purchase-money security liens), there is no need to proceed with the calculation: None of the liens can be eliminated. However, once a determination is made that elimination can be done, the *exact amount* of the lien that can be eliminated must be calculated.

Calculation of the amount that a lien impairs an exemption becomes especially important in a bankruptcy proceeding, because there is a greater opportunity in that situation to eliminate non-purchase-money, non-possessory liens (as discussed in Chapter 2).

Liens that are dischargeable can be eliminated to the extent that they "impair" an exempt asset. The bankruptcy code provides that a lien shall be considered to impair an exemption to the extent that the sum of all the liens on the property, plus the amount of the exemption, exceeds the value of the property. As a rule, this formula also will be followed in state courts.

Another simpler way of looking at the calculation is this: The total dollar amount of liens that *cannot* be eliminated is equal to the value of the property minus the exemption.

This version of the formula makes it clear that when a particular item of property is subject to an unlimited exemption (e.g., an unlimited homestead exemption in Florida), *all* of the liens on the property can be eliminated, provided, of course, the liens are of a type that can be eliminated if they impair an exemption (e.g., most judgment liens). Here, the value of the property will equal the exemption. Thus, the formula will always yield a result of *zero* for the amount of the liens that *cannot* be eliminated.

Unfortunately, when the property is subject to a cap on the amount exempt, the effect of the rule will be that, in many cases, what appears to be a lien that can be eliminated will not be deemed to impair the exemption. Thus, an "exempt" asset may be lost.

Example

John Smith files for bankruptcy. He owns an item of property that qualifies as household goods in a state that allows him to use his state's exemption, which is $20,000. The value of the property is $40,000. A non-purchase-money, non-possessory lien on the property totals $10,000. As described in Chapter 2, this type of lien is eligible for elimination in a bankruptcy proceeding.

It may first appear that the exemption is impaired, as the lien of $10,000 invades the $20,000 exemption. However, this is not the case. The total of the lien of $10,000, plus the amount of the exemption $20,000, equals $30,000. This does not exceed the value of the property ($40,000). Thus, there is no impairment, and the liens cannot be eliminated.

Looking at it another way, the result is the same. The amount of the lien that cannot be eliminated is equal to the value of the property, $40,000, minus the exemption, $20,000, which amounts to $20,000, when the lien here is only $10,000. Thus, no part of the lien can be eliminated.

If Smith had liens that totaled $30,000, and the property still had a value of $40,000, then $10,000 of these liens would be deemed to impair his exemption, and, thus, could be eliminated. ($30,000 liens plus the $20,000 exemption equals $50,000. $50,000 less the $40,000 value of property equals $10,000. Or, the value of the property, $40,000, less the amount of the exemption, $20,000, equals liens that cannot be eliminated, $20,000. The balance of the liens above $20,000, which is $10,000, can be eliminated).

There can be variations among the states with respect to laws governing liens and calculation of the exemption impairment. States will typically follow the bankruptcy rules described above. However, this may not always be the case.

In the last example, where the liens totaled $30,000, it may be possible in some states to eliminate the entire amount of the liens, on the grounds that elimination of liens is an all or nothing proposition: i.e., if there is *any* impairment of the exemption (here, impairment is calculated at $10,000), then the *total amount* of the liens is eliminated.

Example

John Smith personally owns an item of property that qualifies as a tool of the trade in a state that allows him to use his state's exemption, which is $20,000. The value of the property is $40,000. Purchase-money liens on the property total $30,000. This type of lien cannot be eliminated in, or out of, a bankruptcy proceeding.

Smith suffers a judgment in the amount of $10,000 from a lawsuit for negligence. The judgment creditor places a lien on Smith's tools of the trade. Judgment liens of this type can be eliminated. Further, the judgment lien impairs Smith's exemption under the formula, and can be discharged.

The total of the liens of $40,000, plus the amount of the exemption $20,000, equals $60,000. This amount exceeds the value of the property, $40,000. Thus, up to the amount of this difference, $20,000, can be eliminated. The judgment lien is for $10,000. Thus, it can be eliminated in its entirety.

Looking at the calculation another way, the result is the same. The liens that cannot be eliminated are equal to the value of the property, $40,000, minus the exemption, $20,000. Here, that amounts to $20,000. A consensual lien of $30,000 already consumes more than this amount. Thus, any liens beyond the consensual lien can be eliminated, provided they are subject to elimination, as in this case.

In any case involving lien impairment of an exempt asset, it is wise to consult with an attorney before concluding how much of a lien can be eliminated in the particular state in question.

Plan Smart

The prior two examples demonstrate that, in some cases, encumbering an asset with a consensual lien may make a subsequent judgment lien dischargable. This type of planning is discussed in Chapter 3.

Timing the Calculation. Most states calculate lien impairment only when there is an attempt at a forced sale of the property (i.e., foreclosure of the lien). In some states, however, the calculation may be done at the time the property is attached. In this situation, the judgment debtor may be able to have the lien removed in advance of any foreclosure proceeding. This would allow the owner to sell the property free of the judgment lien.

For the most part, judgment liens will represent the most significant example of liens that can be eliminated when they impair an exemption. But the fact that a judgment lien is usually valid for 10 to 20 years can have planning implications.

Plan Smart

A crafty judgment creditor could attach a debtor's home while the home was exempt, but wait to foreclose until the value of the home went up and the amount of the first mortgage went down, so that, according the formula used to calculate lien impairment, the judgment lien no longer impaired the exemption.

In that case, the best solution for the debtor may be a Chapter 7 bankruptcy proceeding. There, calculation is determined as of the date the proceeding is filed. This strategy eliminates the waiting game that some creditors may play.

Of course, in states such as Florida with an unlimited exemption for residences, this strategy would not be necessary, as the home will always remain immune from judicial liens, regardless of how long the judgment creditor waits.

Note, however, that the Chapter 7 filing also eliminates a related problem. If a judgment creditor places a lien on property (e.g., a home), the debtor will find it impossible to sell the property. Because liens run with the property, any buyer would take the property subject to the judgment lien. Thus, there would be no buyers. A bankruptcy proceeding terminates the judgment lien, which allows the owner to sell the property at a later date.

The following example illustrates different results due to specific state laws:

Example

Nancy Wagner, a Nevada resident, owns a residence worth $150,000 with a first mortgage of $100,000. Nevada exempts a residence in the amount of $125,000.

A judgment is rendered against Wagner in the amount of $80,000. At this time, the judgment creditor cannot foreclose on the property because the lien impairs the exemption, and could be eliminated: the value of the residence, $150,000, less the exemption, $125,000, equals the amount of liens that cannot be eliminated, $25,000. Already, the first mortgage exceeds this amount. Thus, the judicial lien can be eliminated in its entirety.

Now let's say that 10 years later the home is worth $250,000 and the first mortgage totals $30,000. The results are different: the value of the residence, $250,000, less the exemption, $125,000, equals the amount of liens that cannot be eliminated, $125,000. The first mortgage totals only $30,000. Thus, another $95,000 of liens cannot be eliminated ($125,000 less $30,000). This means that no part of the judicial lien can be eliminated, and Wagner will lose her home to foreclosure.

In this situation, Wagner should have considered filing a Chapter 7 bankruptcy proceeding 10 years earlier, when the entire judicial lien could have been eliminated.

Now let's say that Wagner is a Florida resident. Florida has an unlimited exemption for a residence.

Due to the unlimited exemption, the home will always be exempt. A waiting strategy by a judgment creditor would be ineffective. The value of the home, and the value of the exemption, will always be equal. As a result, the calculation will always result in the full value of the judicial lien being subject to elimination.

In this situation, Wagner would only need to consider a bankruptcy filing if she were interested in selling the home, and she were unable to have the lien removed before a forced sale of the property by the judgment creditor. However, luckily for her, Florida is one of the states that provide that creditors cannot attach an exempt asset. Judgment debtors do not have to wait until there is a forced sale to calculate lien impairment or have a lien removed. Thus, the lien can be removed immediately, making a bankruptcy action unnecessary.

Lien Stripping or Bifurcation

A small business owner may at some point find it necessary to consider filing bankruptcy to protect an exempt asset. Therefore, every small business owner should have an understanding of some bankruptcy basics (see Chapter 2). However, one specific bankruptcy rule regarding lien elimination can be an important factor if you are a small business owner trying to decide how to *finance* your business.

The bankruptcy code contains an unusual rule not found in state laws regulating liens, which is termed bifurcation of liens, or "lien stripping." This can be a very significant asset protection tool for debtors in a bankruptcy proceeding.

Under the bankruptcy code, a lien, other than a lien secured solely by a personal residence, is deemed secured only to the extent of the value of the property, at the time of the bankruptcy filing. Any excess balance is deemed unsecured and is "stripped away."

Remember, only a secured lien can impair an exemption. Thus, to the extent the loan is deemed unsecured, it cannot impair the debtor's exempt property.

The lien in this situation will still be valid, but only *to the extent of the full value of the property*. Thus, if the lien is of a type that cannot ordinarily be eliminated, the excess of the debt above the value of the property will be discharged.

Note that this rule applies against exempt and nonexempt property, as only the excess above the value of the property is eliminated.

In short, the effect of this provision will usually be to reduce, but not eliminate, liens that impair both exempt and nonexempt assets. Liens in either case will be reduced to an amount equal to the value of the secured property. Therefore, bifurcation can result in significant savings.

Example

John owns a car with a value of $20,000, which is subject to a lien of $28,000 for a car loan.

In a bankruptcy proceeding, under the bifurcation concept, the lien will be valued at $20,000. The balance of the lien, $8,000, is "stripped" away. This excess is not automatically eliminated. Instead, it is simply no longer secured by the car. However, because the excess is unsecured, it usually will be eliminated in a bankruptcy proceeding.

As a result, the creditor holds a secured loan in the amount of $20,000, and an unsecured loan for $8,000.

Of course, a purchase-money security interest lien cannot be eliminated, even when it impairs an exempt asset. The real value of bifurcation is that John, in all likelihood, will only have to pay back $20,000 of the loan, as unsecured debts are typically discharged in bankruptcy. Thus, John will save $8,000.

When bifurcation is applied, the choice will be to pay back the secured portion in one lump sum in a Chapter 7 bankruptcy, or over three to five years in a Chapter 13 bankruptcy. (A comparison of these two bankruptcy chapters is discussed in Chapter 2.)

Because most debtors can't raise the required lump sum payment, and do not want to surrender the property to the creditor, bifurcation of liens takes place most often in a Chapter 13 filing.

Plan Smart

For many years, courts struggled in deciding how to value property for purposes of lien stripping. Some courts held that the value should be the wholesale value, while other courts ruled that replacement value (a much higher value) should be used.

Recently, the U.S. Supreme Court ruled (to the cheers of creditors) that replacement value must be used because, in most cases, debtors end up keeping the property by paying the stripped down amount of the lien. The appropriate value, the court reasoned, should be replacement value, because this is the cost the debtor would pay if he or she lost the property to the creditor, and then had to replace it.

Bifurcation, or lien stripping, is not available in any state. It is entirely a creature of federal bankruptcy law. (However, in very limited circumstances, a homeowner in some states does not have to pay a deficiency judgment, which occurs when his or her home is lost through foreclosure and a balance remains on the loan after the home is sold.) The deficiency also could be discharged as an unsecured debt in a Chapter 7 bankruptcy proceeding (see Chapter 2). Note that, in contrast to this narrow exception, bifurcation, when it's available in a bankruptcy proceeding, allows the debtor to strip the lien *and keep the property,* provided the stripped-down lien is paid.

Lien Stripping for Personal Residences

It's important to note that lien stripping is not available for a lien secured solely by a personal residence. This provision was added to the bankruptcy law in 1994. During the late 1980s, a secondary market developed for mortgages: Banks would write mortgages, and then sell the mortgages to investment companies that, in turn, would sell stock to investors. In effect, investors would buy into the mortgages, and the mortgages would be traded as securities, similar to stocks and bonds.

Congress clearly had these investors, and not debtors, in mind when it added this restriction on lien stripping for personal residence loans. The intent here is to prevent debtors in bankruptcy from voiding *any portion* of a lien on a mortgage, even when the amount owed on the loan greatly exceeds the value of the residence, and when the owner intends on keeping the home. The result is that the full amount of the loan must be repaid. (Of course, if the owner gives up the home, the excess debt above the value of the home will be discharged as unsecured.) In doing this, Congress intended to make the market for the mortgages more secure and thus more attractive to investors. Thus, a so-called "125 percent home equity mortgage"—wherein a homeowner borrows, against the home, 100 percent of its value, plus an additional 25 percent—represents an extremely risky way to finance a business.

Warning

The small business owner will frequently consider funding a business through a second mortgage, or a refinancing, on a personal residence. However, because of the previously stated provision, you would be wise to heed this advice: Don't do it, or at least do it only after serious consideration of the possible consequences.

Specifically, consider this option only if you are completely *sure you can pay the mortgage (without a return from your business) or you are prepared in the event that you lose your house. Here, in a worst-case scenario, the small business owner would lose the home to foreclosure. You could then file a Chapter 7 bankruptcy proceeding to eliminate any deficiency (balance left after sale of the home), and thus be completely free of any remaining portion of the mortgage.*

Clearly, if you had a spouse, children, pets, etc., you would be taking a significant risk here unless you were completely sure you could pay the loan.

The risks of home loss would not be as great for a single person who could easily move to an apartment, or a family that could easily move into a home supplied by a relative.

The rule to remember is this: Be prepared to pay the full balance of the mortgages, or you will lose your home.

Despite the general rule, two exceptions may apply so as to allow lien stripping of a mortgage on a personal residence:

1. **Loans based on a home plus other collateral** — Lien stripping is prevented only when the lien is secured "solely" by a personal residence. Court decisions have made it clear that when the debtor has given other collateral (in addition to the personal residence; e.g., office equipment) as security for the mortgage, lien stripping will be allowed. Thus, if you will be taking out a second mortgage or refinancing your home, you should consider offering additional collateral, such as furniture, as security for the loan. This can be done under the guise of seeking better terms from the lender, such as a lower interest rate.

2. **Some second mortgages** — Many (but not all) bankruptcy courts follow a rule that makes a second mortgage totally unsecured if the first mortgage balance equals or exceeds the value of the personal residence. This exception will not apply in the case of a refinancing of a mortgage, since in a refinancing the new mortgage pays off the first mortgage. The exception is predicated on there being two distinct mortgages (a first and a second mortgage). For this reason, if you have the option of financing your business through a second mortgage or refinancing your first mortgage, the second mortgage may be the better choice, especially where the amount of the first mortgage is close to the value of the home.

In addition, remember that the general rule applies only to a lien secured solely by a *personal residence*. Thus, lien stripping will be allowed for a mortgage on a building used in a business.

If you own a small business, you must consider a number of different factors in deciding how to finance it. Be especially wary of misleading advertisements regarding second mortgages or refinancing.

When financing a business, a second mortgage or refinancing can offer a lower interest rate than a credit card. However, this is not always the case, and there are other considerations. For a "125 percent home equity" loan, expect to see an interest rate double the rate available on a conventional mortgage.

Even where the rate on a new mortgage is lower than that on a credit card, you need to weigh this benefit against the risks engendered by the mortgage: Credit card debt is unsecured and fully dischargeable in a bankruptcy proceeding, while the mortgage, of course, is not.

Furthermore, while most home mortgage interest is deductible if you itemize deductions on your tax return, IRS rules provide that the mortgage interest is only deductible to the extent it is attributable to the value of the property. If you take out mortgages or home equity loans that exceed the value of the property, interest on the excess portion of the loans is not deductible. Thus, in a 125 percent loan, only $^{100}/_{125}$ (80 percent) of the interest is deductible.

A second mortgage or refinancing to consolidate bills does not save you money by eliminating bills. They merely substitute one bill for others. While your monthly bills may well be lower than the bills they replace, they are paid over a longer period of time. This will usually cost you more money because interest, usually at a high rate, will apply for a much longer period.

Overall, however, the inability to strip and thus reduce the lien, or eliminate the lien against a homestead exemption, in or out of bankruptcy, is one of the most important factors to consider. This factor, alone, should give you pause before considering a second mortgage or refinancing as a source of funding for a business. A conventional second mortgage, which when added to the first mortgage typically doesn't exceed 80 to 90 percent of the value of the home, may offer advantages, including a low interest rate, low monthly payments and a tax deduction for the interest paid. These advantages must be weighed against the risk of foreclosure and loss of the home.

There is one other situation where a second mortgage on a home may represent an excellent exemption planning strategy: namely, where the value of the home exceeds the amount of the homestead exemption in your state. In that case, a second mortgage can bring your equity in the home below the exemption amount, thus making the home judgment-proof. Even here, however, all of the above factors must still be weighed against the benefits of this form of exemption planning. In this respect, a 125 percent home equity loan presents a very risky alternative. A conventional second mortgage, however, might be an attractive choice in this situation. See Chapter 3 for details on this homestead strategy.

Invalidating Liens

Liens that are invalid, of course, cannot impair any assets, whether they are exempt or nonexempt.

Mechanics' liens and tax liens will be invalid unless they have been filed with the appropriate government office ("perfected"), and then foreclosed on within a certain period of time. The time limitations vary from state to state.

In the case of mechanic's liens, these periods are very short. Typically, these liens must be filed within 60 or 90 days after the work is performed, and then foreclosed on within one year.

Tax liens usually have to be filed within 2 to 3 years, and expire after 10 or 15 years.

Even judgment liens have time limitations. Usually, judgment liens must be foreclosed on within 10 to 20 years.

If any of these liens have not been filed, or foreclosed on, within the prescribed periods, the liens are invalid and unenforceable.

Example

 Peter Jones, a Connecticut resident, has a contractor put a $40,000 addition on his residence, but has not yet paid the bill. Jones' residence, worth $120,000 after the addition, is subject to a $100,000 first mortgage.

The residence is an exempt asset in Connecticut under these facts. However, mechanics' liens are valid, even when they impair an exempt asset.

Fortunately for Jones, however, the contractor failed to record his mechanic's lien of $40,000 within 90 days of the job being completed, as required by Connecticut law.

Accordingly, the contractor's lien is invalid and therefore of no consequence. Jones's home is completely exempt from the claims of the contractor.

In addition, the Federal Trade Commission's (FTC) Credit Practices Rule makes invalid any non-purchase-money, non-possessory security interest liens in household necessities such as clothing, appliances, and linens, as well as some items of little economic value to a consumer.

Using FTC Credit Practices Rule to Invalidate Liens

The Federal Trade Commission's (FTC) Credit Practices Rule can be used to invalidate certain liens against household property. Remember, an invalid lien can be eliminated whether it is attached to exempt or nonexempt property.

Under the Rule, certain non-purchase-money, non-possessory security interest liens are invalid: specifically, liens attached to household necessities and goods.

This provision affects only *consumer goods* and not liens on business property. Most importantly, because consumer goods often would be entitled only to limited protection as exempt assets, the rule can offer real protection.

As discussed previously, a non-purchase-money security interest lien arises where the proceeds from the debt were not used to purchase the property. In other words, this type of lien arises when you *already own* some type of property and put it up as collateral for a loan, the proceeds of which are used for some other purpose. Loans involving purchase-money security interest liens (where the creditor finances the purchase of the asset that is the collateral for the loan) are more common, and are not invalid under this rule.

The lien must *also* be non-possessory to be invalid. This means that the debtor, as opposed to the creditor, has possession of the property. In contrast, an example of a possessory lien would be a pawn shop loan, where the creditor holds the collateral. Possessory liens in these types of property also remain valid under this rule.

The rule's definition of household goods includes household necessities such as clothing, appliances and linens, and some items of little economic value but of unique, personal value to the owner. These may include items such as family photographs, personal papers, the family Bible, and household pets.

The following types of property are *excluded* from the definition of household goods: works of art, electronic entertainment equipment (except one television and one radio), items acquired as antiques (more than 100 years old), jewelry (except wedding rings), pianos or other musical instruments, boats, snowmobiles, bicycles, and cameras. Liens on these types of property remain valid.

In practice, most commercial lenders and merchants will steer clear of liens that come under this rule because they are aware the liens would be invalid. However, some lenders who are either unscrupulous or ignorant of the rule may try to attach a lien to these assets. Therefore, you should be aware that liens that fall within the rule are invalid, and thus cannot impair any exempt or nonexempt assets.

Avoiding Liens Through Persuasion

All of this asset protection planning has another ancillary benefit that serves your goals: The more judgment-proof you make yourself, the less likely a creditor may be in pursuing a case. Or at the least, you may be able to influence a settlement, possibly sooner than later. All of these options have their obvious benefits.

Many times, judicial liens can be avoided through the power of persuasion; that is, by convincing the other party that bringing the lawsuit would be a waste of time. This could eliminate the need to file a bankruptcy action.

In a court proceeding, there are three parts to a lawsuit: factually proving the elements of the case (e.g., negligence), proving the existence and amount of monetary damages, and collecting the judgment. The plaintiff has the burden in each of these three parts.

In many cases, the first part is not an issue. For example, if an employee making a delivery runs into the back of a vehicle stopped at a red light, there really is no issue as to whether the employee was negligent. The employee *was* negligent. However, the amount of monetary damages suffered will almost always be an issue.

Actually collecting a judgment can be the most difficult obstacle for a plaintiff to overcome, particularly where there are no assets to attach, either because there are no significant assets, or all of the assets are protected by exemptions and other means.

As stated above, most states provide that a judgment expires after 10 to 20 years. This may seem like a long time. However, in practice, judgment creditors rarely continue to pursue the collection of a judgment after an initial attempt fails when they realize that the effort will be fruitless.

Plan Smart

In practice, if someone with a claim learns that the other party has no reachable assets, usually the matter will be dropped, and no lawsuit initiated. The relevant saying is, "You can't get blood from a stone."

No lawyer would take a case on a contingent fee basis for a plaintiff under these circumstances. Thus, the plaintiff will be faced with the prospect of paying his or her attorney by the hour (at rates of $150 and upward per hour), with the likelihood that he or she will collect nothing. Faced with these dim prospects, even individuals who would otherwise sue on principle will usually choose not to pursue the matter further.

Thus, informing the other party that the lawsuit will be fruitless, before it is filed, can be a very effective strategy. If you do not have resources that could be reached by a judgment creditor, let the other party know immediately of your situation. Because of the costs and time involved in bringing a lawsuit, most parties will forego the claim when presented with these facts.

One word of caution is necessary, however. Phrasing can be important. Don't elaborate on the asset protection plan you have in place. General statements usually are better. Simply tell the other party, or his or her lawyer, that you will defend against the lawsuit if necessary, but that you don't have any assets that would be available in any event. When questioned, simply point out that your only real asset is your home (or your ERISA qualified retirement plan), which is exempt. Tell the other party that you will vigorously defend against the lawsuit, but it will be a waste of time anyway. If you do not feel comfortable doing this, hire a lawyer. The fees spent will usually be worth the results achieved in this situation.

Chapter 2

Bankruptcy—An Overview

As a last resort in your asset protection plan, you may have to file for bankruptcy. Therefore, it is important that you have a basic understanding of the bankruptcy code in order to properly structure your exempt assets. In many cases, you may be able to discharge most or all of your unsecured debts, such as credit card debts, while preserving all of your assets. In addition, as previously suggested, at times, the most efficient way to eliminate a portion of a lien may be to file a bankruptcy action.

Generally, the bankruptcy code follows the rules on eliminating liens that impair exempt assets, which are described in Chapter 1. In addition, however, the bankruptcy code allows for the elimination of certain liens that impair exempt property that cannot be eliminated in a state court proceeding.

Then, once you understand the lien elimination rules, we'll examine the types of bankruptcy filings available to small business owners and their implications. There are major differences among Chapter 7, Chapter 13 and Chapter 11 filings, as well as the eligibility for each of them.

Before filing such an action, you'll want to consider the after-effects of bankruptcy for you and your business, and how currently proposed bankruptcy reform legislation in Congress may affect you.

SPECIAL LIEN ELIMINATION SITUATIONS

In a bankruptcy proceeding, it is possible to eliminate a non-purchase-money, non-possessory security interest lien in exempt property, if the property consists of:

- household furnishings, household goods, wearing apparel, appliances, books, animals, crops, musical instruments, or jewelry held primarily for the personal, family or household use of the debtor or a dependent of the debtor

- implements, professional books, or tools of the trade of the debtor or a dependent of the debtor

- professionally prescribed health aids for the debtor or a dependent of the debtor

Remember, a non-purchase-money security interest lien arises where the proceeds from the debt were not used to purchase the property. Loans involving purchase-money security interests are more common. This fact means lien elimination will not apply to very many loans.

The requirement that the lien must be on a specific and narrow class of property also means that this exemption will not apply to many cases.

And the lien must *also* be non-possessory. This means that the debtor, as opposed to the creditor, must retain possession of the property. This condition will not usually be difficult to meet, except, for example, in the case of a loan from a pawn broker.

The bankruptcy code imposes one other condition on this rule: If the debtor uses the state's exemptions, rather than the federal bankruptcy code exemptions, and the property exempted consists of implements, professional books, or tools of the trade of the debtor or a dependent of the debtor, or farm animals or crops of the debtor or a dependent of the debtor, then the lien cannot be eliminated to the extent the value of such implements, professional books, tools of the trade, animals, and crops exceeds $5,000.

The cap exists because, while the federal exemptions for the property covered by the rule are not that generous, the analogous state exemptions can be significant.

It's important to note that the courts have typically interpreted this $5,000 limitation as a cap on *the amount of the lien* that can be eliminated. However, a Texas bankruptcy court has ruled that this limitation actually means the debtor must be left with a *minimum equity* in the property of $5,000.

The difference between the two interpretations can be significant, when the loan exceeds the value of the property.

In addition, a mechanic's lien that is filed within the 90 days before the bankruptcy action commences (or is for rent owed) can be eliminated as a "preference" under the bankruptcy code.

John Smith personally owns office furniture valued at $20,000 with a non-purchase-money, non-possessory lien against it in the amount of $80,000. Thus, Smith has no equity in the furniture.

Smith files a bankruptcy action and elects his state's exemptions, so that the $5,000 limitation applies (due to the federal cap). Further, Smith's state exemption for the office equipment makes it completely exempt.

Under the most common interpretation, Smith can eliminate $5,000 of the lien, and he still owes $75,000. He still will have no equity in the furniture.

Under the recent interpretation by a Texas bankruptcy court, the balance of the loan will be reduced to the difference between the value of the property, $20,000, and the $5,000 limitation. Here, that amount is $15,000. In this way, the debtor is left with a minimum equity of $5,000 in the property.

Thus, in this example, under the second interpretation, Smith's loan is reduced to $15,000, and he has $5,000 equity in the furniture ($20,000 less $15,000).

Under this second interpretation, Smith saves $60,000 (lien of $75,000 vs. lien of $15,000).

CHAPTER 7 FILINGS

Chapter 7 is the most common type of bankruptcy proceeding. It is available to individuals and business entities.

In a Chapter 7 (also known as a liquidation) bankruptcy, the debtor's assets are sold and converted to cash, with the proceeds going to pay the cost of administering the case and paying the filer's creditors. Debts that are not paid are discharged—that is, eliminated.

That's the theory, anyway. Exempt assets are, of course, excluded from the assets that must be sold, up to the dollar amount of the particular exemption (see Chapter 3 for a complete discussion of exemptions). Because consensual liens on assets, such as mortgages or car loans, cannot be eliminated even on exempt assets, debtors either continue to pay these debts or surrender the property. Usually, these consensual liens will encumber enough of the value of the property so that the remaining value will fit within an asset exemption.

For example, your home may have mortgages and home equity loans that cover 90 percent of its value, and the remaining 10 percent may be protected by the homestead exemption. Thus, a sale of the asset would generate no proceeds for the other creditors. Accordingly, in typical cases, these assets are not sold, and in fact are retained by the debtor, who continues to pay off the liens.

With the exempt assets and encumbered assets removed from the pool, there are usually no assets available to the unsecured creditors who, in most cases, will be banks holding credit card accounts. The end result will be that these unsecured creditors will receive nothing, and the debts they are owed will be discharged.

Among the issues to be considered in a Chapter 7 filing:

- Certain income and assets acquired after a Chapter 7 filing may be included in your bankruptcy estate if you do not plan properly.

- Any recent transfers of assets will be examined, and may be undone, so you should proceed carefully.

- Personal liability for some debts will never be dischargeable under current law.

- Personal liability for most debts can be discharged, but most liens survive after the completion of a Chapter 7 filing.

Exclusion of Income Received After Chapter 7 Filing

Wages and other sources of income, including self-employment income, earned and received after the Chapter 7 action begins are excluded from the proceeding.

Plan Smart

Given this fact, a debtor who works on a contract basis (e.g., a building contractor) could postpone forming any lucrative contracts until after the proceeding commences. Similarly, where only one spouse works, planned employment for the other spouse should begin only after the action is filed. In these situations, it is better to wait until after the action is completed (not just filed), if at all possible, to avoid any allegation of fraud.

In fact, *all* assets earned and received after the proceeding begins are excluded from the bankruptcy, subject to the following exceptions:

- property received through inheritance

- property received as a result of a divorce decree settlement

- life insurance or other death benefits

These assets are brought back into the bankruptcy action if they are received during the proceeding or within six months of the final discharge. Thus, if an inheritance were anticipated, the debtor should obtain a legal opinion establishing the inheritance, and then consider filing the action immediately so that the inheritance would be received after the six-month period. Similar timing issues revolve around divorce. There is generally little you can do about the timing of life insurance payments or death benefits.

Preferential Transfers in Chapter 7

"Preferential transfers" will also be brought back into the bankruptcy action. These include transfers of cash or assets to insiders (family members and controlled business entities) within the year before the action is filed. For transfers to persons or entities, other than insiders, the time period is 90 days.

Ordinarily, then, transfers to insiders should be planned and carried out more than a year before the action is filed. In theory, however, bankruptcy courts can go back in time (in some cases as much as four years) and undo transfers proved to be fraudulent.

However, in practice, courts do not often go back this far. Use one year as a guideline, but plan further in advance if possible (time limitations are discussed more fully in Chapter 4).

Nondischargeable Debts in Chapter 7

Certain debts will not be discharged in a Chapter 7 bankruptcy. These include:

- alimony and child support

- most student loans

- most federal, state and local taxes

- debts incurred through fraud within one year (and possibly as much as four years) before the bankruptcy action

- fines and penalties for violating the law

- debts for purchases of more than $1,000 in luxury goods or services (or loans of more than $1,000 on an open-end credit plan) from a single creditor within 60 days of filing for bankruptcy

- debts not listed on the bankruptcy petition.

Discharging Personal Liability in Chapter 7

As was stated before, the debtor's personal liability for dischargeable debts is erased in a Chapter 7 filing. However, liens that are not subject to elimination (i.e., most consensual and statutory liens) survive the discharge. This fact explains why a homeowner must continue to pay the mortgages on his home, or face foreclosure, after a Chapter 7 action is completed, even though personal liability for the mortgages is eliminated.

This distinction also can be important when the debtor surrenders the property, and the amount of the liens exceeds the value of the property.

Example

 John Smith owns a home with a value of $100,000 that is subject to mortgage liens totaling $150,000.

Because these liens cannot be eliminated, or (generally) even bifurcated, if Smith intends to keep his home, he will have to pay the $150,000 in mortgages.

However, once his Chapter 7 discharge is final, Smith will have no personal liability for the mortgages. The liens will, nevertheless, still attach to the home. Thus, if Smith wants to retain the home, he will still have to pay the mortgages. If he has defaulted on the mortgages, and he wants to reinstate them by paying the arrearage over time, he may have to file in Chapter 13 (see below).

Alternatively, Smith can surrender the home. If he does so, he will not be liable for the $50,000 mortgage deficiency, as he has no personal liability for the mortgages after the discharge.

Some states provide a somewhat similar provision. For example, in California and some other states, a debtor has no personal liability for a deficiency judgment that results from a foreclosure of a purchase-money mortgage. Note that this state provision is very narrow in scope because:

1. *It only applies in some states.*

2. *It only applies on purchase-money (first) mortgages. It usually does not apply to second mortgages, or refinancings, which are far more likely to cause a deficiency.*

3. *For the provision to apply, the debtor must lose his or her home in foreclosure.*

Nevertheless, debtors who face the loss of their home through foreclosure of a first mortgage should be aware that, in some states, it may be possible to eliminate any deficiency judgment, without resorting to bankruptcy. Debtors in this situation should consult an attorney on the best way to proceed in the particular state in question.

Chapter 7, on the surface, seems harsh to debtors. However, in practice, many debtors retain all of their assets and shed all (or almost all) of their unsecured debt, including credit card debts.

This favorable outcome (along with a surge in credit card debt, second mortgages and refinancing of homes) explains why hundreds of thousands of families have filed Chapter 7 bankruptcy actions each year, for the past several years.

In addition, any bankruptcy filing causes an automatic stay of any collection efforts by creditors. This is welcome relief for beleaguered debtors. However, debtors should be aware that creditors, especially those with secured claims who are not being paid, can request that the automatic stay be lifted if foreclosure or repossession is an inevitability.

CHAPTER 13 FILINGS

In a Chapter 13 proceeding, an individual debtor with regular wages or income agrees to pay back a portion of his or her debts over a period of three to five years. This chapter is available only to individuals.

The debtor proposes a plan that usually involves paying secured creditors the value of their liens, and paying unsecured creditors a fraction of their claims (e.g., 20 percent) or nothing at all. The plan must treat each creditor within a class (e.g., secured creditors) the same, but it may treat creditors in separate classes differently.

Why would a debtor choose Chapter 13? Most don't. However, Chapter 13 may be the better alternative when the debtor has defaulted on secured loans (e.g., a home mortgage, or car loan) and is unable to make up the default, or pay off the lien, in one lump sum payment (as would be required in Chapter 7), but is also unwilling to surrender the property to the secured creditor. In Chapter 13, the debtor can make up the default or pay off the lien over three to five years, rather than immediately in one lump sum.

Absent this one particular circumstance, Chapter 7 will almost always be the superior alternative. A major disadvantage of Chapter 13 is the fact that the debtor must account for all of the income or assets received during this three- to five-year period.

CHAPTER 11 FILINGS

In a sense, Chapter 11 is to business entities what Chapter 13 is to individual debtors. Chapter 11, or the business reorganization chapter, is used primarily by larger corporations that intend to continue operations after restructuring. A small business owner, or the business entity, is much more likely to be involved in a Chapter 7 proceeding or, in the case of the owner, a Chapter 13 proceeding.

AFTER-EFFECTS OF BANKRUPTCY

When concluded, a bankruptcy filing remains on the debtor's credit report for 10 years. However, even the damage to the debtor's credit rating may be mitigated by other factors.

For example, most debtors are unaware that FHA, the federal agency that insures millions of mortgages, has one of the most liberal polices concerning bankruptcy and home mortgages. Generally, the FHA only precludes debtors from obtaining a new FHA mortgage for two years, not 10 years, provided the debtor has an otherwise acceptable credit standing during the two-year period.

Because a home is typically the largest purchase individuals make, debtors should realize that financing for a new home may still be available shortly after the bankruptcy action is completed.

It is important to list all debts in a bankruptcy filing, as debts not listed cannot be discharged. However, some debtors retain a credit card with a very low (or no) balance, but a large credit line, by purposely omitting the debt from the filing, to ensure they will have future credit available. On the other hand, many banks periodically check customer's credit reports. If this is done, the card will likely be cancelled anyway.

In addition, any recent shuffling of debt from the card retained to the listed cards is likely to be attacked as fraudulent. This is especially true if it happened in the year leading to the bankruptcy. However, if planned well in advance, and before any financial difficulties arise, an extra card held in reserve will be effective. This card can be used only infrequently, and then only for small purchases, to keep it active. (See Chapter 4 for timing and related issues involving transfers.)

PROPOSED BANKRUPTCY REFORM LEGISLATION

Congress has been trying, for a number of years, to come to a consensus on reforming the U.S. bankruptcy code. Pressure from creditor lobbies and a perceived need to toughen the standards is at the root of this effort.

The bill is a direct response by Congress to the massive increase in the number of individual bankruptcy actions (primarily Chapter 7) that have been filed since the mid-1990s, and the perception by some in Congress that the code is unfair to creditors. The driving force behind the bill, of course, is the credit card industry.

At this time, the fate of bankruptcy reform legislation is uncertain. President Clinton vetoed one bill that was passed by Congress. In contrast, President Bush is likely to sign such a bill, if it can make its way out of a divided Congress. For this reason, many analysts predicted that a bill would finally become law in 2002. However, near the end of 2002, it became clear that contrasting versions of the bill passed by the House and Senate could not be reconciled.

Essentially, the impasse pitted Democrats against Republicans, and was limited to just two issues. Democrats favored language making non-dischargable the personal liability for damages incurred as a result of anti-abortion protests, and limiting the homestead exemption to $100,000. Republicans favored language that would allow for exceptions on the issue of dischargability of damages in this situation, as well as on the limitation of the homestead exemption. So after a multi-year battle, with resolution on many other issues and the bill within a whisker of becoming law, it was felled by just these two issues.

So what does the future hold for bankruptcy reform? Predictions by analysts are mixed, with most forecasting that the bill will not become law in the near future, especially in light of a poorly performing economy and other issues consuming Congress's attention. However, the credit card industry is not likely to give up the fight. For this reason, informed business owners, who are interested in asset protection, should be aware of the more important proposed changes and should monitor the status of the proposed legislation.

Some of the more important changes under consideration for reform of the bankruptcy code include:

- Debtors would be forced to file in Chapter 13, rather than Chapter 7, if, under a "means testing" formula, the debtor would have at least $100 of disposable income available each month and the ability to pay back at least 25 percent of the unsecured debt, or if the debtor would have at least $166.67 of monthly disposable income. This provision would likely apply to a significant number (perhaps even the majority) of debtors who currently file in Chapter 7. In addition, debtors would have to commit their disposable income to pay off creditors for five years. The current three-year period would be eliminated.

- The residency requirement that must be met to claim a state's exemptions would be increased from the current six months to two years. This is directed primarily at debtors who felt the urge to move to Florida or Texas just over a year before filing for bankruptcy.

- A Chapter 7 filing could not be made if the debtor had

received a discharge in Chapter 7 or Chapter 11 within the last eight years. Currently, Chapter 7 actions must be seven years apart. In addition, debtors would be precluded from filing in Chapter 13 if they received a discharge in any Chapter within the last four years. Currently, Chapter 13 actions can be filed successively, or immediately after a Chapter 7 action. The later option is sometimes called a "Chapter 20" (7 + 13) action, and is currently available where the debtor wants to first eliminate all unsecured debt in Chapter 7, and then follow this with a Chapter 13 action to reinstate liens, and pay them over time. This option would be eliminated.

- States' homestead exemptions would be capped. A $125,000 cap has been proposed. Competing proposals would make the cap mandatory; or impose the gap only in the event that the debtor was convicted of a felony violation of the bankruptcy code; or if a debt arose from violations of securities law, fiduciary fraud, racketeering, or intentional or reckless physical harm. Proponents of the conditional cap would also impose the $125,000 cap on any value that was added to the homestead during the three years and four months prior to the filing, unless the value was added from a prior homestead in the same state.

- All value to the homestead that was fraudulently added during the 10 years prior to the filing would be excluded.

- A uniform and restrictive definition for "household goods" would be imposed.

- Bifurcation would be eliminated, both in Chapter 7 and in Chapter 13, on any loan incurred within one year of filing the action, or on a motor vehicle loan incurred within $2^1/_2$ years of the filing. Because bifurcation is normally not available for mortgages on a personal residence, it usually takes place on loans of shorter duration, typically loans of five years or less, such as car loans. The effect of this provision, then, would be to require debtors to pay the full amount of a loan, even when that amount exceeds the value of the property, or, alternatively, surrender the property. Where bifurcation did occur, property would be valued at replacement cost, which is usually the highest of several alternative ways to value the property.

- Currently, bifurcation is not possible for a lien secured "solely" by a personal residence. This allows the strategy (advanced in Chapter 1) of offering additional collateral to the bank when taking out the loan, to remove the mortgage from this exception and thus make it susceptible to bifurcation. The reform proposal would change the word "solely" to "primarily," and thus eliminate this strategy.

- The prohibition against "luxury" purchases or loans from a single creditor would be changed to reduce the triggering amount of purchases or borrowing to $250, as opposed to the current $1,000, and to increase the time period of the prohibition to 90 days before the bankruptcy filing, as opposed to the current 60 days. This provision is especially designed to prevent discharge of large credit card purchases (defined as $250 or more) made within three months of filing the action.

- The location for a bankruptcy filing by a business entity would be changed to the state in which it conducts most of its business, rather than the state in which it was formed. This proposal is designed to stem the tide of business bankruptcy filings in Delaware by businesses formed, but not operating, there.

- The retirement plan exemption would be extended to all retirement plans and IRAs, with a $1 million cap for IRAs. On a positive note, the $1 million IRA cap would not be extended to either SEP or SIMPLE IRAs. In short, protection afforded to IRAs formed withing these plans would be unlimited, thus negating any possible advantage the SIMPLE 401(k) may have over the SIMPLE IRA. Moreover, under earlier reform proposals, Coverdell Education Savings Accounts (education IRAs) would receive less protection, subject to a $50,000 per dependant limitation, and an overall limitation of $100,000 for all dependents. In addition, deposits to a Coverdell Education Savings Account within one year before the bankruptcy action would not be protected. Funds contributed more than one year before filing would be protected only if the beneficiary is a child, stepchild, grandchild or step-grandchild, and then be subject to a cap of $5,000 for funds that were contributed between one and two years before filing. For these reasons, the conventional IRA or Roth IRA may be better options.

- Creditors, including credit card companies, would be allowed to secure from customers a waiver of their exemption for retirement benefits, in a bankruptcy proceeding, and possibly a state court proceeding. This proposal is especially controversial, and therefore its inclusion in any bill that becomes law is uncertain. However, if included, it may be the most damaging provision for filers to emerge out of bankruptcy reform.

- Generally, the proposals would become law six months after enactment. In other words, the law would not apply to filings made the first six months after enactment. This delayed effective date would provide a window for filers to take advantage of the more generous provisions in the existing law. However, new limits on the homestead exemption would go into effect on the date of enactment, which would limit this planning opportunity.

Plan Smart

Should a reform bill be signed into law with a delay for its effective date, debtors considering bankruptcy should probably file before the law goes into effect, all other things being equal. Check out CCH Business Owner's Toolkit™ *for the latest news regarding bankruptcy reform legislation (http://www.toolkit.cch.com).*

Once you have a general understanding of asset exemptions and bankruptcy, you can explore planning opportunities that exploit particular exemptions, and that is the subject of next chapter, "Asset Exemption Planning."

Chapter 3

Effective Asset Exemption Planning

When placing assets out of the reach of creditors, the primary strategy centers on most effectively using the asset exemptions allowed under federal and state codes. This exempted property is declared untouchable in the eyes of the law, should you find yourself in the undesirable position of having a creditor's lien liquidating your assets.

Every state has a list of assets considered "exempt" from legal judgments and unreachable by creditors. The federal bankruptcy statute also has its own list of exempt assets, although in some states you may substitute your state's exemptions for the federal ones in a bankruptcy action.

States Allowing Either Federal or State Exemptions

In the following states, residents may choose between the federal exemptions and their states' post-judgment exemptions, in a bankruptcy proceeding:

Arkansas	Minnesota	South Carolina
Connecticut	New Hampshire	Texas
District of Columbia	New Jersey	Vermont
Hawaii	New Mexico	Washington
Massachusetts	Pennsylvania	Wisconsin
Michigan	Rhode Island	

If you reside in one of these states, you should examine both your state's post-judgment asset exemptions and the federal bankruptcy exemptions, in comparing your inventory of assets to the exemptions.

In the other states, you can only use your own state's post-judgment assets exemptions in a bankruptcy proceeding. These states have opted out of the federal exemption system. Remember, too, that in a state court proceeding, only your state's post-judgment asset exemptions will be available.

To effectively plan for maximum asset protection, you'll need to understand the limits of exempt asset status and the exemption options available.

Understanding Exempt Asset Status

No state has one single dollar exemption that covers all of your property. Rather, the exemptions are sometimes termed "pigeon holes," into which you must try to fit as many items of property as possible.

For example, Florida and Texas, two debtor-friendly states, each offer over 35 separate exemptions. Knowing what the exemptions are, and fitting a particular item of property into an exemption, can be a very effective asset protection strategy, because the exemptions can be quite generous.

Example

In one case, a California physician, operating his practice in the form of a corporation, filed a Chapter 7 (liquidation) bankruptcy proceeding. In Chapter 7, "all" of the debtor's assets are sold, with the proceeds used to pay the creditors.

The physician had accumulated nearly $2 million in a retirement plan. California, like many other states, exempts assets in a retirement plan from liquidation.

The physician's creditors challenged the $2 million exemption, on the grounds that it was unfair. While agreeing with the creditors that the exemption was unfair, the court acknowledged that it was powerless to ignore the exemption.

The result was that the physician eliminated all of his debts and, at the same time, walked away from the "liquidation" bankruptcy proceeding with $2 million.

Had the physician simply withdrawn the $2 million from the business and invested it in a personal portfolio outside of a retirement plan (as many small business owners would have done), he would have lost $2 million.

As noted above, transferring your assets into exempt categories will be effective, but only if the transfers are done well in advance of the onset of financial difficulties.

In one case, a Wisconsin couple moved to Florida and then, a little over a year later, filed a bankruptcy action there. They had liquidated their Wisconsin assets and invested the proceeds in a Florida home that cost over $200,000. Wisconsin recognizes only a $40,000 homestead exemption, while Florida is well known for its unlimited homestead exemption.

The bankruptcy court ruled that the conversion of nonexempt assets into exempt assets was fraudulent, as the move was really motivated only by a desire to use Florida's more generous homestead exemption. The court limited the couple to Wisconsin's $40,000 exemption. Had the move and conversion occurred much earlier, the couple would have saved over $160,000. This story should highlight the fact that timing and motive are important factors in asset exemption transfers *(these factors are discussed in Chapter 4).*

(As discussed further in Chapter 4, the case involving the Wisconsin couple may no longer represent the law in Florida. Recently, the U.S. Court of Appeals ruled that Florida's homestead exemption, which is embodied in Florida's Constitution, is absolute, and protected even when purchases or transfers are fraudulent. This decision is unique, and unlikely to be followed even in other states, such as Texas, where the homestead exemption is provided by the state constitution.)

In contrast, in another case, a state judge filed a bankruptcy proceeding in his home state, which offered only a limited homestead exemption. He attributed his financial condition to large losses he suffered in the real estate market.

The value of his residence was close to $1 million, meaning that it would not be exempt in the bankruptcy proceeding. However, the judge had planned well. He had previously transferred his interest in the family residence and other property to his spouse. She was not a party to the bankruptcy proceeding.

Because the transfers occurred well before the bankruptcy proceeding (about 10 years earlier), and during a period when the debtor was financially healthy, the bankruptcy trustee could not reach these assets.

The judge mentioned above saved $1 million. Clearly, transfers can be a significant part of an asset protection plan.

You can effectively plan for asset exemptions only when the nature of asset exemptions is well understood. Unfortunately, in practice, this understanding is frequently lacking.

John Smith, a Nevada resident, owns a home with a value of $110,000. He has a first mortgage on his home of $100,000.

John is starting a business. He knows Nevada exempts a residence in the amount of $125,000. Because his home is worth only $110,000, he concludes that his home is an exempt asset.

Smith takes out a second mortgage in the amount of $30,000 to finance the startup costs for his new business. Because his home is an exempt asset, he believes he is not risking his home, as a creditor cannot levy on an exempt asset.

While it is true that Smith's home is an exempt asset, this exemption will not help Smith. Consensual liens, such as first and second mortgages, cannot be eliminated in state court or in a bankruptcy action even when they are secured by an exempt asset.

Essentially, the exempt status of the home is meaningless in this situation. If John does not pay his second mortgage of $30,000 and his first mortgage of $100,000, he will lose his home.

As another example, Peter Jones, a Florida resident, owns a home with a value of $300,000. The home has no mortgage.

Jones has failed to pay his real estate taxes and motor vehicle taxes for several years. Accordingly, the town in which he resides places a lien against his residence and begins foreclosure proceedings to collect the delinquent taxes.

Jones knows he enjoys an unlimited homestead exemption in Florida. Accordingly, he concludes that, because his home is an exempt asset, he can ignore the foreclosure proceeding.

However, in this case, Jones will lose his home. Statutory liens, including liens for delinquent taxes, cannot be eliminated in state court or in a bankruptcy action even when the liens are secured by an exempt asst. The exemption offers no protection whatsoever. The result is essentially the same as if the asset was not exempt.

Consider this third example: Mary Black, a Connecticut resident, forms an LLC to operate her new business. She contributes a car to the LLC, subject to a lien against it for a car loan. The car has a value of $9,000, and the amount owed on the loan is $8,000. Thus, there is $1,000 equity in the car.

Black concludes her car is an exempt asset, because Connecticut exempts the first $1,500 of equity in a car. She is confident that the car will be protected if her business experiences financial difficulties.

Black is wrong. As discussed below, asset exemptions are available only to "natural persons" (i.e., real people). Corporations, LLCs and even partnerships are considered "persons" for many purposes in the law, but not for asset exemption purposes. Black's car is fully subject to the claims of the business creditors.

In this chapter, we'll cover the more general rules about how asset exemptions work, and what they can and can't do for you. In addition, we'll discuss the specific exemptions (such as a personal residence, pension plan assets, business tools of the trade, etc.) in more detail, and how to best make them work for you. In the next chapter, we will show you how to use asset transfers, and other "adjustments," to further take advantage of the exemptions.

Who Is Eligible for Exemptions

Asset exemptions are available only to "natural persons" (i.e., real human beings). Corporations, LLCs and even partnerships are considered "persons" for many purposes in the law, but not for asset exemption purposes.

Asset exemptions were designed to ensure that families could emerge from a financial crisis with the ability to provide for their basic necessities, such as food, shelter and clothing. Artificial entities have no such needs and, accordingly, cannot use the asset exemptions.

Of course, this conclusion is lacking a certain logic. Small business owners do in fact rely on their business's assets to provide for their family's basic necessities. Nevertheless, the law in many cases seems to defy logic, as illustrated below.

Example

In a recent Texas case, a family claimed that the Texas homestead exemption protected their family farm, which consisted of their home and several large tracts of land. Texas provides an unlimited homestead exemption.

The family had previously transferred ownership of the farm to a family limited partnership as an estate planning device.

The creditor produced copies of the deeds proving the limited partnership, and not the family members, owned the farm. Accordingly, even though the farm was the family's home, the court ruled that the homestead exemption, which otherwise would have protected the farm, was not available. Instead, the interest in the limited partnership was an item of personal property, which would have to be protected as such, subject to the less generous exemptions available for interests in personal property.

Keep Personal Exemptions Personal

As a general rule of thumb, a home should never be transferred to a business entity, such as a limited partnership, LLC or corporation, because usually the homestead exemption offers one of the more important and useful asset exemptions. This rule, of course, does not apply to a commercial building.

In contrast, if you transfer your home to a revocable living trust, you should not face this problem. Such transfers are common estate-planning tools where the goal is to avoid probate court or federal estate taxes (using a trust to protect a homestead is discussed later in this chapter, and see Chapter 5 for a complete discussion of trusts).

On the surface, the availability of asset exemptions only to natural persons may seem to be an argument in favor of operating a business in the form of a sole proprietorship (if there is one owner), since the sole proprietor is automatically deemed to be the personal owner of all the business's assets. It also may seem to be an argument in favor of the owner personally owning and leasing all of the assets to the business.

Either of these approaches, however, would be a mistake. As discussed in Chapter 6, the sole proprietor has unlimited, personal liability for all of the business's debts. This one fact makes the sole proprietorship untenable as a form in which to operate a business with maximum levels of protection, as discussed later.

No Exemptions for Business

A business entity, such as a corporation or LLC, *must* be funded with assets. If you don't contribute any assets to the business entity (i.e., you fund the entity *entirely* with leases and loans), you would be likely to lose the limited liability ordinarily enjoyed by the owners of these businesses forms.

But the investment in a business entity's assets can be protected from liability even in the absence of asset exemptions, through strategic structuring and funding practices, including the use of a holding entity and a separate operating entity; leases and loans; and the encumbering of the operating entity's assets with liens that run in favor of the owner or holding entity (see Chapter 8 for a detailed discussion).

That the business's assets can be protected from liability, even though asset exemptions will be unavailable to the business entity, illustrates an important point in asset protection planning: If you are to effectively protect your business and personal assets, a comprehensive, or multi-layered, approach is required. One strategy alone, such as exemption planning, will usually be insufficient.

Be cautious when reading other material on the topic of asset protection and relying on information in some other exemption tables. Since exemptions are available only to natural persons, and not to business entities, do not be misled by tables listing partnership assets as exempt.

Partnership assets are not exempt. Asset exemptions are not available to business entities. Thus, these assets are fully subject to the claims of the business creditors.

Further, the business owner possesses a personal property interest (i.e., his or her interest in the partnership), but does not own any of the specific assets in the partnership. The partnership itself owns these assets. Accordingly, the owner cannot claim any exemptions in these specific assets, either.

What providers of these tables really mean to say is that a partner's personal creditors can't directly attach the specific assets owned by the partnership. However, they can attach the partner's ownership interest in the partnership itself, which is deemed to be a type of personal property. In a general partnership, the creditors might then be able to foreclose on the interest and liquidate the business. Thus, in this way, they can reach the business's assets (note that in most states, an LLC offers better protection from the claims of the owner's personal creditors; see Chapter 6 for a detailed discussion).

YOUR ASSET EXEMPTION OPTIONS

Now that we've introduced the concept of asset exemptions—which are established by every state's laws and the federal bankruptcy code, in order to shield certain types of assets from being reached by unsecured creditors—it's time to explore strategies that take advantage of them.

This discussion focuses on ways you can exploit the most important asset exemptions common to most states, including:

- Homestead exemption, as well as the options to consider if this exemption is not available to you, or if you want to use a trust to protect the home

- Retirement plan exemption

- Wage exemption

- Annuity exemption

- Wild card exemption

- Tools of the trade and household goods exemptions

The focus here is a narrow one—comprehensive coverage of each category of asset exemptions offered by the states is unwarranted, as many categories yield unimpressive protection. The Appendices contain tables listing asset exemptions for each state, as well as the federal bankruptcy exemptions.

Also, we'll cover exemption doubling for spouses, what happens to the proceeds of the sale of an exempt asset, and other exemption planning strategies.

In addition, timing and motive are critical factors in avoiding creditor challenges to asset transfers (these factors are addressed in Chapter 4).

The Homestead Exemption

In many states, the most important exemption is provided for a homestead— a personal residence.

As suggested earlier, exemptions vary widely from state to state. The homestead exemption provides a good example of this variation.

Kansas, Florida, Iowa, South Dakota and Texas provide an unlimited dollar value homestead exemption. Florida and Texas, in fact, are well known as debtor-friendly states because of their homestead exemptions. The Florida homestead exemption is especially valuable because a U.S. Court of Appeals recently held that the exemption will apply even when the owner acquired or enlarged it with the intent of defrauding creditors.

States with no dollar cap on their homestead exemption do limit the exemption to a certain area of land, which is much larger in rural areas. For example, in Florida the exemption is limited to half an acre in a city and 160 contiguous acres elsewhere. In practice, this area limitation will only rarely be a factor.

In contrast, Delaware, the District of Columbia, Maryland, New Jersey, Pennsylvania and Rhode Island provide no specific homestead exemption.

Most states offer exemptions between these extremes. Even here, however, the exemption can be anywhere along the spectrum. For example, the exemption is $5,000 in Ohio, $80,000 in North Dakota, and $125,000 in Nevada.

The federal bankruptcy homestead exemption is $17,425. Where a state's homestead exemption is lower than $17,425, a debtor contemplating a bankruptcy filing should consider using the federal exemptions (if the state law permits it), all other things being equal.

The homestead exemption is considered such a basic and important right in some states, including Florida and Texas, that it is mandated by the state's constitution. This prevents the state's legislature from modifying or repealing the exemption by statute.

Generally, consensual liens, such as mortgages, cannot be eliminated inside or outside of bankruptcy, even when they are attached to property subject to an exemption. Thus, the homestead exemption can actually be worth nothing to the debtor if the home is very heavily mortgaged. In addition, remember that bifurcation or lien splitting usually will not be possible in a bankruptcy proceeding with respect to mortgages secured solely be a residence (see Chapter 1).

Nevertheless, where the homestead exemption is generous (e.g., in

Florida or Texas), it will probably provide the greatest opportunity to shield wealth from creditors.

To exploit this exemption most effectively, the small business owner should employ the following strategies:

- When the homestead exemption is unlimited, or the amount of the exemption exceeds the value of the home, consider paying off the mortgages on the property.

- Where the value of the home exceeds the exemption amount, consider the opposite strategy; that is, encumbering the home with an additional commercial mortgage, or private mortgage from your business's holding entity.

- Where there is no homestead exemption, or the homestead exemption is extremely low, consider owning the home with a spouse in tenancy by the entirety, if the state allows this. It's important here that you consider this option only after carefully weighing the risks of divorce.

These strategies are discussed in detail later in this chapter.

Plan Smart

Some states require individuals to record their homestead exemption at the county recording office, or wherever legal documents are normally recorded in the state. If the exemption is not recorded, you may not be able to use it. In some of these states, recording must take place before a bankruptcy filing, while in others, recording must occur before a forced sale of the home.

In some states, recording is optional, and may give you no greater rights than if you hadn't filed the papers.

It isn't necessary to sort out all of the differences. If recording is allowed or required, you should simply record your homestead exemption.

The following states allow, or require, the recording of the homestead exemption:

Alabama	Massachusetts	Texas
Arkansas	Michigan	Utah
California	Montana	Virginia
Florida	Nebraska	Washington
Idaho	Nevada	Texas
Iowa	South Dakota	

If the Exemption Exceeds Your Home's Value

In states where the homestead is unlimited, ideally, you should pay off all consensual liens (i.e., first and second mortgages) secured by the residence.

This rule also applies in states where the exemption exceeds the value of your home.

There are two major benefits to this action. First, the cash used to make the payment will be converted from a nonexempt asset (cash) to an exempt asset (a paid-off home). Second, at the same time, you will still be able to remove judicial liens (and other liens subject to elimination) from the residence since these kinds of liens impair the exemption.

Example

John Smith, a Florida resident, owns a home worth $225,000 that is subject to a $150,000 mortgage. The homestead exemption in Florida, of course, is unlimited.

Smith should consider paying off his $150,000 mortgage. By doing this, Smith will convert $150,000 of cash to an exempt form.

In addition, after paying off the mortgage, Smith will still be able to remove any judicial liens (as well as other types of liens subject to elimination) attached to the property, as these liens will always be deemed to impair his homestead exemption.

This is powerful protection for the small business owner who may face judgment liens from personal guarantees he or she provides for the business entity's contracts, or from torts, such as negligence or malpractice, committed while carrying out the business activities.

The same strategy will be equally effective when the homestead exemption is limited, but the exemption amount exceeds the value of home.

For example, in Nevada the exemption amount is capped at $125,000. Let's say Peter Jones owns a home in Nevada valued at $100,000 that is subject to a mortgage in the amount of $70,000.

By paying off the $70,000 mortgage, Jones will convert this amount to an exempt form, while still ensuring he can eliminate judicial liens applied against his home.

If Your Home's Value Exceeds the Exemption

When the homestead exemption is limited and the value of the home exceeds the exemption, the opposite strategy should be employed: You should keep the home encumbered with first or second mortgages. The amount of consensual liens (and other non-removable liens) on the property should always equal or exceed the difference between the value of the home and the exemption amount.

Because this difference represents the total amount of liens that *cannot* be eliminated, any judicial liens then added to the property will be subject to elimination. Essentially, this practice makes the home judgment-proof, even though the homestead exemption is limited.

Example

Refer to the preceding example, but now let's say Jones' Nevada home is worth $225,000, and is subject to the same $70,000 mortgage.

The amount of liens that cannot *be eliminated is equal to the value of the property ($225,000) less the amount of Nevada's homestead exemption ($125,000), or $100,000 in this case (see Chapter 1 for details on lien elimination).*

Jones is carrying only a $70,000 mortgage at this time. Thus, at this time, the home may potentially be encumbered by an additional judicial lien of up to $30,000.

For every dollar that Jones pays off the mortgage, another dollar becomes potentially available to a judgment creditor.

Instead of concentrating on paying off the mortgage, Jones should consider encumbering the home with a second mortgage in a minimum amount of $30,000. Then, the two mortgages would consume the full $100,000 of liens that can't be eliminated. Thus, this strategy would mean any judicial liens that were added to the home later could be eliminated.

Because the principal due on each mortgage will decrease as it is paid off, an even better approach would be to take out a second mortgage in an amount above the minimum.

Extreme caution, however, is required when taking out second mortgages or refinancing a home, *because mortgage liens cannot be eliminated in or out of bankruptcy, and they cannot be bifurcated in a bankruptcy proceeding.*

The risk here is obvious: If the second mortgage were not paid, the residence would be lost to foreclosure. A second mortgage should only be considered when you are absolutely sure you can pay back the loan.

If you choose, you could combine this strategy with even more advanced strategies. One strategy involves using a holding entity and an operating entity to operate your business (as described in Chapter 8). In that case, the wealth of the business would reside in the holding entity, which has no exposure to liability, while the operating entity, due to its exposure to liability, would not contain vulnerable assets.

In employing this strategy, you may want to consider taking a personal loan from your business's holding entity, while providing the holding entity, in return, with a demand promissory note secured by a mortgage on your residence.

In this strategy, the holding entity would normally not demand payment on the note, thus ensuring that the lien will remain on the residence. The holding entity would end up holding a valuable asset (i.e., the note and mortgage). However, because the holding entity does not conduct operating activities, the risk of loss here is minimal.

In other respects, the strategy described above is the same. Thus, in the last example, Jones would take a $30,000 loan from his holding entity, granting the holding entity a $30,000 mortgage in his residence.

In either case (a bank mortgage or a private mortgage), the business owner would have to consider how to employ the proceeds from the loan. One possibility, as advocated in Chapter 8, is to use the cash to make a loan to the operating entity, in which the operating entity grants liens on its assets to the owner (i.e., the holding entity) as security for the loan. This use of the proceeds ensures that the operating entity's assets are protected from creditors (because they are encumbered by secured loans from the business owner), despite the lack of asset exemptions, which are only available to natural persons, not business entities.

Warning

 The strategy of obtaining a private loan from your business that is secured by a mortgage on your home should never *be executed if only one business entity (an operating entity) is used to operate a business.*

A mortgage on your home in favor of an operating entity would create a significant asset (i.e., the mortgage on your home) in the operating entity that would be exposed to liability, in the form of the claims of the business's creditors. If the operating entity's creditors were able to secure a judgment against the operating entity, they might be able to reach, and therefore foreclose on, your home mortgage.

If No Homestead Exemption Exists

Where a state provides for no homestead exemption, or an extremely small exemption, the form in which you own the home may determine the extent to which your home will be protected from creditors. Your best options are:

- tenancy by the entirety

- transferring ownership to the spouse with less legal exposure

In addition, there are other forms of ownership, but they do not offer enough protection. They are presented here for illustrative purposes:

- joint tenancy

- tenancy in common

- community property

Tenancy by the Entirety

Where state law permits it, owning your home in the form of tenancy by the entirety may offer you the greatest protection.

Tenancy by the entirety is not available to all homeowners. It is available only to married couples who take title to their home in this ownership form. As discussed later, it also is not available in all states.

The theory behind tenancy by the entirety is that the married couple is one single unit. Thus, neither spouse may voluntarily, or involuntarily, convey their interest in the home without the consent of the other. This rule places the home out of the reach of the creditors of one of the spouses. Tenancy by the entirety applies only to your personal residence; you can't use it for other real estate or for other types of assets.

It's important to know that the protection afforded by this form of ownership only applies when a creditor attempts to collect on a debt that is in the name of just one of the spouses. Where both spouses are jointly liable on a debt, this form of ownership offers no protection.

Since tenancy by the entirety is a creature of state law, in order to take advantage of it in a bankruptcy action, you would have to use your state's exemptions as opposed to the federal exemptions. Even then, the exemption will be valuable only if both spouses do not file for bankruptcy together, and only if the filing spouse is solely liable for the debt resulting in the lien on the home.

Plan Smart

The following states permit a husband and wife to own a home in the form of a tenancy by the entirety:

Delaware	*Maryland*	*Pennsylvania*
District of Columbia	*Massachusetts*	*Tennessee*
Florida	*Michigan*	*Vermont*
Hawaii	*North Carolina*	*Virginia*
Indiana	*Ohio*	*Wyoming*

Because many of these states offer either no homestead exemption, or a relatively low exemption, the small business owner may want to consider using this ownership form to protect a home.

However, this form of ownership is not available in all of the states that offer only a limited homestead exemption. For example, New Jersey and Rhode Island offer no homestead exemption, but also do not provide for the tenancy by the entirety form of ownership.

Tenancy by the entirety can offer significant protection, especially in the case of the small business owner. In practice, usually one spouse will own or operate the business. This spouse may incur debts from personal guarantees extended on the business's debts, or the personal commission of torts such as negligence while carrying out the business's activities. Because the other spouse will not be a party to these debts, the home will be protected from liability for the debts if it is owned in tenancy by the entirety.

Where both a husband and wife are actively involved in operating a business, caution must be exercised. This ownership form offers no protection for debts on which the couple is jointly liable.

Thus, great efforts should be made to ensure that only one spouse guarantees the contracts of the business entity, if the business's creditor demands a personal guarantee.

Note that, as discussed in Chapter 6, other strategies can protect assets when spouses operate a business together. For example, if either spouse commits an act of negligence, the other would not be liable, provided they are operating the business in the form of an LLC or corporation.

Warning

In contrast, both spouses would be liable for an individual spouse's negligence if the business is a general partnership and both spouses are owners. Only tenancy by the entirety could protect the couple's home if no homestead exemption is available. As discussed in Chapter 6, the general partnership is a business form that should be avoided, precisely because of the tremendous exposure to liability that it involves.

Finally, using this ownership form usually requires that the married couple take their interest in the home through the same deed at the same time. Thus, a transfer by a husband of a half-interest in a home to his new spouse cannot create a tenancy by the entirety. To correctly convert property to this form, the sole owner should transfer, by deed, the entire interest in the property to himself and his spouse, so that they both take their interests at the same time and through the same deed. Have an attorney draft or review the deed to make sure it accomplishes your purposes.

Don't confuse tenancy by the entirety with joint tenancy, tenancy in common, or community property. These forms of ownership do not offer the kind of protection as does tenancy by the entirety.

Warning

If your homestead is already jointly owned with your spouse, converting it to tenancy by the entirety carries no additional risks. However, when the small business owner holds the home as separate property and conveys an interest in the residence to the other spouse solely to take advantage of tenancy by the entirety, an additional risk is created—namely, loss of the home (or a half-interest in it) if a divorce should occur.

The homeowner in this situation should weigh the risk of loss of the home to his or her individual creditors against the risk of loss that may occur as a result of a divorce.

Moreover, if a bankruptcy action is filed by one spouse, the property will become part of the bankruptcy estate if the nonfiling spouse dies, or receives a final decree of divorce, within six months after the bankruptcy action is completed.

If a divorce is a real possibility in the future, it may be possible to delay the divorce long enough to avoid this provision.

Transferring Assets to the Non-Business-Owner Spouse

An asset protection strategy similar to tenancy by the entirety involves transferring personal assets, such as a home, to the non-business-owner spouse. It carries the same risks previously discussed in the case of divorce, but with additional risks as well. Some business owners make these transfers so that the business's creditors will not be able to reach those assets. This strategy adds an extra layer of protection if the business creditors are able to reach the owner's personal assets outside the business, which is possible in certain circumstances, such as where the owner makes a personal guarantee of a business debt or personally commits a tort such as negligence.

Thus, this strategy can be quite effective in shielding assets from creditors. If you go this route, be careful of the timing of the transfer—if it occurs while you are being hounded by creditors, they may be able to attack the transfer as fraudulent (see Chapter 4 for more information).

However, the risks inherent in this strategy are usually not worth the benefits. In a divorce action, the other spouse will own all the assets at the time of the proceeding. While judges in divorce actions normally have the power to make an equitable division of property acquired during marriage regardless of whose name is on the property, separate individual ownership creates a strong presumption in making the ultimate allocation of property between the spouses.

Worse yet, as the sole owner of the property, a spouse can sell and use the property at will, regardless of the wishes of the nonowning spouse. This can be particularly perilous in the case of a home or business property.

Therefore, this strategy is not recommended, especially in light of all of the other strategies available to business owners.

Joint Tenancy

In states that do not allow ownership in tenancy by the entirety, married couples typically own their home in joint tenancy.

Joint tenancy is available to any combination of individuals, and not simply spouses. Moreover, the number of co-owners is not limited to two. However, as with a tenancy by the entirety, the owners usually must take equal interests, at the same time, and through the same deed or other instrument.

This form also shares the following characteristic with tenancy by the entirety: If one owner dies, the survivor automatically, by operation of law, inherits the decedent's interest, regardless of any provisions in a will.

However, a co-owner in joint tenancy, including a spouse, may freely sell his or her interest without the other's consent. Thus, it follows that creditors of one of the joint tenants can reach *the debtor's interest* in property owned in this form. Thus, joint tenancy does not offer the protection that is provided by tenancy by the entirety.

In the case of a married couple owning a home in joint tenancy, the creditors of one spouse could reach the half-interest owned by the debtor-spouse. Once this was done, the creditor could force a sale of the property, through a partition proceeding in state court, and use half of the proceeds (the debtor's share of the property) from the sale to pay off the debt. (This all assumes, of course, that a homestead exemption did not protect the property.)

Warning

Sometimes, individuals who solely own property create a joint tenancy in the property with another person, usually a close relative, to avoid probate court.

Because joint tenancy includes a right of survivorship, this strategy works. Upon the death of one owner, the survivor automatically, by operation of law, acquires the decedent's interest. No probate court proceeding, and no deed or other transfer document, is necessary.

However, this strategy also can carry significant risks. For example, let's say a widow with two children creates a joint tenancy in her home and bank account with one of the children for the purpose of avoiding probate court. A joint tenancy creates immediate rights in the other owner. The one child could now force a sale of the home through a partition proceeding, pocket half of the sales proceeds, and possibly leave the mother homeless.

In addition, this one child could withdraw 100 percent of the bank account, and the bank would have no liability, because any owner in joint tenancy has the right to use the property (even if they are only a half-owner).

Upon the death of the mother, the other child would be left with nothing. A verbal agreement (a common occurrence in these situations) among the three that the co-owner would share the inheritance with his or her sibling would usually be unenforceable.

Keep in mind, too, that a joint tenancy overrules provisions in a will. A common error is for individuals to leave certain property in their wills to designated beneficiaries, not realizing that the property is owned in joint tenancy and will automatically pass to the surviving owner of the property regardless of anything in the will.

If this probate court avoidance strategy is to be used, the transferor should be aware of the risks involved. Moreover, it must also be understood that for the transfer to be effective, the transferor usually should transfer equal shares in the property to himself and the other party. Technically, a conveyance of a half-interest to the other party only creates a tenancy in common, with no right of survivorship (however, banks will frequently ignore this technicality in their treatment of bank accounts).

Plan Smart

If your goal is to avoid probate court, there are better alternatives. For example, you can quickly establish a simple trust for bank accounts by asking your banker to set up a Totten trust. All that's necessary is filling out a simple form.

This type of trust makes the owner of the account the trustee of the account, but importantly gives the owner of the account exclusive rights to the property during his or her life. At the owner's death, the account automatically passes to the named beneficiaries. This is superior to a joint tenancy in this situation, as the beneficiaries have no rights in the property during the account holder's life.

A similar type of simple trust can be used for ownership of a home, where the intent is to avoid probate court. However, in that case, the owner would have to pay an attorney to have the trust form drafted (see Chapter 5 for a discussion of trusts).

Tenancy in Common

When property is owned as tenancy in common and one of the parties dies, the decedent's interest passes to the beneficiary under the decedent's will, or to the closest heirs as directed by state statute. In fact, the main difference between this form and joint tenancy (or tenancy by the entirety) is the lack of a right of survivorship in a tenancy in common. However, as with joint tenancy, property is not protected from creditors when ownership is in the form of tenancy in common.

In addition, in this form, the "unities" do not apply, so that the co-owners can hold unequal interests, and can take their ownership interests at different times and through different instruments. Thus, if there is an attempt to create a joint tenancy that fails because the co-owners did not take possession at the same time and by the same legal document, the result will be a tenancy in common.

Community Property

From an asset protection standpoint, the results are the worst when property is owned as community property. In that case, the creditors of one spouse can reach the entire value of the property, not just that spouse's portion.

States with Community Property Laws

Community property law exists in only a relatively small group of states:

Arizona	*Louisiana*	*Texas*
California	*Nevada*	*Washington*
Idaho	*New Mexico*	*Wisconsin*

In these states, property acquired by a married couple during marriage, other than through individual gift or inheritance, is presumed to be owned in community property, regardless of which spouse's name is on the title or other ownership document. What's more, property that was acquired before the marriage, or during the marriage by gift or inheritance, may be transformed into community property if it is mixed or "co-mingled" with other community property.

Also, if you have ever lived in a community property state and later move out of it, your existing community property retains its character despite your change in residence.

Plan Smart

Married couples who own property, such as a home or investments, in a community property state may want to consider converting the ownership to joint tenancy, at least where only one spouse will be incurring the majority of debts. This will shield half of the value of the property.

Alternatively, the entire interest might be conveyed to the other (non-business-owner) spouse. As described above, this can be quite effective, but also quite risky due to the possibility of divorce.

It is also possible to remove the property from community property status so that each spouse owns one-half of the asset as his or her separate property, or jointly own the property in the tenants in common form of ownership previously described.

If you live in a community property state, in order to opt out of the community property law with respect to some or all of your property, both spouses must sign what is known as a "transmutation agreement." This document, which must be carefully drafted by an attorney, can transform your property ownership into whichever form you wish, and can be written to apply to your existing property as well as property you acquire in the future.

Any change in ownership here must be carefully considered. The community property ownership form was designed to accord equal property rights to spouses. Thus, planning here may involve giving up some of these rights, and the cost of doing this must be weighed against the benefits derived.

You should be aware that community property can impart an income tax advantage, despite its extreme disadvantage from an asset protection perspective: When one spouse dies, and the other inherits the other half of the property, the survivor receives a "stepped up" basis for the *whole interest* in the property rather than just the half he or she received. This means that any appreciation in the value of the property—between the time the couple had purchased the asset and the date of the first spouse's death—will not be taxed when the property is later sold.

By contrast, in joint tenancy, upon the death of one spouse, the other gets a stepped-up basis for only that spouse's half-interest. (Nevertheless, with the first $250,000 of capital gain per person from the sale of a home now automatically tax-free, for most taxpayers there may be no real advantage here with respect to a home.) The advantage may still exist for investments and other assets that appreciate in value. Still, the risks in this ownership form may outweigh any income tax benefits.

Using a Trust To Protect a Homestead

The homestead should never be contributed to a business entity, such as a corporation, LLC or partnership. Asset exemptions are available only to natural persons, and not to business entities.

In contrast, transfers of a home to a revocable living trust ordinarily should not create this same problem. Such transfers are common estate-planning tools where the goal is to avoid probate court.

In tax cases, the courts have already ruled that, after a transfer to a revocable living trust, the individual can still claim the personal exclusion of the first $250,000 of gain from the sale of a residence, as if it were still owned by the taxpayer personally. In a revocable living trust, the trustor (trust creator) can cancel or amend the trust at will, and the trustor is usually also the trustee and the beneficiary. Thus, the trustor still has complete control over the property.

While there is no guarantee, this same reasoning should extend to asset exemption cases.

However, there is one situation where transfers to a revocable living trust require special attention. In many cases, this type of trust takes the form of an estate-tax-saving bypass or "credit-shelter" trust. Here, a married couple transfers assets to the trust. While both are living, the trust is revocable.

When the first spouse dies, that spouse's share of the trust assets flow into a new, irrevocable trust, under which those assets are managed for the surviving spouse. The survivor has limited powers with respect to the new trust's assets and therefore will escape estate tax on those assets when he or she eventually dies.

The surviving spouse may not be able to claim any exemptions in the assets in the irrevocable trust. The irrevocable trust will be recognized as a separate entity and, in fact, will pay its own income taxes, according to a separate schedule for trusts and estates.

This is especially important to understand because, in many cases, an interest in a home, IRA or other exempt asset may have been contributed to the irrevocable trust. Exemptions would have continued to be available for these interests, had the transfers been outright to the surviving spouse. The bottom line: The exemptions will likely be lost. However, protection may still exist, through a different strategy.

Specifically, this type of trust can immunize trust assets from the claims of creditors through a spendthrift clause. While in certain circumstances this type of clause can be invalid, in the case of the irrevocable trust described here, it should be valid (see Chapter 5 for details on asset protection trusts and spendthrift clauses).

Plan Smart

If you have a bypass trust and are unsure whether the trust contains an effective spendthrift clause, ask an estate-planning attorney to review the document.

The Retirement Plan Exemption

Retirement plans represent a significant planning opportunity for the small business owner. In states with a small or nonexistent homestead exemption, this category may provide the best protection available for assets. Even in states with a significant or unlimited homestead exemption, the amount that can be accumulated and protected inside a retirement plan will often exceed the value of the homestead exemption.

Every small business owner should be aware of some basic retirement plan concepts. Today, self-employed individuals operating limited liability companies (LLCs), sole proprietorships, general partnerships, and S corporations can form retirement plans on virtually the same terms as large C corporations.

A popular retirement plan among small business owners is the SIMPLE (Savings Incentive Match Plan for Employees). The SIMPLE can be formed as an amendment to an existing standard 401(k) plan or as an IRA (Individual Retirement Account).

Each year you may contribute up to the lesser of 3 percent of your net earnings or $8,000 (in 2003) to your own account in a SIMPLE plan, and you must permit your employees to make salary-reduction contributions as well. All these contributions must be matched by the business, dollar for dollar.

The IRA version is easier to set up. However, as discussed below, the 401(k) version may be a better choice, because it may offer better protection from the claims of creditors.

The SIMPLE plan is exempt from the usual pension anti-discrimination and top-heavy rules that govern pensions. This makes administration of the plan much simpler (hence the name).

Warning

If you use a SIMPLE plan, it must be the only retirement plan the business offers.

As an alternative, you may choose to form a SEP (Simplified Employee Pension), under which up to the lesser of 15 percent of your salary or $40,000 (in 2003) may be contributed to an IRA. You must also contribute the same percentage of each employee's pay to individual IRAs established for each employee, but the plan is flexible: The contribution percentages can vary from year to year and you can even skip years if you wish.

Finally, small business owners may establish "regular" pension plans, including defined-benefit, defined-contribution, and conventional 401(k) salary-reduction plans. An advantage of the conventional plan is the high contribution limit of $40,000 per year (in 2003), for your own account for defined-contribution plans (or even more, if you use a defined-benefit pension plan), and the fact that you can contribute less for lower-paid or younger employees. You may also combine types of plans to get the best features of each.

Plan Smart

While using conventional types of pension plans allows you to combine different plans to get the maximum advantage from each of them, don't forget about the complexity that can be involved for these retirement plans. The administrative costs for a conventional plan may be cost-prohibitive for the small business owner.

Effect of ERISA on Exemption Status

When a retirement plan is subject to ERISA (the federal Employee Retirement Income Security Act), its assets will be excluded from a bankruptcy proceeding and a state court proceeding. Most retirement plans are covered by ERISA, although there are a few notable exceptions discussed below.

The U.S. Supreme Court has specifically ruled that ERISA-qualified retirement plans are not an issue in a bankruptcy proceeding. The assets in such plans are *excluded* from the filer's bankruptcy estate, rather than exempted. Thus, the small business owner does not have to claim a state or federal exemption to exclude these assets.

In a state court proceeding, usually these assets will be expressly exempted by statute. However, this is not the case in all states. Some states offer no protection or limited protection (see the Appendices for specific state information). Where the state does not exempt these assets in their entirety, the small business owner may be able to rely on a doctrine termed "preemption" to protect the assets.

In other words, a very strong argument can be made today that ERISA preempts, or overrules, state law, and thus protects qualified pension assets in a state court proceeding.

If a creditor attempts to attach ERISA-qualified retirement assets in a state court proceeding, and the state does not exempt the assets, it is advisable to hire an attorney and fight the attachment on the grounds of ERISA preemption.

A U.S. Court of Appeals ruled that ERISA preempted an Hawaiian statute that did not protect assets deposited to an ERISA-qualified plan within three years of a bankruptcy proceeding.

The court ruled that ERISA offers complete protection for these assets, and that ERISA overruled state laws to the contrary. Many other federal courts, as well as state courts, have ruled this way.

Unprotected IRAs

SIMPLE and SEP retirement plans can represent an excellent strategy that small business owners can use to shield assets from creditors. However, the exemption available for ERISA-qualified retirement plans will not apply to IRAs established through these plans. IRAs that are established privately, or by business owners in a SIMPLE or SEP plan, are not considered ERISA-qualified.

However, IRAs are usually protected by state statute. This exemption can be relied on in a state court proceeding, or in bankruptcy by claiming the state's exemptions. However, many times, the exemption for IRAs is not complete, as it may not extend to all types of IRAs, or may be limited in the amounts that it covers.

For example, because Roth and Coverdell (education) IRAs are new, not all states have updated their statutes to include these IRA forms. However, this can be expected soon, at least in the case of Roth IRAs. Further, the following states currently offer no clear-cut exemptions for IRAs: District of Columbia, Iowa, Michigan, New Hampshire, New Mexico, and Wyoming. (See Appendix A for details on the types of IRAs your state exempts.)

For these reasons, a SIMPLE 401(k) may be a better choice, especially in states that offer no protection, or very limited protection, for SIMPLE or SEP IRAs. However, because of its simplicity, a SIMPLE or SEP IRA may be a better choice in states that completely exempt IRAs established through these plans.

Court decisions may also exempt IRAs and provide an alternative to statutory exemptions. Some state and federal courts have ruled that provisions within the Internal Revenue Code (IRC) make IRAs, and plans based on IRAs, exempt in state court proceedings and bankruptcy proceedings. They hold that the IRCs provisions preempt state law. However, many other courts have ruled the opposite way, holding that IRAs are protected only if they are expressly exempt under state statute. Because of this uncertainty, it is still best, at this time anyway, to form a SIMPLE 401(k) plan when state statutes do not completely exempt SIMPLE and SEP IRAs, unless a legal opinion is obtained indicating that case law applicable in the particular state can be relied on to exempt IRAs.

Finally, Roth IRAs offer excellent tax benefits. Where a state also exempts Roth IRAs, this investment also represents a valuable asset protection device. However, as the Appendices indicate, many states exempt Roth IRAs, but not Coverdell IRAs. So, it may be advisable to avoid Coverdell IRAs, at least where asset protection is a primary objective.

ERISA Eligibility Requirement

There is a very important exclusion from ERISA, which has a direct effect on the small business owner. A retirement plan that includes only the business owner and his or her spouse as participants is not qualified under ERISA.

Example

In one case, a husband and wife were the only participants in a retirement plan established by their corporation.

They had accumulated $1.6 million in the plan. Because the plan did not cover any employees other than the business owner and his spouse, the plan was not qualified and therefore not protected under ERISA.

The result: The entire $1.6 million was made available to the couple's creditors.

On the other hand, if the plan has at least one other participant, it is protected under ERISA.

Plan Smart

An effective strategy would be for the business to hire a child of the business owner and include the child as a participant in the plan. A child as young as seven or eight can perform simple tasks like dusting, emptying wastebaskets and making copies, and therefore can be a legitimate employee.

This simple strategy qualifies your retirement plan under ERISA and thus protects all of the plan's assets from the reach of creditors. It also has other advantages. The child's earned income will not be subject to income taxes, to the extent of the standard deduction, currently $4,750 for singles (in 2003). In addition, 3 percent of the child's income, plus another 3 percent matching contribution by the business, could be contributed to a SIMPLE 401(k) plan, where it will accumulate tax-deferred.

At least one court has held that once a plan becomes ERISA-qualified because it has one other participant besides the business owner and his or her spouse, it remains qualified, even after that other participant terminated employment and participation in the plan.

Finally, where an individual controls, directly or indirectly, more than one business entity, all of the entities will be combined in assessing whether at least one other person participates in any one of the entity's retirement plans.

Example

In one case, a physician was successfully sued for malpractice. The plaintiff obtained a judgment of over $60,000, and sought to attach the physician's retirement plan.

The physician and his spouse were participants in the plan. However, the physician also employed one other person. This was sufficient to bring the plan within the protections offered by ERISA.

While this other employee was actually employed by a corporation separate from the entity that offered the retirement plan, the two entities were both owned by the physician and his spouse, and thus were combined under the Internal Revenue Code's rules governing controlled entities.

Retirement Planning

Every business owner with the necessary resources should establish a retirement plan. The funds in a retirement plan are, of course, tax-deferred for income tax purposes. This benefit alone usually justifies the establishment of a retirement plan, offsetting the administrative costs of starting it.

More importantly, however, for the small business owner, forming a retirement plan is an extremely effective asset protection strategy. In theory, the exemption for retirement plan assets is unlimited. The small business owner can shield millions of dollars in this way.

In practice, the exemption will be limited only by how much money you have available each year to contribute to the plan and by the Internal Revenue Code's limitations on contributions. However, the tax law's limitations on contributions are actually quite generous. From an asset protection perspective, this means that, in a thriving business, every year a sizeable amount of your cash can be converted to an exempt asset.

Of course, some small business owners voice concerns over the relative unavailability of retirement benefits before they reach a certain age, as withdrawals prior to the mandatory age are usually subject to a 10 percent penalty. (In a SIMPLE plan, the penalty would be 25 percent during the first two years of a plan, and 10 percent thereafter).

Think of the penalty this way: If you personally own $800,000 of securities and suffer an adverse court judgment, or file for bankruptcy, you could lose the entire $800,000. In contrast, if the same $800,000 of securities is owned through a retirement plan, the entire $800,000 is protected. If you later need these resources, and withdraw the entire amount before the required age, at the very least you still save $720,000 ($800,000 less the 10 percent penalty). This amounts to a very good bargain.

Warning

All retirement plan assets can be attached to collect alimony and child support, as well as federal taxes. ERISA specifically provides for these exemptions.

However, these are the only exceptions where attachment is allowed.

The Wage Exemption

Typically, states exempt 75 percent of the debtor's disposable income. In other words, a judgment creditor could only attach 25 percent of your disposable income, which is defined as gross wages less amounts required by law to be withheld, including federal income and Social Security taxes.

Plan Smart

Some states provide for no specific wage exemption. However, federal law imposes on each state this same 25-percent restriction on wage attachment. This federal law preempts or overrules state laws.

In addition, federal law provides for a minimum wage exemption, which is equal to 30 times the current federal hourly minimum wage. With a federal minimum wage of $5.15, this means that at least the first $154.50 of weekly wages is exempt ($5.15 x 30).

In the case of a wage attachment for child support or alimony, the restriction on wage attachment is increased to 50 percent.

If you reside in Florida, you'll have a much more generous exemption if you are the "head of a family." There, *all* of the disposable earnings of a head of family are exempt. A head of family includes any natural person providing more than one-half of the support for a child or other dependent. Even where the head of a family has voluntarily agreed to a wage attachment (an unlikely occurrence), the first $500 of weekly disposable earnings is still exempt (see the Appendices for state specific information on wage exemption). In addition, Florida provides that up to 6 months of accumulated wages that have been deposited into an account also are exempt. This provision applies to wage earners.

Paying Yourself

In planning for the wage exemption, you primarily must ensure that your earnings from the business will constitute exempt "wages."

You should always take an authorized and regularly scheduled salary from the business, regardless of the form in which the business was organized.

In most states, "earnings" includes compensation paid or payable, in money of a sum certain, for personal services or labor, whether denominated as wages, salary, commission, or bonus.

Typically, owners of a regular C corporation draw a salary from the business. However, in the case of other business forms, this is usually not the case.

The failure to take a salary in these other business forms will likely mean the earnings from the business will not qualify for the exemption. The definition of exempt "earnings" would exclude a business owner's share of earnings in a limited liability company (LLC), subchapter S corporation, or partnership, when the business owners merely divide up the net income of the business. Taking a salary solves this problem.

A salary is also an important way of withdrawing vulnerable funds from the business entity. This is another example of a multi-layered approach to asset protection (see Chapter 14 for more details on structuring withdrawals from the business).

Plan Smart

Small business owners in the state of Florida should ideally deposit into a bank account, and retain in the account, the last six months' wages. Remember, too, that in Florida, the wage exemption for a head of household is unlimited in amount. In theory, it makes sense to deposit and retain all of the wages earned during the prior six months, to establish a record of the amount of compensation you earned. In practice, the limit for this account will be based on the availability of cash and your other personal needs. Withdrawals from the account can be based on deposits that occurred more than six months ago.

This strategy comports with the advice offered by most financial advisors—homeowners should keep an emergency bank account consisting of approximately six months of wages.

In other states, the same strategy can be used. Here, however, the amount deposited will be limited by the state's exemption statute, and the shorter exemption period will dictate how long wages should remain in the account (see the Appendices for information on each state's exemption for wages statute).

Bankruptcy Provisions

In a Chapter 7 bankruptcy proceeding, generally only assets owned at the start of the case are included in the bankruptcy estate.

Thus, the debtor retains wages earned during the proceeding, in their entirety. This is one of the many reasons that debtors typically file in Chapter 7. Wages earned prior to the proceeding, but unpaid, can be exempted only if the state's exemptions are claimed.

In a Chapter 13 proceeding, the debtor commits all disposable income, after accounting for reasonable living expenses, to paying off creditors over a three- or five-year period. The difference between the treatment of wages earned during the proceeding will usually, but not always, make Chapter 7 a better choice than Chapter 13 (bankruptcy categories are compared in Chapter 2).

The Annuity Exemption

Many states exempt annuities, although there is no federal bankruptcy exemption for annuities. An annuity is a fund that provides an equal periodic (usually monthly) amount of money to the purchaser. In most states the exemption for annuities is limited to a fixed dollar amount per month (e.g., in Idaho the exemption is limited to $350 per month). However, in some states, for example, Florida, the exemption for annuities is unlimited in most cases.

Defined-benefit pension plans pay retirement benefits as an annuity. In that case, the receipts are exempt under the retirement plan exemption discussed previously.

Many individuals purchase commercial annuities from insurance companies, typically as a supplement to their retirement earnings. The annuity exemption is primarily intended to cover commercial annuities. Thus, the purchase of a commercial annuity also serves as an asset protection device. It's particularly useful if you find that conventional retirement plans are too costly to set up, or you don't wish to fund a retirement plan that includes your employees.

Essentially, the cash used to purchase the annuity is converted to an exempt asset. Of course, as the cash is received back each month, it is re-converted to a nonexempt asset. The advantage to the annuity is that, during the entire period it is outstanding, you have a protected source from which you can draw income.

Private Annuities

Moreover, a planning opportunity exists because the exemption usually extends to private annuities. This is an arrangement, established by contract, between two individuals, who are usually family members.

Private annuities are frequently used in estate planning. Usually, an older family member (e.g., a parent) "sells" property, such as interests in the family business or other securities, to the younger family member (e.g., a child) in exchange for a private life annuity.

The transfer eliminates gift and estate taxes on the amount transferred. Because the older family member receives a private annuity of equal value in return for the transfer, no gift tax is due on the transfer. In addition, the value transferred is removed from the taxable estate of the older family member, because the life annuity held by the older family member terminates upon his or her death. The gift and estate tax savings created by the transfer can be significant.

For many parents, the process of reducing the size of their taxable estate presents a dilemma. To reduce their estate taxes, parents must, many times, transfer wealth to children during the parents' lifetime. Yet, they are reluctant to give up all rights in the property, because they believe they may need some of these resources in the future. The private annuity solves that dilemma.

Example

John Smith has operated a very successful business for many years. He now owns a stock portfolio valued at $1 million.

He transfers $500,000 of the securities to his daughter in exchange for a private annuity that will pay him $1,000 per month for life. (It is assumed here that the $1,000 per month makes the exchange of equal value).

The $500,000 has been removed from Smith's taxable estate. This transfer, alone, could have saved Smith $200,000 or more in estate taxes, depending on the value of other assets he owns. In addition, no gift taxes are due, because no gift was made, as there was an even exchange.

Finally, Smith has now converted the $500,000 of securities, which formerly were within the reach of his creditors, to an exempt asset.

You should consider a private annuity if you hold substantial nonexempt assets and live in a state that exempts annuities, or if federal estate taxes are an issue for you. These assets can be transferred to a child or other family member in exchange for a private annuity, which would convert nonexempt assets to exempt, as well as eliminate estate and gift taxes.

While this may not be a first-line strategy for the average business owner, as time passes and more wealth is generated by the business, it becomes a very attractive strategy. The annuity contract must be drafted, and the annuity valued, so that no gift tax is due on the transfer. This will normally require the services of an estate planning attorney.

The private annuity is also a common strategy used to transfer interests in a business from parents to children. Nonvoting interests can be transferred in this way to reduce that parent's taxable estate, while allowing the parent to maintain control of the business (see Chapter 10 for more details on this topic).

Finally, it must be remembered that the assets transferred will be owned by the transferee (e.g., the child), and thus within the reach of *that* individual's creditors. Even here, however, the assets can be protected if the transfer is made to a trust (with a spendthrift clause) that will manage the assets for the beneficiary (see Chapter 5 for a discussion of asset protection trusts).

It's important to note that if the annuity you establish is especially valuable, you would have to claim your state's exemptions in a bankruptcy proceeding, because there is no federal exemption for annuities.

The Wild Card Exemption

Many states provide a wild card exemption that can be used to protect various types of personal property. Usually the wild card exemption is a small, specific dollar amount, averaging around $1,000. Some states also allow some or all of an unused homestead exemption to be used as a wild card. The federal bankruptcy code adopts both of these approaches.

The state of Texas provides the most generous wild card exemption: $60,000 for heads of household ($30,000 for others) that can be applied, at the debtor's discretion, to various types of personal property (see the Appendices for specific state wild card exemptions).

Exempting an Ownership Interest in a Business

A wild card may be the most effective way, or the only way, *from an exemption viewpoint*, to protect an ownership interest in a business, which is considered an item of personal property.

Because of the limited dollar value of the wild card exemption, however, the best approach to protecting the ownership interest in a business is the strategy explored in detail in Chapter 8—form the business as an limited liability company (LLC), and then minimize the amount of vulnerable capital within the operating entity through: a strategic initial investment, leases of assets to the business, a practice of regular withdrawals from the business, and liens on the business's assets in favor of the owner in exchange for extensions of credit from the owner.

These practices will shield the business's assets, and the owner's personal assets, from the claims of the business's creditors. In addition, the use of an LLC will offer the greatest possible protection for the owner's interest in the business from the claims of the owner's personal creditors.

In addition, another estate planning strategy involves creating the business as an LLC, and then conveying nonvoting ownership interests to family members (i.e., children), either outright or in trust (the main advantages of this strategy are outlined in Chapter 10).

However, this strategy also has significant advantages in terms of exemption planning. As discussed above, the wild card exemptions available for general items of personal property are usually quite limited. By conveying ownership interests in this manner, you will retain complete control of the business, but at the same time reduce the monetary value of your particular ownership interest to a level that is likely to fit within the wild card exemption.

At any rate, you should examine the wild card exemption available in your state, and the analogous federal exemption if your state has not opted out of the federal exemptions, and consider the extent to which it would protect your personal property, including your interest in the business.

Tools of the Trade and Household Goods Exemptions

"Tools of the trade" and "household goods" are exemption categories that provide good examples of the pigeon-hole concept, into which a particular item of property must somehow be fitted in order to be exempt.

For example, individuals have successfully argued that valuable diamond rings are exempt as wearing apparel treated as protected household goods, rather than jewelry that would not be protected. Debtors in other courts have lost this same argument.

"Tools of the trade" are frequently exempt and can be widely interpreted to include any property reasonably necessary to carry out a business. Sometimes a vehicle can be qualified under this provision only if it is uniquely put to use in the business, such as a delivery van. If a vehicle were not qualified under this category, it would have to fit under a specific exemption for motor vehicles, which could offer less protection.

Keep in mind that the "tools of the trade" exemption will not ordinarily apply to the property owned by a business entity, such as a limited liability company (LLC) or a corporation, as exemptions are available only to natural persons. Thus, the exemption may not be as significant as first appears.

Plan Smart

As discussed in Chapter 8, a business owner should own assets personally or in a holding company, and lease them to the operating company, to shield the assets from the claims of the business's creditors.

When the assets to be leased fit under one of the exemptions, the owner should consider personally owning them so that he or she can rely on the exemption for the assets. This can be done with respect to tools of the trade, including office equipment and motor vehicles used in the business.

The one exception to this rule may be assets that carry a high risk of causing injury. Here, the owner ordinarily should contribute these assets to the operating company, because liability may run to the owner. An example would be motor vehicles used by other employees of the business.

When only the owner uses a motor vehicle, the risk is reduced, and the strategy of personally owning the asset becomes more attractive.

The same reasoning applies to the other tools of the trade. Manufacturing machinery may be too risky to personally own, while office equipment may be an ideal candidate for this strategy.

In either case, but especially when the owner personally owns the asset, the owner should ensure that there is more than adequate liability insurance coverage on the asset.

Finally, this strategy does not apply to nonexempt assets such as a commercial building. In the case of a commercial building, the risks would usually be too high to justify this strategy in any event. Nevertheless, in many cases, a lease of a commercial building makes sense. However, the lessor (and owner) should be the holding company.

The classification of exempt "household goods" usually involves various subcategories. States sometimes create separate categories for items that another state would include within the household goods category as a subcategory. As a result, the states vary widely in terms of what categories and subcategories they make available. Further, even with subcategories, the term "household goods" suffers from the same problem as the term "tools of the trade"—it is subject to court interpretation.

Subcategories are sometimes subject to caps, as are the controlling categories. For example, there is a federal bankruptcy exemption for household goods, but there is an overall cap of $9,300, and a separate cap of $450 per item. In some states, the categories have no caps. In others, the debtor has to prove certain items qualify as basic necessities.

In many cases, the dollar caps are relatively low. Nevertheless, all debtors will want to protect this type of property and, in particular, personal effects, many times simply for sentimental reasons.

For this reason, you should examine your state's particular exemptions (see the Appendices for your specific state information). In doing so, it is a good practice to conservatively include items within particular categories that indisputably fit there, while keeping in mind that it may be possible, if necessary, to stretch the definition of certain categories.

Doubling of Exemptions

States sometimes provide that *each* individual owner can claim an exemption for their property. Thus, a husband and wife can double the exemptions listed in the state's law, provided that (1) they are joint owners of the property, and (2) each of them is liable on the debt in question. Sometimes, only a married couple is allowed to double the homestead exemption.

Some states only provide one singular exemption, regardless of how many owners there are for the piece of property (the Appendices indicates the states' positions on doubling of exemptions). Where doubling is permitted, take this into account when determining to what extent particular assets will be protected.

The bankruptcy code allows for the doubling of *all* of the federal exemptions, when a husband and wife file for bankruptcy together, *regardless of who is the debtor.* Who actually owes the debts is irrelevant when spouses file together, because both the husband and wife are parties to the same petition.

In a state court proceeding, normally only one spouse will be a party to the case, when only that one spouse owes the debt in question.

This feature of the bankruptcy code makes the federal bankruptcy exemptions preferable when a husband and wife file together, and the state's exemptions are not significant. Where the state exemptions are claimed, the state's laws on doubling would apply.

Proceeds from Exempt Assets

Exemption planning involves the conversion of nonexempt assets into exempt assets. While the *opposite* of exemption planning should never be voluntarily undertaken, in reality it will sometimes be inevitable. For example, life insurance will be converted to cash upon the death of the insured. Exempt wages will be received, and become simply "cash," a nonexempt asset. In each of these cases, what was once an exempt asset loses its exempt status.

Ideally, when this happens, a plan will be in place to apply the cash proceeds to an exemption (e.g., by paying down a mortgage on a home with an unlimited homestead exemption, by making a contribution to a retirement plan, by making a gift in return for a private annuity, etc.).

Nevertheless, because of the unfairness of an involuntary conversion to a nonexempt form, many states provide that the proceeds from certain exempt assets are, in turn, exempt for a certain period of time.

This exemption applies only to certain listed exempt assets, usually life insurance (subject to restrictions) and, in some states, the homestead and earned but unpaid wages. The exemption is relatively short-lived, typically being in a range of two to 18 months, with six months an average for homestead proceeds. The exception here is life insurance proceeds, which, subject to certain restrictions, are simply exempt in many states regardless of the time that elapses, or the number of times that the proceeds are re-invested into different forms.

Plan Smart

Even where there's a generous exemption, it is doubtful that life insurance proceeds will remain exempt forever. Assume that, even in this situation, the exemption will expire eventually, but at the same time save records as if the exemption will never expire, on the outside chance that an asset acquired with the proceeds, even years later, may still be exempt.

In every case involving exempt proceeds, it is important to be able to trace and separately identify the proceeds, in whatever form they exist in the future. Records should be established that detail the trail of the proceeds. They should be retained, along with copies of supporting documentation, for at least the life of the new exemption or, in the absence of a fixed expiration period, indefinitely.

In Hawaii, sales proceeds from an exempt homestead are exempt for six months. Idaho follows this same six-month rule, while the period is one year in Illinois, and 18 months in Montana.

Many states do not exempt proceeds from the sale of an exempt homestead. Thus, caution should always be exercised before selling any exempt asset—in particular, the homestead—because of its value.

Florida exempts the amount of allowable wages received in the six months prior to an attachment or bankruptcy action, provided the proceeds have been deposited into a bank account. This is an especially generous exemption, because the wage exemption in Florida is unlimited for heads of household; in most other states, only earned but unpaid wages will qualify for this exemption (you can examine your state's exemptions in the Appendices to determine whether, and to what extent, your state exempts the proceeds received from the disposition of exempt assets).

Other Exemption Planning Strategies

There are other exemption planning strategies you should consider, such as changing your state of residence and converting secured debt into unsecured debt.

Change of Residence

A change of residence may be a prelude to a conversion of assets into an exempt form. A change in residence can be very effective, because individuals can always claim their state's exemptions, in or out of bankruptcy, and because states vary widely in terms of the exemptions they offer.

While states often have residency requirements (usually six months to a year) with respect to divorce or voting, most are silent on the issue of establishing residency for purposes of claiming asset exemptions. In most cases this is not an issue because it usually arises in a bankruptcy action. There, the federal bankruptcy code controls, which establishes a six-month residency requirement.

Conversion of Secured Debt into Unsecured Debt

As discussed earlier, consensual liens, such as mortgages and car loans, generally cannot be eliminated even when they impair an exemption. Another effective strategy consists of paying down secured debt with unsecured debt. This can be especially effective prior to a bankruptcy action (if planned far enough in advance). For example, you could make a mortgage payment with a credit card. The amount of cash represented by the payment is effectively converted to an exempt form (equity in your home, which is presumably protected by the homestead exemption). Because the unsecured credit card debt can be discharged in bankruptcy, the debtor protects this amount of cash as if it were an exempt asset.

Example

John Smith, a Texas resident, is carrying a $160,000 mortgage on a home worth $180,000. Smith's monthly mortgage payment is $1,600.

Smith is short of funds, and anticipates, sometime in the future, that he may have to file for bankruptcy.

He makes two mortgage payments using his credit card's "access checks," for a total of $3,200, and files for bankruptcy 14 months later.

Smith has converted the $3,200 to an exempt form. The credit card debt, including the $3,200, will likely be discharged. In short, Smith has protected and saved $3,200.

It's important to know that each of the strategies presented in this chapter must be executed so as to avoid creditor challenges. Avoiding creditor challenges to asset transfers is the focus of Chapter 4.

Chapter 4

Avoiding Challenges to Asset Transfers

It is often possible to use carefully planned transfers to place your assets out of the reach of potential creditors. This can done in two ways: asset exemption planning and strategic funding practices within your business entity.

Effective exemption planning can take many forms: using any of your available cash to purchase exempt assets; paying down mortgages on homes if your state provides an unlimited homestead exemption, or if the amount of the homestead exemption exceeds the value of your home; adding a mortgage to a home when the value of the home equity exceeds the amount of the homestead exemption; or converting secured debt into unsecured debt by, for example, using a credit card to make a mortgage payment. A change of residence to a more debtor-friendly state is a more dramatic way to facilitate asset exemption planning.

Strategically funding your business entity means minimizing the amount of vulnerable capital within the business. You can accomplish this by making leases and loans of assets to the business entity; by making a practice of regularly withdrawing funds from the entity as salary, lease and loan payments to yourself; and by encumbering the entity's assets with liens that run in favor of yourself, and that result from extensions of credit from you to the business (Chapter 3 discusses effective use of select asset exemptions, while Chapter 8 addresses strategic funding practices).

In each situation, it's still possible for creditors to challenge your asset transfers. Through proper planning, these challenges usually can be blocked effectively. This chapter will discuss the primary theories and strategies your creditors may use to challenge transfers under the Uniform Fraudulent Transfers Act (UFTA), as well as the steps you can take to minimize the risks of such challenges.

In addition, we'll examine how transfers can have an impact on your Medicaid status later in life, and how to preserve assets when planning for the medical issues that affect old age.

Plan Smart

 Besides the Uniform Fraudulent Transfer Act (UFTA) and bankruptcy code rules that restrict asset transfers, special provisions in state limited liability company (LLC) and corporation statutes also restrict distributions from the business entity to an owner. If your business takes either LLC or corporate form, you'll need to consider the impact the laws may have on you.

While the UFTA and bankruptcy code apply to all types of transfers, the reach of these other statutes is limited to distributions made on account of the ownership interest. These distributions include dividends or other distributions of earnings, and ownership buy-outs such as stock redemptions. Ordinarily, these statutes will not *apply to payments of salary, or for leases and loans, to the owner, because these distributions are not made to the owner simply because of ownership (i.e., they are made to you in your capacity as an employee, lessor or lender). This fundamental tenet of asset protection is addressed in Chapter 14.*

Note that when distributions of earnings and ownership redemptions are planned, the business owner must be aware of the separate *rules (including the* separate *solvency tests) that will apply under these statutes. These rules are also covered in Chapter 14.*

HOW UFTA AFFECTS TRANSFERS

All states have enacted a version of the Uniform Fraudulent Transfers Act (UFTA). It is primarily through this act that creditors will challenge your asset transfers. Under the act, timing and motive (or intent), along with solvency, are critical factors in avoiding creditor challenges.

The UFTA outlaws two types of fraud:

- constructive fraud

- actual fraud

When the transferor (e.g., the business entity) is solvent, actual fraud, in which the creditor must prove motive or intent, will likely be the more important of the two provisions, both in cases involving exemption planning transfers and transfers from the business entity. Each type of fraud is discussed later in this chapter.

Timing the Transfers

The UFTA has a four-year statute of limitations (although some states apply a shorter period). Thus, if more than four years have elapsed since a transfer, ordinarily the transfer will be beyond challenge. Clearly, there is an advantage to planning any transfers before a business is formed, or at least while a business is thriving; once four years have passed, your transfers will be "safe." With transfers that occur in the midst of a financial crisis, it is doubtful that four years will elapse before the transfer is challenged.

However, this is not to say that effective transfers cannot be made within the four years preceding a challenge. In that case, however, the transfer will be open to court scrutiny, and you will have to be able to justify it. This is where motive (or intent) and solvency become the important factors. In contrast, transfers made more than four years prior to a challenge will not be subject to court examination.

Timing Before a Bankruptcy

The federal bankruptcy code has specific time limitations when it comes to transfers. The code provides that debts incurred through actual fraud within one year of the bankruptcy filing cannot be discharged. Bankruptcy courts usually (but not always) interpret this power broadly enough to allow a challenge to *any* fraudulent transfer within the time frame, including exemption planning conversions.

Thus, one year emerges as a critical time period in pre-bankruptcy planning, and many times you will be advised to take a certain action, then wait for a little over a year to file for bankruptcy. Once again, transfers within the one-year period before the filing are not automatically invalid. However, bankruptcy courts will apply special scrutiny to transfers that occur within this one-year period, and you would have to answer questions concerning such transfers in writing, and under oath, on the bankruptcy petition.

On the other hand, this is not to say that transfers made more than one year before a filing are totally secure. In fact, the code also provides that bankruptcy courts may apply a *state* statute in determining whether transfers were fraudulent. Here, this means the UFTA with its four-year statute of limitations.

Warning

An important exception to the one-year rule is that in a federal bankruptcy setting, residency will be determined as of six months prior to the filing of the action. Effectively, this requirement prevents you from expanding your exemptions by moving to a new state during the six-month period prior to filing the action.

In two situations under the federal bankruptcy code, transfers are *automatically* invalid. The code provides that "preferences" paid to insiders (family members and controlled business entities) within one year of filing are invalid. The period is 90 days for preferential transfers to non-insiders. Virtually all transfers by small business owners will be to insiders, and thus will come under the one-year provision.

Also, in a bankruptcy setting, under the rule governing "luxury purchases," debts incurred for purchases on credit or loans, of more than $1,000 from a single creditor, within the 60 days prior to filing, can not be discharged.

Note that in the cases of preferential transfers and luxury purchases, the rules govern the covered transactions, regardless of the debtor's motive.

Timing Under State Law

Some states have specific provisions dealing with conversion of nonexempt assets into exempt assets, apart from their version of the UFTA. Typically, these provisions exist in states that provide generous exemptions, such as Florida and Texas, where conversions occur on a regular basis. These specialized statutes will take precedence over the general provisions of the UFTA.

While it may first appear that such statutes create a disadvantage for debtors, the opposite is true when the specialized statute provides a shorter statute of limitations. For example, in Texas, a creditor must mount a challenge within two years after the transfer. This compares, of course, to four years under the UFTA. Thus, in Texas, asset exemption transfers made more than two years before a challenge will escape scrutiny. Other types of transfers are still subject to the UFTA.

Plan Smart

As was discussed in Chapter 3, the homestead exemption is established by the constitution in some states, including Florida and Texas.

Due to this fact, the Florida Supreme Court declared unconstitutional, and therefore invalid, a specialized statute that Florida had enacted to regulate fraudulent asset exemption transfers.

A legislature may not, by statute, take away a constitutional right. This is a fundamental principle of law. A similar argument can be made in Texas.

Constructive Fraud

In a constructive fraud case, your motive or intent is irrelevant. To establish that the transfer was fraudulent, the creditor must only prove two things:

- The debtor was insolvent when the transfer was made.

- The debtor did not receive adequate consideration (that is, something of equal or greater value) in return for the transfer.

The strategies advocated in this book will, in most cases, ensure that you don't meet the second criterion, and thus eliminate any claim based on constructive fraud.

Asset Exemption Transfers and Constructive Fraud

The law governing asset exemption transfers is muddled. Most exemption planning occurs in a bankruptcy context. The *legislative history* to the bankruptcy code clearly indicates that Congress's intent was to allow pre-bankruptcy exemption planning. Further, the code has no *specific* provision outlawing such transfers. Accordingly, some bankruptcy courts routinely allow such transfers, except in the most egregious cases.

On the other hand, despite the legislative history of the code and the lack of a specific provision outlawing these transfers, *most* bankruptcy courts apply the standards of the UFTA to asset exemption transfers in the same way the UFTA is applied to any other transfers. So some uneven results have been achieved.

Most debtors considering bankruptcy will be insolvent (see below for a detailed definition of this term) and will automatically meet the first criteria for constructive fraud. Thus, it is important that you be able to establish that you received adequate consideration in return for the transfer to avoid a constructive fraud claim.

This will not present a problem in most cases, because asset exemption transfers usually involve the conversion of nonexempt assets into exempt assets—that is, an equal exchange of value. For example, the purchase of an exempt home for cash involves the receipt of adequate consideration in return (i.e., the home).

The result should be the same when a mortgage is paid down on an exempt residence. However, one bankruptcy court has ruled that, in this situation, the home does not provide any return consideration, and, thus, the transfer is made without the receipt of adequate consideration. This is true, according to the court, even when the mortgage is completely paid off, and the mortgage lien on the home is released.

In reality, of course, when you make a payment for a release of a lien, or simply for a release of part of the debt, the payment is made in return for valuable consideration. How many debtors would believe they received nothing in return in this situation? None. Accordingly, other courts may not follow this rationale. Nevertheless, under this interpretation, the transfer can be undone if the debtor is insolvent, as is likely in pre-bankruptcy exemption planning.

Is it a "Transfer?"

The same bankruptcy court that ruled above acknowledged another way to defeat the charge of constructive fraud. The UFTA only applies if a "transfer" is made. The court made a distinction between a transfer made by an individual to himself (or a married couple to themselves), on the one hand, and a transfer from a husband to a husband and wife, on the other. The first situation does not involve a "transfer," as there is no change in ownership. Therefore, since there is no transfer, there can be no constructive fraud.

In contrast, a transfer of the second type does involve a transfer, as there *is* a change in ownership.

Example

In the case in question, the husband inherited approximately $160,000 from his father. Immediately *after receiving this inheritance, he used it to completely pay off two mortgages on his home, which he owned in tenancy by the entirety with his spouse.*

The husband also individually *owed more than $100,000 in unsecured debt. Accordingly, about $1^1/_2$ years after he paid off the mortgages, he filed an individual bankruptcy action. His wife was not a party to this action.*

As discussed in Chapter 3, a creditor of only one spouse cannot reach property owned in tenancy by the entirety, when only the debtor spouse files in bankruptcy.

However, the bankruptcy court found that the mortgage payoff was fraudulent, and entered a judgment against the husband and the wife in the amount of the $160,000.

According to the court, there was a transfer from one entity (the husband) to a different entity (the husband and wife). Had the payment been from joint funds, rather than from the husband's inheritance, there would have been no "transfer," and therefore no fraud.

As shown in the previous example, one way to avoid a constructive fraud claim may be to ensure the transferor and transferee are one and the same. A payment on a mortgage secured by a jointly owned exempt home should come from joint funds, such as a joint checking account or a joint credit card.

In the example discussed above, the debtor received an inheritance, which is a source of funds attributable to only one spouse.

Had the debtor deposited the funds in the joint account, *and* left the funds in the account for a long period of time (the longer the better), so that the funds co-mingled with other joint funds in the account, it is possible that he would be considered to have converted the inheritance to joint funds, and thus the transaction would not have been a "transfer" according to the definition of the term adopted by the court in question.

In contrast to an inheritance are wages, which are usually deposited by a couple into a joint account on a regular basis and used to pay joint bills. These wages are likely to be considered joint funds much more rapidly than, say, an inheritance. Note that in the above example, the husband deposited the inheritance in a joint account for just a few days before paying off the mortgages. This was apparently insufficient to convert the funds to joint ownership, according to the court. This was probably due, in large part, to the unique character of an inheritance.

Thus, conversion of wages should not necessarily face the same outcome. However, it would be a mistake to pay down a mortgage on a jointly owned home from an account owned by only one spouse.

Plan Smart

In short, the small business owner should follow this rule in making asset exemption transfers: A solely owned nonexempt asset should be converted to a solely owned exempt asset, while jointly owned nonexempt assets should be converted to jointly owned exempt assets. While not foolproof, this strategy helps to make the transfer resistant to challenge, on the grounds that it is not actually a "transfer" subject to the UFTA.

This strategy can be used to purchase an exempt asset (such as an exempt homestead), to pay down a mortgage when the exemption amount exceeds the home's value, or to encumber the home with another mortgage when the value of the home exceeds the homestead exemption.

In some cases, following this rule won't be practical. In the case of a newly married couple, for example, it would be expected that a residence owned by one spouse might by transferred into tenancy by the entirety. Here, to defeat a claim of constructive fraud, the transferor would need to ensure that he or she is not insolvent at the time of the transfer.

Note that, in cases involving fraud within one year of a bankruptcy filing, the court will not have to rely on the UFTA to invalidate a fraudulent act. In this situation, whether or not the fraud was in the form of a "transfer" will probably be irrelevant, because the transfer occurred within one year of filing a bankruptcy action. Where, however, the alleged fraud occurred before the one-year period, or the action is in state court, whether or not the fraud took the form of a transfer can affect the outcome.

The moral of the story is that caution must be exercised, especially in pre-bankruptcy exemption planning, because the debtor will usually be insolvent. In this situation, if you do not receive adequate consideration in return for the transfer, there is the possibility that the transfer will automatically be deemed fraudulent, regardless of intent, under the constructive fraud theory.

Warning

When a debtor is insolvent, a "gift" will always be deemed fraudulent under the constructive fraud theory. A gift is a transfer to another person or entity, where the transferor receives nothing (or something inadequate) in return.

The UFTA does not expressly define the term "adequate consideration." However, essentially the term means something of approximately equal value.

Transfers by the Business

Creditors can challenge payments to the owner of a business for salary, lease payments and loans, as well as liens placed by the owner on the entity's assets. However, each of these transfers involves the owner providing adequate consideration to the entity, so they will not meet the second test for constructive fraud.

Lease and loan payments are made in return for assets provided by the owner to the entity. Liens result only from extensions of credit from the owner to the entity. Payments to the owner for services actually rendered, or for assets actually leased or loaned to the entity, should pass muster, provided that the amounts of the liens or payments are not outrageous in comparison to what the owner provided the entity.

In particular, with respect to salary, the owner has great leeway. As discussed in Chapter 14, owners can justify salaries amounting to hundreds of thousands of dollars as "reasonable" in many cases. Thus, each type of transfer is beyond reproach in any action based on constructive fraud.

Because creditors must prove *both* criteria for constructive fraud, the use of adequate consideration makes the issue of your insolvency irrelevant in a constructive fraud case. Note that insolvency can still be important in an actual fraud case, as discussed below.

Actual Fraud

The UFTA also outlaws actual fraud—that is, transfers made with the intent, or motive, of avoiding a debt. As was suggested above, you should be more concerned with this type of claim.

Both the UFTA itself and the courts have identified factors that tend to establish fraud. With the exception of the first factor (motive or intent), which must be proved in every case based on actual fraud, no one factor is necessarily more important than the others. Factors are weighed by the particular court, and the relative importance of a given factor varies on a case-by-case basis. Notwithstanding that, the most important factors, in most cases, are as follows:

- the motive or intent of the debtor

- whether the debtor was insolvent at the time of the transfer, or could reasonably anticipate becoming insolvent thereafter

- whether the transfer was concealed from the creditor

- whether, at the time the transfer was made, the debtor had been sued, was threatened with a lawsuit or was otherwise in the midst of a financial crisis

- whether the debtor received adequate consideration in return for the transfer

- whether, at the time the transfer occurred, the debtor had incurred a substantial debt

Other factors that are given weight include:

- whether the transfer was of all or substantially all of the debtor's assets

- whether the transfer was to an insider (i.e., family member or controlled entity)

- whether the debtor fled the vicinity or tried to hide assets

- whether the debtor transferred assets to a lien holder, who then transferred the assets to an insider of the debtor

Motive (Intent)

Actual fraud is predicated on a court's finding that the debtor intentionally transferred assets to avoid a creditor's claim. Absent proof of such an intent, or motive, the creditor's challenge fails.

Simply put, to avoid actual fraud, the debtor must be able to convince the court that the transfer was motivated by some legitimate reason, unrelated to the desire to place the asset out of the reach of creditors.

Explanations are derived from common sense and will vary depending on the nature of the transfer. For example, you might pay down a home mortgage to avoid interest charges, which, over the life of a mortgage, can double or even triple the cost of a home. You might take out a second mortgage on a home to invest the funds in a new business, make improvements in your family's home, enable the family to take a vacation or invest the proceeds, etc.

With respect to the business entity, courts have sometimes ruled that payments were not fraudulent when they were made for legitimate business expenses, including payments to the owner for services actually rendered to the entity, or capital leased or loaned to the entity.

Plan Smart

Payments from the business entity to the owner can be legitimized if services and capital are actually provided to the entity. Here, it is essential that these payments be regular and supported by written agreements between the owner and the entity.

Payments that occur only when a financial crisis arises, or that are not supported by written agreements, have the appearance of being fraudulent.

Frequently, a debtor incurs a debt when he or she does not have the resources to pay it back. Courts have ruled that if, at the time the debt was incurred or a transfer was made, the debtor had a reasonable expectation of receiving future resources, there is no fraudulent intent in the transaction. After all, that's the nature of taking on debt—you borrow money now with the intention of paying it back later when you have greater resources. Using this theory, it is possible to sustain a purchase on an unsecured credit card, or an asset transfer, at a time when the debtor was insolvent. You could show, for example, that you reasonably anticipated receiving a bonus or a raise, or perhaps an inheritance.

A business entity could show that it anticipated excellent results from a new marketing plan or contacts the owner had made. That the results were not achieved is not important, provided that the *expectation* had some basis in fact.

Similarly, an individual or a business entity that is solvent at the time of a transfer, but becomes unable to pay a debt, can disprove fraudulent intent by establishing that it could not reasonably anticipate the events that led to the insolvency. For example, fraudulent intent is disproved by an unexpected loss of a job; pay cut; loss of a major customer, client or contract; or default on receivables of significant value.

In these ways, you can preserve the validity of a transfer even in the face of a finding of insolvency, at least in an actual fraud case.

Another effective strategy, of course, is to establish that these other factors do not apply to the case (e.g., the debtor was actually solvent at all relevant times).

Relationship of motive and timing. Sometimes the timing of a transfer reveals the real intent behind it.

Example

Chapter 2 presented the case of the Wisconsin couple who liquidated all of their property and moved to Florida, investing the $228,000 they raised into a Florida home, which, of course, was an exempt asset due to Florida's unlimited homestead exemption.

A little more than one year after the conversion, they filed for bankruptcy. The court ruled that the move and conversion were fraudulent, and relegated the couple to the lower $40,000 homestead exemption that had been available in Wisconsin.

The couple tried to explain that the move was motivated by a desire to find better jobs. The court was not convinced.

Given the importance of the one-year period prior to filing a bankruptcy proceeding, what do you think the bankruptcy judge inferred from the timing of the move?

Don't expose motive by filing a bankruptcy action just after the one-year time period. Doing so gives the court the very evidence it needs to prove fraudulent intent.

This case also illustrates the fact that courts can examine transfers more than a year before filing (but not more than four years prior to filing).

(Note: This may no longer represent the law in Florida. Recently, a U.S. Court of Appeals ruled that the Florida homestead exemption, as embodied in the state's constitution, is absolute and protected even when transfers involving the homestead are predicated on actual or constructive fraud. This decision is unique and not likely to be followed even in other states, such as Texas, where the homestead exemption is provided by the state's constitution.)

Two UFTA factors specifically provide that motive can be inferred from the timing of transfer. Thus, fraudulent intent can be inferred if a transfer occurs when a lawsuit is threatened or initiated, or if it takes place at the time a substantial debt is incurred.

Similarly, transfers that suddenly occur on the eve of a bankruptcy filing, when the debtor receives notice of a lawsuit, or is in the midst of a financial crisis will only rarely succeed, because the courts can infer fraudulent intent from the circumstances and, in particular, the timing of the transfers. This is why transfers from the business entity to the owner must be ongoing and supported by written agreements.

Plan Smart

 It is essential that the debtor be able to prove that the transfer was motivated by legitimate reasons unrelated to a desire to protect the asset from a creditor.

As discussed above, some bankruptcy courts recognize the validity of asset exemption planning, in general. However, the majority of courts do not follow this same rationale.

Most transfers can be explained in a rational way unrelated to asset exemption planning. Of course, this is a lot easier if the transfers occur well in advance of a bankruptcy filing or, for example, notice of a lawsuit.

Within the business, a record proving that payments to the owner have been ongoing, regular and supported by written agreements will be important in convincing a court that the transfers are legitimate.

Salary, lease and loan payments from the entity to the owner that meet these requirements can be sustained in the face of creditor challenges even when other factors, such as insolvency, work in the creditor's favor.

Relationship of motive and future creditors. The UFTA outlaws fraud as to existing *and future* creditors. In other words, to make a claim based on a fraudulent transfer, a creditor does not have to prove his or her claim existed at the time of the transfer.

Some courts have narrowly construed this provision to require proof that the debtor had that *particular* future creditor in mind when he made the transfer. However, most courts simply require that *any* future creditor must prove that he or she could have made a claim based on the law that existed at the time of the transfer.

Thus, absent some new enactment of law after the transfer that, for the first time, creates a right to sue, generally you will not be able to defeat a claim based on the fact that the creditor did not exist at the time of the transfer.

Nevertheless, a transfer made to protect assets from existing creditor, or in anticipation of a specific future creditor, is much more likely to be ruled fraudulent because intent can be inferred from the circumstances.

Insolvency

Insolvency is a key factor in establishing fraudulent intent in many actual fraud cases, and one of two determining factors in constructive fraud cases.

Because insolvency can be an important factor in asset transfers, you should be familiar with the two different ways to gauge insolvency. Specifically, the UFTA provides that you are insolvent if:

- your liabilities exceed your assets (i.e., a balance sheet analysis shows a negative owner's equity, or net worth), or

- you cannot pay your debts as they come due (i.e., a cash flow statement shows the debtor has a negative cash flow)

As discussed below, although either version can be important, the cash flow analysis will usually carry more weight.

Plan Smart

Don't confuse insolvency in a constructive fraud case with insolvency in an actual fraud case.

Insolvency is defined in the same way in both situations. However, the effect of a finding of insolvency is very different in each case.

In the constructive fraud theory, insolvency, when coupled with a lack of adequate consideration in return for the transfer, automatically renders the transfer fraudulent, regardless of motive or intent.

In contrast, under the actual fraud theory, insolvency is weighed by the courts as just one of the factors. Here, it is not absolute proof when it comes to the issue of fraud.

As discussed above, because transfers advocated in this book generally will be for adequate return consideration (thus making constructive fraud a non-issue), insolvency will usually be more important in an actual fraud case, where it is just one factor (albeit usually an important factor) that will be weighed by the court.

Nevertheless, because a finding of insolvency will control the outcome of a constructive fraud case, whenever there is an absence of adequate return consideration, the business owner who is, or anticipates becoming, insolvent, must ensure that transfers are either supported by adequate return consideration or that they do not qualify as "transfers" covered under the UFTA.

When making transfers, you should prepare a balance sheet that indicates your financial position (assets minus liabilities) and cash flow statement that shows your liquidity as of the date of that transfer.

However, it must be understood that the UFTA applies to existing and future creditors. Accordingly, any analysis of insolvency also must project your financial position and cash flow (for you and your business) for at least the next three months after a transfer, and preferably for the next year as well. Thus, a second balance sheet and a second cash flow statement should be prepared based on these projections. A finding of insolvency based on either the financial situation on the date of the transaction or under the projections can be significant.

Separate statements for the owner and the business entity. Determinations of insolvency (or, hopefully, the lack of it) will have to be made for you as an individual, based on your individual financial situation when you make a transfer, as in the case of asset exemption planning. They also may have to be made for the business entity, as in the case of liens placed on the entity's assets in favor of the owner or payments from the entity to the owner.

Great care must be taken to separate the owner's personal finances from those of the business entity. If the small business follows the advice in Chapter 16 of this book, this separation will already exist in the recordkeeping system for the business. This separation is essential if you are to preserve your limited liability for the business's debts (see Chapter 16 for details).

Balance sheet analysis. This analysis involves subtracting liabilities from assets. Assets should be valued at fair market value, and not original cost, for purposes of this projection. Note that, in a conventional accounting system, most assets will remain in the accounting records at historical cost. For our purposes here, these assets must be adjusted to fair market value. Thus, an adjustment may be necessary for an asset such as an office building, which has appreciated significantly in value. The fair market value of depreciated assets should be used and not the book value, as an estimate of fair market value already includes adjustments for depreciation.

Liabilities should normally be subtracted at face value. This includes any liens established on the assets by the owner, which should always be recorded on the entity's books as liabilities in any event.

Exempt assets must be excluded from the balance sheet equation. In the business entity, this will not affect the calculation because asset exemptions are available only to natural persons (as discussed in Chapter 3).

For an individual, exempt assets are excluded because they are not available to the creditors. However, exempt assets are available to the holders of consensual and statutory liens on exempt assets (as explained in Chapter 1). Thus, when exempt assets are excluded, the corresponding consensual and statutory liens on the exempt assets also should be excluded.

This will make a significant difference in an individual's balance sheet calculation. Among the assets that must be excluded are the homestead to the extent of its exemption, ERISA-qualified retirement plan assets and, in many states, IRAs.

When the face value of a liability insurance policy would be available to a particular creditor, this amount should be included as an asset in the balance sheet calculation. This would be appropriate when, for example, a claim was made by an injured party in the form of a negligence lawsuit, and the plaintiff, after securing a judgment, alleged that a transfer from the defendant was fraudulent. This can make a dramatic difference in the calculation results, turning the results into a finding of solvency.

It would be inappropriate to include the face value of the policy in the calculation when the policy could not be paid to the creditor in question (e.g., a breach of contract claim). Thus, the calculation should initially be made without inclusion of the face value. A second determination, made by plugging this amount into the equation, should also be made. This determination will be relevant only with respect to those creditors who could make claims covered by the policy (i.e., usually claims based on the commission of a tort, such as negligence).

Ultimately, the effect of the exclusion of exempt assets will mean that, in many cases, individuals will be deemed insolvent. Similarly, financing the business entity with leases and loans and encumbering the entity's assets with liens in favor of the owner, all of which are extremely effective asset protection strategies, will also mean that in many cases the business entity will be insolvent, according to the calculation.

In these situations, it is essential to exchange adequate consideration when making transfers, to avoid application of the constructive fraud theory. Then, actual fraud can be avoided through proof that the debtor is not insolvent *from a cash flow perspective,* plus proof that the transfer was motivated by a legitimate reason, as explained above. In addition, the absence of findings on the other factors, as addressed below, can help to disprove an allegation of actual fraud.

The forward-looking (sometimes called projected, or pro forma) balance sheet should include any assets and liabilities (subject to the rules discussed above) that the individual or business, as the case may be, can reasonably expect to materialize. As discussed above, this projected statement should be in addition to a balance sheet based on the individual's or business entity's existing financial position.

The forward-looking balance sheet is important because an anticipated change in circumstances can be used to prove or disprove insolvency. A debtor who is solvent at the time a debt was incurred can be ruled insolvent at a future date, when he or she fails to pay the debt. If it can be shown that the debtor could have reasonably anticipated this result, this can be important evidence of fraudulent intent.

Conversely, a debtor who is insolvent at the time a debt is incurred can disprove intent of fraud by proving that he or she reasonably anticipated being able to pay the debt through future earnings. This strategy is discussed in more detail above.

Cash flow statement analysis. Measuring cash flow for an individual amounts to adding up the individual's monthly sources of income, and then subtracting the monthly expenses. A home finance program such as Intuit's "Quicken" or Microsoft's "Managing Your Money" will be helpful here. A cash flow statement is a standard feature in every business accounting software program. Thus, for the business entity, you can generally rely on the business entity's accounting software to make such calculations.

Did You Know?

Ratios can be used to quickly gauge an entity's current and future solvency from a cash flow perspective.

The current ratio is calculated by dividing the entity's current assets by its current liabilities. Current assets are those that will be converted to cash or used up within one year. Current assets include cash, receivables, marketable securities, inventory and prepaid expenses. Similarly, current liabilities are those that will be paid within the next year. This should include the next 12 monthly payments for any installment loans (such as mortgages, or car loans).

A result of 2:1, or better, is desirable. A ratio of 1:1 means the entity is solvent, but on the border of being insolvent in the sense of being unable to pay its debts as they come due.

A different version of the ratio, called the quick ratio or acid test ratio, excludes inventory and pre-paid expenses from the definition of current assets, on the grounds that inventory can be difficult to quickly convert to cash. This ratio should normally be 1:1 or better.

Take into account any source of income that can reasonably be expected to materialize. As was suggested above, courts generally hold that, if such sources do not materialize, there is no fraud, as long as the original projections had some basis in fact. Here, again, offering a reasonable explanation, with supporting proof, can be an effective strategy.

Example

Let's say Linda Jones had a reasonable expectation, based on past experience, that she would receive a sizable bonus in the last quarter of the year. Accordingly, in anticipation of this bonus, she makes substantial charges on her credit card, even though at the time of the purchases she is insolvent. Here, the future projection of solvency, if reasonable, would negate any finding of fraudulent intent.

Similar conclusions are warranted when a business incurs debt or makes transfers at a time when it is insolvent. If such transactions are based on reasonable projections that the entity would be solvent in the future (e.g., from increased sales, decreased operating expenses, etc.), these projections can negate a finding of fraudulent intent even if the projections do not materialize.

Conversely, debts incurred on a date when the individual or business was solvent can be shown to be the result of fraudulent conduct, when reasonable projections would have indicated future insolvency.

Proof that the debtor was not insolvent from a cash flow analysis can negate a finding of insolvency from a balance sheet analysis, as illustrated in the examples below.

Examples

John Smith, a Florida resident, owns a home worth $180,000, which is subject to a mortgage in the amount of $100,000. He also has an ERISA-qualified retirement plan with assets worth $140,000.

His only nonexempt asset is cash in a savings account of $19,000. His only other liability is for several credit cards that total $20,000.

Smith makes mortgage payments with his credit card, totaling $4,000. This leaves Smith with a balance on his credit cards of $24,000.

Smith is insolvent under the balance sheet analysis ($19,000 less $24,000). The home and the retirement plan must be excluded from the calculation because both are completely exempt. The corresponding mortgage loan on the exempt home must also be excluded.

If Smith is paying his monthly bills as they come due, he will not be insolvent from a cash flow perspective. For example, Smith earns $4,000 per month, has monthly expenses of $2,000 and he has been paying his bills each month.

Smith is not insolvent, despite the results from the balance sheet analysis. The cash flow analysis makes more sense in this case, and it should, accordingly, bear more weight in any court proceeding.

Now let's say Smith has a limited liability company (LLC). The LLC has $210,000 of assets it owns, including cash in a checking account of $20,000. Smith has liens on these assets from various extensions of credit he made to the entity. The LLC also has $100,000 of assets in its possession that it leases from Smith.

The LLC also has $80,000 of other liabilities, from open accounts it has with suppliers.

Also, the LLC pays Smith's monthly salary of $10,000.

The LLC is insolvent, from a balance sheet analysis: $200,000 of assets less $280,000 of debt.

The lease of assets must be excluded because the LLC does not own these assets and they are, thus, unavailable to its creditors. The $200,000 of liens created by Smith ($210,000 - $10,000 monthly salary) will be for liabilities the LLC owes Smith, for extensions of credit Smith made to the LLC (loans, unpaid wages, etc.). Thus, these liabilities must be included in the total liabilities.

Nevertheless, the LLC can escape any allegation of insolvency based on the same rationale as in the first example. If the LLC is paying its bills as they come due, it will not be deemed insolvent, despite the results under the balance sheet analysis.

Regardless of whether you're planning to make a transfer in the near future, you should periodically make separate determinations of solvency for yourself personally and for your business, being careful to separate your resources from those of the business entity.

Your personal analysis will be relevant for asset exemption planning and personal borrowing, while the business entity's analysis will be relevant when the entity makes payments to, and creates liens in favor of, you, and otherwise engages in borrowing.

Concealment

Cases indicate that concealment can be an extremely important factor in proving fraudulent intent. Lying on a loan application or in a bankruptcy petition is usually conclusive proof of fraud. Worse, yet, of course, it also is a crime that is taken very seriously by the courts.

Conversely, the opposite of concealment—disclosure—can negate a finding of fraud. Actual disclosure will almost always defeat a creditor's claim, absent some specific act of fraud on the part of the debtor.

Example

If a bank or other lender provides a 125-percent mortgage loan, by definition, the liability created exceeds the asset that secures the loan. Because many of the debtor's other assets may be exempt, the debtor technically, from a balance sheet analysis, may be insolvent at the time of the loan.

However, the debtor's financial situation would be fully disclosed to the creditor before the loan was granted, on the loan application, tax returns, credit report, etc. Of course, the lender will charge an especially high rate of interest in this situation to cover the additional risks it knows it is taking. Here, the creditor cannot complain later that it was defrauded, as it knew exactly what it was doing at the time of the loan.

In addition, *constructive notice* of a debtor's financial situation can negate any allegation of fraud. "Constructive notice" means information that the creditor received or could have received. If a debtor's credit report, income tax records and home finance reports were *available* to the creditor, or even obtainable by the creditor, the debtor can show that the creditor knew or should have known about the debtor's financial situation. Thus, the creditor cannot now claim that he or she was defrauded.

Plan Smart

Use your business's accounting software program to generate monthly financial statements. These statements and the entity's income tax returns can serve as constructive notice of the entity's financial condition to the creditors of the entity.

A creditor may not be able to mount a claim of fraud later if it could have accessed this information at the time credit was extended.

Similarly, an individual could use a finance software program that allows the tracking of income and expenses. These records, along with the individual's tax returns, can serve as constructive notice to creditors who extend credit to the individual.

Note that this argument is likely to be more acceptable when a one-time extension of credit is made, such as a loan, as opposed to the use of a credit card or other open account.

Other Factors

Other factors will usually be of less importance in actual fraud cases. Transfers by the small business owner usually will be to an "insider," and the debtor usually will be in control of the property after the transfer. However, these factors tend to be relatively unimportant in the overall analysis. Other factors should not apply at all. For example, your leaving the jurisdiction with a large amount of cash should not be a necessary part of any asset protection strategy!

SPECIAL MEDICAID TRANSFERS

Transfers of assets also are used to protect assets from the extreme expense of nursing home care. Nursing home care costs $70,000 a year or more in many parts of the country. Therefore, you should be aware of some of the basic issues involved in asset transfers relating to nursing home care.

Just as a creditor can challenge transfers of personal or business assets, the government may challenge transfers of assets if you apply for Medicaid benefits.

Warning

Before transferring any assets, you should always seek professional advice from an attorney or financial advisor. The following information should be used strictly as a guideline. Exemptions can be different depending on the state you're in and are subject to change. The consequences of making transfers that are not eligible for exemption can be severe and include rendering the applicant ineligible for Medicaid.

Medicaid is the federal program that pays for long-term nursing home costs. Don't confuse Medicaid with Medicare. Medicaid is a social welfare program available only to individuals with extremely limited means. Basically, under Medicaid, a single individual can only have $1,600 in assets and $50 per month in income in order to be eligible for benefits.

In contrast, Medicare is the federal program that *everyone*, regardless of income or assets, qualifies for at age 65 by paying Social Security taxes when they were working. Unfortunately, Medicare only pays for the first 100 days of a stay in a nursing home, and then only when skilled nursing care is medically required.

When this period expires, or if nursing home care is needed to provide help with daily living activities, the individual must begin personally paying the $70,000 (or higher) per year bill or qualify for Medicaid.

This expense would quickly consume most families' personal wealth. Accordingly, Medicaid-qualifying asset transfers are an important asset protection strategy. However, such transfers, with some exceptions, will be effective only if they are executed well in advance of the need for long-term nursing home care. Unfortunately, the first time most individuals consider such transfers is when they realize Medicare will only pay a few months of bills. At this point, planning may be too late.

Timing of Transfers under Medicaid

Federal law provides for a three-year "look-back" period for transfers made to individuals. The period is five years for transfers into a trust. Some time ago, transfers into a trust for the benefit of the applicant were acceptable planning tools. However, federal law has been changed to make trusts largely ineffective here. To be effective, the transferor must relinquish all control, interest and incidents of ownership in the property transferred to a trust. This, coupled with the longer look-back period, may make transfers to individuals the better alternative.

Transfers to individuals during the three-year period *do not automatically* disqualify the applicant from qualifying for Medicaid benefits. Certain transfers are exempt, and others, because of their limited size, may disqualify an applicant only for a limited period of time of less than three years. These situations are discussed below.

Of course, transfers to an individual more than three years prior to an application for Medicaid will escape scrutiny entirely. This is the best course of action, when planning can be done that far in advance, and the transferor is amenable to parting with some assets in favor of children or other relatives.

Exempt Assets under Medicaid

Federal and state laws exempt certain assets in determining an individual's eligibility for Medicaid. In other words, ownership of these assets will *not* affect an individual's eligibility.

Warning

The dollar amounts of many of the exemptions discussed below are changed each year. In addition, the amounts and types of exemptions may vary from state to state. Use these exemptions only as guidelines. Check with the social service agency in your state for your current exemptions.

A Medicaid applicant first would have to use all of his or her assets in excess of the exempt amounts to pay the costs of nursing home care before becoming eligible for Medicaid. The assets of a married couple are *combined* in determining eligibility, as an individual is legally liable for the nursing home costs incurred by his or her spouse. However, the exemptions for a married couple are accordingly larger than what are available for a single applicant.

Importantly, an applicant who believes he or she should have been granted larger exemptions is allowed to request a hearing to present his or her case. Generally, an applicant should immediately seek legal advice in this situation, as the law requires that a request for a hearing be filed promptly or otherwise be barred by law, meaning the applicant would not be able to challenge the assigned exemptions later.

The following assets are exempt:

- $1,600 owned by the applicant

- between $17,400 and $87,000, but only for a married couple where the applicant's spouse continues to live in the couple's home; these amounts are the minimum and maximum exemptions; the actual exemption is equal to one-half of the married couple's total assets, subject to the minimum and maximum amounts (this exemption is in addition to the $1,600 exemption for assets owned by the applicant)

- a home, but only if the applicant is likely to return home or one of the following individuals continues to live in the home:

  — the applicant's spouse

  — a child under age 21

  — a child over age 21 who is disabled

  — a brother or sister who owns part of the house and has resided there for at least one year

- essential household items (furniture, appliances, etc.)

- personal effects (clothing, jewelry, etc.)

- burial plots

- burial funds of up to $1,500 each for a married couple, and up to $1,200 for a single applicant; for an irrevocable burial fund, these amounts are raised to $5,400 each for a married couple, and $5,400 for a single applicant

- one motor vehicle up to $4,500, except a married applicant can keep one motor vehicle owned by either spouse, automatically, with no limit on the value; others can keep one motor vehicle, with no limit on value, only if the vehicle is used for any of the following reasons:

  — transportation to and from employment

— transportation for medical treatment

— transportation of a handicapped person

- cash surrender value of life insurance, only if the face value of all polices is less than $1,500 (an unlikely occurrence); note that term life insurance does not have a cash surrender value and is, therefore, completely exempt

- the dollar amount of nursing home costs paid by a long-term-care insurance policy (This is a relatively new type of specialized insurance designed to pay nursing home costs, not to be confused with an ordinary health insurance policy or an insurance policy that pays for the gaps in Medicare, which do not pay for nursing home costs. While the premiums for long-term-care insurance can be substantial, so can the savings. For example, if an applicant had a policy that paid for $200,000 of nursing home costs, then when later applying for Medicaid after the policy ran out, $200,000 of the applicant's assets would be exempt. Long-term-care insurance policies vary significantly in their coverage and premiums. Therefore, it may be advisable to seek legal advice before purchasing such a policy.)

Exempt Income under Medicaid

Certain income is exempt from consideration in determining the applicant's eligibility for Medicaid. Income that is *not* exempt must be used to pay nursing home costs. The following income is exempt:

- $50 per month earned by the applicant, for support of the applicant

- unlimited income earned by the applicant's spouse

- $1,326.25 to $1,975.50 per month earned by the applicant for support of the applicant's spouse, only if the applicant's spouse continues to reside at home; these amounts are the minimum and maximum for this exemption (This exemption is designed to allow the applicant to continue to make a contribution toward supporting the family home after entering a nursing home. A complicated formula is used to determine the exact amount. Basically, the applicant is allowed to add the excess costs of operating the home above $397.88 to the minimum exemption amount of $1,326.25 per month, subject to a maximum exemption of $1,975.50 per month.)

Note that a single applicant is only allowed to keep $50 per month of earned income.

Transfers of Assets under Medicaid Rules

Applicants can transfer assets before entering a nursing home, intending to protect those assets and make the applicant eligible for Medicaid. Transfers within three years (to individuals) or five years (to trusts) of application can be very carefully structured to fall within one of the permissible exceptions. However, a *warning* is in order. This area is extremely complex and requires the advice of an attorney. Transfers outside an exception can actually make an applicant totally *ineligible* for Medicaid.

Certain transfers are permissible, such as:

- transfers of assets to the extent value was received in return; thus, payments by the applicant for goods and services purchased have no effect on eligibility, because the applicant receives equal value in return

- direct transfers of assets to individuals more than three years before application (This forms an important basis for asset transfer planning in this area.)

- transfers into an irrevocable trust more than five years before application; generally, if trust assets or income are available to or under any direct control of the applicant, the trust assets or income would not be exempt (unless one of the other exemptions applied), so this type of trust usually has to be irrevocable, meaning it cannot be cancelled or altered after it is created; further, this type of trust usually would require an independent trustee (someone other than the applicant or his spouse) and someone other than the applicant as the beneficiary (see below)

- any transfer to a spouse, but because the couple's assets are combined anyway, such a transfer does not serve a useful asset protection function

- any transfer to disabled child

- transfers of a home, only if the transfer was to one of the following individuals:

  — the applicant's spouse

  — a child under the age of 21

  — a child over the age of 21 who is disabled

  — any other child who was residing at the home at least two

years immediately before the application and who provided care for the applicant during those two years

— a brother or sister who is part owner of the home and has resided in the home for at least one year.

Note that the home is exempt, as long as the other spouse continues to reside there. Thus, a transfer of the Medicaid recipient's family home is not necessary, in these circumstances.

However, a problem arises if the other spouse dies. This takes the home out of the exemption. One approach here would be for the spouse residing in the nursing home to transfer the interest in the home to another individual, who qualifies under the rules described above, such as an adult child who resided in the home with, and took care of, the applicant for the past two years. This must be done cautiously, if the other spouse continues to reside in the home, as such a transfer gives the transferee important ownership rights in the home. Always consult an attorney before making this or any type of transfer.

Penalized Transfers under Medicaid

You should seek legal advice *before* you make any transfer of assets. A transfer that is *not* exempt makes the applicant *ineligible* for Medicaid for a certain period of time.

The calculation of the ineligibility period is complicated. However, basically, the period of ineligibility is equal to the time period the nursing home costs would have been paid for, had the transfer *not* been made.

For example, assume a home with a value of $144,000 is transferred as a gift (with no value received in return) in a way that is *not* exempt. The applicant would be *ineligible* for Medicaid for a period of two years from the date of the transfer, assuming the average cost of a nursing home in that state was $6,000 per month ($144,000 divided by $6,000, the assumed average monthly cost of a nursing home, yielding 24 months, or two years of ineligibility).

Transfers in Trust for Others under Medicaid

When individuals choose to transfer assets, as a pre-Medicaid planning tool, these transfers can be made outright to the recipient or in trust for the benefit of the recipient. As discussed above, the transferor would have to relinquish all rights in, and direct control over, trust assets, or the trust assets will be deemed owned by the transferor for Medicaid qualification purposes.

Perhaps the biggest disadvantage to a transfer in trust for the benefit of others is the extension of the "look-back" period from three to five years. Thus, such a transfer would have to be planned almost impossibly far in advance.

However, transfers in trust do have advantages. Transfers into a properly drafted irrevocable trust with an independent trustee, more than five years before application for Medicaid, would protect those assets by keeping them out of the reach of the applicant. Of course, to be effective, the transferor would have to relinquish all control, interest and incidents of ownership in the property.

With an irrevocable trust and an independent trustee, there is a loss of control over the assets, but to nowhere near the extent encountered with an outright transfer.

With an outright transfer, the recipient is free to do whatever he or she wants with the property. With a trust, the transferor can set out conditions and restrictions concerning the beneficiary's use of the property and the income it may generate, formally writing these into the trust document. Control over the ultimate disposition of the property also can be ensured through a trust.

The cost of a trust must be weighed against the benefits. An independent trustee (someone other than you or your spouse) would be required. If some other family member were unwilling or otherwise unable to serve as a trustee, the cost of a professional trustee would have to be taken into account. The trust would be an entity for tax purposes, meaning a tax return would have to be filed for it each year. However, with the cost of a nursing home around $70,000 per year, these costs may be very quickly recouped.

Chapter 5

Using Asset Protection Trusts

Trusts are useful for many purposes, including avoidance of probate court, elimination of federal estate taxes, and management and control of property for a beneficiary when direct ownership of the property by the beneficiary is not desired. They also can be very useful for asset protection purposes, where the creditors of the beneficiary are prevented from reaching the trust's assets. This chapter is concerned with the last objective—namely, the use of the trust as an asset protection device.

A trust can be an effective way to place assets outside the reach of creditors. However, not all forms of a trust will function as an asset protection device. Further, even a properly structured asset protection trust can be challenged by creditors. Before these issues can be addressed, you must understand some basic ideas about the nature of a trust. Common forms of trusts, and their objectives, are also briefly considered in this chapter, with special emphasis on the asset protection trust.

THE NATURE OF A TRUST

A trust is a legal agreement among three parties:

1. the trustor (or settlor or grantor)

2. the trustee

3. the beneficiary

A trustor, or settlor, transfers legal title to some property to a trust, then a trustee manages the property for a beneficiary. A trust can have more than one beneficiary, trustee or trustor. Moreover, one individual may assume two or even three of the roles as trustor, trustee and beneficiary. Usually, in this case, the trust will provide for at least one contingent beneficiary, who will become an active beneficiary upon the death of the trustor.

For example, a husband and wife could, as co-trustors, transfer property to a trust with themselves as co-trustees, with the husband and wife both as life beneficiaries, and perhaps with their children as contingent beneficiaries of the remainder interest.

Further, a single trust instrument can establish multiple trusts. For example, the previously mentioned trust could provide that, upon the death of the husband and wife, individual trusts would be established for each child. Again, one person may assume all three roles in the trust, as discussed below.

Common trust factors to consider include the use of a revocable vs. irrevocable trust, as well as whether the legal agreement is a living or testamentary trust.

Revocable vs. Irrevocable Trusts

A revocable trust is a trust that can be amended or revoked by the trustor after it is created. In contrast, an irrevocable trust cannot be amended or revoked by the trustor after it is created. A revocable trust becomes irrevocable upon the trustor's death, since the trustor is no longer able to change or revoke the trust.

Trusts designed to avoid federal estate taxes are often drafted to be irrevocable (but not always, as in the case of the bypass trust, discussed later), while trusts designed only to avoid probate court frequently are revocable.

Probate Court and Federal Estate Taxes

It's important to realize that avoidance of probate court and elimination of federal estate taxes are two different issues. Separate rules apply to each situation. Generally, it's much easier to avoid probate court than it is to avoid the estate tax collector. For example, a funded revocable trust (one supplied with assets before death) will always avoid probate court, because ownership is transferred outside of the grantor's will. On the other hand, a revocable unfunded trust—later given assets through a will—by definition will go through probate court.

However, neither type of trust will avoid federal estate taxes, because the trustor's control over the trust (due to the fact that he or she can amend or revoke it) means the trust's assets must be included in the trustor's taxable estate.

Similarly, co-ownership of property in joint tenancy, POD (pay on death) designations for securities and bank accounts, and beneficiary designations for life insurance and retirement benefits mean that these assets will avoid the probate court process, because title passes to the designated heirs outside of the will. However, absent any specific additional strategy to eliminate the federal estate tax (e.g., creating an irrevocable life insurance trust), these assets are still included in the owner's taxable estate.

Living or Testamentary Trusts

A living trust (sometimes called an *inter vivos* trust) is one created by the trustor during his or her lifetime, while a testamentary trust is a trust created by the trustor's will.

Only a funded living trust avoids probate court. In a testamentary trust, property must pass into the trust by way of the will and, thus, must go through the probate court process. Similarly, an unfunded living trust technically does not exist until it receives some assets. If you attempt to create a living trust but do not transfer any assets to it except through your will, the property must go through probate just like a testamentary trust.

Avoiding probate court, and the costs and delays associated with this process, is a distinct advantage of the living trust. On the other hand, funding of the living trust means that the trustor must transfer assets into the trust during his or her lifetime, and provide for management of those assets by a trustee. This creates its own burdens. These burdens can be lessened when the trustor also acts as the trustee. However, in some instances, this can cause the trust's assets to be included in the trustor's taxable estate. In many cases, an estate planning attorney can structure the trust to prevent this outcome.

COMMON TYPES OF TRUSTS

Trusts can be created for almost any purpose imaginable and can include practically any conditions and requirements that you desire. Over the years, however, a number of types of trusts especially useful for common purposes have been developed:

- The Grantor Trust (and by extension, the Totten Trust)

- The Bypass or Credit Shelter Trust

- The Marital Deduction or QTIP Trust

- The Irrevocable Living Children's Trust

- The Irrevocable Life Insurance Trust

The Grantor Trust

Where a living trust is irrevocable, the trust will generally be treated as a separate taxpayer, which adds additional complexities and costs. Such a trust will be taxed according to a special rate schedule designed for estates and trusts, which is extremely compressed—that is, it imposes high tax rates on very low levels of income. Furthermore, the trust and estate tax scheme does not allow for personal exemptions. Thus, in addition to the administrative burden, higher taxes are a very likely result.

However, language can be used in the trust to make it a "grantor trust" under the IRS definition. Here, the term "grantor" means the same thing as the term "trustor." In the grantor trust, the trust is not recognized as a separate taxpayer. Instead, the grantor, or trustor, reports the trust income on his or her personal income tax return, as if he or she owned all the trust assets personally and the trust did not exist.

This greatly simplifies the administration of the trust. At the same time, other precautions can be taken so that the trust still removes the assets from the taxable estate of the trustor. In short, the grantor trust takes advantage of exceptions to the separate income tax and estate tax rules that apply to trusts.

Warning

Planning to eliminate federal estate taxes requires special considerations and the services of an estate planning attorney. For example, in some situations an independent trustee may be necessary, or special language must be used in the trust when the trustor is also the trustee, to prevent the trust assets from being included in the trustor's taxable estate.

Chapter 10 contains a more detailed discussion of federal estate taxes.

The Totten Trust

A very simple form of a revocable grantor trust used to avoid probate court is called a Totten trust. Most banks have a simple form that a depositor can use to create this trust form for a bank account. In a Totten trust, the depositor is the trustor, the trustee and the only beneficiary during his or her life. A contingent beneficiary is named in the trust instrument who takes over ownership of the account upon the death of the trustor.

The trust is revocable. Thus, the trustor can amend or revoke the trust during his or her lifetime. The easiest way to do this is simply to spend the money in the account.

Because the contingent beneficiary has no rights in the account during the trustor's life, the Totten trust is much safer than, for example, a common alternative way of avoiding probate court with a bank account: namely, opening or converting the account to joint tenancy. When the joint tenancy alternative is used, the joint owner takes an immediate interest in the account, including the right to withdraw some or all of the funds.

In the Totten trust, the beneficiary has no immediate rights in the account, so the creditors of the beneficiary cannot reach the account. On the other hand, the creditors of a co-owner of an account held in joint tenancy can attach the co-owner's interest in the account.

The Totten trust is just one example of the fact that one person may assume multiple roles in the trust.

The Bypass or Credit Shelter Trust

The bypass trust, also called a credit shelter trust, is used to eliminate or reduce federal estate taxes and is typically used by a married couple whose estate exceeds the amount exempt from federal estate tax. In 2002, every individual is entitled to an estate tax credit, which essentially exempts the first $1 million in assets from tax; this amount is scheduled to rise to $1.5 million in 2004 and to $2 million in 2006.

Of course, a married person may leave an unlimited amount of assets to his or her spouse, free of estate taxes and without using up any of the estate tax credit (see Chapter 10). The problem is that if the second spouse then dies with an estate worth more than the exempted amount, his or her estate would be subject to estate tax. Meanwhile, the first spouse's estate tax credit was unused and, in effect, wasted.

The bypass trust was created to take care of this problem. This type of trust may be revocable or irrevocable, and living or testamentary. Typically, the trust instrument initially creates a single living trust that is revocable.

Upon the death of the first spouse, the instrument establishes a separate, irrevocable "bypass" trust with the deceased spouse's share of the trust's assets. The surviving spouse is the beneficiary of this trust, with the children as beneficiaries of the remaining interest.

The irrevocable trust is funded to the extent of the first spouse's exemption. Thus, the amount in the irrevocable trust is not subject to estate taxes on the death of the first spouse, and the trust takes full advantage of the first spouse's estate tax credit.

At the same time, special language is used in the irrevocable trust so that the assets in the irrevocable trust will not be included in the taxable estate of the beneficiary (i.e., the other spouse). Generally this involves giving the second spouse only limited powers to control the trust assets. Thus, the bypass trust is aptly named, as the assets in the irrevocable trust "bypass" the estate tax that would be assessed when the second spouse dies.

The Marital Deduction or QTIP Trust

This type of trust is designed not to avoid federal estate taxes upon the death of a surviving spouse, but rather to provide management and control of assets for a surviving spouse after the first spouse dies.

The trust is designed so that all assets in the trust qualify for the unlimited martial deduction, as would outright gifts to a spouse. Thus, the trust avoids estate taxes upon the death of the first spouse. The real advantage of the trust is the ability to have an independent trustee control and manage the assets for the surviving spouse, and the ability to determine the contingent beneficiaries, who usually are the children.

The trust frequently is used when the trustor has children from prior marriage, and the trustor wants to ensure that a certain portion of his or her estate will pass to children from the prior marriage. This cannot always be assumed when the property is left outright to the surviving spouse. The trust also is used when professional management of the assets is desirable for the surviving spouse.

The Irrevocable Living Children's Trust

This type of trust is often used where the objective is management and control of the assets in the trust, and outright gifts to the children would not be desirable because the assets might be wasted.

Importantly, the trust avoids probate court and the costs, delays and challenges associated with that process. In addition, this trust serves as an asset protection trust. Because a spendthrift clause is used in this type of trust, assets in it are shielded from the children's creditors in the event of a major court judgment, bankruptcy, divorce, etc. An explanation of a spendthrift clause appears later in this chapter.

While management and control also can be achieved by establishing a custodial account for the child under the Uniform Transfers to Minors Act (UTMA), the disadvantage of the UTMA is that the assets must be distributed outright to the child at an early age, usually age 21. In contrast, in a children's trust, the assets can continue to be managed in the trust well past age 21; for example, the trust could continue until the child finishes college, gets married, produces grandchildren, or attains a certain age such as 25, 35, etc. Provisions can be written into the trust that require mandatory periodic distributions, or that give the trustee complete discretion over distributions. The trustor also can choose the exact circumstances in which distributions can be made (e.g., for education, new home, etc). Importantly, the entire time the assets remain in the trust, the assets are shielded from the beneficiary's creditors. When the assets remain in the trust for the beneficiary's lifetime and for, perhaps, successive descendents' lives, in order to take advantage of this protection, the trust is sometimes termed a "Dynasty Trust."

Parents can act as trustees, thus eliminating administration costs and issues that arise from having someone else manage the assets.

The trust can be set up as a grantor trust to simplify administration (see above); on the other hand, you may want to avoid the grantor trust rules so that the trust is a tax-paying entity. In the latter case, the trust may be able to offer income tax-splitting advantages (see Chapter 10 for details).

The irrevocable children's trust also can be used to eliminate estate taxes on the future appreciation in the underlying assets. Where elimination of estate taxes is not an issue, the trust can be revocable. The trust also can be established by way of a will (i.e., be testamentary in origin).

Finally, the trust can be revocable, which gives parents the flexibility to amend or revoke the trust. This option also avoids probate court, but not federal estate taxes, and thus is not recommended where the trust will be funded with substantial assets.

The Irrevocable Life Insurance Trust

Ordinarily, the face value of life insurance is included in the taxable estate of the owner of the policy. This can represent a significant source of estate taxes. However, you can create a special type of trust that eliminates estate taxes on the life insurance benefits because the trust, and not you, will be deemed to be the owner of the policy.

It is usually desirable to establish the life insurance trust first, and then have the trust purchase the policy in its own name. The trustor funds the trust, which in turn, purchases the policy in its own name, and pays the policy's premium against its own account. An independent trustee is absolutely required in this case.

It is possible to transfer an existing life insurance policy to such a trust; for example, where the trustor is older or has health problems that make a new life insurance policy cost-prohibitive. However, caution must be exercised so that the trustor irrevocably relinquishes to the trust absolutely all control over the policy. An estate planning attorney can ensure this is done properly. The idea is that the trust takes over ownership of the policy; the trustor then makes contributions to the trust, which, in turn, uses the contributions to pay the policy's premium against its own account.

THE ASSET PROTECTION TRUST

Did you know that you can place your assets in a trust for your children, *and completely shield the assets from the children's creditors?* The law is very clear in this situation. Assets in this type of asset protection trust are out of the reach of children's creditors in all circumstances, including court judgments, bankruptcy and divorce. An asset protection trust is equally effective when a trustor establishes the trust with beneficiaries other than children.

However, when a trustor places assets in a trust for his own benefit, the law is less clear as to whether the assets can be shielded from the trustor's/beneficiary's creditors.

If the trustor is also a beneficiary, a trust can *potentially* function as an asset protection device, provided that the trust:

- is irrevocable

- has an independent trustee

- does not provide for mandatory distributions of income or principal (i.e., such distributions are subject to the discretion of the trustee)

- has a spendthrift clause

Given these circumstances, a number of asset protection strategies are available. Most common are the use of offshore trusts. But since 1997, Alaska and Delaware have changed their state laws to allow similar trusts here in the U.S., thereby preventing the flight of capital overseas.

The Spendthrift Clause

A spendthrift clause prevents the beneficiary of a trust from voluntarily or involuntarily transferring any current or future rights in the trust. In other words, among other things, it prevents the creditors of the beneficiary from reaching the trust's assets.

The term "self-settled spendthrift trust" refers to a trust with a spendthrift clause, where the trustor also is a beneficiary.

The only impediment to using such a trust has been the fact that until

1997 every state (with relatively minor exceptions) has provided that a self-settled spendthrift trust clause is invalid.

States based this rule on the grounds that it is against public policy for an individual to put property into a trust and out of the reach of his or her creditors, when the individual still can benefit from the property.

Significantly, as of 1997, Alaska and Delaware allow such trusts to operate. See below for a full discussion of the merits of these trusts.

On the other hand, the use of a spendthrift clause in a trust established for a different beneficiary (e.g., a child) has always been recognized as valid. Thus, in a children's trust, a bypass trust, a QTIP trust, a life insurance trust, etc., a spendthrift clause should always be used.

Note that, when the trust is established for a separate beneficiary, the fact that the trust is revocable does not invalidate the spendthrift clause, as it imparts no rights in the beneficiary. However, the beneficiary should not be a trustee, and the trust should not provide for mandatory distributions of income or principal. Where mandatory distributions of income or principal exist, a creditor would be able to reach the distributions when they occur.

The Delaware and Alaska Asset Protection Trusts

In the last decade, nearly a billion dollars has flowed out of the United States and into offshore trusts situated in Nevis, St. Kitts, the Bahamas, the Cook Islands and other offshore jurisdictions. Why? The primary reason is that, unlike most states, these jurisdictions do not prohibit the use of a self-settled spendthrift trust.

In an effort to capture some of this investment capital, Alaska, in mid-1997, modified its trust statutes to legalize a spendthrift clause in a self-settled trust. Not to be outdone and, in particular, to preserve its status as the premier site for business and investment, Delaware immediately followed Alaska's lead with a similar change.

Plan Smart

When, in mid-1997, Alaska and Delaware modified their trust statutes to legalize a spendthrift clause in a self-settled trust, they created a significant departure in American law. Up until that time, the only effective way to create a self-settled spendthrift trust was to form it offshore, outside of U.S. jurisdiction.

Alaska and Delaware also eliminated the rule against perpetuities. This antiquated rule limits the duration of a trust to the life of some person living at the time the trust is created, plus 21 years. As a result, the Alaska and Delaware asset protection trusts can continue indefinitely.

Missouri has a more limited exception to the rule that makes a self-settled spendthrift trust invalid. In that state, the exception does not apply where the trustor is the sole beneficiary of either the income or the principal, or the beneficiary of a fixed portion of the income or the principal. This exception has existed since the 1980s. However, because of the limited nature of the exception, Missouri has not been considered a significant option for opening an asset protection trust.

The Full Faith and Credit Clause

The Full Faith and Credit Clause in the U.S. Constitution requires each state to recognize a judgment entered in another state. Thus, as the argument goes, Alaska or Delaware would have to recognize another state's judgment, and thus allow a creditor access to the trust's assets despite the spendthrift clause.

Therefore, a serious question exists as to the effectiveness of the changes Delaware and Alaska made to their trust laws. The question can really be reduced to one word: jurisdiction. If the trustor resides in a different state, a creditor could sue the trustor/beneficiary outside of Alaska and Delaware, in the state in which the trustor resides. The state in which the suit is filed would likely rule that, under its laws, the assets are reachable by the creditor, consistent with the general rule in most states that a spendthrift clause in a self-settled trust is invalid.

The same result might occur where the creditor was able to file suit in its home state, rather than in Delaware or Alaska. Normally, a lawsuit can be filed in the state in which a contract is formed or a tort (e.g., negligent act) is committed.

Unfortunately, to date, there have been no reported cases on this issue involving an asset protection trust in Alaska or Delaware. A few cases, involving tax issues, have produced mixed results and, thus, do not offer firm guidance. The above argument can be extrapolated from these few cases. However, this argument oversimplifies the issues.

Each of these cases turned on its own unique facts and involved other issues. Moreover, if a challenge ended up in federal court, which is likely with this type of conflict-of-laws issue, the federal court would have to decide which state's laws to apply—the law of Alaska or Delaware, or the law of the trustor's or creditor's home state.

Both Alaska and Delaware require that the trustee reside in the state, that some or all of the trust's assets be located there, and that the trust administration and paperwork be located there. Arguably, these requirements were enacted to attract capital into these states. However, a secondary goal was to establish grounds for a court to find that the law of Alaska or Delaware, rather than the trustor's or creditor's home state, should be applied to the trusts.

Both states' statutes also expressly provide that they have jurisdiction over the trusts. Further, the trust document itself also will have a choice of law clause that establishes Alaska or Delaware as the controlling law. While none of these facts can assure a favorable outcome, they do buttress the argument that the law of Alaska or Delaware should control the outcome.

Some states assert jurisdiction over any trust where the beneficiary is a resident of the state. Thus, for example, Connecticut imposes an income tax on a resident's share of income from an out-of-state trust. This provision recently was upheld as valid by the courts. In doing so, the courts have concluded that Connecticut has jurisdiction, because Connecticut law dictates that jurisdiction is not determined by where the trust is set up, but instead by where the beneficiary resides. This conclusion, according to the courts, is justified because the interest in the trust is deemed to be personal property owned by the resident beneficiary.

Real Property vs. Personal Property

Probably one of the most secure ways to establish jurisdiction over the trust in Alaska or Delaware is to have the trust invest in real property (land and buildings) situated in that state. It is clearly established that jurisdiction over real property is accorded to the state in which the real property is situated. Thus, the trust could invest in a rental apartment building or a condominium located in Delaware or Alaska, depending on the site of the trust. While using this strategy would limit investment choices and reduce liquidity, it would also make it very difficult for creditors from outside these states to challenge the validity of the trust.

Warning

Because a state can assert jurisdiction over real property located within the state, it would be a mistake for an Alaska or Delaware trust to invest in real property located outside of one these states. Doing so would likely ensure that the state in which the real property is located will have jurisdiction, and that the trust, at least to the extent of this asset, is invalid.

Combining the Trust with a Business Entity

In theory, the greater the contacts with Alaska or Delaware, the greater the likelihood that a court will uphold the validity of the trust. Therefore, because Delaware, in particular, represents a very favorable place to form a business entity (see Chapter 9 for a discussion of choice of state issues), the business owner could first form the business entity there, and then have the business fund an asset protection trust in the same state. The entity could fund the trust as part of the compensation package for the owner of the business.

While certainly not a guarantee that the state will have jurisdiction over the trust, this strategy does at least offer support for this conclusion. For example, as discussed previously, in a recent case the right of Connecticut to tax a Delaware trust was upheld on the grounds that Connecticut had jurisdiction over the trust. Connecticut was found to have jurisdiction, in large part, because the beneficiary of the trust was a resident of Connecticut.

Thus, by extension, it can be argued that Connecticut would assert jurisdiction over a Delaware *asset protection* trust where the beneficiary resided in Connecticut. This is a more likely outcome where the beneficiary is also the trustor, which is the usual scenario in an asset protection trust. If Connecticut law were to apply to the trust, the trust would be invalid, in accordance with the general rule (outside of Delaware and Alaska) that a self-settled asset protection trust is invalid.

In contrast, if a Delaware entity created the Delaware trust, there is less likelihood that another state would be deemed to have jurisdiction, because the trustor exists in Delaware. It is possible, however, that a court would "collapse" the transactions and hold that the owner of the business entity effectively created the trust, or rule that the residence of the beneficiary alone would be determinative of the issue of jurisdiction. The only sure conclusion is that the use of the business entity to create the trust increases the possibility that Delaware law would be applied to the trust and that, accordingly, the trust will be declared valid.

Should a judgment be rendered in Alaska or Delaware upholding the validity of the trust, an argument also can be made that the trustor's home state will then be compelled by the same Full Faith and Credit Clause of the U.S. Constitution to honor this judgment.

Bankruptcy Considerations

While federal bankruptcy courts have jurisdiction that stretches across the states, it is an oversimplification to state that a domestic asset protection trust could not survive in a bankruptcy proceeding. Federal bankruptcy law requires that the court honor any exemption established under state law. Thus, in a bankruptcy proceeding, the same issue is presented—which state's laws will be applied? If the bankruptcy court finds that Alaska or Delaware law applies to the trust, according to the above analysis, for example, then the trust will be upheld as valid and exempt from the bankruptcy proceeding.

At this time, the outcome cannot be safely predicted. Arguments can be made that support either position. Because of the distinct advantages of these new asset protection trusts, and, as discussed below, the significant protections offered particularly by Alaska's statute, one thing probably can be safely predicted—when a significant sum is at stake, a creditor is likely to challenge the validity of the trust on the grounds discussed above.

Warning

To date, there have been no reported cases on the validity of an Alaska or Delaware asset protection trust against a challenge mounted outside one of these states. For this reason, some planners still recommend offshore asset protection trusts rather than domestic trusts.

However, offshore trusts are more expensive to establish. Further, many individuals are hesitant about investing offshore, because of concerns (mostly unfounded) about the jurisdiction's stability, currency valuation issues, etc. Finally, offshore trusts also can be challenged, as discussed below.

You should consult with an estate planning attorney before deciding whether to establish a self-settled asset protection trust, and, if such a trust is to be formed, whether to use Alaska, Delaware or an offshore jurisdiction for the trust's establishment.

If the decision is made to establish a domestic asset protection trust, consideration should be given to using the strategies previously outlined (e.g., investing in real property) to bolster the argument that Alaska or Delaware law should be applied to the trust.

Note that if the trustor is a resident of Alaska or Delaware, an issue can still exist as to validity of the Alaska or Delaware asset protection trust when the creditor is a resident of a different state, or the creditor's claim is based on an event that occurred in another state. An Alaska trust might, for example, be challenged by a former spouse, pursuant to a court judgment of alimony or child support from another state. Or the trust might be challenged by a creditor based on an auto accident that occurred in another state.

However, if you are a resident of Alaska or Delaware, it is probably less likely that the trust will be successfully challenged. Your residency will make it more likely that a federal court will find that Alaska or Delaware law should apply to the case. Nevertheless, because of the absence of direct rulings on the issue, this result is far from guaranteed.

Requirements of the Alaska and Delaware Trusts

By statute, both the Alaska and Delaware asset protection trusts require that the trust:

- must be irrevocable

- must have an independent trustee

- must not provide for mandatory distributions of income or principal (i.e., such distributions are subject to the discretion of the trustee)

- must have a spendthrift clause

These conditions are the standard requirements that must be met for any self-settled spendthrift trust. In addition, however, the statutes require that:

- the trustee must be an individual who is a resident of Alaska or Delaware, or a bank and trust company licensed in that state

- some or all of the trust assets must be located in the state (a bank account will suffice, so that the other assets can be invested by the trustee elsewhere)

- the trust documents and administration must be in the state

- certain creditors can reach the assets

With respect to this last requirement, significant differences exist between the Alaska and Delaware statutes. In short, the Alaska statute offers significantly better protection against the claims of creditors.

Creditor's Rights: Comparing Alaska and Delaware Trusts

The Alaska statute contains only two very narrow exceptions, under which creditors can reach the trust's assets. A creditor can breach the trust if:

- the trustor transferred assets to the trust intentionally as a means of defrauding the creditor, and the creditor brings suit within one year of the time he or she learned, or should have learned, of the transfer, but within four years in any event, or

- at the time of a transfer, the trustor was in default by more than 30 days under a court order of child support, and the creditor is attempting to enforce an order of child support

With respect to the first exception, the grounds that can be used by the creditor are actually narrower than it first appears. The Alaska statute requires that the creditor prove actual fraud—that is, intent, *factually*. This means the creditor is *prohibited* from using the "badges of fraud" that the courts have established, upon which intent can be *inferred* (see Chapter 4). Instead, the creditor must prove what the trustor was actually thinking at the time of the transfer. This is a very difficult burden.

The second exception is so narrow that it is quite easy to avoid. This narrowness also means that the trustor can immunize his or her assets against the alimony, child support (in most cases) and property claims of a past, present or future spouse. The effects of this provision are two-pronged: The protections offered by the statute are *extremely* significant, as these types of claims can exhaust wealth; since the protections are so extreme and seem to go against the trend, especially in terms of enforcement of child support orders, it means the provisions also will generate controversy, and thus challenges by creditors will be likely.

The Delaware statute creates much wider exceptions than the Alaska statute. Specifically, in Delaware, a creditor can reach the trust assets if:

- actual fraud (intent) can be proved; here, unlike in Alaska, creditors *can* use the badges of fraud to establish intent; the same time limitations that apply in Alaska also apply in Delaware

- the claim is made by a current, or former, spouse, and is for alimony or a property distribution

- the claim is for child support

- the claim stems from personal injuries or property damage, and the claim arose before the transfer

Plan Smart

A common misunderstanding is that the Alaska and Delaware asset protection statutes are identical. This is incorrect, especially where the statutes provide exceptions that allow creditors to reach the trust's assets.

As discussed above, the Alaska statute offers significantly greater protection than the Delaware statute. In Alaska, absent actual fraud, current and former spouses cannot reach the trust's assets for claims of alimony, claims based on property distributions or virtually all claims for child support. Also, claims based on personal injury or property damage occurring before the transfer will not be successful in Alaska. In Delaware, all of these claims are specifically allowed by statute.

While the chances that the Delaware statute will be challenged are somewhat lower, this really is not an argument in favor of establishing the trust in Delaware. If the trust is formed in Alaska and a challenge is successful (e.g., for child support), the trustor will likely be no worse off than if the trust were set up in Delaware. However, in Alaska, there is at least a possibility that the creditor's claim will be defeated.

Generally, consideration should be made to forming the trust in Alaska rather than Delaware if child support, alimony and marital property distributions are important issues, or there is the possibility of a claim based on an earlier act of negligence.

If the business entity is formed in Delaware, the entity could establish the trust there. As previously discussed, this may make it more likely that Delaware law will be applied to the trust and that, accordingly, the trust will be upheld as valid. This would be even more likely if the business entity had actual contacts there (e.g., an office, bank account, etc.).

In short, the choice of a trust in Alaska or Delaware will depend on the individual's particular circumstances.

Other Considerations

Fees. There will be legal fees for drafting the trust and fees charged by the trustee for administration of the trust. These costs, in many cases, will pale in comparison to the savings that can be generated if the trust protects you from a major judgment creditor—provided, of course, that the trust is upheld as valid.

The irrevocable nature of the trust. Because the trust will have to be irrevocable, the decision to establish the trust should be well thought out. Once established, you cannot change your mind as to particular provisions (for example, you can't remove your wayward son from the list of contingent beneficiaries) or as to whether the trust should have been created in the first place.

Discretionary distributions. Further, because the trust should not be structured to make mandatory distributions of income or principal, you will have to depend on the trustee's judgment in deciding whether to make a requested distribution.

However, you will have provided the trustee with guidance in making discretionary distributions in the trust document. Further, many clients use a letter addressed to the trustee requesting, but not requiring, that distributions be made when requested under certain circumstances. While not bound by such a letter, trustees know they will not be in business long if they gain a reputation as being unresponsive to client's requests. Thus, in practice, requests generally are honored.

Estate tax and income tax considerations. Assets within a properly constituted asset protection trust should escape federal estate taxes. Thus, the trust also functions as an estate planning device.

Transfers to the trust should be deemed completed gifts. Such transfers would reduce the unified estate tax exemption (at $1 million for 2003). However, the trustor could transfer up to $11,000 in 2003, per beneficiary of the trust (other than to himself or herself), without reducing the exemption (see Chapter 10 for details on this annual gift tax exclusion).

The trust ordinarily would be a separate tax-paying entity, absent special language that establishes a different result. This may not be desirable, as it creates additional administrative burdens and costs, and usually results in higher taxes. However, special language can be used to make the trust a grantor trust. In that case, the trust's income would all be taxed to the trustor, at his or her individual rates, and reported on the trustor's individual income tax return, Form 1040. This option is likely to lower the tax burden and administrative costs of the trust.

Other clauses. A domestic asset protection trust should have a trust protector clause, anti-duress clause and change of situs clause. These clauses are most commonly found in offshore trusts and are discussed below, in that context.

Risk. Finally, as previously discussed, the law concerning the validity of domestic asset protection trusts is not yet settled. You need to be aware that the trust may be challenged, and there is a possibility that the trust will be declared invalid. For this reason, some consideration should also be given to establishing an offshore asset protection trust rather than a domestic one.

The Offshore Asset Protection Trust

An offshore asset protection trust represents an alternative to a domestic asset protection trust formed in Delaware or Alaska. Prior to 1997 and the enactment of new trust legislation in Delaware and Alaska, the offshore asset protection trust was the only real way to create an effective self-settled spendthrift trust. Popular offshore jurisdictions for these trusts include Nevis, St. Kitts, the Cook Islands and the Bahamas. These jurisdictions have long recognized the validity of self-settled asset protection trusts.

Warning

You need to be aware that offshore "tax shelters" are prime targets of the IRS's stepped up campaign to discover unreported taxable income. Therefore, exercise extreme caution and consult a professional advisor before considering the use of an offshore trust.

As with their domestic counterparts, self-settled offshore asset protection trusts must:

- be irrevocable

- have an independent trustee

- provide only for distributions that are subject to the discretion of the trustee

- have a spendthrift clause

However, offshore asset prediction trusts can offer significant advantages over domestic asset protection trusts established in Delaware or Alaska. While the laws differ in each offshore jurisdiction, the Nevis trust statute is illustrative of these advantages.

Nevis law provides that an asset transfer can be challenged *only* by *factually* proving actual fraud. The broader grounds available to attack a transfer to a trust in Delaware are not available in Nevis. In this respect, the law in Nevis is similar to that found in the Alaska trust statute. However, as discussed below, Nevis places significant restrictions on the rights of a creditor that do not exist in Alaska or Delaware.

The general statute of limitations in Nevis for challenging transfers to the trust is two years, rather than the four years available in Alaska and Delaware.

Nevis will not recognize a foreign judgment. Instead, the creditor must file a new lawsuit in Nevis and prove actual fraud in the new case there. Further, the creditor must hire a Nevis-licensed attorney, and post a $25,000 bond to bring the suit. In contrast, in the United States, every state is compelled by the U.S. Constitution to recognize a sister state's judgment, as previously discussed.

The fact that no international law compels a sovereign nation to accept the laws of a foreign government really represents the essence of an offshore asset protection trust: The offshore jurisdiction is simply immune from U.S. laws. While the trustor/beneficiary will be a resident of a U.S. state, and thus subject to U.S. court jurisdiction, the trustor/beneficiary cannot compel the offshore trustee to make a distribution, because all distributions are subject to the trustee's discretion. Thus, when a U.S. court orders the trustor/beneficiary to compel a distribution, the trustor/beneficiary can invoke what is termed the "impossibility" defense. Until recently, this defense has been successful (as outlined in an example later in this chapter).

Moreover, once the new required lawsuit is filed in Nevis, the creditor must prove actual fraud by a "beyond a reasonable doubt" standard. In the United States, this standard applies only in criminal cases. It equates to the creditor establishing there is a more than 90 percent probability that his or her allegations are true. By contrast, in the U.S., the standard to win in a civil case by a creditor challenging an asset transfer is proof by a "preponderance of the evidence." This standard is much lower; the creditor needs only to establish that there is a more than a 50 percent probability that the allegations are true.

The intent of the U.S criminal standard is to prevent, to the greatest extent possible, innocent people from being convicted of crimes they did not commit. The standard is based on the theory that it's better to let nine guilty people go free, than to convict one innocent person. To achieve that effect, it is acknowledged that the use of such a high standard also may serve to protect guilty persons. This is perceived as the cost of protecting the rights and liberty of innocent persons. The use of this standard in a Nevis offshore trust case will make it extremely difficult for a creditor to prevail in a claim.

Foreign jurisdictions do not require that any of the trust's assets be located there. This is in contrast to the Delaware and Alaska trust laws, which require that at least some assets (perhaps a bank account) be located there.

Common Clauses in Offshore Trusts

Typically, offshore asset protection trusts will contain the following clauses in addition to a spendthrift clause:

- **Anti-Duress Clause** — This clause, when triggered, provides that the trustee is not to make a distribution from the trust when the trustor/beneficiary is under "duress"—that is, when a creditor has made a claim, or obtained a judgment against the trustor/beneficiary, outside of the foreign jurisdiction. This clause effectively prevents the creditor from enforcing the claim against the trust's assets without obtaining a new judgment in the offshore jurisdiction, as a result of a new lawsuit that was filed there. When this clause is invoked, it automatically removes the trustor/beneficiary from the positions of trust protector or co-trustee, if he or she held such positions. See below for the definition of trust protector.

- **Trust Protector Clause** — This clause names a "trust protector" and allows him or her to remove the trustee and, in some cases, to veto some or all of the trustee's actions. The trust protector is a very useful concept derived from British law, which is one reason that former British colonies are among the more popular locations for offshore trusts. In many offshore trusts, the trustor/beneficiary is the trust protector. When this is the case, usually the anti-duress clause (see above) also will trigger removal of the trust protector, when the trustor/beneficiary is under duress from a U.S. court. As discussed in the example below, it may be desirable to have an independent trust protector.

- **Flight Clause** — This clause allows the trustee to move the site of the trust to another jurisdiction. In theory, this might be used if the creditor hired a local attorney and filed suit in the foreign jurisdiction. The suit could be thwarted by removing the trust to another foreign jurisdiction, so that the creditor would have to start anew by filing suit yet again in the new jurisdiction.

- **Choice of Law Clause** — This clause directs that the trust is to be governed by the laws of the jurisdiction in which it is sited. While not necessarily conclusive on the issue of jurisdiction, such a clause is recommended.

Warning

 On the surface, it appears that an offshore trust represents an ideal way to shield assets from the reach of creditors. In fact, in many cases, offshore trusts have proved successful, often to the frustration of U.S. judges. This frustration culminated in a recent case, which has caused some practitioners to re-evaluate the risks inherent in offshore trusts. In this case a U.S. court used what is perhaps its only available weapon against an offshore trust—a criminal contempt citation against the trustor/beneficiary.

In 1999, the 9th Circuit Court of Appeals sustained a lower court ruling in a Cook Islands trust case that had held the couple who created the trust in criminal contempt of court and jailed them for six months, because they failed to obtain a withdrawal of funds from the trust pursuant to the court's order. The couple had relied on the impossibility defense (discussed above).

The court rejected the defense because it did not believe it was impossible for the trustors/beneficiaries to cause a withdrawal from the trust, despite the clear-cut provisions in the trust that made all withdrawals completely subject to the control of the trustee, and the anti-duress clause that automatically caused the removal of the couple from their positions as trust protectors and co-trustees of the trust.

The court based its conclusion on the following facts:

The couple had previously received distributions from the trust of about $1 million, which seemed to imply the couple had liberal access to the trust's assets. The court no doubt also was aware of the well-known fact that, in practice, trustees of offshore trusts virtually always distribute assets to the trustor/beneficiary upon request.

The couple served as the trust protectors for the trust. As such, they had not only the power to remove the trustee, but also the power to veto all of the trustee's actions. The court found these powers evidenced the significant control the couple exerted over the trust.

In accordance with the trust's anti-duress clause, the couple was immediately removed from this position, as soon as the trustee learned about the U.S. judgment. However, the court found this fact unconvincing, even though it meant that the couple was, in fact, powerless to force the trustee to make the distribution.

Similarly, the couple served as co-trustees of the trust. This too, the court found, was significant proof that the couple exercised control over the trust.

When the trustee learned of the U.S. judgment, the couple also was automatically removed from this position, in accordance with the trust's anti-duress clause. This, once again, did not move the court, thus indicating the couple's position relative to the trust, prior to the U.S. judgment, was the more important factor.

The court rejected the invocation of the anti-duress clause, which worked to prevent the trustee from making distributions to the couple and which also caused the removal of the couple as trust protectors and co-trustees of the trust. The court concluded that the couple themselves triggered the clause by contacting the trustee to inform him of the judgment. Of course, the couple did this ostensibly to request a distribution to satisfy the judgment. The court believed the notification was really done only to obtain protection under the anti-duress clause. The court concluded that this was self-serving, and thus something the court would censure.

In this case, the original court judgment against the couple was made pursuant to a Federal Trade Commission action. The couple had earned substantial sales commissions in a fraudulent investment scheme. While there was no finding that the couple directly engaged in the fraud, the court concluded that their actions bordered on fraud.

There is little doubt that the court was motivated by the fact that the couple apparently conceived of the trust as a means of shielding their profits from the fraudulent investment scheme. Had the couple's actions been honorable, it is possible that the couple would have not have faced the wrath of the court. (It should be noted that an action was subsequently filed in Nevis. The Nevis court ruled in favor of the trustee and the couple. This result was expected, given the provisions in the Nevis trust statute, as discussed above).

The decision in this case instills additional risks in the offshore trust option and provides some guidance as to the proper parameters of such a trust.

Plan Smart

Planners are split on how to interpret the case. Some planners believe that, given this case, the risks of a finding of criminal contempt against the trustor/beneficiary of an offshore trust are too significant to warrant the continued use of this planning strategy.

However, many other planners believe that the case is simply an example of the old legal adage, "bad facts make bad law." Thus avoiding the "bad facts" could mean that the fate the couple suffered in the previously discussed case can be avoided.

In light of the U.S. Court's decision in the case discussed above, it would be wise to:

- *Avoid being the trust protector or a co-trustee of the trust. Ideally, the trust protector (or a co-trustee if this is used) should be someone outside of the U.S. court's jurisdiction. A U.S. person may be acceptable, provided this person is not the trustor/beneficiary and is, in reality, independent of the trustor/beneficiary. By doing this, the trustor/beneficiary will be laying the groundwork for a finding that he or she did not have the ability to control the trust and thus his or her ability to force a distribution from the trust was impossible.*

- *Avoid personally notifying the foreign trustee of a U.S. court judgment. Let the judgment creditor or the court notify the trustee. In this way, the trustor/beneficiary cannot be accused of personally triggering the anti-duress clause.*

- *Avoid engaging in fraudulent or disputable conduct. Courts are likely to display extreme hostility toward a trustor/beneficiary who is either trying to shield assets that were acquired through illegal conduct, or where the trust's assets were legitimately acquired, but the creditor's claim is based on illegal conduct on the part of the trustor/beneficiary.*

In addition, because U.S. courts can assert jurisdiction over any *property* actually located within the United States, caution must be exercised to ensure that none of the assets acquired by the trust are located within U.S. borders.

Thus, ownership by the offshore trust of real estate located in the U.S. would be the worst possible choice. However, ownership of stock in U.S. companies also could present a problem. This risk might be avoided if the stock certificates are not held in "street name"—that is, they are not held by a U.S. broker. Instead, the certificates should be physically held by the trustee, in the trustee's name, in the offshore jurisdiction.

It is still possible, if the ownership is discovered, that the interest could be attached, as the obligation to honor the stock certificate emanates from a U.S. company. Luckily, many foreign jurisdictions also have secrecy laws that would make it difficult for the trust's actual investments to be uncovered.

In short, while offshore trusts may still provide planning opportunities, this option must be cautiously approached.

Estate and Income Tax Aspects

Generally, the offshore trust will be deemed to be a "foreign grantor trust." The trust will be deemed a "grantor" trust because there will be a U.S. beneficiary. This status means that the contributions to the trust will be free of income tax consequences. Such contributions *will* reduce your unified estate/gift tax exemption ($1 million for 2002), unless you take advantage of the annual gift tax exclusion ($11,000 for 2002). (See the previous discussion regarding this issue and Alaska and Delaware asset protection trusts).

This status also means that the trust's income will be taxed to you as the trustor/beneficiary, and you can report it on your personal income tax return, Form 1040. This will serve to simplify the reporting of the trust's income.

Remember, a U.S. resident is taxed on all worldwide income. Further, as discussed above, when an offshore trust has a U.S. beneficiary, the trust will be deemed a grantor trust, which means that the trustor/beneficiary will be taxed on all of the trust's income even if the income is not distributed, as if the income were earned directly by the trustor/beneficiary.

Representations that an offshore trust is an effective means for a U.S. resident beneficiary to avoid U.S. income tax are false and misleading.

Given the nature of the offshore trusts' provisions, its assets should normally be excluded from the estate of the trustor/beneficiary. This result is identical to that of the domestic asset protection trusts.

That the trust will be a "foreign" trust has certain implications. As long as the foreign trust has a U.S. beneficiary, the income tax consequences will be as described above. However, upon the death of the U.S. beneficiary, the trust's assets will be deemed to have been contributed to a foreign trust without a U.S. beneficiary. The result will be that all of the appreciation in the value of the trust's assets, *since the assets were first purchased by the trustor*, will be treated as taxable gain.

While the law in this area is not settled, it may be possible to avoid this outcome by requiring that the trust distribute all of its assets to a U.S. beneficiary upon the trustor/beneficiary's death or, of course, if there is another surviving U.S. discretionary beneficiary of the trust.

This result also would be avoided if the foreign trust were deemed to be a "domestic" trust. This result seems contradictory, but is a possibility under the federal tax code.

A provision added to the Internal Revenue Code in 1996 provides an objective test to determine when an offshore trust will be deemed, for tax purposes, to be a domestic trust. Basically, the trust must consent to the U.S. courts' having primary jurisdiction over the trust and to primary control by a U.S.-based trustee. Complying with either of these requirements means that the very purpose for which the offshore trust is designed (i.e., asset protection) will no longer exist.

Similarly, a safe harbor exists to qualify the trust as domestic. Among other things, the safe harbor requires that the trust not have a "flight clause." As discussed above, a flight clause is a standard, as well as a desirable, feature of an offshore trust.

In short, qualifying the offshore trust as domestic usually will not be advisable. However, you should discuss this issue with the attorney who will be drafting the trust.

In addition, a 1997 provision added to the Internal Revenue Code repealed a 35 percent excise tax that previously applied to contributions to a foreign trust without a U.S. beneficiary.

Trust Planning Issues

The offshore trust shares certain characteristics with domestic asset protection trusts. Thus, if you're thinking of setting up such a trust, you must carefully consider the irrevocable and discretionary nature of the trust.

However, the offshore trust has unique characteristics not found in domestic asset protection trusts. Thus, political stability, the financial strength of the foreign trust company, foreign currency gains and losses, and additional drafting costs are other issues that must be considered when examining an offshore trust as an asset protection strategy.

Offshore jurisdictions in which these trusts are commonly established have developed reputations as safe places to invest assets. However, some small business owners may be uncomfortable with the idea of placing investments outside of the U.S.

Legal fees for drafting an offshore trust can be expensive—more expensive than fees incurred for a domestic asset protection trust. The added fees must be weighed against the greater protection that potentially can be achieved with an offshore trust.

Also, ongoing maintenance fees payable to the offshore trust company can be substantial. These fees, combined with the initial setup fees, usually mean it is not cost-effective to establish an offshore trust until you have $1 million or more that you need to shelter.

In summary, each of these strategies involves its own unique risks. These risks, and the cost of setting up the trust, must be weighed against the potential benefits. The best way to do this is through consultation with an attorney who practices in this specialty.

Part II

Limit Liability in Your Business Structure

Whether you're a current or future small business owner, asset protection planning extends well beyond protecting your personal assets by being aware of and maximizing your personal exemptions, as discussed in Part I.

Since your business is likely to be your riskiest undertaking, you'll need to consider carefully the organizational form in which your business is conducted. While you can choose to run your business as a sole proprietorship, partnership, corporation or limited liability company, in most cases the LLC will offer the most effective protection for both your personal assets outside the business and your investment in the business itself.

But there is much more than that to consider when structuring your business. Part II sorts out all the specific considerations that must be examined when making an entity choice, including the best way to set up your financing, what tax and securities issues should be addressed, and how best to secure the protections afforded to you by law.

Chapter 6: Choosing an Organizational Form for Your Business examines the characteristics of all of the business forms available to you, including the newest business entities, such as the limited liability limited partnership (LLLP), and an alternative and superior form of the corporation: the statutory close corporation. This chapter also covers the most recent developments in laws governing LLCs, which make LLCs more widely available to business owners, and which add to the LLC's advantages over other forms.

Chapter 7: Comparing the LLC and Corporation builds on the material that is presented in Chapter 6 by providing a more detailed and comprehensive comparison of these two most useful business forms.

This chapter compares and contrasts the two forms, including discussions of protection from liability, costs of formation and operation, income and self-employment taxes, retirement and fringe benefits, securities and estate planning issues, etc.

Chapter 8: Using Holding and Operating Companies details an important strategy that should be considered by every small business owner— using a two-entity structure. In this type of arrangement, an operating entity will carry out the actual business functions and a holding entity will own the major capital assets of the company, often including the operating entity itself. In this way, you can provide a nearly impermeable shield for your business assets against the claims of business and personal creditors. It is possible for business owners who desire a simplified structure to personally act as the holding entity, although in that case the liability shield will not be as strong.

The discussion of funding strategies includes a description of which assets should be invested within the business form, and which assets should be owned outside of the form, as well as the proper mix of assets between an operating entity and a holding entity.

Chapter 9: Choosing a State allows you to make an informed decision when deciding on the state in which your business entity will be formed. The liability and internal affairs of a business entity are governed by the laws of the state in which it is formed, not the state in which it operates. While forming the business in your home state may offer simplicity and cost savings, states such as Delaware and Nevada may, in some cases, offer superior liability and other offsetting advantages.

Chapter 10: Planning for Federal Estate Taxes examines an often-overlooked, but important, issue in business formation. A business that thrives and grows will produce tremendous wealth for its owner. Yet, in the absence of effective estate planning, much of this wealth may be paid to the federal government in the form of estate taxes, rather than to the owner's family, when the business owner dies. The strategies contained within this section will help to preserve that wealth.

Chapter 11: Securities Law Issues includes an examination of the complexities of federal and state securities laws. An understanding of this is essential because solicitations of capital from even small numbers of individuals can result in civil, and even criminal, penalties, if you do not comply with the restrictions imposed by these laws.

Chapter 12: Tax Aspects of Funding Decisions completes the discussion of issues that surround structuring and funding your business. In particular, funding a business entity with services or assets subject to liabilities can have important tax consequences, in terms of the immediate recognition of taxable income, as well as the tax basis of your investment in the business. Tax basis, in turn, affects the allocation of the entity's income among its owners, and the amount of gain that owners realize when they sell their interests.

Chapter 13: Forming the Business Entity is the capstone chapter to this section. After you have chosen a particular business form, the particular state in which you will create the entity, and the structure for the business, you must actually form the entity or entities that will make up this structure by completing certain documents, filing them with the proper authorities and paying the appropriate fees.

This chapter describes the actual process of forming an entity, registering to do business in other states and using a fictitious name. This chapter also emphasizes the use of proper documentation when forming a business entity.

Chapter 6

Choosing an Organizational Form

At first glance, as a small business owner, you are faced with a somewhat confusing array of organizational forms in which you can operate your business:

- sole proprietorship

- general partnership

- limited partnership

- limited liability company

- limited liability partnership

- several types of corporations

This chapter will dispel the confusion by giving you an overview of the major characteristics of these forms, and then providing discussions on the nature of limited liability for business debts, as well as the impact of both business and personal liability on structuring/funding issues. Finally, we'll conclude with your likely options.

BUSINESS FORMS: AN OVERVIEW

The following summary of business forms, with an emphasis on the nature of liability in each form, will help you understand why most business owners should operate as a corporation or an LLC. More detailed examinations of the various forms follow the chart.

Common Organizational Business Forms

Form	Characteristics
Sole Proprietorship	*One owner. Simplest business form. No formal requirements to create or operate this form. Owner has unlimited, personal liability for all of the business's debts. Owner personally hires all employees, and thus the owner has unlimited, personal liability for the acts of employees. For these reasons, this form should usually be avoided.*
	Not a separate taxpaying entity: Income is reported on the owner's personal tax return, which may result in lower taxes, and does not require the filing of a separate tax return.
General Partnership	*Must have two or more owners. No formal requirements to create or operate this form. All owners have unlimited, personal liability for all of the businesses debts. All owners personally hire all employees, and thus all of the owners have unlimited, personal liability for the acts of employees. In addition, each owner has unlimited, personal liability for the acts of all of the other owners. Exposure to liability is so great in this form that, simply put, it should not be used.*
	Not a separate taxpaying entity: Income is reported on the owners' personal tax returns, which may result in lower taxes, and the business files only an information return with the IRS. Relatively simple business form to create and operate—basically a sole proprietorship with two or more owners.
Limited Partnership (LP)	*Must have two or more owners. Formally created under state law. At least one owner must be a general partner who has unlimited, personal liability in all of the same ways as in a general partnership. At least one owner must be a limited partner (frequently all of the other owners will be limited partners) who has limited liability, similar to owners of a corporation or limited liability company (LLC). However, unlike those owners, limited partners are prohibited from participating in the management of the business. This form has been used mostly for tax planning purposes (tax shelters) and estate planning purposes (transfer of discounted ownership shares to children).*
Corporation	*May have one or more owners. Formally created under state law. All of the owners have limited liability for the business's debts. Usually more costly than LLC to create and maintain. Subject to many formal statutory rules ("corporate formalities") regarding officers and directors, meeting and recordkeeping requirements. A regular corporation, termed a "C corporation," is a separate taxpaying entity, which may result in higher taxes and requires the filing of a separate tax return.*

Corporation (continued)	*When the corporation elects to be treated as a "conduit" for tax purposes, so that its income and loss flow to the owners, it is termed a "subchapter S" corporation. Note that this is merely a federal income tax election made by filing a form with the IRS. The corporation is formed in the normal manner under state law, and the subchapter S election has no other effect on the character of the corporation, except for the different tax scheme.*
	In a small group of states, the corporation may be formed as a statutory close corporation, which operates more like a partnership or LLC. This option can offer significant advantages over a conventional corporation.
Limited Liability Company (LLC)	*Newer business form. May have one or more owners. Formally created under state law. All of the owners have limited liability for the business's debts. Usually less costly than a corporation to create and maintain. Relaxed, less burdensome rules governing operation compared to a corporation.*
	Not a separate taxpaying entity: Income is reported on the owner's personal tax returns, which may result in lower taxes, and does not require the filing of a separate tax return when there is only one owner. The LLC combines into one form the best elements from the corporation (limited liability for all of the owners) and the general partnership (absence of formalities, low costs, tax benefits).
	Finally, in many states, the business interests of the owners of an LLC are protected from the claims of the owners' personal creditors. This advantage is not enjoyed in the corporation or the Limited Liability Partnership (LLP).
Limited Liability Partnership (LLP)	*Requires two or more owners. Similar to an LLC, but with important differences. Formally created under state law. All of the owners have limited liability for the business's debts, but in many states, the limited liability offers less protection than what is afforded to the owners of an LLC or a corporation.*
	Generally, anyone can form an LLP. However, California and New York limit the use of the LLP to professionals. Finally, some states use the term "Registered" Limited Liability Partnership (RLLP) because the LLP is really a general partnership that has "registered" in the LLP form to achieve some version of limited liability for all of the owners of the business.
Business Forms for Professionals	*Formally created under state law, the options include professional corporations (PCs), LLCs, professional limited liability companies (PLLCs) and LLPs. Each are explained in detail later.*

Sole Proprietorships and General Partnerships

If you are the sole owner of a business, and you have not formally created either a corporation or an LLC, you are operating a sole proprietorship. Sole proprietorships cannot themselves own any assets; therefore, all of the business assets will be considered your personal property. All of your assets—business and personal—are subject to the claims of all of your creditors—business and personal.

If you are a co-owner of a business, and you have not formally created a corporation, LLC, LLP, LP (or LLLP), you are operating a general partnership. Again, you have unlimited, personal liability for all of the businesses debts, including the acts of employees. In the case of the general partnership, you also have unlimited, personal liability for the acts of all of the other owners.

If you are already operating a business as a sole proprietorship or general partnership, you should seriously consider converting the business to an LLC or corporation. This simple change converts your liability from unlimited, personal liability for the business's debts to limited liability, and the conversion may be accomplished tax-free. In some cases, there may be a tax bill due upon the conversion of a general partnership to a corporation, so consult a tax professional first if you are considering this step.

The IRS will automatically treat a single-owner LLC as a sole proprietorship for tax purposes, so you would retain all the simplicity and tax savings of the simpler business form. Similarly, a multiple-owner LLC will be treated as if it were a partnership for tax purposes, so after a conversion you would continue to file a partnership tax return and retain the favorable pass-through tax treatment that goes along with partnership status. You can elect to forego the more favorable treatment and have your LLC taxed as a corporation, though this is rarely done.

Finally, what can you do to protect assets if you decide that you *still* want to operate in the form of the sole proprietorship? You must rely on other asset protection strategies discussed in this book, including post-judgment and bankruptcy asset exemptions, asset protection trusts, use of independent contractors, insurance, etc.

As for the small business owners who *still* want to operate in the form of a general partnership, here is some general advice: *Don't do it.* The general partner experiences all of the same exposures to liability as the sole proprietor, *plus unlimited, personal liability for the acts of all of his co-owners.* This should make even the biggest risk-taker reconsider that decision. It has been said that when the biggest accounting firms were operating as general partnerships, they relied on one asset protection strategy in particular: a whole lot of insurance. Today, all of these firms are organized as LLPs, LLCs or corporations.

Small business partnerships should follow the lead of these firms. Remember that the costs of forming an LLC or corporation with more than one owner will be lower, as the costs will be shared by all of the owners.

Limited Partnerships

A limited partnership (LP) is a partnership in which there must be at least one general partner who has unlimited personal liability, and at least one limited partner whose liability is limited to the investment he or she has made in the business.

Did You Know?

To achieve limited liability for the owner who is assuming the general partnership interest, it was once common strategy to make the general partner be a corporation or LLC owned by the individual who otherwise would have directly owned the general partnership interest. Today, this once common strategy, which requires the creation of two entities, is obsolete. The same objective, limited liability for all of the owners, can be accomplished through the use of one entity—the LLC.

Limited partners are really "silent partners" who make an investment of capital in the way that a passive shareholder does in a large, publicly traded corporation. Along with the positive aspect of limited liability, limited partners have a negative to contend with, in that they are prohibited from making day-to-day management decisions. Because all of the owners usually want to participate in the management of the business, this is not a suitable form in most cases.

On the other hand, the fact that limited partners cannot participate in management means that this form can be useful for estate planning. Parent/owners who don't want to lose control of the business, but who want to reduce the size of their taxable estate, can transfer ownership shares to children in the form of limited partnership interests. (Actually, the same objectives can be accomplished with an LLC, but in that case *all* of the owners enjoy limited liability for the business's debts. Both objectives are discussed in more detail below, in the context of the LLC.)

Because the LP is not a taxpaying entity, losses from the business can be passed on to the owners' personal tax returns, where they can "shelter" or offset other passive income that the limited partners might have. The general partner's losses are not usually considered passive, so they can be used to shelter other income up to the value of the partner's investment in the partnership.

As discussed later in this chapter, the LP can represent an effective shield for the owners' business interests against the claims of the owners' personal creditors. In many states, this can also be achieved in the LLC (but not in the corporation or LLP). In states where this is not possible in the LLC, the LP may represent a viable alternative to the LLC under the right conditions.

Did You Know?

A recent Tax Court decision added to the growing line of cases that delivered both good news and bad news if you use an LP as a family wealth transfer device. The good news is the court found that the partnership was bona fide, *that the liquidation restrictions were valid and that some substantial discounts for lack of marketability and lack of control could be applied in valuing the partnership interests that a father later transferred to his children. The bad news? The Court would not recognize extreme discounts that could never reasonably take place even for the most carefully constructed LPs.*

This line of decisions just proves further that, while LPs can be used for asset protection and estate planning (see Chapter 10 for estate planning ideas), they do have their limitations no matter how carefully constructed.

Finally, as discussed below, states are beginning to allow the LP to register as an LLLP (limited liability limited partnership), in which all of the owners, including the general partner, have limited liability. This form is different from the LLP, also discussed later. The entity otherwise continues to be subject to the state's limited partnership law (usually the Revised Limited Partnership Act). This change will bolster the use of the limited partnership as an alternative to the LLC.

Warning

Do not confuse a limited liability partnership (LLP) with a limited partnership (LP). The LLP is similar to an LLC, in that all *of the owners have limited liability (though, as discussed below, the quality of this limited liability in the LLP varies from state to state).*

In contrast, in an LP, at least one owner must be a general partner, who has unlimited personal liability.

Further, in an LLP, all of the owners can participate in management. In contrast, in an LP, limited partners are prohibited from participating in management.

The LLC and the Corporation

Two important organizational forms of business to consider are the limited liability company (LLC) and the corporation. Only the LLC and corporation offer the protection of full limited liability to *all* of the owners of the business in every state.

For tax purposes, the IRS treats the LLC as a sole proprietorship when there is one owner, and a general partnership when there are two or more owners, unless an election is made to treat the LLC as a corporation.

Today, all states allow one-owner LLCs. In addition, there is no tax reason that would require an LLC to have a life of a fixed duration, as once required in some earlier versions of certain state LLC statutes.

Generally, these two forms provide the greatest levels of asset protection, compared to the other entity options discussed in this chapter. Expanding on this concept, Chapter 7 examines the relative advantages of the LLC and the different types of corporations, in order to explain in greater detail why these are your best organizational choices as a small business owner.

The Statutory Close Corporation

Special note should be made of the statutory close corporation. In a strict sense, this is not a separate business form. It is, instead, a corporation that is regulated by a special state law. This statute, a supplement to a state's regular corporation statutes, governs most of the operations of this type of corporation.

The close corporations statutes relax many of the formalities normally applicable to a corporation. Basically, these statutes allow the corporation to be operated in a way similar to an LLC. The statutory close corporation may do away with a board of directors. Generally, shareholders do not have to hold meetings. Shareholders can run the corporation, by way of a shareholder agreement, which is similar to an LLC or a partnership operating agreement. Shareholders can agree to have one vote per person, as in a partnership, as opposed to one vote per share, if they so desire.

Warning

Don't confuse a statutory close corporation with the generic term "close corporation." The statutory close corporation is created under a supplemental state corporation statute.

The generic term close corporation is often used to refer to any corporation formed under a state's regular corporation statutes where the stock is not traded on an exchange, such as the New York Stock Exchange. That a corporation is called a close corporation does not mean it is a statutory close corporation. Unless the corporation is created in state that allows this option, with the required special language in the articles of organization, it will not be a statutory close corporation.

By contrast, in a regular corporation, directors and shareholders must hold regular meetings. Formal requirements exist regarding notice, quorums, waiving meetings, etc. The elimination of these and other formalities by the statutory close corporation statutes has important asset protection implications.

A failure to follow the required formalities can form the basis for a court piercing the veil of limited liability, and imposing unlimited, personal liability on the shareholders of a regular corporation (see Chapter 16). With the reduction or absence of such formalities, the likelihood of this doctrine being applied is reduced significantly. The statutory close corporation shares this advantage with the LLC.

Where the special statute is silent on an issue, the regular corporation statutes apply. Thus, the statutory close corporation will be subject to restrictions on retained earnings, dividends and other aspects of its operations that will not apply to the LLC.

Moreover, even the statutory close corporation statutes do not eliminate the fact that personal creditors of the owner will be able to attach, and then vote, the shares in favor of a liquidation of the business. In many states this cannot occur in the case of an LLC. Nevertheless, as discussed in Chapter 7, in very limited cases, a corporation *may* offer advantages over the LLC in terms of self-employment tax and possibly fringe benefits. Therefore, if you do intend to form a corporation, generally you should form it as a statutory close corporation. (An exception to this rule is the business owner who intends a broad-based public offering of securities or one that will exceed the 30 or 50 shareholder limits in effect in the states' statutory close corporation statutes).

Plan Smart

The following states (along with the District of Columbia) recognize the statutory close corporation:

Alabama	*Georgia*	*Maryland*
Arizona	*Illinois*	*Missouri*
Delaware	*Kansas*	*Montana*

Nevada	*Texas*	*Wyoming*
Pennsylvania	*Vermont*	
South Carolina	*Wisconsin*	

In addition, California, Maine, Ohio and Rhode Island have provisions within their regular corporation statutes that permit election to statutory close corporation status, but do not have special statutory close corporation statutes.

If your home state does not allow for the creation of a statutory close corporation, you can simply form the entity in one of the above states, and then register it to do business in your home state. As discussed in Chapter 9, the laws of the state in which the entity is formed will govern its legal affairs. The benefits derived from forming a statutory close corporation in one of these states, and then registering the corporation in the home state, will usually outweigh any additional costs involved.

The special statutory close corporation statutes require that there be a limited number of shareholders (under 30 or, in some states, under 50), and that certain transfer restrictions appear on the stock certificates. The statutory close corporation must be formed under the special statute with particular language used in the articles of organization. A regular corporation also can be converted to a statutory close corporation in states that allow this type of corporation.

The LLC generally will provide greater asset protection and other benefits. Chapter 7, which compares the corporation and the LLC, discusses how the small business owner can combine the LLC and the statutory close corporation.

The Limited Liability Partnership (LLP)

The limited liability partnership (LLP) is one of the newest business forms. While the LLP is similar to the LLC, there are some important differences that may make the LLP an inappropriate choice for the small business owner.

In many states, owners of an LLP have only a *reduced* form of limited liability from the claims of the business's creditors. This "limited shield," as it is sometimes called, does not afford the owners the same protection they would enjoy in either the LLC or the corporation. The nature of this limited shield version of limited liability is discussed later in this chapter.

In addition, in *many* states, the business interests of the owners of an LLP are afforded less protection from the claims of the owners' *personal creditors,* as compared to the LLC. This form of liability also is discussed later in this chapter.

Finally, California and New York limit the use of LLPs to professionals, thus eliminating the LLP as a choice for other business owners. (In California, the term "professionals" is defined narrowly to include only lawyers and accountants, further restricting the availability of the LLP there).

Many years ago, the law prohibited professionals such as accountants and lawyers from operating in the corporate form. As a result, virtually all of the largest and oldest CPA and law firms in this country were formed and operated as general partnerships.

This, of course, meant that the general partnership had unlimited personal liability for all of the business's debts, but professionals who wanted to form a business with each other had no other choice.

When the law was finally changed to allow professionals to incorporate, many firms were reluctant to make the change for tax reasons, since the federal tax law deems a conversion from one form (partnership) to another form (corporation) a potentially taxable event. In addition, such a conversion would involve re-titling all of the firm's assets from the general partnership to the new corporation. These large general partnerships have offices in every major city in the country, hundreds of partners and millions of dollars of assets. Accordingly, the transfer process alone would be complex and expensive enough to dissuade these forms from making the conversion.

Similarly, it was believed that the Internal Revenue Service might deem conversion from a general partnership to an LLC to be a conversion to another form, and thus a taxable event. Through lobbying by accounting firms, law firms and other professionals operating in the general partnership form, the limited liability partnership (LLP) was developed.

The conversion process from a general partnership to an LLP is unique in the law. The general partnership simply registers as an LLP. Technically, the old entity does not dissolve, and a new entity is not created. The old entity continues to exist, but is now subject to a new set of laws (i.e., those governing the LLP). The conversion does not trigger a taxable event because there is no change in the entity. Moreover, because of this registration process, none of the assets needs to be re-titled, making the conversion especially simple and inexpensive.

The LLC vs. the LLP. An LLP is not the same form as an LLC. Important differences generally make the LLC a better choice for the small business owner.

While all of the owners of both an LLC and an LLP have limited liability from the claims of the business's creditors, in many states the quality of the limited liability is not the same.

Warning

Many states only offer what is termed a "limited shield" in an LLP. In these states, limited liability protection is significantly reduced. These states include:

Alaska	*Louisiana*	*Ohio*
Arkansas	*Maine*	*Pennsylvania*
District of Columbia	*Michigan*	*South Carolina*
Hawaii	*Nevada*	*Tennessee*
Illinois	*New Hampshire*	*Texas*
Kansas	*New Jersey*	*Utah*
Kentucky	*North Carolina*	*West Virginia*

Since your business entity does not have to be created in the same state in which you reside or do business, it's best to avoid creating an LLP in one of these states.

Other states afford the LLP the same "full shield" protection as that enjoyed in the LLC and corporation. Because the LLP is so new, the law here is rapidly evolving. Expect more states to change the liability shield in the LLP from limited to full. For example, Florida made this change in 1999. (The specific differences between "full shield" and "limited shield" versions of limited liability are discussed later in this chapter).

In addition, in many states, the business interests of the owners of an LLP are afforded less protection from the claims of the owners' *personal* creditors, as compared to the LLC. Specifically, an LLC can be formed in a state that protects the owner's business interest against the claims of his personal creditors. This is not possible with the LLP, as no state affords this protection to LLP owners. (This difference also is discussed later in this chapter.)

Technically, the LLP is a partnership; therefore, it must have two or more owners. While states formerly required two or more owners to form an LLC, today one owner is sufficient.

The small business owner should generally avoid the LLP in "limited shield" states, because it offers less protection from liability there, as compared to either the LLC or the corporation. In addition, the IRS has clarified that an LLC would be treated like a partnership for tax purposes. Thus, today, a general partnership may be converted directly to an LLC tax-free. Accordingly, one of the main purposes of converting a general partnership to an LLP, rather than an LLC, no longer exists.

There is still one instance when an LLP makes sense: When the business owner is operating a very large, complex general partnership, conversion to an LLP rather than an LLC will be less expensive and less burdensome. Even here, however, it makes sense to form the LLP in a "full shield" state, even if that is not where the business's operations are conducted.

Where professionals operate in the LLP form, many states impose mandatory insurance requirements on the owners (see Chapter 18 for a discussion of insurance). These requirements are not usually imposed on the owners of an LLC, although this may be an oversight that will be changed in the future.

Plan Smart

If you are operating a business in the general partnership form, consider converting the business to an LLC, rather than an LLP. This simple change converts all of the owners' liability from unlimited, personal liability for the business's debts to limited liability, and affords the owners greater protection from liability than what is offered in the LLP. Even when the LLP is formed in a state that offers full shield limited liability for the business's debts, the owner of the LLP will still enjoy less protection for the business interest against the claims of personal creditors, as compared to the LLC.

This conversion now may be accomplished tax-free. Further, in a small or modestly sized general partnership, generally re-titling assets will not be that complex or expensive so as to justify the lower level of protection offered by the LLP.

If you are forming a new business with a co-owner, you can simply form it as an LLC (or corporation), rather than an LLP. The LLP was really designed to make conversions from a general partnership tax-free and less burdensome.

The Limited Liability Limited Partnership (LLLP)

As if business owners did not have enough "initials" to contend with (LLC, LLP, PLLC, LP, PC), a new business form, the LLLP, is beginning to emerge in the law.

What is an LLLP? It is a limited liability limited partnership or, more specifically, a limited partnership (LP) that registers under state law so the general partner will have limited liability, similar to the limited partners. This is similar to the process of a general partnership registering to be recognized as a limited liability partnership (LLP), so that *all* of the owners have limited liability.

The LLP is a general partnership that registers in the LLP form. Likewise, an LLLP is a limited partnership that registers in the LLLP form.

The LLLP form primarily is used to *convert* an existing limited partnership previously created under state law. However, it also will probably prove popular as an alternative to forming an LLC in those states that allow foreclosure of an owner's business interest, and forced liquidation of the business, by the owner's *personal* creditors (this issue is discussed later in this chapter).

Plan Smart

Colorado, Delaware, Florida, Georgia, Maryland and Texas recognize the LLLP as of 2002. In the future, it is likely that other states will follow suit.

Because of the LLC, LLP and LLLP, in the future, the general partnership and the limited partnership (LP) will likely become obsolete.

Business Forms for Professionals

When state laws were changed to allow professionals, such as doctors, lawyers, engineers, etc., to form corporations, the laws imposed certain conditions on this choice. Specifically, the laws require that:

1. All owners of the corporation be licensed within the same profession. However, some states allow individuals in similar professions (e.g., psychiatrists and psychologists) to own shares in the same corporation.

2. The business must use the term "PC" (Professional Corporation) in its name.

All states, except California, now allow professionals to form LLCs as well as corporations. All of these states impose on the LLC the same *first* condition imposed on the PC (i.e., all of the owners must be licensed in the same profession). However, curiously, many states do not impose the second condition on LLCs. Accordingly, in these states, no special designation other than the standard LLC is required in the name of the business. In some states that do impose the second condition on LLCs, the term "PLLC" (professional limited liability company) is used.

If you are considering a professional LLC, find out if the state in which you are forming requires you to use the term "PLLC" in the business's name. In addition, it is always a good idea to check with the professional association in your state to determine if there are any special ethical rules regarding the operation of an LLC.

In California, professionals cannot operate in the LLC form, and a one-owner professional business must be formed as a corporation. However, in California, two or more professionals have the choice of operating in the form of an LLP (in the case of accountants and lawyers) or a corporation. Despite its many shortcomings, California does offer full shield protection in the LLP.

Both New York and California limit the use of LLPs to professionals, and in California this means only lawyers and accountants.

Finally, where professionals operate in the LLP form, many states impose mandatory insurance requirements on the owners. Because mandatory insurance is likely to be expanded in the future, professionals in LLP states that do not require it now, and professionals operating in the form of LLCs or corporations, should check with state authorities or their professional association for updates in this area.

THE NATURE OF "LIMITED LIABILITY"

Only in the corporation and LLC form do *all* of the owners enjoy full "limited liability" in every state. But what, exactly, is limited liability? It is sometimes mistakenly said that a corporation or LLC has limited liability. In fact, the corporation and LLC have unlimited, personal liability for their debts. They can lose everything they own.

It is the *owners* who enjoy limited liability: The owner's liability for the *business's debts* is limited to what he or she has invested in the business (i.e., the *business's assets*).

The business can lose everything it owns, and this includes the owner's investment in the business. *It is wise, therefore, to invest and maintain as little capital as possible within the business form.* This tenet of asset protection, which may be carried out in a number of different ways, is discussed in more detail below and in other chapters. Because of limited liability, of course, the owner's *personal assets*, outside of the business form, are shielded from liability for *business debts*.

Example

Let's say the owner of a sole proprietorship or a general partnership has a personal net worth of $1 million, outside of his business, as well as outside of post-judgment and bankruptcy exemptions. His business suffers severe financial difficulties, resulting in a debt of $1.5 million, due to a loss of market share, default on loans, loss of a major lawsuit, etc.

Further, if the owner, at the time of the loss, has $2,000 invested in the business. What does the owner stand to lose? His entire personal net worth of $1 million, in addition, of course, to his $2,000 business interest.

Now if the owner had been operating his business as a corporation or LLC, due to limited liability, his loss now would be limited to his investment in the business, $2,000, and his entire personal net worth of $1 million would be preserved.

Exceptions to Full-Shield Limited Liability

As previously discussed, many states grant the owners of an LLP less liability protection than the owners of an LLC.

Specifically, many states only offer what is termed a "limited shield" of liability. This means that limited liability is reduced. In particular, a limited shield means that the owners the LLP will have *limited liability only with respect to actions of their co-owners; owners will still have unlimited, personal liability in all other cases,* meaning all of their personal assets outside the business will be exposed to liability.

For example, if the business sold a defective product that injured a customer, the owners could be sued *personally.* Similarly, if an employee of the LLP injured someone while carrying out the LLP's business, all of the owners of the LLP would have unlimited, personal liability. (A list of states that afford owners of an LLP only a limited shield of liability appears earlier in this chapter).

The reluctance by many states to grant the owners of an LLP a "full shield" is probably due to the fact that nearly all LLPs were general partnerships that have been converted to the LLP form. It was probably too radical of an idea for legislators in many states to go from unlimited, personal liability for all the owners of the business (i.e., general partnership) to full limited liability.

Further, as discussed below, even when a "full shield" is offered, the business interests of the owners of an LLP are still not offered the same protection from the claims of their personal creditors that the owners achieve in the LLC. For this reason, the LLP is usually not a good choice for the small business owner.

Warning

Unknown to many small business owners, there are, in fact, major exceptions to limited liability, and they are discussed throughout this book (especially see Chapters 15 and 16). When an exception applies, the owners of the business have unlimited, personal liability for all of the business's debts.

With planning, the potential damage caused by these exceptions can be reduced or eliminated (identifying your vulnerabilities is the focus of asset exemption planning explained in Chapter 3).

IMPACT OF LIABILITY ON STRUCTURING/FUNDING

There are two types of liability to consider when deciding how to structure and fund your LLC or corporation:

- liability for business debts (i.e., debts that arise from business transactions)

- liability for personal debts (i.e., debts incurred from activities outside of the business entity).

Business Debt Liability

Most business owners mistakenly believe that assets *within* a corporation or LLC are shielded from liability. This is certainly not the case with respect to business debts. In fact, most business owners face the greatest risk of liability from business transactions, and not personal dealings. Thus, these assets, which can be significant in a successful business, will be exposed to the greatest risk of loss. Yet, a corporation or LLC can be *structured, funded and operated* so that the business's assets are not exposed to *any* liability.

Unfortunately, today, most small business owners are not structuring, funding or operating their businesses to avoid liability. Thus, owners are unknowingly exposing their personal and business assets to a high risk of loss, many times under the illusion that their corporation or LLC will afford them protection. Typically, owners find out the truth only when financial troubles strike. At that point, usually it is too late, or extremely difficult, to preserve wealth, and the result is a significant loss of personal and business assets and, in the worst case, financial disaster.

Plan Smart

You should invest and maintain as little vulnerable capital as possible within the business form, so that your "limited liability" is, in essence, further limited because you expose little or no assets to liability. This principle of asset protection is explored more fully later in this chapter and in the remaining chapters of Part II.

However, you should be aware that this strategy can trigger an exception to limited liability, in which a court "pierces the veil" of limited liability and imposes unlimited, personal liability on the owners, on the grounds that the capitalization was inadequate and was a fraudulent scheme against the business's creditors.

Fortunately, an LLC or a corporation can be adequately capitalized so as to avoid this exception, without exposing business assets to liability.

This exception, and the strategies that can be used to eliminate the exception, are discussed in more detail in Chapter 16. As discussed there, balancing the initial capital structure is critical in avoiding application of this exception. Be sure to examine Chapter 16 before you make a decision on funding your business.

Personal Debt Liability

Placing assets within a business entity (i.e., LLC, corporation or partnership) is sometimes touted as an asset protection device, with respect to *personal* debts. While this strategy has considerable merit, it is misleading because, when used by itself, it dangerously and unnecessarily exposes these assets to a high risk of loss to the *business's* creditors. In order to understand how protection of your business from personal debts is possible, you need to understand something called a "charging order."

The charging order concept stems from a theory involving partnership property. For example, a partner in a general or limited partnership incurs a large personal debt from activities outside the partnership. Further, this debt cannot be satisfied from the partner's personal assets outside the partnership.

According to this view, the personal creditor of the partner can obtain what is termed a "charging order" against the partner's interest in the partnership, and become an "assignee" of this interest. In effect, the creditor attaches the partner's interest in the partnership.

However, according to the law, a partner does not actually own any specific assets in a partnership. His property interest is, in fact, his partnership interest itself, which is deemed a type of personal property. Because of this theory regarding partnership property, a personal creditor of a partner may attach the partner's interest, but the creditor may *not* directly attach the underlying partnership assets.

Charging Orders for Limited Partnerships

In the case of the limited partnership (LP), the law takes the theory a step further. The creditor with the charging order cannot foreclose on that interest and force a liquidation of the partnership to reach the specific partnership assets.

Where does that leave the creditor? The creditor is given the rights of an "assignee." As an assignee, the creditor takes over the rights of the partner to receive any income or assets that otherwise, in the normal course of business, would have been distributed to the partner.

However, the relationship among partners is a personal one. For example, new partners may not be admitted except upon the consent of all of the existing partners. Because of this concept, *the creditor does not become a partner and, accordingly, cannot participate in management of the business (by voting or otherwise); therefore, the creditor cannot legally force a distribution of income or assets that otherwise would not have taken place.*

The business owners can simply stop making ordinary distributions of income. Typically, a distribution of the business's *assets* (other than undistributed income) would take place only on liquidation, which would not occur in the normal course of business. Thus, if no *income* is being generated, or no income or assets are being distributed, the creditor will be holding an interest that will provide no benefit whatsoever.

Worse yet for the creditor is the fact that a holder of a partnership interest in an LP must pay federal incomes taxes on his or her allocated share of earnings, *even if they are not distributed*. Thus, a creditor with a charging order will be taxed on the owner's share of earnings, even though the creditor *receives* no income.

Many creditors, knowing that this is a likely outcome, may decide not to pursue the matter, give up collection efforts, or accept a reduced settlement, especially after the debt goes uncollected for a long period of time.

Plan Smart

All states (except Louisiana and the District of Columbia) have enacted the Revised Uniform Limited Partnership Act (RULPA), and will follow these rules with respect to charging orders and limited partnerships. Because the limited partnership laws of Louisiana and the District of Columbia are based on the older Uniform Limited Partnership Act, they are likely to follow the "liquidation view" discussed below that applies to general partnerships.

The special rules regarding charging orders described above do not apply to other entities such as general partnerships, LLPs, sole proprietorships or corporations. Further, the LLC has special rules of its own.

Charging Orders for General Partnerships

General partnership law as reflected in the Uniform Partnership Act (UPA) has always embraced the liquidation view—the doctrine that the personal creditor with a charging order may foreclose on the debtor's partnership interest if the creditor can prove that it isn't fair and equitable to allow the debtor to carry on the business, with the creditor acting as a mere assignee of the business interest. This usually will not be difficult to prove in a small business setting, as discussed below.

The UPA also specifically allows the courts to make all orders necessary to enforce this right, including an order forcing a liquidation of the business. Specifically, the courts are empowered in these states to make all orders, directions, accounts and inquiries which the debtor owner might have made, or which the circumstances of the case may require. This is a very broad power.

Most states have enacted the UPA to govern general partnerships. A few states have enacted the Revised Uniform Partnership Act (RUPA) to govern general partnerships. However, even this version of general partnership law reflects the liquidation view.

Note that in the general partnership, the law deems the relationship among the partners to be a personal one. Thus, even there, the personal creditor with a charging order cannot become a partner (without the unanimous consent of the other partners) and, accordingly, cannot vote or participate in management. More importantly, however, general partnership law does *not* take the extra step afforded by limited partnership law. Thus, despite the personal relationship, the personal creditors who attach a general partnership interest can foreclose on the partner's interest and force a liquidation of the business.

In a small business, this is more of a possibility, because the courts will look at the size of the creditor's debt in relation to the size of the business, as well as the effect a forced liquidation would have on the other owners, before deciding whether or not a liquidation is equitable. In the case of larger businesses, or ones with multiple owners, forced liquidation is less likely to be deemed equitable. However, the power is broad enough to allow the court to take all actions that the owner could have taken, including voting, or selling, his interest to a third party.

Charging Orders for Limited Liability Partnerships

Registering a general partnership as a limited liability partnership will not be much help in avoiding a forced liquidation through a charging order because of an owner's personal debt. The LLP is simply a general partnership that registers to achieve limited liability for all of the owners. In all other respects, the LLP is subject to general partnership law (i.e., the UPA or RUPA) regarding charging orders. Thus the owner's personal creditors can attach and then foreclose on an LLP interest, and seek a forced liquidation of the business.

Charging Orders for Sole Proprietorships

The sole proprietorship is not recognized as an entity for any purpose and, accordingly, cannot own any property. Thus, the sole proprietor's business assets can always be foreclosed on and liquidated by his personal creditors, because the assets are really personal assets.

This is yet another reason why the small business owner should avoid operating in the form of a general partnership or sole proprietorship.

Charging Orders for Corporations

In theory, the relationship among corporate shareholders is an impersonal one (as opposed to that in a partnership or LLC). Therefore, the law allows a creditor who has acquired the shares through attachment to participate in management of the corporation. Thus, the creditor may vote the shares in favor of liquidation, or in other ways unfavorable to the debtor's interests. In a small, closely held corporation, this is a real possibility.

Warning

When you hold a majority interest in the corporation, and this interest is attached by a creditor with a charging order, your creditor may vote to liquidate the business to satisfy the debt.

Even setting up your corporation as a statutory close corporation does not eliminate the risk that personal creditors of the owner will be able to attach and then vote the shares in favor of a liquidation of the business.

Charging Orders for Limited Liability Companies

The LLC is a hybrid—a combination of the best elements from the corporation and the partnership. The LLC derives a non-liquidation benefit from its partnership heritage.

Many states, in enacting LLC statutes, have followed the RULPA limited partnership (LP) heritage in enacting rules preventing foreclosure of an owner's interest and forced liquidation of the business to satisfy a *personal debt* of the owner. In short, these states now prohibit foreclosure and forced liquidation of an LLC.

The unfavorable outcome that can occur in a corporation cannot occur in the LLC because a creditor with a charging order does not become a member of the LLC and, accordingly, has no voting or management rights. However, this conclusion must be tempered by several facts.

Not all states follow the RULPA view with respect to LLC interests. Instead, some still take the "liquidation view," under which the creditor can, in fact, foreclose on the partnership interest. In short, the creditor can force a liquidation of the partnership, so that the partner's personal debt can be paid from his or her share of the liquidated assets.

Plan Smart

The following states have LLC statutes that follow the RULPA view prohibiting foreclosure and liquidation:

Arkansas	Illinois	Oklahoma
Connecticut	Louisiana	Rhode Island
Delaware	Maryland	Virginia
Idaho	Minnesota	
Iowa	Nevada	

Other states are likely to follow the general partnership view—liquidation. Note that the Uniform Limited Liability Company Act, which has been adopted in some states, reflects the general partnership view.

You should consider forming an LLC in one of the states listed above, even if that is not the state where the business will be conducting its operations (see Chapter 9 for a choice-of-state analysis). In these states, the protection afforded to your business interest, against the claims of any personal creditors, is significant.

Note that, under the RULPA view incorporated into the LLC statutes in the states listed above, courts are not given the power to make any orders, except the mere granting of a charging order. In fact, the courts that have interpreted the RULPA charging order provision have concluded that the charging order is the only remedy available to the personal creditor. This should also extend to LLCs in the states listed above.

As we've seen, a personal creditor of an LLC owner who obtains a charging order against the owner's LLC interest will not have an effective remedy in states that apply the RUPLA charging order concept in their LLC statutes.

This also may be the result in a federal bankruptcy proceeding. However, the federal bankruptcy courts have other powers that come into play. Further complicating the exercise of these powers is the fact that the bankruptcy code does not yet have specific provisions that apply to LLCs. This often leads to uneven results across the states in bankruptcy cases.

The LLC operating agreement is likely to be deemed an "executory contract" in bankruptcy parlance. The trustee appointed by the bankruptcy court can, under the federal bankruptcy code, exercise powers over the debtor's interests in an executory contract. This power can be used to sell or assign the owner's rights under the agreement. This right *should* only apply to the extent a creditor with a charging order could exercise these rights. Thus, an LLC statute with a RULPA charging order provision should work to prevent the bankruptcy trustee from usurping, or assigning, any management rights in the LLC, or naming an assignee of the interest as a full-fledged owner.

In other words, the trustee should have no greater rights than could be exercised by a creditor with a charging order under state law. However, because of a lack of express provisions in the bankruptcy code related to LLCs, this result is not assured. It is possible that bankruptcy courts in some states could reach a different conclusion.

For this reason, a properly drafted LLC operating agreement may contain a clause that expels, or gives the LLC the power to expel, an owner who files a bankruptcy action. This clause, if it is exercised to trigger expulsion, severs the filing member from the contract and allows the remaining owners to regroup and continue the LLC without bankruptcy court interference. (Note that this is the default rule under the Delaware LLC statute—one more reason to consider forming your LLC in Delaware.)

The right to expel might include the requirement that it can only be exercised if the bankruptcy court concluded the trustee had the power to exercise or transfer the management rights of the owner. In the event of an expulsion, management and voting rights could, under the agreement, be vested in the existing voting/managing owners, or if none exist, in the owners who originally held nonmanager/nonvoting interests.

The expulsion clause may further provide for a diminished payout (e.g., equal to book value, rather than fair market value) to an owner who is so expelled. The clause also can provide that the bankruptcy action amounts to a material breach of the agreement by the debtor/owner, entitling the LLC to recover damages from the owner. Further, the clause can provide that this diminished amount be reduced further on account of the damages caused to the LLC by the breach. These provisions reduce any amount that would be paid into the debtor/owner's bankruptcy estate and could persuade the trustee to abandon the executory contract.

Because of the fairly severe consequences triggered by an expulsion clause, it is wise to seek professional guidance in this matter. For example, an expulsion clause may be more appropriate in a family owned LLC, where expulsion, and a diminished payout, would not, in reality, reduce the family's overall wealth.

As you may have guessed, trustees sometimes challenge these clauses. A court may uphold the clause, however, if applicable state law incorporates the RULPA charging order concept, and thus prevents a judgment creditor from assuming all the rights of an owner, and allows the remaining owners the power to reject admitting the creditor as full-fledged owner. Thus, it is essential that the LLC be formed in a state that incorporates the RULPA charging order concept, and that the operating agreement contain a clause along the lines described above.

YOUR LIKELY OPTIONS

Most small business owners will usually want to form the business as an LLC or a corporation. The LLC will usually be a better choice when it comes to protecting the owner's business assets from the claims of personal creditors. Note that care must be taken to form the LLC in a state that follows the RULPA view in its LLC statutes.

However, if the business is to be formed in a state that allows foreclosure and liquidation in an LLC, the owner may want to consider a limited partnership (LP) as an alternative to the LLC, at least where the owner is especially concerned about protecting assets from the claims of *personal* creditors and the business will be family-owned, so that all of the owners will not necessarily be interested in managing the business.

If this is done, care must be taken to insulate the general partner from personal liability (by making the general partner a corporation or LLC owned by you). Of course, this will undermine the very purpose of the strategy—preventing foreclosure and liquidation by a personal creditor, because the strategy will have been undertaken in a state that allows foreclosure and liquidation in both the corporation and the LLC. Nevertheless, the *limited partnership interests* will still be protected from foreclosure and liquidation.

As more states begin to recognize the limited liability limited partnership (LLLP), this strategy will be an even more effective alternative to the LLC.

Plan Smart

Even when state law reflects the RULPA view prohibiting foreclosure and liquidation, is the result really satisfactory to a business owner? Assume the personal creditor does not give up or accept a reduced settlement. Under the modern view, the personal creditor of the owner attaches the owner's interest in the business and, thus, becomes entitled to all of the distributions of assets and income to which the owner would have been entitled.

The owner works in the business, but derives no benefits whatsoever. Any distributed income goes to the creditor, and when the business is finally voluntarily liquidated, all of the assets go to the creditor. How many small business owners would find this outcome satisfactory?

Nevertheless, the personal creditor, in many or even most cases, will *give up or accept a reduced settlement. In particular, the fact the* creditor *will be taxed on the LLC's earnings, even though he or she receives nothing, usually will persuade the creditor to drop collection efforts, to cut his or her losses. Be sure to take care when drafting the entity's documents to avoid making any distributions to the owner mandatory (see Chapter 14 for a discussion of withdrawal strategies).*

Since you can obtain protection from your personal creditors for assets owned by your LLC, some business owners think that they should convert as many assets as possible into business assets. Placing assets within a *single LLC* (in contrast to a single *corporation*), can offer significant protection from the claims of the owner's *personal creditors*, because, in many states, these creditors will *not* be able to foreclose on the interest and force a liquidation of the business.

However, the benefits of this strategy, within a *single* LLC, are very small, because most business owners are more likely to face a business debt or judgment than a personal one. The *business's assets,* as opposed to the owner's personal assets outside of the business, are usually at the greatest risk of loss, which means this strategy actually *increases* the risk of loss.

A better approach would be to use two entities, an operating entity and a holding entity (as discussed in Chapter 8). In this way, you can protect your assets against the claims of both your business and your personal creditors.

Chapter 7

Comparing the LLC and the Corporation

Both the corporation and the limited liability company (LLC) provide limited liability for all of the owners of the business, among their other advantages. Usually the LLC, rather than the corporation, will present a better choice for the small business owner. This is mainly because the LLC is a low-cost, simpler alternative to the corporation. This accounts for the fact that the LLC is the fastest growing business form in the United States.

Warning

Don't confuse the LLC with the LLP. There are some important differences between the two forms in terms of liability. See Chapter 6 for a detailed discussion of these two types of business ownership forms.

Typically, the LLC's advantages over the corporation include:

- Lower state formation and renewal fees

- Less complex and burdensome operating rules

- Simplified taxation

- Better asset protection for the owner's business interest against the claims of *personal* creditors, because of the RULPA lineage of the charging order concept applied in many states (see Chapter 6)

- Better protection for the owner's personal assets outside the business, as the doctrine of piercing the veil of limited liability is less likely to be applied to the LLC due to its simplified operating rules (see Chapter 16)

- Better integration with other planning techniques, including domestic asset protection trusts and estate planning strategies, such as the family limited liability company (these techniques are discussed briefly below and in more detail in Chapter 10)

The corporation *may* have the edge in three limited situations:

- **Going Public** — When the small business owner intends to make a public offering of securities that is broad-based (e.g., an Internet offering), a corporation may be more appropriate than an LLC. While the same objective can be accomplished with an LLC, the investing public is more accustomed to purchasing common stock in a corporation, and state securities regulators are more familiar with an offering of common stock. In future years, this probably will not be the case. Securities law, as it affects the small business owner, is discussed in Chapter 11.

- **Self-Employment (Social Security) Tax** — As discussed later, it is possible, although not likely in most cases, that the corporate form would result in lower self-employment taxes than the LLC.

- **Fringe Benefits** — Currently, the regular C corporation can provide a greater amount and more kinds of fringe benefits, tax-free, to its owners, as compared to an LLC. However, as discussed later, generally, small business owners operating a corporation will elect subchapter S corporation status. This election will mean that the business will enjoy *no* fringe benefit advantage over the LLC. Further, the most important fringe benefit, tax-free health insurance, is currently being phased-in for LLC owners (and all self-employed individuals) by federal law. Finally, the LLC can simply elect to be taxed as a C corporation and enjoy the same tax-free fringe benefits advantage, although the benefits derived from such an election will almost never outweigh the disadvantages associated with being taxed as a C corporation.

In short, the small advantages the corporation may seem to have over the LLC usually turn out to be illusory. In this chapter, we'll examine state fees, simplicity and low cost of operation, and tax implications and explain why the LLC will generally hold the advantage.

STATE FEES FOR LLCS AND CORPORATIONS

State fees to form an LLC are usually lower than the fees charged to form a corporation.

Example

In Connecticut, the corporate fees are $275 for formation and $85 for annual renewal, while the LLC fees are only $60 and $10, respectively.

Similarly, in Rhode Island, the corporate fees are $150 for formation and $85 for annual renewal, while the LLC fees are only $50 and $10, respectively.

The fee structure in Connecticut and Rhode Island is consistent with the intent of LLC law, which, in part, is to make the LLC a lower-cost alternative to the corporation.

Our Appendices contain a table comparing the fees charged by each state for forming an LLC and a corporation.

However, this is not always the case. Some states charge fees for forming and renewing an LLC that are significantly higher than what is charged for a corporation. These states seem to have completely distorted what is supposed to be a principal advantage of the LLC over the corporation—low cost of formation and operation. Nevertheless, it is the law.

Example

In Massachusetts, the fees for forming and renewing (annually) a corporation are $200 and $85 respectively, while for an LLC, there is a $500 formation fee and a $500 annual renewal fee.

In any event, in *most* states, the fees charged for the LLC are lower than those charged for a corporation. Further, in Delaware and Nevada, two key states for business formation, the fees charged by the state are the same for the formation of a corporation and an LLC ($50 in Delaware, and $125 in Nevada).

If you live in one of the states that charge higher fees for forming and renewing an LLC than a corporation, you may want to consider forming a corporation, rather than an LLC, at least where fees are an important deciding factor. However, the fee savings may be misleading.

The small business owner intending on forming a corporation should usually form it as a statutory close corporation (as discussed in Chapter 6). However, this form is not legally recognized in Massachusetts and some other states that charge high LLC fees. So, the fee for forming the statutory close corporation out of state, plus the fee for registering the corporation in the home state or wherever it will be doing business, will probably be equivalent to the fee charged by the home state for an LLC there.

While the small business owner should consider that other factors may, in fact, be more important than the relative fees charged, nevertheless, special note should be made of publication fees that three specific states charge when an LLC is formed or when a foreign LLC is registered.

New York, Pennsylvania and Arizona require that an LLC publish the information from its articles of organization in a newspaper. For example, in New York, this information must be published once per week, for a total of six weeks, in two different newspapers. This can cost anywhere from $1,000 to $2,000, and this may make the LLC a cost-prohibitive option in these states.

Similarly, any out-of-state LLC that will be doing business in one of these states must satisfy the same publication requirements, with information from its registration. This cost can be expected to be in the same range, as described above.

Plan Smart

When a small business will be formed in one of these states, or will be formed out of state, but will be doing business in one of these states, consideration should be given to forming a statutory close corporation, as opposed to an LLC. At the very least, the small business owner who intends on using an LLC in one of these states should first attempt to gauge the cost of publication, by contacting state officials, before the entity is formed or registered to do business in the state.

SIMPLICITY AND LOW COST OF LLC VS. CORPORATION

The LLC was created precisely to provide a simpler and lower-cost alternative to the corporation. The best element of the corporation, limited liability for all of the owners, was combined with the simplicity and low cost of operation of the general partnership (and sole proprietorship). The concepts of simplicity and low cost of operation are not simply restricted to low fees charged by a state. The statutory framework that governs the operation of corporations, termed the "corporate formalities," is much more complex and burdensome than what is imposed on LLCs.

Specifically, the statutory rules governing corporations impose fairly strict requirements regarding directors, officers, meetings, etc. In an LLC, these rules are usually relaxed. Thus, in the LLC, the cost of compliance is lower, and there will be less likelihood of costly mistakes. Remember, a failure to comply with the applicable formalities of your entity choice can lead to a court's "piercing the veil" of limited liability and imposing unlimited, personal liability on the owners. With the LLC, this result is much less likely.

As discussed in Chapter 6, a statutory close corporation enjoys some of these same advantages. For this reason, where a corporation is considered, it should usually be organized as a statutory close corporation.

Plan Smart

The Delaware LLC statute, in particular, provides incredible flexibility and simplicity in forming and operating the LLC. It has no counterpart in statutes governing corporations (or for that matter, in LLC statutes) found in other states.

For instance, Delaware allows the forming of an entity within an entity, thus eliminating the need to form separate LLCs (or corporations) for each separate operating activity carried out by the business.

This and the many other benefits of the Delaware LLC statute are discussed in Chapters 8 and 9.

TAX IMPLICATIONS OF LLCs AND CORPORATIONS

For tax purposes, the LLC is treated as a sole proprietorship when there is one owner and as a general partnership when there are two or more owners. Neither the sole proprietorship nor the general partnership is a taxpaying entity. They are termed "pass-through entities," or conduits. The owners report their share of profit and loss (whether or not it is actually distributed) on their personal income tax returns.

The owner of a one-owner LLC must fill out Schedule C and add it to his or her personal income tax return (Form 1040); members of a multiple-owner LLC must use Schedule E with their returns. A multiple-member LLC also must file a partnership information return, Form 1065, which shows how the money came in and was distributed to members, but no entity-level taxes are imposed. "Salary" to the owner of an LLC is really just a way of dividing profits, or an owner's withdrawal in a one-owner LLC (Chapter 14 covers the different ways of dividing profits in the LLC).

In contrast, a corporation must file a separate tax return, Form 1120, and pay its own taxes. Salary for the corporation's employees, including owner/employees, is reported on their own tax returns, as are any corporate dividends.

The owner can reverse this taxation scheme, in both the LLC and the corporation. The LLC owner can elect to have the LLC treated as a corporation for tax purposes, by filing Form 8832 with the IRS.

Similarly, an owner of a corporation may elect to have the corporation treated similarly to a sole proprietorship or partnership for tax purposes, by filing Form 2553 with the IRS (the so-called "subchapter S" election). In this case, the S corporation would still have to file a tax return for the business (Form 1120S), but no taxes would be imposed on the business itself; the profits, losses and other tax items would be passed through to the owners and reported on their own Schedules E and Forms 1040.

Did You Know?

In 1997, the IRS clarified that, for tax purposes, *the LLC would be treated as a sole proprietorship when there is one owner and a general partnership when there are two or more owners, unless an election is made to treat the LLC as a corporation for tax purposes under the so-called IRS "check-in-the-box" regulations.*

As discussed in Chapter 6, prior to this, there was some confusion as to how the LLC would be taxed, because the LLC has attributes of both a sole proprietorship/general partnership and a corporation. Accordingly, state laws and operating agreements artificially sought to achieve today's classification by requiring that the LLC have two or more owners, and a life of a limited duration (as opposed to the perpetual existence of a corporation).

Today, you don't need to take any action at all if you want your LLC to be treated as a sole proprietorship or partnership for tax purposes.

A common misunderstanding by small business owners concerns the relationship between taxation and limited liability. Many owners mistakenly believe that, because their LLC is treated as a sole proprietorship or general partnership *for tax purposes*, somehow this means that liability in the LLC mirrors liability in these other business forms. The same misunderstanding arises when a corporation elects subchapter S tax status.

Really, there is no relationship. Taxation has nothing to do with liability. All of the owners of the LLC and corporation enjoy limited liability. How the LLC or corporation is *taxed* is irrelevant to the question of *liability*.

Plan Smart

A number of states have announced that they will follow the lead of the IRS with respect to LLCs in assessing state income taxes. Thus, the LLC automatically will be presumed to be a conduit for state tax purposes in these states, and no state corporate tax is imposed. These states include:

- *Arizona*
- *California*
- *Maine*
- *Maryland*

- *Minnesota*
- *New Jersey*
- *Tennessee*
- *Utah*

While other states are likely to take the same lead, this is a fast-developing area of law. It is wise to check with the state tax department in your state for the latest information.

If you form a corporation and then file an election to be taxed as an S corporation for federal purposes, don't automatically assume your state will recognize the federal election. In fact, while most states will follow the election in assessing state taxes, a few do not. In addition, a very few states impose a special tax on the income of every business, whatever its form. Always check with state taxing authorities in the state in which the entity will be formed, and the state in which it will be doing business, *before* choosing a business form and a state of formation.

Plan Smart

If a corporation is to be used, forming it as a statutory close corporation in Nevada completely eliminates the issue of state taxation, as Nevada has no income tax on corporations. Delaware has a corporate income tax, but it does not apply it to subchapter S corporations that are formed there but do no business there.

When making your ultimate decision on entity form, these specific tax issues should be considered:

- S corporation election
- sheltering taxes
- avoiding double taxation
- accumulated earnings tax

- personal holding company tax

- professional service corporations tax

- income tax rates

- self-employment taxes

- retirement plans

- fringe benefits

S Corporation Election

While the election by the LLC is straightforward and uncomplicated, in contrast, the subchapter S election by the corporation can be more troublesome. The subchapter S election can only be made when, among other requirements, the corporation has 75 or fewer shareholders, there is only one class of stock (though there may be voting and nonvoting shares) and any trust holding stock meets certain conditions.

While the first two conditions will only rarely present a problem for the small business owner, the last requirement can preclude other planning opportunities.

Moreover, the tax rules governing subchapter S corporations are especially complicated and difficult to implement, adding more complexity and costs to operation of the corporation when the subchapter S election is made. When one subchapter S corporation owns 100 percent of a subsidiary subchapter S corporation, the subsidiary reports its income on the parent corporation's tax return, which should simplify the tax return process. Here, the subsidiary is termed a qualified subchapter S subsidiary (QSSS).

In asset protection planning, when a holding entity and an operating entity are used (as discussed in Chapter 8), and the owner has chosen to form two corporations as opposed to two LLCs, the owner usually will have the holding corporation form and own the operating corporation, and then elect subchapter S status for both corporations.

Sheltering Taxes

Many small businesses will *report* losses, especially in the early years, although this does not necessarily mean the business will not have a positive cash flow. Because the LLC is a pass-through entity, or conduit, for tax purposes, these losses can be passed on to the owners' personal tax returns, where they can offset, or shelter, other sources of taxable income. For single-owner LLCs, the losses can offset any other type of income reported on your individual income tax return, including income earned by your spouse. For multiple-owner LLCs, the losses also can offset your other income, up to the amount you have invested in the business.

While the corporation also can elect to be treated as a conduit by making a subchapter S election, there are some restrictions, and the rules governing taxation of the subchapter S corporation are very complex.

Historically, tax shelters have been organized as limited partnerships. The LLC shares the same tax-shelter qualities as the limited partnership, but with limited liability for *all* of the owners of the business. Moreover, a tax shelter established as a limited partnership enjoys another benefit—the limited partners cannot participate in management. As discussed in Chapter 10, the LLC may be structured as a manager-managed LLC, so that this same benefit is achieved in the LLC.

Avoiding Double Taxation

Many commentators suggest the fact that, since "double taxation" of dividends applies only in the corporation, the LLC enjoys a tax benefit over the corporation. While this is true, in practice the absence of "double taxation" of dividends in the LLC probably offers only minimal benefits.

The corporation is a separate taxpayer. It computes its taxable income before deducting or paying any dividends to shareholders. Therefore, the dividend is taxed at the corporate level. In addition, when the corporation pays a dividend (a distribution to the owners of current year earnings or accumulated earnings), the dividend is taxable to the owner upon receipt. Thus, in effect, the dividend has been taxed twice.

Example

Let's say a corporation has taxable income of $800,000 and will pay a $100,000 dividend out of these earnings. If the corporation's tax rate is a flat 40 percent, it will pay $320,000 in taxes ($800,000 x 40 percent).

Had the corporation been able to deduct the dividend, it would have paid only $280,000 in taxes ($700,000 x 40 percent). Its taxable income would have been lowered by $100,000, and its taxes lowered by $40,000 ($100,000 x 40 percent).

Another way of looking at it is that the corporation is taxed on the $700,000 plus the dividend of $100,000. In other words, the dividend is taxed at the corporate level because it is not deductible, but it is also taxed when it received by the shareholder.

The LLC is not a separate taxpayer, and it does not pay dividends. Thus, the double taxation concept does not apply to LLCs (unless, of course, an LLC elected to be treated as corporation for federal income tax purposes, which would be a rare occurrence).

Nevertheless, in a small corporation, the owners can avoid paying dividends and instead can withdraw cash from the business in deductible ways, as salary, lease and loan payments, etc. *Very* large salaries for small business owners have been upheld as deductible expenses. Most small corporations, in fact, do not pay any dividends, and yet distribute all of the disposable income to the owners in this tax-deductible way. In addition, most small corporations elect subchapter S status, which means that the corporation itself will pay no income taxes, and double taxation of dividends will not apply. Thus, for small corporations, the double tax on dividends is seldom a problem.

In short, the absence of double taxation of dividends in the LLC may not be of much benefit to the small business owner because double taxation can usually be avoided in the corporation too, through payments of salary to the owner. In this respect, the real benefit in the LLC is in not having to avoid the double taxation in the first place.

Accumulated Earnings Tax

You may have heard that a corporation can accumulate its earnings: Once it pays tax on them at the corporate level, it need not pay them out as dividends and can thus avoid the second part of the double tax. This is true with some caveats.

The IRS imposes an "accumulated earnings" tax, at a rate that approaches 40 percent, on earnings a corporation accumulates above $250,000. The limit is $150,000 for certain "personal service corporations" (i.e., corporations in the fields of health, law, engineering, architecture, accounting, actuarial science, performing arts or consulting, where the owners provide the services). This tax does not apply to LLCs.

This tax is designed to dissuade corporations from accumulating earnings just to avoid paying taxable dividends. However, this tax is usually easy to avoid, for three reasons:

1. Earnings can be reduced to zero, through the withdrawal of earnings in deductible ways such as higher salaries for the owners.

2. The corporation can accumulate earnings beyond these limits, provided it can prove it has a business need to do so, such as payment of anticipated future operating expenses, a planned business expansion, etc.

3. The corporation can elect to be treated as a conduit for tax purposes, by making a subchapter S election, which eliminates this problem.

Personal Holding Company Tax

A personal holding company is a regular "C" corporation that derives 60 percent or more of its earnings through passive income (interest, dividends, rents, royalties, etc.), where more than 50 percent of the value of the stock is owned by five or fewer individuals. The personal holding company tax rate is 39.6 percent of the corporation's undistributed earnings, *and is in addition to the regular corporate income tax.* The tax does not apply to LLCs.

The tax is extremely complicated due to its many exceptions. In practice, the tax will not usually apply to small business owners. While the typical small business may be owned by five or fewer individuals, in most cases its income will not be passive, or will fall within some of the exceptions.

However, in an arrangement where a holding company and an operating company are used (as discussed in Chapter 8), the tax may very well apply to the holding company unless a consolidated tax return is filed. That consolidated return opens its own set of complications and complexities.

This tax can be avoided by making a subchapter S election, since S corporations are not subject to the tax. Once again, however, with an LLC you don't have to worry about dealing with this tax, or avoiding it.

Professional Service Corporations Tax

A professional service corporation is a designation created by law. Professionals in the fields of health, law, engineering, architecture, accounting, actuarial science, performing arts, or consulting (where the owners provide the services) may elect this business form. The professional service corporation has to pay a flat tax of 35 percent on its earnings, rather than using the progressive rate structure that normally applies to corporations. The result will be higher taxes. This tax scheme can be avoided by making the subchapter S election.

Plan Smart

The accumulated earnings tax, personal holding company tax and professional service corporation tax are all examples of the complexity associated with operating in the corporate form, a complexity that is not present in the LLC.

These taxes also illustrate why the subchapter S election is so popular. This election avoids these three taxes. However, the subchapter S election is, itself, governed by complicated rules and restrictions. This helps explain why the LLC was developed. If the subchapter S election had been completely satisfactory, it is doubtful the LLC would have been created. Not having to avoid these taxes in the first place is an example of the simpler scheme of taxation associated with the LLC.

In addition, these taxes, and their complicated rules, also help explain why LLC owners normally do not elect to have their LLCs taxed as corporations.

Income Tax Rates

Both individual and corporate tax rates start at 10 or 15 percent and approach a top rate of nearly 40 percent, although the levels of income that are subject to each rate vary in each tax schedule. Whether your taxes on a given level of income would be lower in the LLC at the individual rates or in the corporation at the corporate rates will depend on a number of factors, including your filing status, personal and dependency exemptions, and your other sources of income.

Of course, when earnings are being distributed by the corporation as a deductible salary to the business owner, the corporate earnings will be reduced to zero and, instead, taxed at the individual level anyway. This is a likely scenario in the small business corporation, as the owner seeks to avoid double taxation of dividends. If the earnings are distributed in a non-tax-deductible way (i.e., through the payment of dividends), the owner will experience the problem of double taxation of dividends.

Self-Employment Taxes

The LLC is not a taxpaying entity and, accordingly, does not pay Social Security or any other employment taxes on the "salary" of the owner. The LLC owner is really self-employed, and the "salary" is only an owner's withdrawal from the business. However, the LLC owner must, on his or her personal income tax return (Form 1040), pay a "self-employment" tax, which is in reality the *Social Security tax and the Medicare tax* that would ordinarily be paid by the employer *and* the employee.

In contrast, it is sometimes said that the owner of the corporation can avoid the payment of self-employment taxes by not taking a salary from the business. This idea may not prove out in practice, because paying out all earnings as salary is the principal way that owners of corporations avoid double taxation on dividends. However, it is true that the corporation can allow earnings to accumulate in the corporation (subject to the accumulated earnings tax limitations discussed above, in the case of a regular "C" corporation). To this extent, the corporation could provide an advantage over the LLC.

But one reason that there's no real advantage in either the LLC or corporation when it comes to self-employment taxes is that the *owner* ultimately bears the cost of the tax in any event, whether it is paid through the business, or directly by the owner, and this cost will be the same in both cases.

In 2003, the corporation pays Social Security tax of 6.20 percent on the first $87,000 of salary paid to the owner, *and* the owner has to make a matching contribution (through a payroll deduction) of 6.20 percent.

On the other hand, the LLC owner is self-employed. The LLC owner must pay a "self-employment tax" at the rate of 12.40 percent of the first $87,000 of self-employment income. This tax is, in reality, a combination of the Social Security tax that would be paid by the employer (6.20 percent) *and* the employee (6.20 percent.).

Similarly, in 2003, the corporation pays a Medicare tax on your salary at the rate of 1.45 percent, with no limit on the earnings to which the rate applies, while you must pay a matching 1.45 percent contribution through a payroll deduction. In the LLC, you would pay 2.9 percent on your self-employment income (equal to the contribution made by the corporation and the employee-owner combined).

In *each* case, you effectively pay the *same total rate of 15.3 percent* on *the same base of earnings.* (In the corporation, 6.2 percent + 6.2 percent + 1.45 percent + 1.45 percent = 15.3 percent; in the LLC, 12.4 percent + 2.9 percent = 15.3 percent).

Self-Employment Tax Planning for Accumulated Earnings

The corporation *might* provide an advantage over the LLC, in terms of self-employment taxes, if you intend to retain earnings within the business for some special purpose.

In a corporation, owners pay no self-employment taxes if they do not receive salary from the corporation, even if the subchapter S election has been made. In contrast, in an LLC, *all* of the owners must pay self-employment taxes *on their share of the business's earnings* (whether or not distributed).

This may be a distinct disadvantage if you want to let earnings accumulate in the entity, free of self-employment taxes, which is not possible in an LLC at this time. In particular, owners of corporations primarily accumulate earnings in anticipation of an owner retiring. The owner's shares can be redeemed with the accumulated earnings. If done properly, the redemption qualifies for capital gains treatment, and thus lowers taxes for the owner. The LLC owner can do the same thing, except that he or she must pay self-employment taxes on the earnings as they are generated.

This also may be a disadvantage in the manager-managed LLC because in many cases the non-manager owners may not be paid any salary or distributions. Yet, unless careful steps were taken, all of the owners would have to pay the self-employment tax anyway, on their share of the entity's earnings, even though they receive no distributions. The way to avoid this problem is to be sure that the LLC operating agreement provides that income is shared on some basis other than the ratio of capital accounts, so that the non-manager owners will be allocated little or no income, and, thus, pay little or no self-employment taxes. This can be accomplished by having the LLC pay the manager-owner salary, lease payments, loan repayments, etc.

Of course, this only shifts the payment of the self-employment taxes to the owner-manager. It does not solve the problem of the owner who wants to accumulate income in the holding LLC, free of these taxes.

Proposed Rule Change

The IRS has proposed *regulations that would exempt LLC owners from paying self-employment taxes, provided they work less than 500 hours per year in the business. This would apply primarily to holding companies and non-manager owners in operating companies because of the 500-hour limitation. Note that the regulations have yet to be enacted. In addition, a proposed exception exists for personal service businesses, such as accounting firms. There, providing even minimal services would subject the owner to self-employment taxes.*

The fate of these proposed regulations remains unclear because of their negative impact on limited partners in a limited partnership (LP). Currently, limited partners do not pay self-employment tax on their share of earnings, unless they receive "guaranteed payments" (i.e., salary) for services rendered. Then, they pay the self-employment tax only on the salary received. In short, currently, limited partners in an LP can avoid the self-employment tax if they do not receive any salary.

The proposed regulations, designed to produce relief for LLC owners, would also apply to LPs. This would mean that limited partners would end up paying self-employment taxes on their full *share of earnings* whenever they worked more than 500 hours, *even if they did not receive any salary, or received only a small salary. For this reason, LP owners have generally opposed the proposed regulations.*

Self-Employment Tax Exceptions in Favor of the LLC

Despite the many drawbacks for the LLC form when it comes to self-employment taxes, there are some factors in favor of the LLC to consider.

If you are an LLC owner, you can deduct half of the self-employment taxes you pay on your personal income tax return, Form 1040. This can be done even if you don't itemize deductions. This fact may lower the effective cost of the taxes and, thus, shift the advantage to the LLC. While the corporation can deduct its half of these taxes on its own tax return, this does not yield a direct benefit to the owner because the corporation files a separate tax return and pays its own taxes.

Furthermore, in the LLC, federal and state unemployment taxes are avoided on the owner's income, including guaranteed payments received for salary. In contrast, the corporation must pay these taxes on the salary that it pays to the owner, at a rate that, in most cases, effectively amounts to 0.8 percent of wages paid.

The LLC owner can avoid the self-employment tax if payments are made by the LLC to the owner as lease payments and loan repayments.

The Internal Revenue Code imposes the self-employment tax on profits derived from ownership of the business, plus any guaranteed payments for salary. The owner will not be "in the business" of leasing real estate (or equipment, furniture, etc) or making loans. Thus, the tax will not apply to these receipts. (In addition, the Code also specifically exempts lease payments received from anyone except a real estate dealer).

Lease payments and loan repayments are paid to the LLC owner for a reason other than his or her capacity as an owner. Accordingly, they are deducted by the LLC in computing its distributable income. Because the LLC does not pay taxes itself, this really represents a way to allocate income to a particular owner, but avoid the self-employment tax.

"Guaranteed payments" made to an LLC owner, for services rendered (i.e., salary) are also deductible by the LLC. However, these payments *are* subject to the self-employment tax with respect to the partner who receives the payments. They are added to his or her distributable share of the LLC profits, and he or she pays the self-employment tax on the total.

Warning

Division of profits in the LLC is covered by the LLC's operating agreement. Different schemes exist that can involve payments made to owners for leases of assets, loan repayments, and salary. Whether or not salary is deemed a "guaranteed payment" can affect how much net income is left to be divided among the LLC owners. In addition, some allocation schemes can have adverse income tax consequences.

These topics are covered in Chapters 12 and 14 and should be examined before you undertake to create an allocation scheme in your operating agreement.

Combining the LLC and the Statutory Close Corporation

It may be possible to combine the LLC and the statutory close corporation to achieve both the asset protection benefits afforded by the LLC and the possible self-employment tax savings attributable to the corporation.

You can do this by forming two entities: a holding company and an operating entity.

As you recall, assets in a corporation will be subject to less protection than those in an LLC, with respect to claims of your personal creditors. This risk can be mitigated by making the holding entity an LLC and the operating entity a statutory close corporation. The holding LLC would be the owner of the operating corporation. Thus, the owner's personal creditors would have to make claims against the LLC, to reach the operating entity's assets.

One problem that may arise is that allowing income to accumulate in the operating corporation will make these assets vulnerable to the claims of the business creditors. This problem can be mitigated by encumbering the operating corporation's assets with liens that run to the holding entity (these and other strategies are covered more fully in Chapter 8).

However, the accumulation of earnings may not be an issue, or even a possibility, for the small business owner. The chief reason corporate earnings are accumulated is to redeem (i.e., buy back) a retiring owner's stock. The redemption, if done properly, will result in capital gains treatment, and thus lower taxes for the retiring owner.

As a practical matter, most small business owners will not be concerned immediately with retiring and cashing out of the business. Further, most small business owners are not likely to be in a position to accumulate earnings in the business.

The upshot then is that the small business owner seeking to avoid self-employment taxes probably will want to use two LLCs as the operating and holding companies, and withdraw funds through lease and loan payments. In addition, the IRS is likely to provide some type of exemption for self-employment taxes in LLCs in the near future.

Retirement Plans

At one time, perhaps the biggest tax advantage enjoyed by the corporation was the ability to establish retirement plans. During this period in the law, businesses treated as sole proprietorships or partnerships for tax purposes could not establish tax-qualified retirement plans.

Back then, many tax advisors recommended establishing a corporation to take advantage of this one important tax planning opportunity. However, the law was changed many years ago to allow self-employed individuals—and thus, owners of LLCs—to establish retirement plans (so-called Keogh or SEP plans) with essentially the same tax deductibility benefits as those enjoyed by corporations (for more on retirement plans and protecting their assets, see Chapter 3).

Fringe Benefits

On the surface, the corporation enjoys a slight advantage over the LLC when it comes to providing certain tax-free fringe benefits to its owners. For example, this includes company-paid life insurance (to $50,000), 100 percent of health insurance, and dependent care assistance. However, this advantage only exists with a regular C corporation. It does not apply to S corporations.

Any owner of a 2-percent-or-more interest in a subchapter S corporation is treated the same as an LLC owner and, thus, enjoys no advantages at all over the LLC owner.

The good news is that the most important fringe benefit of all, tax-deductible health insurance, is now being phased-in for LLC owners and S corporation owners, as well as sole proprietors and partners, under federal law.

Plan Smart

In recent years, LLC owners, other self-employed individuals, and 2-percent-or-more owners of subchapter S corporations have been able to deduct a portion of health insurance premiums. Deducting the cost is the same, in outcome, as not reporting the cost as income in the first place.

In 2002, the deductible amount was 70 percent. For year 2003, these individuals are able to deduct 100 percent of the cost, making health insurance a tax-free benefit to these owners as well.

Where providing fringe benefits to the owner and his or her family is an important issue, consideration should be given to forming the operating entity as a statutory close corporation in Nevada, or one of the other states that offer the special statutory close corporation forms.

Another simple alternative would be to elect to have the LLC taxed as a corporation.

Plan Smart

In fact, the LLC may have an advantage over the corporation when it comes to health care insurance. The IRS has agreed that self-employed business owners, including LLC owners, can deduct 100 percent of the cost of a health insurance policy for a spouse who works for the business. This policy may be a family policy, which covers employees' spouses and dependents; therefore it may cover the business owner and any dependents, as well as the spouse. If you take advantage of this loophole, make sure that the spouse/employee is not also an owner of the business.

This benefit is not available for 2-percent-or-more S corporation owners. Special rules treat the spouse of a 2-percent S corporation owner also as a 2-percent owner. Thus, deductibility of the premium had been limited to a percentage until the year 2003, as discussed previously. Because most small business owners operating corporations elect subchapter S status, the corporation used to put the small business owner at a disadvantage, but now the schedule allowing deduction of the premiums has reached 100 percent for year 2003.

Thus, forming the business as an LLC, and having the LLC employ the spouse of the owner, used to be one effective way to provide tax-free health insurance benefits for the business owner and his family. This strategy became necessary, beginning in the year 2003.

Because the LLC can elect to be taxed as a corporation, it can, in this way, achieve the same benefits enjoyed by corporations. Because of all the tax advantages, described above, LLC owners almost never make this election. Simply put, the benefits achieved by this election usually would be small, especially in comparison to the cost. However, for those small business owners interested in providing the extra tax-free fringe benefits, this election may be preferable to forming a corporation. As discussed in detail in Chapter 6, the LLC offers better protection for the business owner's interest against the claims of his personal creditors. This is a significant protection. It is not available even in the statutory close corporation, which, in other respects, resembles the LLC.

WHY THE LLC MAY BE THE BEST ENTITY CHOICE

As we've shown, an LLC will usually be the best choice for most small business owners for the following reasons:

Protecting your business assets from personal creditors. As discussed in Chapter 6, the LLC offers significantly better protection from the claims of the owner's *personal* creditors. Many states follow the RULPA view (developed from limited partnership law) in *preventing* a *personal* creditor from foreclosing on an owner's LLC interest and forcing a liquidation of the business.

This view has never applied to corporations. Thus, in contrast, a personal creditor may attach *and* vote the interest of an owner of a *corporation*. A creditor may force a liquidation of the business to satisfy the debt if the debtor's interest was a majority interest, but at any rate it can vote the shares in other ways disadvantageous to the business owner.

Protecting your personal assets from business creditors. The relatively few rules about how to operate an LLC means there is a much smaller likelihood that the doctrine of piercing the veil of limited liability will apply in the LLC. When this doctrine applies, unlimited, personal liability is imposed on the owners for the business's debts. One common way this doctrine is applied is by proving that the owner has not followed all of the statutory formalities applicable to corporations, regarding division of authority among the shareholders, officers and directors; the holding of regularly scheduled meetings; notice, quorums and waiver requirements for meetings; etc.

As discussed in Chapter 16, a statutory close corporation can achieve some of these same benefits. However, even the statutory close corporation does not change the fact that your personal creditors can attach and then vote your shares to liquidate the business, when this would not be possible in an LLC, in most states. Thus, the statutory close corporation probably should be used in place of the LLC only when self-employment taxes represent an important issue or state registration fees for the LLC are excessive.

Use with other asset protection strategies. The LLC is better suited to being combined with other assets protection strategies, including domestic asset protection trusts and estate planning.

If you expect your business to be lucrative (most small business owners do!), you should consider forming a holding entity in Delaware, in part to facilitate the creation of an asset protection trust there (see Chapter 5). These trusts are formed as an overall part of an asset protection plan. Thus, it makes sense to form the business entity as an LLC, because the LLC offers better asset protection, at least with respect to the claims of the owner's personal creditors against the owner's business interest.

The LLC is also a better choice when it is part of an estate planning strategy of transferring wealth to the next generation, free of estate taxes. While a complete discussion of estate planning is beyond the scope of this book, the small business owner interested in protecting assets should at least be familiar with some of the basics of estate planning, and how the LLC can play a role in eliminating estate taxes. These issues are discussed in Chapter 10. In particular, the use of a family limited partnership has proved to be an effective device to transfer wealth to the next generation free of federal estate taxes. The family limited liability company is now being used for this purpose.

In addition to choosing a business form, the owner must also decide how to structure and fund the entity, and in which state to form the entity. These decisions can also have important asset protection implications (Chapters 8 and 9 cover these topics).

Chapter 8

Using Holding and Operating Companies

Clearly, the limited liability company (LLC) and corporation emerge as the two best choices for the small business owner, from the discussion in Chapter 6. Ultimately, the LLC emerges as the better choice in most cases, and in particular as an ideal vehicle for asset protection purposes.

However, the business owner faces an asset protection dilemma, even when the business is formed as an LLC or corporation. Specifically, protecting the owner's assets against the claims of *personal creditors* and against the claims of *business creditors* are competing interests. Assets placed within the business form are vulnerable to the business's creditors, but protected, to some extent anyway, from the owner's personal creditors. However, assets kept outside of the business form are vulnerable to the owner's personal creditors, but protected from the business's creditors.

So, how can you protect *all* your assets from *both* business and personal creditors? Both objectives can be accomplished simultaneously through the proper funding and structuring of the business.

The ideal business structure consists of two entities: an *operating entity*, which has possession of the assets, but does not own the assets (unless they are encumbered in favor of the holding entity or owner), and a *holding entity*, which actually owns the business's assets.

A simpler option for your business structure is the one-entity approach. While it may be suited to some situations, generally it does not provide the flexibility and asset protection of the multiple-entity approach. Moreover, once you adopt the multiple-entity approach, you'll need to balance the funding of these entities through both equity and debt, using leases, loans and liens.

USING MULTIPLE BUSINESS ENTITIES

An ideal business structure consists of an *operating entity* that does not own any vulnerable assets and a *holding entity* that actually owns the business's assets.

With this structure, the small business owner can eliminate (or, at the very least, substantially limit) liability for both business debts and personal debts.

The operating entity conducts all of the business's activities and, thus, bears all the risk of loss. The owner's limited liability for *business debts* is limited to no liability at all, because the operating entity contains little or no vulnerable assets, and the holding entity is not legally responsible for the other entity's debts. In short, even limited liability can be enhanced.

At the same time, the owner's liability for *personal debts* is reduced because assets are within the protective framework of a business form (i.e., the holding entity).

Clearly, this strategy is more suited toward the operation of two LLCs, as opposed to two corporations, where the holding LLC is formed in a state that has adopted the RULPA view preventing foreclosure and liquidation of the business interest to satisfy a personal creditor (as discussed in Chapter 7).

However, a statutory close corporation, formed as the operating entity, coupled with an LLC, formed as the holding entity, can still work. Two corporations will not accomplish both objectives, because the law will allow personal creditors to attach, and then vote, the owner's interest, to force a liquidation of the business (Chapter 7 contains a detailed comparison of the LLC and the corporation).

Plan Smart

The LLC is best suited to accomplish these dual objectives because it offers greater protection from the claims of the owner's personal creditors. As discussed in Chapter 7, the small business owner may want to use a statutory close corporation as the operating entity, in combination with an LLC organized as the holding entity.

The individual owner can create and fund the holding entity. The holding entity can then create and fund the operating entity. Technically, the individual owns the holding entity, and the holding entity owns the operating entity. This is frequently the approach taken in a corporation, where the operating entity would be termed a "subsidiary" of the holding entity. However, the same approach also can be used with respect to the LLC.

Alternatively, the owner could personally create and fund both entities, so that he directly owns both entities. The better approach will usually be for the holding entity to own the operating entity.

As discussed later in this chapter, the Delaware LLC statute presents an ideal and unique opportunity to form all of the separate entities within a single LLC.

Operating Entities

Your operating entity is your primary business entity. All business functions occur within that company. Likewise, all of the risks to the business will occur within that entity as well.

Therefore, it is important, from an asset protection standpoint, to minimize vulnerable assets and cash within the entity, should an unanticipated event take place.

In addition, separate operating entities should be formed for each operating activity, so that any liability runs only to that particular entity's assets (formation issues are discussed in Chapter 7). The Delaware LLC statute is especially suited for the use of multiple entities, as explained below.

Also, as discussed later in this chapter, the operating entity's assets could be separately protected through leases, loans and liens, as well as through the use of a separate holding company. This is an example of multi-layered protection.

The Delaware LLC Statute—The Entity Within an Entity

The Delaware LLC statute provides for incomparable flexibility and simplicity in operating LLCs. It clearly allows for the establishment of different classes of interests, including voting and nonvoting interests.

It also allows a single LLC to house multiple separate entities. Each unit can have separate owners and its own classes of ownership interests. Each unit can own its own assets and incur its own liabilities. Each unit should have its own accounting system, which could simply consist of separate files within a single accounting system. Importantly, the recordkeeping must be done as if each entity were organized as a separate LLC.

The designation of the units, or "series" of separate entities within the single LLC as they are referred to in the statute, must be done in the articles of organization. This designation serves as constructive notice that each unit is a separate legal entity and that, accordingly, the other units are not liable for its debts. When the single LLC registers to do business in the owner's home state, or wherever it will conduct operations, this registration will also serve as constructive notice in those states, as the registration is a link to the original articles that were filed in Delaware.

It is essential that the registration be done properly to separate liability among the entities. Consistent with the flexibility in the Delaware LLC statute, each unit does not have to be funded. They can be held in abeyance for future use.

The holding entity and each operating entity can be formed within a single LLC. However, as explained below, if the business is a professional service business, the holding LLC will have to be formed separately, in the event that some owners are not licensed in the same profession, such as in the case of family members and the family LLC.

Warning

Remember, professionals can form an LLC, LLP or a corporation only if all of the owners are licensed within the same profession. Keep this in mind if you're a professional forming a holding entity and an operating entity.

Only the operating entity has to meet this requirement. The holding entity, which will contain nearly all of the wealth of the business, will not be engaged in the practice of any profession. Thus, children or other family members, for example, can still be co-owners of the holding company, even when it is formed by professionals. However, in this case, the professional would have to form each entity directly, because the holding entity could not be the owner of the operating entity.

If the entities were being formed within a single LLC in Delaware, the holding entity would have to be formed as a separate LLC in this situation. Each operating entity could still be formed within the single LLC.

Obviously there are additional costs involved in creating two entities rather than one. However, the Delaware concept of an entity within an entity, embodied in its LLC statute, can significantly lessen these costs. Moreover, these costs, which really are relatively modest, represent a type of inexpensive insurance against the risk of loss.

Plan Smart

Strategies that rely on the use of an operating entity and a holding entity also are used by large businesses. For example, one of the fast growing areas in corporate finance is called "securitization."

A corporation, the operating company, sells its receivables to a second corporation, which is created as the holding company. The only real asset of the holding company is the receivables it purchases. The holding company sells stock to the public, in effect allowing the public to buy an interest in the receivables, through the purchase of the stock. This is what is termed securitization. This trend started with the sale of mortgages by banks. Large corporations now sell accounts receivable in this way.

The holding company is completely insulated from liability for all of the activities of the operating company that created the accounts receivable. Commentators have said that, if it were not for the creation of a holding entity, securitization could not work, because the risk of liability exposure from the operating entity's activities would be too high to enable this kind of stock offering to the public.

At this same time, the operating entity has protected its assets against the claims of its creditors. Cash that is brought in from the sales of the receivables is quickly drawn off to pay the operating entity's expenses, including the salaries of its owners. As discussed below, the small business owner can use a version of this strategy in withdrawing assets from the operating entity.

Holding Entities

In the multiple-entity approach, the holding entity is where all wealth is located within the business structure. But because the holding company conducts no business activities, it has almost no exposure to liability, and therefore these assets are protected.

The small business owner or owners create the holding entity, then in turn the holding entity creates and owns the operating entity, where actual business operations (and risks) occur. Limited liability for the operating company runs to the holding entity and is limited to its investment in the operating entity, stopping short of the owners of the holding company because they do not own the operating company. One holding entity may be used to operate many different operating companies, but care should be taken to keep each operating company and its activities separate from one another.

Ideally, a business's most valuable assets should be owned by the holding company and leased to the operating company, which secures the assets from creditors and provides a way of taking vulnerable cash out of the operating company.

Further, the holding entity can loan money to the operating company to buy other business assets, but it should secure the collateral for the mortgage with liens that run to the holding company. Again, the assets are secured because the holding company is a priority lien holder, and vulnerable cash is taken out of the operating company through loan repayment (withdrawal methods are discussed in detail in Chapter 14).

When properly structured, the multiple-entity approach is successful because it seeks to maximize wealth within the entity with no liability issues, and minimize assets with the entity taking all the risks. And because the holding company itself, and not its owners, creates and funds the operating company, the holding company is liable for the operating company's debts, but only up to the amount it has invested, if it is in a business form that offers limited liability, such as an LLC.

One-Entity Approach

A simpler and less expensive (but sometimes less effective) alternative exists to using a holding entity and an operating entity, where leases, loans and liens can be used, but with only one entity. The small business owner, himself, may act as the "holding entity," personally owing the assets that otherwise would be placed within the holding entity.

However, while this simpler approach is less expensive, in that a second entity needn't be created and operated, it has its drawbacks. This strategy offers no protection to the business owner from his *personal creditors*. By contrast, assets within the holding entity are protected, to some extent, from the claims of the owner's personal creditors (as discussed in Chapter 6).

The business owner can implement all of the funding strategies outlined later in this chapter, with the owner personally acting in place of the holding entity. Thus, the owner can personally own and lease exempt assets to the operating entity, strategically invest a combination of equity and debt, encumber the operating entity's assets with liens that run in favor of the owner, and regularly withdraw vulnerable funds, as they are generated.

However, caution should be exercised with leasing. Some assets by their nature carry an inherent risk that they might cause injury. Examples include buildings, land, machinery and equipment used in a factory, etc. In a case where an asset carries a high potential of liability, it may be unwise to hold ownership in the owners' personal capacity. Liability may run to the owner, in addition to the lessee.

This may expose the owner to unlimited, personal liability. It may be better to place this type of asset within a business form, in exchange for an equity interest, and expose *the asset* to potential loss, rather than run the risk of unlimited, personal liability. Even here, however, the asset can be protected by, for example, encumbering it with liens in favor of the owner, as described later. Of course, with only one entity, the option of placing this asset in the holding entity so that any liability would run there, rather than to the owner personally, is lost.

Example

Joe Smith forms one LLC to operate his business. He purchases a building in his own name, which he leases to the LLC. His theory in owning the building personally is that the greatest risk applies to assets in the business form, which is true.

What he doesn't realize is that liability for any injuries attributed to improper maintenance of the building may run back to him, because he is the owner of the building. Thus, all of his personal assets outside the business may be exposed to liability. These assets, almost assuredly, are more significant than the building itself. If the building is contributed to the LLC, only this one asset is exposed to liability.

A clause in the lease contract should impose the duty to maintain the building on the lessee (i.e., the LLC). However, courts usually will not allow a party to delegate certain duties, such as the duty to reasonably maintain his or her property.

Because the building is a high risk when it comes to injuries, Smith should consider contributing the building to the LLC, in exchange for his equity interest. The building could then be protected by liens that run to the owner.

Alternatively, Smith could own the building personally, and lease it to the LLC, if he is sure that his insurance liability coverage is more than adequate to cover all potential claims.

Where an asset, such as office equipment, has a low potential for liability, personally owning and leasing may be a suitable alternative. In short, this alternative may not be suitable for a small business owner who operates a machine shop with dangerous equipment, but it may be suitable for a professional, such as an accountant.

Of course, the machine shop owner could employ this strategy with respect to some of the assets used in the business, such as the office equipment. In addition, the owner could consider personally owning and leasing to the entity high-risk assets, if he is sure that he has adequate insurance liability coverage. In this type of business, however, the risk of loss is probably high enough to warrant the creation of a second entity.

Plan Smart

A one-entity strategy is more appropriate for a smaller business operated by an owner with a modest net worth. In that case, the owner can initially limit his equity investment in the business to contributions of high-risk assets and cash, which can be quickly withdrawn in the payment of operating expenses, including salary to the owner.

In addition, the owner can personally purchase and then lease low-risk assets (e.g., furniture or office equipment) to the entity, and then withdraw funds from the entity as lease payments, in addition to salary. This also allows the owner to claim an asset exemption in the personally owned "tools of the trade."

As the business grows, the high-risk assets can then be encumbered with liens in favor of the owner, that result from loans and other extensions of credit from the owner to the entity.

As the business continues to grow, the owner can create and fund a holding entity, which then takes over the funding of the operating entity. In this case, the owner will directly own the equity interest in the holding entity.

He also can continue to directly own the equity interest in the operating entity or fund the holding entity with this interest in exchange for the equity interest in the holding entity. In the latter case, the operating entity would become a subsidiary of the holding entity.

Obviously, in situations where the business owner concludes the risk is high enough to contribute the asset, then the asset will not generate lease payments to the owner. Alternatively, the owner could then withdraw vulnerable funds as lease payments attributable to other assets, loan payments and salary. The effect on withdrawals when contributing an asset should be weighed when making a decision as to whether to contribute or lease the asset.

Finally, personally owning and leasing "tools of the trade" to the business entity may offer an asset protection advantage. As discussed in Chapter 3 and later in this chapter, this strategy may allow the business owner to preserve an exemption in these assets.

FUNDING YOUR ENTITIES

To be effective, any asset protection plan must include a strategy of minimizing the amount of vulnerable capital invested within the operating entity. Specifically, the operating entity's business assets can be protected through:

- the owner personally owning and leasing exempt assets to the operating entity

- a strategic combination of equity and debt funding

- encumbering the operating entity's assets with liens that run in favor of the holding entity or owner

- a practice of regular withdrawals of vulnerable funds as they are generated

Personally Owning and Leasing Exempt Assets

The small business owner would be wise to personally own, and lease to the operating entity, exempt assets such as office equipment, furniture, automobiles and other "tools of the trade," at least where these assets are not at a high risk of causing personal injuries. This strategy adds an extra layer of protection for business assets. If you contribute exempt assets to the business, instead of owning and leasing, you lose this extra layer of protection.

Holding these assets outside the entity allows the owner to continue to claim his asset exemptions under bankruptcy and state court proceedings. Moreover, leases allow the owner to withdraw vulnerable funds from the entity (withdrawal of assets as an asset protection strategy is discussed at the end of this chapter). Clearly, the strategy of personally owning business assets can form the basis for multiple strategies.

Plan Smart

Asset exemptions are available only to natural persons, and not to business entities such as LLCs or corporations.

Thus, a contribution of an exempt asset to the business entity will mean a loss of the exemption. As a rule, then, exempt assets should not be contributed into the business entity, and certain exempt assets, including a home, should never be contributed to a business entity (see Chapter 3 for an example of the consequences of failing to heed this rule).

In general, exempt assets should not be contributed to the business entity, unless they are at a high risk of causing personal injuries. For example, high-risk assets, such as factory machinery or heavy equipment, generally should be contributed to the entity, because liability may run to the owner of the asset. Though the asset exemption is lost, the asset is still protected and the overall risks are reduced.

Note that these assets can be contributed to the holding entity or to the operating entity. Where there is an especially high risk of injury, the assets should be contributed to the operating entity, and then encumbered with liens in favor of the holding entity or owner. Where the assets are especially valuable, and of only moderate risk, the holding entity may be a more appropriate reservoir for these assets.

Alternatively, the owner may personally own, and lease to the operating entity, certain high-risk assets, if he is sure he carries more than an adequate amount of liability coverage. This alternative is somewhat risky, as tort judgments can sometimes be extreme. This alternative becomes more attractive in a state with no cap on its exemption for tools of the trade (see below).

Some assets will be inherently low risk, such as office equipment and furniture. These assets are ideal candidates for the contribution strategy. Other assets can have a high or low risk, depending on the circumstances. For example, an automobile driven only by the owner may be low risk, while automobiles or trucks driven by other employees generally will be high risk. Thus, in the former case, it may be possible to personally own and lease the assets to the operating entity, while in the latter case, it may make more sense to contribute the assets.

These types of assets usually will be exempt as "tools of the trade" (asset exemptions are discussed in Chapter 3). The actual exemption available in the particular state in question also should be determined as well, as states differ significantly in the amounts, and types, of tools of the trade they protect. This strategy will be most effective in states that have no cap on the tools of the trade exemption.

Leases of these, and other, assets also allow the owner to withdraw vulnerable funds from the operating entity. An effective asset protection plan always relies on multiple, integrated strategies.

Note, too, that other strategic funding practices, such as the use of liens, will protect assets that are placed within the business form. These practices will place these assets out of the reach of creditors, effectively *converting these assets into exempt assets.*

Combining Equity and Debt Funding

When the owner forms his LLC or corporation, he will take back an ownership or equity interest, signifying that he is as an owner, as opposed to a creditor, of the entity.

In the LLC, the owner takes back a membership interest as a "member." In the corporation, the owner tales back an ownership interest in the form of common stock as a "shareholder." Certificates, evidencing the ownership interest, should always be used, in both the LLC and the corporation, even though by law they are not always required (formation and management of the LLC and corporation are explored in Chapter 13).

As a general rule, exempt assets should not be contributed to the business entity. The discussion here is assumed to apply to nonexempt assets, such as an office building, cash, etc., or to high-risk exempt assets, that might be contributed as an exception to this general rule.

Note that when high-risk assets are contributed in return for an equity interest, they may be contributed to the holding entity or the operating entity. Where there is an especially high risk of injury, the assets should be contributed to the operating entity, and then encumbered with liens in favor of the holding entity or owner. Any liability would then run only to the operating entity, while the asset would still be protected.

Where the assets are especially valuable, and of only moderate risk, the holding entity may be a more appropriate owner for these assets. The assets can then be leased to the operating entity. Here, the risk of loss associated with the operating entity owning these assets would probably outweigh the risk of any liability running back to the holding entity.

Warning

Funding the equity interest in the holding and operating entities normally can be accomplished tax-free, as can funding the entities with debt (leases and loans).

However, a contribution in return for the equity interest can sometimes be a taxable event or have other unanticipated tax consequences. Tax aspects related to funding of the equity interest are addressed in Chapter 12.

Equity Interest in the Operating Entity

As discussed below in more detail, funding the operating entity with debt (i.e., leases and loans) will mean those assets used by the business will not be vulnerable to loss. Further, exempt assets personally owned and leased to the operating entity will be doubly protected—they will not be exposed to liability with respect to the business's creditors, and the owner can still claim his exemption in the assets with respect to his personal creditors.

However, the owner will have to contribute some assets to the operating entity in exchange for his equity interest. Unless additional steps are taken, these assets will be vulnerable to the business's creditors.

You should always try to minimize the actual amount contributed for the equity interest. This can be done by funding the balance of the investment with debt (leases and loans). There is, in practice, no one ideal formula for determining the ratio of equity and debt. Traditionally, in large, publicly held corporations, analysts have used a ratio of 30 percent debt and 70 percent equity as a benchmark. (These are the relative percentages of the business's assets funded through debt and equity contributions).

In small businesses, the ratio of debt to equity is often much higher. The limit to debt funding, in practice, is usually dictated by the business entity's ability to pay back the debt.

Plan Smart

The small business owner should experiment, on paper, with various funding schemes for the operating entity, including different ratios of debt and equity, before starting or expanding his business. The ideal structure will depend on unique factors, including the amount and type of capital available.

In many cases, it may not be necessary to go beyond a 30 to 70 percent debt-to-equity ratio. The assets contributed for the equity interest can be protected through the use of liens, and you also can invest cash and services. However, remember that debt provides the legal basis for the creation of liens and, in part, for the withdrawal of vulnerable funds by the owner.

Since the purpose of debt funding, *from an asset protection viewpoint*, is to give the owner a priority claim on the assets and to saddle the entity's assets with liens in favor of the owner, monthly repayments of the debt should not necessarily be the main focus of your actions. After all, a demand note can be issued to the owner or the holding entity, depending on the source of the loan. As the operating entity generates funds, the owner or holding entity can demand payment.

However, it would be a mistake to fund the equity interest with nothing, or only a miniscule or token amount of assets. This kind of undercapitalization could trigger an exception to limited liability (see Chapter 16 for details).

A reversal of the traditional ratios, with 70 percent of the funding coming from debt, generally would still be reasonable, provided the entity's ability to service its debt were not impaired. A decision to use debt beyond this ratio should probably be made with the advice of an attorney.

Further, using debt beyond this amount may be unnecessary, for three reasons:

1. As discussed later, the use of debt (leases, loans and other extensions of credit from the owner) provides the basis for another asset protection strategy (i.e., encumbering the operating entity's asset with liens in favor of the owner or the holding entity). These liens protect assets contributed though both debt *and* equity funding. Thus, assets that otherwise would be vulnerable (i.e., assets contributed for the equity interest) are protected.

2. Cash can be contributed in return for the equity interest. This contribution then can be quickly withdrawn from the operating entity in the form of payments for the entity's expenses, including payments to the owner for leases, loans and other extensions of credit, as well as salary. Thus, debt provides yet another basis for protecting assets contributed for the equity interest.

3. Future services can be contributed in return for the equity interest in the operating entity. When services are performed for the equity interest, no specific assets are contributed to the operating entity. With no assets in the business form, protection is not even an issue. Yet, the owner will have established, on paper, a significant equity interest in the business. As discussed in Chapter 12, an entrepreneur can usually justify a substantial salary as being "reasonable."

In addition, when an asset contributed for an equity interest carries an especially high risk of injury, the asset should normally be contributed to the operating entity, and then encumbered with liens in favor of the holding entity or owner. Where the assets are especially valuable, and of only moderate risk, the holding entity should own these assets.

Plan Smart

Another way to look at the relative amount of equity and debt funding is the debt-to-equity ratio. This is the amount of debt divided by the amount of equity.

A debt ratio (debt/assets) of 50 percent is the same as a debt-to-equity ratio of 1. Similarly, a debt ratio (debt/assets) of 60 percent is the same as a debt-to-equity ratio of 1.5 (60/40).

Most large businesses have a debt-to-equity ratio between .5 and 2, with most of these companies averaging less than 1. As discussed above, small businesses will typically have higher ratios.

Equity Interest in the Holding Entity

As explained above, the holding entity's assets will not be vulnerable because the holding entity will not engage in any operating activities. Thus, the holding entity may hold the assets loaned or leased to the operating entity, as well as the liens placed on the operating entity's assets. These assets may be contributed to the holding entity in exchange for the equity interest.

Still, the owner would be wise to personally own and lease to the holding entity exempt assets such as office equipment and furniture, automobiles, and other "tools of the trade," at least where these assets are not at a high degree of risk of causing personal injuries. In short, the rationale for doing this, as previously described, also applies to the holding entity.

Moreover, the owner should remember to purchase liability insurance that will cover assets, especially high-risk assets, owned by the holding entity and leased to the operating entity, because of the possibility that liability for injuries caused by the assets could run to the owner.

For this reason, too, consideration should be given to withdrawing funds from the holding entity on a regular basis. Usually this is done in the holding entity in the form of payments of salary to the owner. While the assets within the holding entity are protected to some degree from the owner's personal creditors, there is some small degree of risk to these assets because of the operating entity's activities. Although the latter risk is usually not significant, by withdrawing funds, the overall risk of loss is reduced. In short, diversification reduces risk.

Formal contribution of assets. A common mistake made by small business owners, which can have devastating consequences, is the failure to *actually* transfer assets into the business form in exchange for the equity interest. This mistake will almost always mean that co-mingling of assets will occur (i.e., the owner will use personal assets for business purposes and business assets for personal purposes).

As discussed in Chapter 16, when a business owner co-mingles business and personal assets, this may form the basis for the courts to pierce the veil of limited liability and impose unlimited, personal liability on the owner. Thus, the business owner must ensure that assets are actually titled to the operating entity when they are contributed in return for the equity interest.

Ownership of certain property is represented by a formal document of title. Examples include real property (land and buildings) and motor vehicles.

Title to real property must be transferred through the execution of a deed that takes a particular form. A quitclaim deed can be used where real property is transferred to a one-owner LLC or corporation. This type of deed contains no warranties as to the validity of the transferor's title. In a two-or-more-owner business, a warranty deed, guaranteeing the validity the title, and a title search should be considered.

Note that a new deed is prepared for each transfer, with the legal description being copied from the transferor's old deed. The deed should be recorded as soon as possible on the land records, at the county courthouse or local town clerk's office, depending on the state. This ensures that the deed is valid against any subsequent transfers of the property by the original transferor.

By contrast, a motor vehicle title is usually transferred by executing the reverse side of the transferor's title. This title is then filed with the motor vehicle department, and a new title is issued in the transferee's name.

Other property, such as equipment and furniture, is not represented by a formal document of title. Here, it is still essential that the owner formally transfer ownership to the entity. The transfer document here, however, may take different forms. But essentially, a document transferring ownership must be executed.

Finally, in all of these cases, care must be taken that the entity formally approves of the receipt of the asset, and then formally authorizes the issuance of the member interests or common stock, as the case may be.

The holding entity (or owner) as a creditor. The holding entity (or the business owner) may serve in two roles with respect to the operating entity: the role of owner established through the equity interest and the role of a creditor established by financing the operating entity with debt.

A creditor has a priority claim on the entity's assets, in comparison to the owner's claim. On liquidation, creditors receive their share of assets before holders of the equity interest. Further, *secured* creditors, have priority over general or unsecured creditors. Secured creditors hold a security interest in assets of the entity that have been put up as collateral for the extension of credit.

If the entity defaults on a secured loan, the secured creditor can, in effect, remove the collateral from the entity, and use it satisfy the debt. If the debt is over-secured (i.e., the value of the assets exceeds the amount owed), the difference is returned to the pool of assets available to unsecured creditors and the owners of the business. If the loan is under-secured (the balance owed exceeds the value of the collateral), the creditor is an unsecured creditor with respect to that excess.

The owner can protect his interests in the business's assets against the claims of the business's creditors by investing in the entity as a creditor and, in particular, as a secured creditor. This can be accomplished through the use of leases, loans and other extensions of credit.

Specifically, the holding entity (or owner) can lease assets to the operating entity. Because the holding entity retains ownership of the assets, but conducts no business activities, the assets are not exposed to liability at the holding entity level.

Further, because the operating entity does not own the leased assets, they are not exposed to liability at the operating entity level. In short, the assets are shielded from liability from *the claims of the business's creditors*. Further, if the assets are within the protective form of an LLC (i.e., the holding entity), they are protected from *the claims of the owner's personal creditors* (as discussed in Chapter 7).

The lease also can be secured by perfecting liens against the operating entity's assets.

Case Study — Funding Multiple Entities, Part 1

John, a Connecticut resident, wants to start a business in Connecticut by investing $100,000 of cash.

If John forms a single entity, *and invests the $100,000, this $100,000 will be exposed to the claims of the business's creditors.*

Instead, John forms two LLCs in Connecticut, a holding LLC and an operating LLC. He first forms the holding entity. The holding entity then forms the operating entity, as its only owner.

John contributes $100,000 to the holding LLC in return for an equity interest. The holding LLC uses the $100,000 to purchase the assets necessary to run the operating LLC. The holding LLC then leases these assets (through an approved written lease agreement) to the operating LLC, which then takes possession of the assets. Ownership of the assets, however, remains in the holding LLC.

As a result of this structure, and funding arrangement, John's $100,000 investment is now protected against the claims of both the business's creditors and John's personal creditors.

The operating LLC does not own the assets. Accordingly, the assets are not exposed to the claims of the business creditors at that level. The holding LLC conducts no operating activities. Thus, the assets are not exposed to the claims of the business's creditors at that level either. In short, the assets are protected against the claims of the business creditors.

At the same time, the assets are protected against the claims of John's personal creditors, *because, as discussed in Chapter 6, Connecticut follows the RULPA rule that prevents personal creditors from foreclosing on an owner's LLC interest or forcing a liquidation of the business to satisfy a personal debt.*

Note that John's holding LLC would have established its equity interest *in the operating LLC though a separate investment, apart from the lease. However, this equity investment would also be fully protected through liens on the operating entity's assets that would run to the holding entity, or to John personally.*

For example, the lease would be used to withdraw funds from the operating entity, and also to encumber its assets with liens. These liens could be established by the lease against the operating entity's assets (the leased assets and other assets contributed for the equity interest) as security for the lease obligations. Liens could also be established as a result of other extensions of credit to the operating entity, as discussed below. Thus, the holding entity would have priority claims on these assets, in the event that the operating entity defaulted on the lease payments, which is a likely scenario if the business runs into financial difficulties.

Executing Liens To Secure Funding

Encumbering the operating entity's assets with liens that run in favor of the holding entity or owner is one way to protect the operating entity's business assets. These liens must be perfected in order for them to be valid. This requirement includes mortgages on real property, which must be recorded to protect the owner's priority claim. Liens against personal property (i.e., property used inside or outside of a business other than real property) are perfected differently. The Uniform Commercial Code Form 1 (UCC1) can be used to perfect a lien when acquiring assets, as well as on existing or future assets.

In addition, there is a less complicated alternative to using a holding entity and an operating entity to protect the operating entity's assets: the one-entity approach. Leases, liens and loans are still used, but the business owner personally acts as the holding entity. This method is simpler than using holding and operating entities, but is not always as effective.

Using Liens When Acquiring Assets

In this strategy, ownership of assets is placed within the operating entity, but in a way so they are not vulnerable to loss. The operating entity obtains ownership of an asset, such as a building, usually through a loan of cash from the holding entity (or owner), in exchange for a mortgage or other lien taken back by the holding entity (or owner).

Case Study — Funding Multiple Entities, Part 2

John contributes $100,000 to the holding entity, which lends the $100,000 to the operating entity, so that the operating entity can purchase a building for the business. The operating entity puts up the building as collateral for the loan, giving the holding entity a mortgage on the building.

Now the operating entity owns the building, but John enjoys the same protections he did before when the holding entity owned the assets.

This type of lien is called a "purchase money security interest" because the cash was loaned specifically to purchase the asset, which is then put up as collateral for the loan. The asset is owned by the operating entity, but it is not vulnerable, as the liability represented by the lien, in effect, cancels the value that the asset otherwise would have to an outside creditor of the operating entity.

On liquidation, because the holding entity (or owner) holds the lien as a secured creditor, he would take the asset, leaving the other creditors with little or nothing. The outcome is the same as if the holding company owned the asset and the operating company owned nothing.

Plan Smart

Another example of this strategy took place in 1994, when Rockefeller Center went bankrupt, apparently jeopardizing $1.3 billion worth of real estate. However, asset protection strategies ensured that none of this real estate was lost to creditors.

Rockefeller Properties, two partnerships that acted as operating companies, owned the real estate. However, the real estate was encumbered by a lien, of approximately $1.3 billion, in favor of a corporation, Rockefeller Center Properties, which acted as the holding company.

This structure employed the use of two asset protection strategies: separate operating and holding entities and ownership of the assets being vested in the operating entity, but with a lien of approximately equal value in favor of the holding entity, which meant the assets were not vulnerable to creditors.

Using Liens on Existing or Future Assets

Liens also can be used when the holding entity (or the owner) makes loans of cash to the operating entity to cover the entity's operating expenses, (i.e., when assets are not being purchased with the proceeds). Liens are then placed on *existing* assets, and even assets acquired in the future.

Similarly, liens can be created when compensation (salary, bonus, retirement and health plan contributions, etc.) or reimbursement of expenses is owed by the operating entity to the owner, but unpaid. Here, both existing and future-acquired assets once again can be put up as collateral.

Recording Liens on a Real Property Mortgage

A lien on real property (land and buildings) must be created by a mortgage, which is recorded along with the related promissory note on the land records. The land records are located at the county court house in many states or in the local town clerk's office. The lien *must* be recorded to give the owner a priority claim. If the mortgage is not recorded, the claims of other creditors on the real property may take precedence.

States have different rules when it comes to priorities for recorded liens on real property. However, many states follow the general rule that the first to record takes priority. Thus, if the owner fails to record, the holding entity's lien may be ineffective, as illustrated in the following example.

Case Study — Funding Multiple Entities, Part 3

Now let's say John contributes $100,000 cash to the holding entity, which lends the $100,000 to the operating entity, so that the operating entity can purchase a building for the business. The operating entity puts up the building as collateral for the loan, giving the holding entity a mortgage on the building.

However, John never records the mortgage. Subsequently, a creditor sues the operating entity, obtains a judgment of $100,000, and records a lien against the building for this amount on the land records.

The judgment creditor's lien takes precedence over the holding entity's lien. As a result, the judgment creditor may be able to foreclose on the building.

Had John recorded the holding entity's lien immediately after it was created, the holding entity's lien would have taken precedence. In this case, the judgment creditor would have been unlikely to foreclose on its lien, because doing so would require that it pay off the holding entity's lien. Either way, John would protect his $100,000 investment—he would keep the building or be paid the $100,000 lien in cash.

Filing the UCC1 Form for Personal Property Liens

Liens against personal property are perfected differently than liens on real property. Here, "personal property" does *not* mean property owned personally by the owner of the business. Instead, the term refers to all property used inside or outside of a business (with the exception of real property), including equipment, furniture, inventory, etc.

To perfect a lien against personal property used in a business, a Uniform Commercial Code Form 1 (UCC1) must be executed and filed either in the secretary of state's office or the county courthouse, depending on the state.

Once recorded, the UCC1 makes the lien valid and serves as notice that the lien exists. Usually, the first to record a lien takes priority.

Plan Smart

Article 9 of the Uniform Commercial Code contains rules on lien priority. Usually, the first lien recorded will take priority. However, there are exceptions:

- *When the operating entity purchases inventory from an outside creditor, on credit, and puts up the inventory as collateral for the purchase (a purchase money security interest), the holding entity that has a perfected non-purchase money security interest in the inventory must give notice of the lien before the purchase, or otherwise the outside creditor's lien will have priority, even though it was not recorded first.*

- *In the same situation, if the property is not inventory, the outside creditor will take priority only if he records the lien within ten days after the operating entity takes possession of the purchased property.*

Two lessons should be learned here: Recording the holding entity's lien immediately will usually protect the owner's interest. If the holding entity purchases inventory on credit, the operating entity should notify the outside creditor, in writing, of the holding entity's lien before the purchasing agreement is signed.

The UCC1 can be used to perfect a lien against existing property, future-acquired property and open accounts (i.e., future debt).

Existing property subject to the lien is specifically listed on the UCC1. The UCC1 also describes the nature of the indebtedness and the lien that has been established.

So-called "floating liens" apply to *future-acquired property* or *future credit*. The agreement, which created the lien, between the holding entity (or owner) and the operating entity may state that all *future-acquired property* of the same class is subject to the same lien. Similarly, the operating entity can establish an "open account" with the holding entity (or owner), whereby any *future credit* extended by the holding entity (or owner), perhaps with credit exceptions, is subject to the open account agreement, and the lien that it established.

The UCC1 can specifically state that the lien applies to *future-acquired property* of the same class, *future credit* extended under an open account agreement, or both. In this way, only one UCC1 statement needs to be filed to cover many different extensions of credit from the holding entity (or owner) to the operating entity.

Warning

 A lien on personal property *can apply to future-acquired property of the same class, future credit extended under an open account agreement, or both.*

A lien on real property *(i.e., a mortgage) also can apply to future extensions of credit. Here, the mortgage is termed an "open mortgage" agreement. However, a mortgage lien cannot apply to future-acquired property. The future-acquired real property would have to be transferred as security under a new mortgage after the property is acquired.*

A UCC1 filing is effective for five years. It can be renewed through the filing of a Continuation Statement, *provided this is done at least six months before the five-year period expires.*

It is important that the owner have the filing officer record the file number, date and hour of filing on his copy of the document. Each state uses it own version of this form.

Although states usually accept a generic version, they will likely charge an additional processing fee if their form is not used.

Note that motor vehicles are treated differently than other types of personal property. A lien on a motor vehicle usually must be perfected by placing the lien on the actual motor vehicle title, and then submitting the title to the motor vehicle department.

It is wise to have an attorney review any document before it is executed. Laws vary from state to state. For example, while states usually require certain exact language be used in an acknowledgement for a mortgage deed, this language differs by state. Moreover, documents should be adapted to the particular needs of the business and the owner.

In short, use the forms provided the Appendices as guides, and have an attorney review and approve the documents before they are used.

In addition, the small business owner may want to consider what effect encumbering assets will have on the business entity's ability to borrow through "asset-backed" loans. These are loans secured by the business's equipment and inventory.

Here, a lender may require that the entity give the lender a priority position. This would enable the entity to secure funds through asset-backed loans and still protect the assets from other creditors.

It's important to understand that neither the recording of a mortgage nor the filing of a UCC1 statement actually creates the lien. The *agreement* between the holding entity (or owner) and the operating entity *creates* the lien.

A lien on real property must be created by a mortgage deed. The promissory note is a separate document detailing the nature of the loan, the repayment terms, etc. The *mortgage* is the lien, securing the promises made in the promissory note. The exact legal nature of the mortgage varies from state to state. In some states, the mortgage actually transfers legal title to the creditor, to secure the note. In most states, the mortgage simply creates a security interest in the property, without an actual transfer of title, similar to the way personal property is secured.

When a loan or other extension of credit is secured by personal property, the promissory note or agreement itself creates the lien. A separate agreement is unnecessary.

This underscores the importance of properly executing the underlying agreements. Of course, execution of all agreements must be formally authorized by the management of the entities.

The Appendices contains sample forms (including explanatory comments) that can be used in funding the operating entity with debt.

Plan Smart

Business owners should remember that they also will be creditors with respect to their customers *when selling them goods on credit provided by the business.*

A purchase-money security interest in consumer goods *(goods purchased primarily for home or personal use) does* not *have to be recorded to be perfected. The UCC1 financing statement must be perfected by filing only if the goods involved are used in a business (this is why liens on the operating entity's* business *assets need to be recorded).*

However, sometimes an asset has a mixed use, part personal and part business. This is common today with many people starting small businesses and using home offices, and purchasing mixed-use equipment such as a home computer.

The primary use *(e.g., business versus personal miles driven for a vehicle, or business versus personal hours of computer usage) will determine whether the lien must be recorded to be perfected.*

In one case, a consumer purchased a $3,000 computer, telling the merchant that it would be used for personal use, as part of her teaching assignments, and in a variety store. The buyer financed the purchase in an agreement giving the merchant a lien on the computer.

The merchant did not record the lien. In a Chapter 7 bankruptcy proceeding, the court held that the lien was not perfected, because the goods were purchased primarily *for business use. Accordingly, the merchant lost the $3,000.*

Small business owners who provide credit for goods they sell should have the buyer specify, in the credit agreement, that the purchase is primarily for personal or household use, or file the lien in a UCC1 financing statement.

Continuous Withdrawal of Assets

Clearly, a strategy that minimizes the amount of vulnerable assets invested in a business will not work unless a plan exists to withdraw, on a regular basis, the assets generated by the operating entity. Otherwise, vulnerable assets will stay within the operating entity, and the owner's liability, while limited, will still be significant.

A number of strategies exist to accomplish this objective, including salary, lease/loan payments, and sale of accounts receivable to the owner or the holding entity (these strategies are discussed in more detail in Chapter 14).

Plan Smart

Creditors can attack the initial capitalization of an entity as fraudulent under a doctrine termed "piercing of the veil" of limited liability (this topic is covered in Chapter 16).

Creditors also can attack withdrawals, as well as the creation of liens, as fraudulent conveyances (this topic is addressed in Chapter 4). Be especially cognizant of the entity's financial position (assets minus liabilities) when creating liens because insolvency can be a basis for creditors to attack these transfers. A good practice is to leave a portion of the assets contributed for the equity interest unencumbered. This practice is insurance that the entity will not be insolvent, from a balance sheet analysis, when liens and other transfers take place.

Examine both Chapters 4 and 16 before funding your entities or planning withdrawal strategies.

Chapter 9

Choosing a State

The small business owner can form a corporation or LLC in any state, even in a state in which he conducts no business activities. Further, even when an out-of-state entity is created, there is no requirement that any assets be located in that state.

So clearly, on a basic level, you have two options: form the entity in your home state or form the business in another state. There are advantages and disadvantages to either option, and among the considerations are complexity of administration, fees and costs.

But from an asset protection standpoint, you'll also want to consider the benefits of forming and registering in a state known as friendly to business ownership. Any additional expenditure of time and money may be inexpensive compared to the unique protections some states offer.

FORMING THE ENTITY IN YOUR HOME STATE

The simplest choice for the small business owner is to form the entity in his or her home state, where, typically, all of the business activities will be conducted.

Forming an entity out-of-state will create additional costs. The out-of-state entity will have to register to do business in the owner's home state (as discussed in Chapter 7). This registration fee is the same fee that would be charged to *form* the entity in his home state.

Thus, the owner would pay two sets of fees to form the entity out-of-state, but only one fee if the entity were formed in the owner's home state.

Example

John is a Massachusetts resident who plans on doing business exclusively in Massachusetts. If he decides to form a corporation in Connecticut, he will pay a formation fee of $275 to the state of Connecticut and a registration fee of $200 to the state of Massachusetts (the fee Massachusetts also charges to form a corporation there).

The simplest choice would be for John to form a corporation in Massachusetts and pay only Massachusetts's formation fee of $200. However, in deciding where to form the entity, the small business owner should consider other factors, aside from the initial state fees involved.

FORMING THE ENTITY IN ANOTHER STATE

The small business owner can choose any state in which to form a business, and it needn't conduct any business activities there. But in whichever state you choose, articles of organization need to be filed with the appropriate state agency, including the name of a resident agent for service of process (i.e., for purposes of consenting to the state's jurisdiction).

The articles are usually filed with the corporations division of the secretary of state's office. A fee is required at the time of the filing. Failure to file means the entity does not exist, and the owner is operating a sole proprietorship or a general partnership (formation issues are discussed in Chapter 13).

In addition, the entity must register as a "foreign" entity in each other state in which it does any substantial business. The activities of a holding entity usually would not rise to the level of "doing business" in a state. Thus, normally, an out-of-state holding entity would not have to register in either the owner's home state or where the operating entity conducts the business's operations.

Failure to register in this regard should be distinguished from failure to file articles of organization. A failure to register as a foreign entity in a state normally does not mean the entity will not be legally recognized. Nor, normally, does it mean that the entity's contracts are invalid. Most states simply provide that the entity must pay the registration fee that was due. However, a few states might provide for far more insidious results, by not recognizing the entity, which would result in unlimited personal liability for the business's debts incurred in that state, or invalidation of the business's contracts. When in doubt, register—or consult an attorney for advice.

Note that the entity-within-an-entity concept, which is embodied in the Delaware LLC statute, eliminates this problem. A single LLC can house multiple separate legal entities. This single LLC is formed in Delaware, and then registers in any state in which the operating entities will do business (see the discussion in Chapter 8 and below for more details on this statute).

Warning

As discussed in Chapter 7, California prevents professionals from operating in the LLC form. California also limits its LLPs to a narrow class of professionals, namely lawyers and accountants.

New York also limits LLPs to professionals, but defines this term more broadly than California.

A business entity's internal matters (voting, management, etc) and liability status will be governed by the state in which it is formed, as discussed below. However, nothing requires a state to recognize a type of entity that cannot be legally formed there. Thus, in the case of professionals who form an LLC or an LLP, and plan on doing business in California or New York, caution must be exercised. If the entity could not be formed in those states, it also will not be recognized if it is formed in another state, and then seeks to register to do business in those states. The end result could be that the business will be recognized, under those circumstances, only as a sole proprietorship or general partnership.

There are other aspects to consider when forming an entity outside of the owner's home state, such as fee considerations and the differences among state laws, as well as the advantages and disadvantages that result from these differences.

Fee Considerations

When choosing a state, the simplest (or cheapest) choice may not be the best choice. Another state's lower formation fee should not be the deciding factor in forming the entity there, when the owner will be doing business in his own home state as well. Clearly, the small business owner cannot avoid his home state's fee by forming an out-of-state entity, because a registration fee, equivalent to a formation fee, must be paid to the owner's home state anyway, if the owner will be doing business there.

If you are doing business in another state, but not in your home state, and you intend to use only one entity, you should consider forming the entity in the state in which you will be doing business, rather than your home state. This will result in only one fee.

If you form the entity in your home state, you will pay two sets of fees: the formation fee to the home state and the registration fee in the other state.

Example

Now let's say John is a Massachusetts resident who plans on doing business exclusively in Connecticut. If he decides to form a corporation in Massachusetts, his home state, he will pay a formation fee of $200 to the state of Massachusetts and a registration fee of $275 to the state of Connecticut (the fee Connecticut also charges to form a corporation there).

The best choice now may be for John to form a corporation outside of his home state, in Connecticut, and pay only the Connecticut formation fee of $275.

If two entities are being formed (i.e., a holding entity and an operating entity), there will be no additional costs involved in forming an entity out-of-state. The holding entity could be formed out-of-state, and the operating entity in the owner's home state.

Because the holding entity will conduct no business activities in the home state, it needn't be registered in the home state. Specifically, the activities of the out-of-state holding entity should not rise to the level of "doing business" in the home state. Thus, the cost of forming two entities, with one formed out-of-state, will be the same as forming both entities in the owner's home state.

Choice of State Law

Fees should not always be the only, or even the main, consideration. Simply put, the laws in each state are not all the same, and some states offer significantly greater asset protection and other benefits as well. The internal affairs (voting, management, etc.) and the liability of the owners for an LLC or corporation will be governed by the state where the business is formed, and not the state where it does business.

In particular, some states have a reputation for developing a body of law and a court system favorable to the business owner. Delaware is perhaps the best example of such as state. Nevada also has gained a reputation as a desirable state in which to form a business. Thus, consideration should be given to forming an entity in one of these states, especially when the business owner's home state is deficient from an asset protection perspective.

Some of the particular advantages available under state law include:

- protection of business assets against personal creditors

- full-shield liability protection

- management flexibility and simplicity

- statutory close corporation option

- asset protection trusts

- tax incentives

- exemption from securities registration

Protection for Business Interests Against Personal Creditors

Some states do not offer adequate protection for the owner's business interest in an LLC against the claims of the owner's personal creditors (as discussed in Chapter 6). These states model their LLC statute's charging order remedy on the general partnership provision that allows for foreclosure of the interest and forced liquidation of the business.

Many states, including Delaware and Nevada, offer protection for the business interest. These states model their LLC statutes on the charging order concept found in the Revised Uniform Limited Partnership Act (RULPA). If the business owner's home state does not offer this business interest protection, serious consideration should be given to forming an LLC in a state that does offer such protection.

Full-Shield Limited Liability Protection

Some states offer only a limited shield (i.e., a stripped-down version) of limited liability for the owners of LLPs (see the discussion in Chapter 6). In particular, the limited shield means that the owners of an LLP will have limited liability only with respect to the actions of their co-owners; the owners will still have unlimited, personal liability in all other cases.

If the home state only offers this limited-shield version, and an LLP is the type of entity that will be formed, consideration should be given to forming the LLP in a state that offers this full-shield protection.

Delaware and Nevada are two states that offer this protection.

Management Flexibility and Simplicity

Some states create mandatory voting rights for all members of an LLC on certain issues, even when the LLC is managed not by all the members, but by a small group of members who are termed the "managers." This can cause confusion and can make certain votes illegal. It also can interfere with an estate planning strategy discussed in Chapter 10—the use of the family limited liability company, where children are given nonvoting interests.

LLC statutes in some states make it clear that members can be accorded no voting rights at all, on any matter whatsoever. Delaware is one of those states. When the law in the home state accords all members certain mandatory voting rights, consideration should be given to forming the LLC in Delaware, or in some other state that allows the owner to completely eliminate voting rights for selected members.

As discussed in Chapter 6, the Delaware LLC statute may also offer greater protection in the event one of the LLC members files for bankruptcy.

Moreover, the Delaware LLC statute provides incredible flexibility and simplicity in forming and operating the LLC. It has no counterpart in statutes governing corporations (nor even in LLC statutes found in other states). For instance, it allows the forming of an entity within an entity, thus eliminating the need to form separate LLCs (or corporations) for each separate operating activity carried out by the business.

Each entity within the single LLC can have its own accounting system, own its own assets and be liable only for its own debts, as if each entity were a separate LLC. Thus, in many cases, a single LLC can be used to manage the holding entity, as well as the multiple operating entities (see Chapter 8 for structuring and funding decisions).

This may lead to fee savings, as the single LLC would require a formation fee in Delaware and a single registration fee elsewhere where it does business. It also eliminates the question as to whether an out-of-state holding entity also must register to do business in other particular states.

This and the many other benefits of the Delaware LLC statute are also discussed in Chapter 7. The Appendices contains Sample Articles of Organization and a Sample Operating Agreement for a Delaware LLC.

Statutory Close Corporation Option

Some states have a special statutory close corporation statute that is very favorable for owners of small corporations (as discussed in Chapter 6). The statutory close corporation statutes relax many of the formalities normally applicable to a corporation. Basically, these statutes allow the corporation to be operated in a way similar to an LLC. Specifically, these corporations may do away with a board of directors, and shareholders can run the corporation, by way of a shareholder agreement, which is similar to an LLC operating agreement. Generally, shareholders do not have to hold meetings.

A failure to follow the formalities normally applicable to a regular C corporation can form the basis for a court's decision to pierce the veil of limited liability and impose unlimited, personal liability on the owners (see Chapter 16). With the absence of such formalities in the statutory close corporation, the likelihood of this doctrine being applied is lessened significantly.

Thus, if a corporation is to be formed, it should usually be formed as a statutory close corporation. This can only be done in the small group of states that allow this option, such as Delaware and Nevada (see Chapter 6 for a complete list of these states).

Plan Smart

Forming an entity out-of-state will not create additional costs if, for example, the holding entity is formed out-of-state and the operating entity is formed in the owner's home state. The activities of the out-of-state holding entity should not rise to the level of "doing business" in the home state. Thus, the holding entity should not have to register in the home state.

Essentially, only the interest in the holding entity requires extra protection, as the holding entity will house the wealth of the business. The holding entity will normally own the operating entity and the most valuable assets used by the operating entity. The assets owned by the operating entity will be protected in other ways, such as with liens that run to the holding entity (as described in Chapter 8).

If additional costs are not an issue, the ideal situation may be to form both the holding entity and the operating entity in an asset protection friendly state, such as Delaware. This may mean three fees (two formation fees, plus a registration fee). Even if additional costs are involved, however, the benefits will outweigh those costs in most cases.

Asset Protection Trust Options

Forming the holding entity in Delaware or Alaska can be part of an overall asset protection plan because these states have statutes authorizing the creation of domestic asset protection trusts (as discussed in Chapter 5). However, this is a significant departure from domestic law in the United States. Accordingly, a trust created under either of these statutes could be challenged on jurisdictional grounds.

One way to bolster the validity of these trusts is to create additional "contacts" in Delaware or Alaska, where the trust is formed. Having a holding entity formed in Delaware or Alaska that funds the asset protection trust located there would create additional contacts in that state (for a complete discussion of this topic, see Chapters 5 and 8).

Plan Smart

If you are forming a holding entity and an operating entity, consider forming the holding entity out-of-state, in particular, in Delaware, and the operating entity in your home state (or where the business's activities will be conducted).

Forming the holding entity out-of-state will produce no additional costs. There will still be only two fees: one to form the holding entity and the other to form the operating entity. The small business owner should take the lead from larger businesses and consider Delaware as the site for the holding entity. This also may help sustain the validity of an asset protection trust formed there.

In addition, if fees are not a significant concern, consider forming both the holding entity and operating entity in Delaware, so that Delaware law will govern each entity. Here, the operating entity will have to register to do business in the owner's home state (or where the business's activities will be conducted), thus creating a third fee. However, this fee may prove to be an inexpensive form of insurance. This option is more attractive when the home state's LLC statute does not effectively protect an owner's interest from his personal creditors.

Note, too, that, as previously described, the Delaware LLC statute allows for the creation of multiple entities within the form of single entity. This can make formation of an LLC in Delaware less expensive.

The Appendices contain a Sample Articles of Organization that can be used to form an LLC in the state of Delaware. They also cover preparation of formation and operating documents, and the specific advantages of the Delaware statute are discussed in more detail.

State Tax Incentives

Ordinarily, an LLC and a subchapter S corporation will not be subject to state income taxes in a state in which they conduct no business and in which the owners do not reside. This may make it desirable to form the entity out-of-state. The owners will be subject to state income taxes in the state in which they reside or the state in which the entity conducts its business activities (usually, but not always, the same state). Delaware and Nevada, two popular states for formation of LLCs and corporations, both follow these rules.

Moreover, most states will follow the presumed tax status of the LLC (as a conduit) and the federal subchapter S tax election of a corporation (to be taxed as a conduit), as discussed in Chapter 6. However, a few states may not recognize the subchapter S election. These states may impose states income taxes on the corporation even when it does no business in the state. It also is remotely possible that a state would still treat an LLC as a corporation for state income tax purposes and impose taxes on it regardless of whether it conducts operations there.

Although these situations are unlikely to be encountered, it's a good practice to check with state taxing authorities before choosing a state in which to form the business—or form the business in a state such as Delaware or Nevada, which provides clear rules favorable to the small business owner.

Did You Know?

According to the most recent statistics, 60 percent of Fortune 500 companies and 50 percent of companies listed on the New York Stock Exchange are incorporated in Delaware. Moreover, many business bankruptcy proceedings are initiated there.

Consistent with this regulatory scheme, which is purposely designed to attract businesses into the state, business formation fees are low in Delaware: $50 for a corporation and $50 for an LLC.

Nevada is also gaining a reputation as a favorable state in which to form a business. A significant number of new businesses are being formed there. For example, Nevada has enacted a statutory close corporation statute similar to Delaware's statute.

Exemption From Securities Registration

Unlike other states, Delaware expressly exempts from securities registration all LLC interests that are not actually traded in a securities market.

This kind of flexibility is particularly advantageous when, in the manager-managed LLC, non-manager interests are to be issued (see Chapter 11 for securities issues in business formation).

Chapter 10

Planning for Federal Estate Taxes

The small business owner must be aware of estate planning issues when forming a business, as these considerations can have important implications when initially structuring the business. Proper initial business formation can save hundreds of thousands of dollars in estate taxes in later years.

Estate planning is, in fact, a type of asset protection planning. Here, assets, which can be quite substantial, are being protected from the claims of the federal government.

This chapter can cover neither estate taxes nor estate planning to reduce these taxes in any comprehensive way. However, as a small business owner, you should be familiar with some of the basics of estate planning, because federal estate taxes can be significant, and a business form can be chosen to eliminate or reduce these taxes.

And, certainly, the rules have recently changed when it come to estate planning. Estate tax reform passed by Congress in 2001 has created new and different opportunities, as well as some uncertainties.

Moreover, this chapter addresses a common estate planning tool called the family limited liability company and how it can be utilized to reduce or eliminate estate taxes when transferring business interests to your family.

Finally, before making the transfers, it's important to be aware of the implications of changes in ownership with regard to taxes and management/control of the business operations.

ESTATE TAX BASICS

Estate planning is a very complex subject, and anyone hoping to successfully shield hard-earned life-long earnings from the tax collector should consult a professional in this area. But this basic understanding of estate taxation is important: Federal estate taxation rates are among the highest tax rates in America. After a fixed exemption amount, assets are taxed at a 37 percent rate that rises to about 50 percent—although recent estate tax reform promises to lower these amounts over the years.

Obviously, this is a sizeable chunk of your lifetime of effort—generations of saving and work cut by a third or a half upon the owner's death. But there are important exceptions written into the estate taxation laws. You can go a long way toward preserving your wealth and business if you take advantage of:

- the unlimited marital deduction
- the unified exemption and gift exemption
- the annual gift tax exclusion
- the family-owned business exemption

The Unlimited Marital Deduction

An individual can give during life, or at death, an unlimited amount to a spouse, free of estate and gift taxes. This is termed the "unlimited marital deduction" and is separate from the regular "unified" exemption or the new "gift" exemption (discussed below).

However, the unlimited martial deduction is deceiving. If everything is left to the spouse to take advantage of the unlimited exemption, a problem arises. The surviving spouse has no spouse and, thus, no unlimited marital deduction. If the surviving spouse remarried and then left everything to the new spouse, few individuals would find this a satisfactory solution either.

Thus, without adequate estate planning, the family will still end up passing on a significant portion of the family's fortune to the federal government when the other spouse dies.

The Unified Exemption and Gift Exemption

As of the year 2002, every individual can transfer a total of $1 million during lifetime or at death, free of estate and gift taxes. This exemption is scheduled to rise to $1.5 million in the year 2004.

Until recently, it was termed a "unified" exemption because gifts made during life also counted against the total (there was one overall exemption, and the individual used it up by making gifts during life *and* at death). Reform of the estate tax laws in 2001 has further divided this exemption into subcategories. The overall, or unified, exemption remains for the entire estate, but a gift exemption limits the amount that can be given during a lifetime.

Once the unified exemption is used up, the tax rates that apply are quite high. In effect, the rates *start* at 37 percent. While the exemption might, at first glance, seem generous enough so as not to even warrant any planning, it must be remembered that the goal of every small business owner is to build the business and amass wealth. While not every small business owner will be successful, many will find that they have accumulated a significant net worth, which will trigger the federal estate tax.

In addition, because of the 2001 reform act, the estate tax itself is being phased out over a 10-year period, but the gift tax will remain in place (see the discussion later in this chapter). The gift tax exemption will be $1 million in 2003, consistent with the estate tax. But in future years, the gift tax exemption will remain at $1 million, while the estate tax exemption rises until the estate tax is fully repealed in 2010. At that time, the top gift tax rate will equal the top income tax rate.

The following table depicts major changes to estate and gift taxes made by the estate tax reform of 2001.

Estate and Gift Tax Rates and Exemptions				
Year	Top Estate Tax Rate	Estate Tax Exemption	Top Gift Tax Rate	Gift Tax Exemption
2002	50%	$1 million	50%	$1 million
2003	49%	$1 million	49%	$1 million
2004	48%	$1.5 million	48%	$1 million
2005	47%	$1.5 million	47%	$1 million
2006	46%	$2 million	46%	$1 million
2007	45%	$2 million	45%	$1 million
2008	45%	$2 million	45%	$1 million
2009	45%	$3.5 million	45%	$1 million
2010	0%	Repealed	35%	$1 million
2011*	55%	$1 million	35%	$1 million

*Estate tax reform of 2001 sunsets in 2011. At that time, the law reverts back to rules in place in 2001.

Congress retained the gift tax out of concern that, with no gift tax, wealthy families would use gifting of assets to family members in lower income brackets as an income tax splitting strategy. Of course, this concern underscores the effectiveness of this strategy—which remains effective, subject to the $1 million lifetime gift tax exemption.

Furthermore, the $11,000 annual gift tax exclusion (see discussion below) is not affected by this legislation. This fact again bolsters gift giving as an effective strategy in reducing income and estate taxes.

Ultimately, many other factors can make a taxable estate larger than it may seem. During the 1990s, for example, the stock market made portfolios, and thus taxable estates, swell in value. In addition, without the use of other estate planning strategies, retirement benefits and life insurance can significantly add to the value of a taxable estate.

At these rates, much of the value of the business, built up through years of hard work, could end up being passed on to the *federal government*, rather than to the next generation, if estate planning strategies are not employed to avoid this outcome.

The Annual Gift Tax Exclusion

The small business owner also should be familiar with the $11,000 annual gift exclusion, which is sometimes used as part of this type of estate planning strategy. This exclusion is scheduled to increase in amount, as it is now indexed to the rate of inflation. Lifetime annual gifts that qualify under this exclusion *do not reduce the unified estate or gift tax exemptions*.

A husband and wife can join together and raise the exclusion to $22,000, even if only one owns the transferred property, through a concept called "gift splitting." This requires that a *Federal Gift Tax Return*, Form 706, be filed, and a gift splitting election be made.

In addition, the $11,000 amount is the exclusion *per donee*. Carefully used, this estate planning strategy can be used to transfer significant amounts without any federal gift taxes.

Family-Owned Business Exemption

As a small business owner, you may be eligible for an additional estate planning exemption. The exemption totals $1.3 million. However, the small business owner must subtract his regular exemption from this amount.

Thus, the *difference* really amounts to an *additional* exemption, beyond the regular exemption. For example, the regular exemption is $1 million in 2003. Thus, this exemption yields an *extra* $300,000 ($1.3 million - $1 million).

However, in 2004, as a result of recent estate tax reform, the family-owned business exemption is scheduled to be eliminated. At the same time, though, the regular exemption will increase to $1.5 million, exceeding the previous family-owned business exemption amount.

This additional exemption is available only to small business owners who meet all of the eligibility criteria. One requirement is that the business be family-owned. One family must normally own at least a 50 percent interest in the business. However, a family can own as little as a 30 percent interest if it aggregates its interest with a second or third family. In that case, the *total* ownership among all the families must be at least 70 percent if there are two families, and at least 90 percent if there are three families. This requirement is seldom a problem for a small, family-owned business.

A second requirement may pose a greater obstacle for the small business owner. The value of the business included in the owner's overall estate must exceed 50 percent of the total value of the estate. If the small business owner has been successful at running the business, presumably there will be significant wealth accumulated *outside* of the business, in the form of an investment portfolio, retirement benefits, life insurance, etc. In many cases, the business will likely represent less than 50 percent of the value of the total estate. In short, this criterion may exclude a large number of small business owners.

Overall, the small business owner usually will find it advantageous to transfer interests to the next generation and, possibly as a result, forego this additional exemption, when:

- The value of the interests transferred can be expected to exceed $300,000 (the value of the additional exemption in 2003), *at the time of the parent's death.*

- The owner expects to have an especially large taxable estate due to *personal wealth accumulated outside of the business.*

Finally, however, even the more successful business owner might be able to take advantage of *both* planning opportunities. While alive, the parent can transfer interests representing a significant portion of the value of the business to the next generation, while other estate planning techniques can reduce the size of the taxable estate that results from *other* assets. As a result, the value of the business interest included in the parent's estate, while relatively modest, may still exceed 50 percent of the total value of the estate, allowing the added exemption.

If you think this exemption may be to your benefit, be sure to consult with an estate planning professional. While we have explained the major requirements that you need to meet to qualify for this additional exemption, other requirements must be met as well.

ESTATE TAX REFORM OF 2001

Many aspects of the estate and gift tax were changed by recent reform measures passed by Congress. This major tax legislation includes a phase-out of the federal estate tax over a 10-year period, as well as major changes to the gift tax and carryover basis rules for inherited assets.

But is the federal estate tax really being phased out? The legislation includes a provision that *automatically reinstates the tax* at the end of the 10-year period, unless Congress passes new legislation continuing the repeal, and this prospect is uncertain. Technically, the "repeal" exists only for one year, 2010.

The phase-out, and possible reinstatement, of the federal estate tax has significant implications. Many sophisticated techniques (some of which are discussed below) have been developed to eliminate, or significantly reduce, the federal estate tax. Many of the strategies center on transferring wealth to the next generation through various types of lifetime gifting. In general, it would not be prudent to abandon these strategies because there is a real possibility the estate tax will return. If no planning is employed, and the estate tax returns, 10 years of opportunities to shift assets to the next generation, free of estate tax, would be lost.

Finally, the uncertainty concerning the future of the estate tax requires that flexibility be built into estate plans. Clauses can be used in existing, as well as new, estate plans that allow the flexibility needed to respond to either a repeal or continuation of the tax.

It is especially important to have existing plans reviewed. Funding clauses in many existing tax-saving trusts, if not amended, may produce undesirable results. A review of your estate plan is absolutely necessary if you have substantial wealth and are interested in avoiding federal estate taxes.

New Gifting Opportunities

The divergence of the estate tax and the gift tax (as previously described) presents new opportunities. You can take advantage of the $1 million lifetime gifting exemption by transferring up to this amount, immediately or over time, free of estate taxes. This produces income tax splitting benefits and reduces the size of a potentially taxable estate upon death.

In addition, your estate later can use the remaining estate tax exemption available at that time, assuming the full repeal is not continued by new legislation before its sunset date in 2011.

Of course, using the $11,000 gift tax exclusion (as described previously), you can continue to transfer wealth that won't count against the new gift tax exemption. However, gifting your assets, whether by annual exclusion or lifetime exemption, has tax basis implications that affect the paying of capital gains tax.

Changes in Stepped-Up Tax Basis

The estate tax reform of 2001 made significant changes to the tax basis of gift or inheritance assets when they are later sold.

The recipient of gifts given during a donor's lifetime also receives the carryover tax basis of the gifts. In short, all capital gains for those assets accumulated during the donor's lifetime are carried over to the recipient, and when this person later sells the assets, capital gains taxes must be paid by the recipient on the entire appreciation in value of the assets. So in this case, estate tax avoidance can result in substantial capital gains taxes for the recipient.

On the other hand, assets left in the estate and exposed to estate taxation—even if no tax is due because of the allowable estate exemption—are given a stepped-up basis for the recipient, usually equal to fair market value. In short, when the recipient later sells the assets, capital gains taxes are only assessed on the difference between the stepped-up basis and the ultimate selling price. But this situation is not permanent.

To further complicate matters, when the estate tax is fully repealed (which is for year 2010 only, according to current law), limits are placed on allowable stepped-up basis, presumably to keep people from taking advantage of a situation where they would pay no estate taxes and also completely avoid capital gains taxes.

Under the terms of a full estate tax repeal, only $1.3 million of inherited assets are eligible for stepped-up basis. The balance retains the carryover basis from the donor. In addition, a surviving spouse is allowed an extra $3 million in stepped-up inherited assets, bringing that total to $4.3 million. The estate's executor can decide which of the assets gets the stepped-up basis and which get the carryover basis.

Clearly, an estate plan involving gifting, exclusions, exemptions and changes in tax basis of assets is extremely complicated and involves carefully balancing a number of objectives. But the tax savings are potentially enormous. For this reason, it is very important to consult an expert in this field before undertaking any of these strategies.

TRANSFERRING BUSINESS INTERESTS TO THE FAMILY

Even with the allowable exemptions and exceptions to estate taxation, there is the real possibility that the remaining assets will be taxed at very high rates. To legally avoid this outcome, a number of strategies have been developed over the years that will allow you to pass on wealth to your family. Consider using:

- the family LLC

- discounted business interests

- tax-free gifts

- trusts and S corporations

- annuities

But before you decide to use any of these strategies, carefully consider the implications of your choice, because you will be diluting your ownership in what you worked so hard to build, as well as affecting the tax status of all the parties involved.

It is always wise to consult an estate planning professional for advice before undertaking any planning strategies.

The Family LLC

Many different estate planning strategies can be used to eliminate or, at the very least, significantly reduce estate taxes, ensuring the family's wealth is passed on to the next generation. One such strategy involves the use of a limited partnership (LP) or a limited liability company (LLC). Parents transfer to their children "discounted" shares in their LP or LLC, *without giving up control of the business.*

Parental control of the business is ensured in the LP because limited partnership interests are transferred to the children, while the parents retain the general partnership interest (as discussed in Chapter 6, limited partners may not participate in the management of the business). Historically, the LP has been used in estate planning strategy because of this attribute.

Today, the LLC can be used to accomplish this same purpose, but with *all* of the owners having limited liability for the business's debts. An LLC can be structured as a "member-managed" entity, wherein all of the owners participate in management, similar to the partners in a general partnership. However, the LLC can also be formed as a "manager-managed" entity, wherein the owners who are also the managers control the business, while the owners who are not managers act in a capacity similar to limited partners. In short, the "manager-managed" LLC is well suited to accomplish this estate planning objective.

Parents can transfer ownership interests, in the form of non-voting/non-manager interests, to the children without giving up control of the business. In the immediate future, many practitioners will continue to use the LP in employing this estate planning strategy, because a body of favorable case law has built up over the years supporting the use of the LP for this purpose. However, many practitioners are already embracing the LLC as a better alternative to the LP, because *all* of the owners of the LLC enjoy limited liability.

Plan Smart

Sometimes an LP is created solely to transfer wealth tax-free. In this case, it is usually funded with the family's securities or real estate holdings. However, its best use exists when the family is using the entity to operate a legitimate business.

As the limited liability limited partnership (LLLP) begins to become more common, the limited partnership form may, once again, be the choice of practitioners employing this estate planning strategy, at least in those states that allow the owner's personal creditors to foreclose on the owner's business interest, and force a liquidation of the business to satisfy the debt (see Chapter 6 for a detailed discussion of how the LLLP avoids this outcome).

In contrast, the corporation has never been used for this purpose. The corporation does not offer the same protection to owners from the claims of the owners' personal creditors (as discussed in Chapter 6, personal creditors of the owner of a corporation, but not an LLC in many states, may foreclose on the interest of the owner and force a liquidation of the business, or simply vote in favor of liquidation).

Moreover, the subchapter S corporation limits estate planning opportunities because it places restrictions on the types of trusts that may be shareholders. This can be a problem especially in the small business, because most small business owners will make the subchapter S election. Therefore, in short, the LLC presents a better choice than the corporation.

Plan Smart

Most small business owners operating a corporation will make the subchapter S election, which requires that there be only one class of stock in the corporation. For this estate planning strategy to work, there would have to be two types of stock—voting for the parents and nonvoting for the children.

In reality, voting common stock and nonvoting common stock are considered, for purposes of this rule, to be one class of stock. Thus, it is possible to employ this strategy in the corporation electing subchapter S status.

However, the S corporation has never been widely used in executing this strategy.

The small business owner should consider creating a manager-managed LLC at the outset, even when the owner does not anticipate immediately making transfers. This can be done even in the one-owner LLC, in anticipation of the possibility of transferring interests some time in the future. This eliminates the need, in the future, to make amendments to the articles of organization and operating agreement, which would be necessary had a member-managed LLC been created.

If a holding entity and an operating entity are created, it is important to use this strategy when structuring the holding entity, which will own the bulk of the assets, as well as own the operating entity—which is the entire wealth of the business. Thus, the operating entity may then be a member-managed or a manager-managed LLC, with the holding entity as the only owner.

When the owner directly creates and owns both entities, each entity should be manager-managed. Clearly, having the holding entity own the operating entity simplifies this strategy.

Finally, professionals can form an LLC, LLP or a corporation only if all of the owners are licensed within the same profession (as discussed in Chapter 6). Only the operating entity has to meet this requirement. The holding entity, which will contain nearly all of the wealth of the business, will not be engaged in the practice of any profession. Thus, children, or other family members, for example, can still be co-owners of the holding company, even when it is formed by professionals. However, the operating entity would have to be directly owned by the professionals, rather than by the holding company.

Plan Smart

Parents may wonder whether interests can be transferred to children who are minors. Or, they may be concerned as to whether their children will responsibly manage their interests. These issues can be resolved.

First, it must be remembered that the children's interests are non-voting/non-manager interests, meaning the children will not have the power to control the business in any event.

In addition, however, the children's interests can be transferred to an irrevocable children's trust, with the parents as trustees. There, the interests can be completely protected from the children's creditors (see Chapter 5 for a detailed discussion on trusts and, in particular, the types of provisions that can be used in a trust to protect assets from the claims of creditors).

Drafting such a trust would require the services of an estate planning attorney. A simpler strategy would be to transfer the interests to the children under the Uniform Transfers to Minors Act (UTM). This requires nothing more than properly titling the ownership interests. The disadvantage here is that, under the UTM, the children gain control over the interests at a relatively young age (age 21 in most states). In contrast, in an irrevocable children's trust, the parents, as trustees, can retain control until the children reach a specific age the parents select.

Finally, an agreement restricting transfer of ownership interests is essential in any small business with multiple owners. Such an agreement effectively gives the parents control over the disposition of the shares owned by the children, even when the children own the shares outright (this agreement is also discussed in Chapter 5).

It is clear that the most effective strategy involves transferring business interests to the next generation, *before the interest become especially valuable.* The more valuable the interest, the more difficult it becomes to make the transfers, while still preserving the $1 million exemption.

Discounting the Interests

Now that we've discussed the entity form best suited for transferring business interests, it's time to explain how best to make those transfers.

A transfer (in excess of the $11,000 annual exclusion per person) will reduce the $1 million lifetime gift tax exemption allowed under federal estate tax laws. This is where "discounting" becomes an important part of the transfer strategy.

The ability to control the business has value. The interests transferred lack the ability to control the business. Consequently, the value of the transferred interests will be "discounted," or lower in amount. Thus, the transferred interest will use up a smaller portion of the exemption.

Warning

Discounts due to a lack of control and marketability should be documented by an appraisal. Law and accounting firms, as well as banks, provide this type of service. While there is a cost involved in obtaining an appraisal, the cost is usually more than offset by the estate tax savings.

The interests also will be discounted because of a lack of marketability. The interests in a closely held business are not worth as much as similar interests in a publicly traded company, because there is no established market in which the interests can be sold. Discounts typically range from 10 percent to 50 percent.

Case Study — Transferring LLC Interests to the Family

John owns an LLC with a value of $600,000 (value of assets less liabilities). He wants to avoid the estate tax, as he knows the value of his business, and his other assets, will steadily increase above his exemption amount. John owns 100 percent of the business, represented by ownership of one share as a member/manager, and nine shares as a member/non-manager.

John transfers the nine member/non-manager shares to his children as a gift. Because this represents nine of the ten outstanding shares, or 90 percent ownership in the business, the transfer should be valued at $540,000 ($600,000 x 90 percent), and would reduce John's exemption by this amount.

However, because of discounting, due to a lack of control and marketability, the interest would only be valued at $378,000, if a 30 percent discount were applied ($540,000 x 70 percent). This discounted amount is what counts against your estate and gift lifetime exemptions. Thus, John will have preserved $162,000 of his exemption, which could be used to make future tax-free transfers. He accomplished this even though, in reality, he transferred 90 percent of his business to his children.

In addition, 90 percent (the children's ownership share) of the future appreciation in the value of the business, which John projects will be quite substantial, will be attributed to the children. In other words, nearly all of the future appreciation in value will be passed on to the children free of estate taxes. John will not have to be concerned about paying hundreds of thousands of dollars in estate taxes when passing this value onto the children.

Note that, in practice, as much as 99 percent of the business can be transferred in this way to the next generation, without a loss of control.

Note, too, that it would be important to form the LLC in a state that protects the business owner's interest against the claims of his personal creditors, and that allows for the complete elimination of voting rights for certain membership interests, such as those held by members who are not managers. For example, Delaware is one state where both of these objectives can be accomplished.

Using Tax-Free Gifts

As an alternative to outright transfers, the $11,000 annual gift exclusion provides a simple opportunity to pass on wealth. The exclusion is now indexed to the rate of inflation, and lifetime annual gifts that qualify under this exclusion *do not reduce the estate or gift tax exemptions.* A married couple can join together and increase the exclusion to $22,000 by "gift splitting." This requires a gift-splitting election and the filing of a form with the IRS (as mentioned earlier in this chapter).

In addition, the $11,000 is the exclusion *per donee*. Thus, parents with four children could transfer to the children interests in the business that total $88,000 *each year*, without reducing the $1 million exemption they each enjoy ($22,000 x four donees). Of course, because of discounting, as previously explained, this $88,000 represents a much larger value to the children. For example, at a 30 percent discount rate, the $88,000 will really represent $125,714 ($88,000/70 percent).

Case Study — Tax-Free Gifts of Business Interests

Let's assume John (from the previous case study) owns an LLC with a value of $600,000, but does not want to reduce his $1 million exemption when he transfers the interests to his children. The discounted value of the interests he plans to transfer is $378,000 (90 percent of the business is $540,000, then $540,000 x 70 percent = the discounted interests).

If John and his spouse join in making the gifts, and they have four children, it will take less than five years to complete the transfers, using only the $11,000 annual gift tax exclusion and, thus, preserving the entire $1 million exemption ($22,000 x four donees = $88,000 per year that may be transferred under the exclusion; at that rate, in five years, they could transfer $440,000 ($88,000 x five years).

Trusts and Subchapter S Corporations

There are restrictions on the types of trusts that may be shareholders in a subchapter S corporation, although recently the rules have been liberalized. In particular, these trusts will qualify as shareholders under current law:

- **Electing Small Business Trust (ESMT)** — The problem here is that all of the trust's undistributed income is taxed at the highest possible marginal tax rate for individuals.

- **Grantor Trust** — Here, the parent will be taxed on all of the trust income. As discussed later, this may be desirable as an option in certain situations.

- **Qualified Subchapter S Trust (QSST)** — The rules here are similar to typical provisions found in trusts established for children. Basically, the rules require that a separate trust be established for each child, and that the income and principal within the trust be managed exclusively for that child. While this may seem to be a burden where there are several children, one trust instrument can create multiple trusts (i.e., only one document, executed once, is actually necessary).

Nevertheless, the limitation here is that the parent will not be able to create a single trust that will "spray" income among all of the children/beneficiaries unless an ESMT (which results in all income taxed at steep tax rate) or grantor trust (all income is taxed to the parent) is used.

Plan Smart

None of these rules apply to the LLC. Thus, even with these changes for trusts and subchapter S corporations, the LLC is a simpler and more flexible alternative than the corporation when transferring interests to trusts.

In addition, if interests in the business are transferred to the next generation during the life of the parents, the remaining value in the estate of the parents at death will be relatively small. This could negatively affect the family-owned business exemption allowed under federal estate tax law (as previously explained). The small business owner must weigh the benefits of this strategy against the possibility that it may possibly contribute to the loss of the additional family-owned business exemption, which is repealed in 2004.

Plan Smart

When transferring the interest to an irrevocable children's trust, income tax rules governing trusts allow an experienced trust drafter to choose whether to have the income taxed to the children or taxed to the parent through the so-called "grantor trust rules."

While income tax splitting can result in tax savings to the family (as explained later), the grantor trust rules provide simplification because all of the income can be reported on the parent's income tax return. This is especially desirable where income is accumulated in the trust, rather than distributed to the beneficiaries. This is a very likely scenario, in this case, because trust income tax rates are higher than those that apply to individuals.

In fact, many trust drafters intentionally make children's trusts subject to the grantor trust rules for this reason, by creating so-called "defective grantor trusts." (The term "defective" is used because, ordinarily, the children would be taxed on the trust's income, absent a defect in drafting the trust).

With a defective grantor trust, the income from the trust is taxed to the parent, but the value of the trust assets is excused from the parent's taxable estate.

Annuities

Other, more advanced strategies exist that allow transfers to be made, without reducing the gift tax exemption. For example, a private annuity may be used. Here, a child promises to pay a life annuity to the parent, in return for the interest in the business.

The annuity is structured so that its value is equal to the discounted value of the business interest transferred to the child. There is no gift, as the child gives the parent an equal value in return, and thus there is no reduction in the $1 million exemption.

If the parent dies before the annuity is paid off, nothing is counted in the parent's estate, because the annuity terminates at that point. Advanced strategies, especially, require the advice of an estate planning professional.

IMPLICATIONS OF THE TRANSFERS

The result of transfers to children will often be income-splitting that lowers the family's income taxes. Traditionally, income in an LLC is divided according to the relative balance in the owners' capital accounts. Because the children will own much, or nearly all, of the business, according to the capital accounts, most of the income would be attributable to the children, if this traditional allocation scheme is used.

The children's share of income would be "passive" income in this instance. In 2003, the first $1,500 of this passive income will be taxed to the children at their lower tax rates, while the parents' top rate could approach 40 percent.

In addition, if the children actually provide services to the business, any payments to them would not be passive income. Accordingly, *all* of this non-passive income would be taxed to the children at their lower rates. For 2003, the first $4,750 (the amount of the child's current standard deduction) would be tax-free. Moreover, it should be noted that parents could provide the cash necessary to pay the taxes incurred by the children.

Further, when children actually work in the business, this will mean retirement plan contributions can be made on their behalf (see Chapter 3). It also will allow the retirement plan to qualify under ERISA, where, otherwise, with only the two parents participating in the plan, it would not qualify. This will mean the retirement plan benefits will be protected as exempt assets in a bankruptcy or state court proceeding (see Chapter 3 for a discussion of asset exemption planning).

Use of this allocation scheme also will mean that the wealth represented by the business's earnings will not be subject to the estate tax. Nearly all of the income drawn out from the business would be attributable to the children and, thus, not taxable in the parents' estate.

Transfers to the children also offer flexibility with respect to income taxes. Because the parent retains control, and provides all of the labor and planning for the business, all (or most) of the business's earnings can be drawn out by the parent as salary, if that is desired. This obviously is an advantage to the parents in terms of control of the cash flow.

Moreover, transferring ownership interests to the children serves a useful asset exemption purpose. The value of the business is divided among the parent and the children, leaving the parent with complete control of the business, but with a lower-valued ownership interest. This makes it easier to exempt the parent's ownership interest (which as discussed in Chapter 3 is personal property).

Finally, when transfers are made into a trust with a spendthrift clause, the interests transferred are protected from the children's creditors.

Ultimately, asset protection strategies should be designed to work together, as part of a comprehensive asset protection plan.

If you are going to use this estate planning strategy of transferring ownership interests to family members, several caveats are in order:

- While the parents retain control of the management of the business, and control over withdrawals during the life of the business, the children in fact will own a significant portion of the business. They will receive this share on liquidation of the business. Some parents would not want this result or would want the ability to revoke the transfers, which is not possible.

- Parents still must plan for the transfer of *control* of the business (i.e., the manager interest) to the next generation. This decision involves many other factors, such as the children's desire, or competence, to operate the business, etc.

- The IRS has approved the transfer of interests both to children directly and to trusts that hold the interests for the children. Accordingly, the children or the trust will be recognized as partners for federal tax purposes. However, in both cases, the IRS will recognize the children, or the trusts holding their interests, as partners, only if *capital* is a material income-producing factor. This rule exists to prevent parents from shifting what really is income from their personal services to the children. If the profits are generated principally by services provided by the parents, the children (or their trust) will not be recognized for federal tax purposes and the income will be taxed to the parents. Note that the IRS cannot control who is a partner under state law, or for any other purpose, except for purposes of federal taxation and, in this case, for purposes of deciding who will be taxed on the business's income.

Plan Smart

This IRS rule on which partners are taxed may not present a problem for the small business owner, even in a personal service business, because the children will be gifted interests in the holding entity. The holding entity will produce income primarily from the provision of capital to the operating entity (providing leased equipment, purchasing receivables, etc.). This is yet another reason to use a holding entity and an operating entity.

Finally, where capital is not a material factor in producing income, there is another option. The IRS will recognize the children, or their trust, as partners if the children provide significant services to the business, and income is allocated according to the relative services provided, rather than on the basis of relative capital interests.

- In addition, where trusts hold the interests of the children, the trustee, especially if this is the parent, must manage the interests solely for the benefit of the beneficiaries of the trusts—the children. This prevents parents from using the principal or income in the trust for their own personal benefit.

Warning

This strategy has recently come under IRS scrutiny, precisely because of its effectiveness in significantly reducing estate taxes. Basically, the IRS has scored successes when individuals have created an entity and transferred interests to their children on their death-bed, as a tax-avoidance tool, and when entities have been formed and funded solely with marketable securities and, thus, had no business purpose. Neither of these situations will be likely to apply to the small business owner.

- This type of planning is really only appropriate for the family-owned business.

- Most importantly, estate planning is an especially complex and ever-evolving area of law. It is wise to consult an estate planning practitioner before undertaking any planning measures.

Chapter 11

Securities Law Issues

The small business owner must consider numerous legal issues before starting business operations. One issue particularly worthy of some discussion is securities law, as it affects the issuance of interests in the LLC and corporation.

An awareness of securities issues is essential to prevent future claims against the business and to allow the business owner to exploit capital markets as the business seeks to expand.

Federal and state securities rules are complex. While this discussion is not intended as complete coverage of this topic, the small business owner interested in asset protection should, at the very least, understand:

- whether or not the entity is issuing "securities"

- whether the offering must be registered or may be exempt

- Regulation D, Rule 504/SCOR (small corporate offering registration) offering—a common route small businesses use to raise up to $1 million from the public

- an alternative route termed a Regulation A/SCOR offering can be used to raise $1 million from the public, with the added advantage of being able to "test the waters" before actually making the offering

- Internet offerings of securities

Issuing Securities

Whenever a corporation is formed, "securities" are issued. The term "security" clearly covers common stock, which will always be issued by a corporation as evidence of ownership. However, preferred stock and bonds, usually issued by larger businesses, also constitute securities.

A limited partnership interest in a limited partnership (LP) is a security. More importantly for the small business owner, a non-manager interest in an LLC is likely to be deemed a security. The key in both of these cases is that the investor puts up capital, expecting a return to be derived solely from the efforts of others (i.e., the manager-owner of the LLC or the general partner in the LP).

The law is much more settled with respect to the sale of securities by a corporation. Securities laws date to the 1930s and were originally developed to regulate offerings of securities by corporations. The LLC is so new that there has not yet been a definitive determination as to exactly what type of LLC interest is a security.

For example, while Delaware law clearly provides that any interest in an LLC will not be deemed a security unless it is traded on a securities market, this kind of clear-cut rule is lacking in other states.

The corporation *may* present a better alternative than the LLC where the small business owner intends to make *a general and widespread public offering* of securities, such as through an Internet offering, for two reasons:

1. Securities law was developed primarily to govern offerings by corporations. Thus, the law there is more settled.

2. Both potential investors, and federal and estate regulators, are more familiar with, and thus may be more receptive to, a sale of common stock in a corporation, as opposed to an interest in an LLC.

However, this recommendation would not apply in the case of a small offering made among a group of private investors. In addition, this issue will seldom be a factor for the small business owner.

SEC REGISTRATION AND EXEMPTION

Generally, *before* an entity can issue securities, it must first register the offering with the federal Securities and Exchange Commission (SEC) *and* with the SEC's counterparts in *each state* in which the securities are being sold, *unless an exemption applies*.

Warning

From the perspective of limiting exposure to liability, it is extremely important that the small business owner either properly register an offering of securities with the federal and state governments, or ascertain that an exemption applies. Failure to comply with federal and state securities laws can result in large civil fines and the likelihood of personal liability for losses suffered by investors.

If a small business owner has raised capital from investors and the business fails, there is a likelihood that the business owner will be sued. One of the first things a plaintiff's lawyer will examine is whether the business owner complied with federal and state securities laws. If there is a failure in this respect, the small business owner will likely lose. Conversely, if the owner has complied with these laws, the small business owner will likely win, even though the investors suffer a total loss.

Fortunately for the small business owner, an issuance of securities to himself, his immediate family members and a few other partners will usually be totally exempt form both federal and state securities laws. In this case, the exemption generally is "self-executing"—that is, the exemption is automatic.

Generally, an automatic or self-executing exemption will apply when the offering of securities has all of these attributes:

1. limited to 10 or fewer individuals who are all organizers of the business or who, alternatively, invested through direct in-person solicitation

2. did not involve any use of the mails, telephones or the Internet in solicitations

3. limited to one state

A self-executing exemption does not require the filing of any documentation with the federal or state governments.

Warning

Unfortunately, each state's securities laws (termed "blue sky laws") are, in fact, unique—even though they are modeled after the federal laws.

Some states may require that a simple notice of a sale be filed when sales are made to individuals who are not organizers of the business, even though all of the conditions for the exemption described above are met. If you are offering securities under this set of circumstances, it is wise to first check with the state agency that regulates securities offerings in the particular state involved.

REGULATION D, RULE 504/SCOR FILING

When the small business owner is interested in raising capital from the public, a federal Regulation D, Rule 504 exemption coupled with a uniform state small corporate offering registration (SCOR) filing will be the most common route taken. Both the federal exemption and the state filing limit the amount raised to $1 million in a one-year period. To prevent abuse, a second offering cannot be made for six months after the first 12 months expire. Effectively, the small business owner could rely on this combination to raise $1 million every 18 months.

Unlike other federal exemptions, the Rule 504 exemption contains no onerous restrictions (other than the $1 million limitation). The issuer is free to advertise the securities and to solicit potential investors. In addition, there are no restrictions on the number or type of investors. Nor are there any resale restrictions on the securities. The SEC requires that Form D be filed after the first sale, notifying the SEC that the issuer has used the exemption. However, it is wise to file this form *prior* to offering the securities for sale, in case the SEC has any questions related to the form, and refrain from any advertising, offers or sales, until the SEC approves the form.

Plan Smart

Until recently, some small businesses used the federal Rule 504 exemption, and then sold securities only in those states that offered a similar exemption without any onerous restrictions.

However, the intent of Rule 504 has always been that the issuer registers the securities in each state in which they are offered for sale, and complies with the strict registration requirements imposed by the states. This is why under Rule 504, the issuer faces no real federal restrictions related to the sale.

Accordingly, the SEC amended Rule 504 to effectively limit the use of Rule 504 only to those offerings made in states where registration is required or is exempt only with severe restrictions, such as bans on general advertising of the securities, limits on the numbers and types of investors, etc. The result is that, today, an issuer who wants to raise capital from the public through a general solicitation, and rely on Rule 504, will have to register the securities in the states through a SCOR filing.

The state SCOR filing is an actual registration, rather than an exemption. But unlike other aspects of state securities laws, the form used is uniform, meaning that one form can be completed and submitted to each state, with a few minor exceptions.

Warning

While nearly all states accept the SCOR filing, the following states do not accept it, at this time:

Alabama	*Florida*	*Minnesota*
Delaware	*Hawaii*	*New York*

Moreover, the SCOR registration, while uniform in appearance, will not be treated identically when it reaches the individual states.

Most states are "merit-review" states. They review the offering to determine whether it is "fair" to investors. However, the following states, do not conduct a merit review:

Connecticut	*Maryland*	*Vermont*
Georgia	*New Jersey*	*Washington*
Illinois	*New York*	

In these non-merit-review states, the offering will automatically *be approved, provided all of the information on the forms is complete and accurate. Note that "non-merit-review" is also the policy embodied in federal securities law.*

In the merit-review states, if the regulators believe the offering is not fair to investors, they will not approve it. The following merit-review states have a reputation as being hostile toward SCOR filings:

California	*Massachusetts*	*Texas*

The following merit-review states have a reputation as being progressive toward SCOR filings:

Arizona	*South Carolina*
Iowa	*Washington*

The small business owner making a public offering of securities may want to consider offering the securities only in the non-merit-review states and the merit-review states with a progressive stance toward SCOR offerings (remember, however, that New York does not accept a SCOR registration at this time; a filing there will have to made on the state's individual registration form).

In particular, it may be advisable to forego an offering in those states perceived as being hostile toward the SCOR registration.

REGULATION A/SCOR FILING

Regulation A allows small business owners to use a simplified form to gain an SEC exemption for an offering of securities. While Regulation A is technically an exemption, it is best thought of as a simplified registration because a filing must be made with the SEC before any offers to sell securities can be made (unlike Regulation D, Rule 504 discussed previously).

Registration A permits an issuer to raise up to $5 million in a 12-month period. However, because the state SCOR registration has a $1 million limit, Registration A effectively is limited to this same amount when it is combined with a SCOR registration in each state.

The most significant advantage of using Regulation A (rather than Regulation D, Rule 504) is that it allows issuers to test the waters for investor interest before undertaking the arduous and expensive process of preparing the required SEC documents.

Plan Smart

Because of the expense of preparing federal and state documentation, testing the waters may be essential, if the small business owner intends to make a public offering of securities. Testing the waters is only available under Regulation A, *which may make it a better alternative than Regulation D, Rule 504.*

The fact that an Internet site—using a coupon that can be e-mailed, or printed and mailed, to the issuer—can qualify under the rules also makes this option very attractive.

The Regulation A form, designated Form 1-A by the SEC, can be prepared in several versions, including a simplified question-and-answer version that uses the SCOR Form U7. *This simplified format, which is a recent option, overcomes what previously had been the biggest impediment to using Regulation A rather than Regulation D, Rule 504—the added complexity and expense of preparing the standard Form 1-A.*

Thus, if the offering is limited to $1 million, Regulation A can be coupled with a state SCOR filing, further simplifying the process of registration.

The SEC imposes strict requirements on an issuer who will be testing the waters under Regulation A. These rules dictate that:

- Solicitation of interest may take the form of written documents or scripted radio or television broadcasts (this would allow the use of a web site on the Internet as a means of determining whether there is sufficient interest to justify an offering).

- Solicitations of interest may not be made after the filing of the Regulation A Form 1-A offering statement.

- No offers, sales or exchange of consideration can take place during the testing process. Sales may not be made until 20 calendar days after the last publication or delivery of the document or radio/television broadcast.

- Any written document under this section may include a coupon, returnable to the issuer, indicating interest in a potential offering, revealing the name, address and telephone number of the prospective investor.

- On or before the date of its first use, the issuer must submit a copy of any written document or script of any broadcast to the SEC's main office in Washington D.C. (Attn: Office of Small Business Policy). Oral communications with prospective investors and other broadcasts are permitted, *after* this submission. Further, the rules require that the written document or broadcast must contain specific information, including:

— the name and telephone number of a person able to answer questions about the document or broadcast

— a statement that no money or other consideration is being solicited and, if sent in response, will not be accepted

— a statement that no sales of securities will be made or commitment to purchase accepted until delivery of an offering circular that includes complete information about the issuer and the offering

— a statement that an indication of interest made by a prospective investor involves no obligation or commitment of any kind

— a disclosure of identity of the chief executive officer of the issuer, as well as a brief and general description of the business and its products

Warning

Not all states have provisions that allow testing of the waters. However, the following states do allow issuers of Regulation A to gauge interest beforehand:

Colorado	*New York*	*Vermont*
Illinois	*North Dakota*	*Virginia*
Indiana	*Oregon*	*Washington*
Iowa	*Pennsylvania*	*Wisconsin*
Massachusetts	*South Carolina*	*Wyoming*
Nevada	*Utah*	

The small business owner should limit testing of the waters to residents of these particular states. If an Internet web site is used, a disclaimer can be used to accomplish this objective (see below).

The following states are considering the adoption of such a provision:

Arizona	*Michigan*
Maine	*Rhode Island*

It is possible other states may follow suit in the future.

INTERNET OFFERINGS OF SECURITIES

Many small businesses are turning to the Internet in raising capital because it represents a centralized and inexpensive way to solicit potential investors from all across the country. While the law in this area is evolving, it is important the small business owner understands that a view is emerging in the law—an Internet offering is an offering of securities in *every* state, unless certain conditions (described below) apply.

Consequently, the small business owner intending to solicit using the Internet will have to first register the securities in every state or find an exemption in particular states.

Of course, a uniform state SCOR registration could be made in the states that accept it. Further, the Internet offering will not be subject to a state's jurisdiction if the offering:

- specifically and expressly disclaims that the securities are being offered to residents of that particular state (e.g., those not accepting the SCOR registration); in that event, no registration or exemption would be necessary in those particular states

- is registered under federal securities laws or relies on some federal exemption, other than Rule 504

Because Rule 504 will be the most common exemption used by the small business owner making an Internet offering, satisfying the second condition is unlikely.

Warning

A complete discussion of securities law is beyond the scope of this book. For example, other exemptions are available, subject to more restrictions than Rule 504, which allow the issuer to raise more capital. However, you should keep the following in mind:

- *The SCOR registrations, Form U-7 and the Rule 504 Form D, while simplified as far as securities registrations are concerned, are in fact complex and technical. Their preparation will normally require the use of an attorney. In any case, where the small business owner questions whether an offering is subject to registration, or eligible for an exemption, it is wise to first consult an attorney.*

- *The SCOR registration must be completed and approved before any offering can be made. Subsequently an offer must be accompanied by a prospectus, which is part of the SCOR Form U-7.*

Chapter 12

Tax Aspects of Strategic Funding Decisions

Funding a business entity with equity or debt normally may be accomplished tax-free. That is, in equity and debt funding, normally neither the owner nor the entity recognizes gain.

However, in some situations, the owner will recognize gain when he acquires his equity interest. And that gain can have significant tax implications.

So a small business owner needs to be aware that certain ownership contributions are taxable events. Moreover, how the business is funded will have an impact on the eventual allocations of income and interests, and how they are taxed.

TAXABLE OWNERSHIP CONTRIBUTIONS

A small business owner *may* have to recognize gain when acquiring an *equity interest* in the business if the owner:

- receives it in exchange for a contribution of past or future services

- receives some kind of property in return for the interest (a "disguised sale")

- contributes property subject to a liability (such as an outstanding mortgage)

- distributes previously contributed property to another owner within 7 years of the original contribution

The first three rules will apply in funding either the LLC or the corporation, although the third rule will be applied differently in either case. The fourth rule applies only in the case of the LLC.

Warning

The rules that apply to subchapter S corporations are separate from those that apply to LLCs. Use this information only as general guidance and always seek a professional opinion specific to your situation.

Payment for Services

When the owner acquires an equity interest in exchange for compensation for services performed or to be performed, the owner will be treated as having received taxable income. The owner is taxed on the value received by the business for the equity interest because it is compensation for services rendered or to be rendered.

Warning

A contribution of future services can seem to be an excellent way to capitalize an entity with an equity interest, where the owner does not have sufficient capital, in the form of cash or other property, to contribute.

This type of funding can serve an important asset protection purpose. Through this option, the owner is able to adequately capitalize the equity interest, and thus perhaps stave off any attack based on "piercing of the veil" of limited liability (see Chapter 16), while at the same time avoiding the necessity of placing vulnerable assets within the business form.

However, owners are personally liable for the value of contributions promised to the entity, in return for the equity interest, until the contribution is actually delivered. Thus, the owner must be cautious in not taking back too valuable an equity interest by promising too much. The actual per hour value of the services will be a function of the going rate for similar services. The entrepreneurial efforts required of a business owner will certainly make this per hour rate much higher than it would be in a different setting.

The owner must determine the per hour rate for his services and then, importantly, determine the number of hours he is willing to commit in return for the equity interest. Too long of a commitment (or too small of a rate) can mean there will be a difference between what was promised and what was delivered, at a time a financial crisis strikes. The owner would have personal liability for this difference.

That such a contribution is taxable to the owner immediately must be taken into account, too. As described above, the full value of the promised services must be included as income on the date the equity interest is received, and not over the time the services are rendered.

Finally, any compensation scheme between the entity and owner must be documented and approved at the entity level, as explained below.

Individuals are always taxed on amounts received for services rendered. However, taxation normally takes place only when the owner receives the salary. Here, the owner is, in effect, prepaid in one lump sum. Thus, he must immediately recognize income equal to the full value of the contribution upon capitalizing the entity with the promise of future services.

It is essential that the amount of services to be contributed is specified, and a mechanism must be set up to value these services. The number of ownership interests (shares) that will be issued in return must be specified and documented. Thus, an agreement must be authorized and executed, which details the rate of pay (an hourly rate or annual salary), the total value of the contribution, and the number of ownership interests issued.

Of course, subsequently, the owner must actually perform the services, and the performance, too, must be documented. This type of documentation should be part of the accounting system in place for any small business.

Plan Smart

"Organizational costs" are the costs of forming the business entity. They are incurred before the entity legally comes into being (i.e., before the articles of organization are filed and approved by the state). Organizational costs cannot be deducted immediately by the business. Instead, the entity must capitalize these costs and expense them over five years.

If the compensation to the owner is for services performed in creating the entity (pre-formation services), they will be organizational costs. If the owner wants an immediate deduction for the business for this compensation, the compensation agreement should specify payment is for services provided after the formation of the entity.

A contribution of services, solely in exchange for an interest in profits, may not be immediately taxable if the recipient does not obtain an equity or ownership interest in the entity. The recipient is, instead, taxed on his shares of profits, as the profits are generated.

Disguised Sales

Normally, the owner acquires an equity interest in the entity by contributing money, other property or services to the entity. In return, he receives *only* his equity interest.

If in addition to his equity interest he receives cash or other property, he really has made a *taxable* sale of the property to the entity (what the IRS terms a "disguised sale"). This ordinarily should not affect the small business owner, as it would be unusual for an owner to take back anything except the equity interest itself.

In addition, the IRS has a "safe harbor" rule for partnerships, which provides that a contribution will not be treated as a disguised sale when a distribution is made to the owner more than two years after a contribution. This exception also should apply to LLCs.

Plan Smart

If the owner of an LLC receives a distribution within two years after his contribution, he must be able to prove it was not consideration paid for a sale of the asset to the entity. This can be done by showing the distribution was for compensation, lease or loan payments, etc.

Property Subject to a Liability

When the owner contributes assets subject to a liability (such as an outstanding mortgage) in exchange for an equity interest, this may be a taxable transaction. Here, the rules differ, depending on whether the contribution is to an LLC or a corporation.

Generally, in the LLC or corporation, the owner's contribution will be taxable if the amount of the liability assumed by the entity exceeds the owner's tax basis in the asset contributed. In the corporation, the liability is subtracted from the owner's basis in the asset contributed, to derive the tax basis of his ownership interest. In the LLC, the liability assumed by the LLC affects the tax basis of *each* owner in the LLC.

Case Study — Property with a Liability

John, Peter and Amy form an LLC. John contributes a building with a tax basis of $80,000 and a fair market value of $170,000. The LLC assumes the $60,000 mortgage liability on the building.

John's tax basis in the LLC normally would be the basis of the property he contributed— $80,000. However, the $60,000 liability assumed by the LLC must be allocated among all the owners, including John. Thus, the tax bases of John, Peter and Amy in the LLC will be increased by $20,000 each.

In addition, John's basis must be decreased by the other owner's allocable share of the liability ($40,000). Thus, John's final basis in the LLC is $60,000 ($80,000 + $20,000 - $40,000).

Note that John would have recognized a gain on the contribution if, and to the extent, the mortgage liability exceeded John's basis in the building. Here, no gain is recognized because the liability of $60,000 is less than John's basis of $80,000 in the building.

Remember Peter and Amy would each increase their tax basis for their investment in the LLC, by $20,000 each. The LLC would have a carryover basis of $80,000 for the building on its books.

Finally, if this were a corporation, John's tax basis for his ownership interest would be $20,000 ($80,000 tax basis for contributed asset less liability of $60,000). Note how, in the corporation, when the entity assumes the liability, there are no adjustments to the bases of the other owners.

Different rules also apply in the case of the corporation, when there is a contribution of property and the transferors do not control 80 percent or more of the corporation.

These other rules could apply, for example, to *subsequent* contributions to a corporation by a single transferor who, alone, controls less than 80 percent of the corporation. Here, when property is contributed to a corporation subject to a liability, or non-cash property is contributed, gain is recognized on the contribution, as if the property were sold to the corporation. In this case, no basis adjustments are required for the liability. Instead, the corporation picks up the asset on its books at fair market value (along with the liability) as if it had purchased the asset.

Warning

Clearly, these calculations are complicated. Professional guidance should be sought before property subject to a liability is contributed to an LLC or a corporation.

Distribution of Property to Another Owner

If an owner contributes property to an LLC, and the business distributes the same property to another owner within seven years of the contribution, the contributing owner must recognize gain or loss on the distribution. This amount is the difference between the property's basis and its fair market value at the time of contribution. This rule does not apply to a corporation.

This really will only apply when a specific asset, other than cash, is contributed, and then that same asset is redistributed in this way. Here, again, this will not ordinarily be an issue of concern to the small business owner.

Again, if you are considering this option, be sure to consult with a tax attorney to make sure you comply with the complexities of these transfers and/or distributions.

TAXABLE ALLOCATIONS OF INCOME AND INTERESTS

The small business owner must be familiar with the different measures of the term "basis," and the effect these different measures have on the allocation of income among the owners of the business. Since tax law is particularly complicated, the owner should seek advice from a tax professional in these matters. However, owners should understand the basic rules governing tax basis.

When contributing non-cash property to an LLC, any difference between the property's fair market value and tax basis to the owner will require that the entity allocate depreciation, related to the item, away from the contributing owner and in favor of the other owners. The allocation of gain and loss from the sale of the asset will be to the contributing owner and away from the other owners.

The building contributed by John in the previous case study would come under this rule. This allocation will usually mean less deprecation expense, but higher gain will be attributed to the transferor when the asset is sold by the business entity.

The critical concepts affecting the taxability of income and interest allocations are tax basis of the owner's equity interest, fair market value of the owner's equity interest and how the operating agreement dictates the division of profits.

Tax Basis of the Owner's Equity Interest

Where only cash or services are contributed to an entity, in return for an equity interest, the tax basis of the owner's equity interest will be the same as the fair market value of the equity interest. In other cases, the two amounts will be different. The differences can have important ramifications, especially when dividing income among the owners.

The *initial* tax basis of the owner's equity interest is equal to the initial cash plus the tax basis of non-cash property contributed to the entity, subject to the adjustments previously discussed when non-cash property with a liability is contributed to an LLC.

Note that, when non-cash property is contributed, the tax basis of the owner's equity interest is based on the owner's tax basis in the asset contributed. This tax basis is carried over. It is equal to the owner's *original cost* in the asset, plus the cost of any capital improvements the owner made to the asset, minus any depreciation he took on the asset. With property that has appreciated (or depreciated) in value, or that has been depreciated, this tax basis will usually be different from the fair market value of the property.

Case Study — Figuring Tax Basis

In the prior case study, John's building, which he contributed to the LLC, had a basis to him of $80,000. This would have been his original cost *for the building, plus the cost of any* capital improvements *he made to the building, such as a new roof, minus any* depreciation *he took on the building. Depreciation will only be an issue where the asset has been used for business purposes prior to the contribution.*

This will be the carryover basis that the LLC will use for purposes of depreciating the asset, or calculating gain or loss on its sale. This would also be the tax basis of the owner's equity interest for John, except that he contributed the building subject to a liability. The adjustments to this $80,000 figure are addressed in the original case study.

Note that the building has a fair market value of $170,000. This would be determined by an appraisal or any other reasonable estimation of its current value based on estimated selling price or, perhaps, replacement value.

Had John contributed $170,000 of cash, or services with a value of $170,000, the tax basis of his owner's equity interest would be the same as the fair market value contributed—$170,000.

The entity also uses this same carryover tax basis in the acquired property for purposes of determining its depreciation, and gain or loss. Also, the holding period for the property, for capital gains purposes, includes the contributing owner's holding period.

If the owner sells his business interest, the gain or loss is determined by subtracting the *tax basis* for the equity interest from the proceeds received from the sale.

Fair Market Value of the Owner's Equity Interest

As discussed above, where only cash or services are contributed, the tax basis of the owner's equity interest and the fair market value of the owner's equity interest will be equal. In other cases, the figures will be different.

These differences arise because the fair market value of the owner's equity interest is based on the fair market value, and not the tax basis, of the property the owner contributes to the entity. When cash or services are contributed, the face value of the cash and the lack of a prior value for the services mean that tax basis and fair market value are equal.

When non-cash property is contributed, *free of any liability*, the full appraised value is the property's fair market value. On the other hand, when non-cash property is contributed, *subject to a liability that will be paid by the entity*, the amount of the liability is subtracted from the appraised fair market value of the property, to determine the actual fair market value contributed.

Case Study — Figuring Fair Market Value

In the prior example, John's building, which he contributed to the LLC, had a basis to him of $80,000. It had a fair market value of $170,000, but was subject to a liability of $60,000, which the LLC will pay.

The fair market value *John contributed, and thus the fair market value of the owner's equity interest, is $110,000 ($170,000 less $60,000). Note how this differs from John's* tax basis *of the owner's equity interest, which is $80,000 before adjustment and $60,000 after adjustment.*

This difference can lead to misunderstandings when profits are divided among the owners.

Division of Profits

LLC owners typically divide profits based on the relative capital accounts of the owners. Subchapter S corporation owners divide profits based on relative number of shares owned. However, the number of shares owned is determined by the relative capital contributed by the owners. Hence, in both cases, the relative amounts credited to each owner for his or her contribution will control the division of profits.

Note that, even in the LLC, the relative amounts credited will translate into the issuance of ownership interests. These ownership interests may be termed shares. Division of profits can then be made according to the relative number of shares owned in the LLC, which will be the same as the relative balance of the capital accounts (the Sample Operating Agreement for a Delaware LLC in Appendix E reflects this approach).

Voting rights in the LLC also are usually dictated by the relative capital accounts of the owners, or the relative number of shares owned, which is based on the relative capital accounts. Voting in the corporation is usually on a per share basis and is unaffected by the ratio. However, relative capital account contributions will, again, dictate how many shares each owner will be issued.

Unfortunately, the issue left open by many small business owners is which capital accounts are to be used in making these assessments: the capital accounts based on the *tax basis* of the owner's equity interest or the capital accounts based on the *fair market value* of the owner's equity interest. As previously discussed, the differences can be significant.

Usually it makes more sense to use the fair market value of the owner's equity interest for each owner, as this is the true representation of what each owner contributed.

Case Study — Dividing Profits According to Interests

In the previous case study, the real value John contributed is $110,000. The building is worth $170,000, but the LLC will have to pay the liability on it of $60,000. Thus, John really contributed something of value to the LLC worth $110,000.

It wouldn't be fair to give him credit, for purposes of division of profits or voting, for only the $60,000 tax basis he will have in his ownership interest.

However, since for tax purposes, records must be maintained based on the tax basis of the owner's equity interest, it is generally easier to simply base assessments on these figures. In short, using the fair market value of the owner's equity interest usually provides a fairer result, but this requires that a separate record for the capital accounts be created and maintained. For this reason, some businesses make all assessments based on the tax basis figures.

Case Study — Recordkeeping and Accounting Using FMV

In the previous case study, John's fair market value of the owner's equity interest is $110,000. His owner's equity account, in the LLC's accounting system, should be credited for this amount.

The building has a value of $170,000, and the liability assumed by the LLC amounts to $60,000. Thus, the entry for the accounting system would be:

Building FMV	*$170,000*
John's Owner's Equity for Contribution	*$110,000*
Liability on Contribution	*$60,000*

This way of recording requires that a separate tax record for the building be established, as the LLC's tax basis for the building will be $60,000 (i.e., the carryover basis from John). This is the amount that must be used for purposes of depreciation, and calculation of gains or losses on the sale of the building by the LLC.

A separate record of the owner's capital accounts, based on tax basis, also will be maintained outside the accounting system. This record will reflect only the following adjustments: an increase in John's account for $80,000, his tax basis after adjustment, and an increase in the accounts for each of the two co-owners of $10,000 based on the liability adjustment.

This separate record will not dictate division of profits and voting in the LLC.

For income allocation purposes, the best approach is usually to record interests within the accounting system based on the fair market value of the owner's equity interest. The agreement among the owners then must clearly specify that profit-sharing and voting (in the LLC) are to be based on this measure. As discussed above, determinations based on fair market value provide a much more equitable result.

For tax purposes, a separate record of the capital accounts based on the tax basis of the owner's equity interest is then maintained *outside the accounting system*.

Case Study — Asset Protection Using FMV

Keeping records in the accounting system based on the fair market value of the owner's equity interest is a better approach from an asset protection perspective, too. The net amount of the asset recorded (asset minus liability) in the LLC's accounting system is $110,000, which is the true value of John's contribution.

This amount also is much larger than the $80,000 that would be recorded, under the tax basis alternative.

The additional amount of net assets has a beneficial effect on the calculation of liquidity (as discussed in Chapter 4). This additional amount will make it less likely that transfers from the business will be deemed fraudulent.

This fair market value approach also is consistent with generally accepted accounting principles.

Alternatively, the owners could record the tax basis in the accounting records. This method is illustrated below. This is *not* desirable because the accounting system does not reflect the true economic effect of the contribution.

Case Study — Recordkeeping and Accounting Using Tax Basis

In the previous case study, John's tax basis of the owner's equity interest is $60,000 after adjustment. His owner's equity account, in the LLC's accounting system, should be credited for this amount.

John's two co-owners each will receive a credit to their owner's equity accounts for $10,000, because of the liability adjustment, as discussed in the original case study. The building will be debited to the LLC's accounts for $80,000—the carryover basis from John. Thus, the entry would be:

Building	$80,000
John's Owner's Equity for Contribution	$60,000
Peter's Additional Owner's Equity	$10,000
Amy's Additional Owner's Equity	$10,000

This way of recordkeeping ensures that the building is recorded for the amount that can be depreciated (i.e., the carryover basis from John). However, in this tax-based approach to recording, the liability is not recorded, as it is accounted for as an adjustment to the owner's equity accounts. This makes it difficult to account for the payments by the LLC on the liability, in the LLC's accounting system.

A separate record of the owner's capital accounts, based on fair market value, would be maintained outside the accounting system. This record will reflect only one adjustment: an increase in John's account for $110,000, the real value he contributed. No adjustments are made here for the co-owners, as the $60,000 liability is simply subtracted from the value of the building, $170,000, and John is given credit for only the true value contributed, $110,000.

This separate record will dictate division of profits and voting in the LLC.

Finally, in this last case study, for the sake of simplicity, the business could forego keeping the separate set of records based on fair market value, as these are not required for tax purposes. Division of profits and voting in the LLC could then be based on the relative tax basis of the owner's equity interests. As previously discussed, this is usually not desirable, as it produces inequitable results. In addition, the amount of net assets recorded will be lower, which may have a negative effect on the ability of the owner to defend against claims that withdrawals from the business are fraudulent.

The one exception might be where present and planned future contributions will only be in the form of cash or services. There, of course, the tax basis of the owner's equity interest and fair market value of the owner's equity interest will be equal. Even here, however, because of the possibility of future non-cash contributions, the best alternative will usually be to record, and allocate income and voting, based on fair market value.

Clearly, the tax implications of funding decisions can be complicated, and extend beyond the immediate tax consequences, at least in certain cases. A Sample Operating Agreement for a Delaware LLC appears in the Appendices. You should not attempt to use this form without first understanding all of the implications and alternatives available, and having it reviewed by an attorney. In other words, the small business owner should use the sample agreement as a guide and have it adapted to suit his particular needs.

Chapter 13

Establishing The Business Entity

Corporations and limited liability companies (LLCs) are formal legal entities created by filing articles of organization and various registrations, as well as by paying fees to the appropriate state agencies.

In addition, sound business planning dictates that a buy-sell agreement and an LLC operating agreement or shareholder agreement are entered into as well, even where it's not required by law.

Of course, other considerations, such as required licenses to operate the business, federal and state tax and employer identification numbers, and various legal issues need to be addressed when establishing the business entity.

FORMING THE LLC OR CORPORATION

The LLC and corporation are creations of law, and as such, a number of legal requirements must be satisfied to formally launch your business entity.

First and foremost are the articles of organization, which lay out the specific formal structure of the business. This "blueprint" of the company is filed with the state in which your business will be formed.

Next is the foreign registration certificate, another state-mandated requirement if you plan on doing business in a state other than the one in which your business is formed.

Of course, with each of these filings comes a state fee. These fees vary by state and by company size/structure.

In addition, to seal the state's jurisdiction over your business and operations, you will need to name an agent for service of process. In essence, this is the company's point person in dealing with that state's legal matters. You will need to name a resident for each state in which you do business. There are several businesses that, for a fee, will act as your agent in every state.

And while only required by law in a corporation, an operating agreement among the business's owners is highly recommended for all business forms. It clearly spells out the division of ownership, labor and profits, and often heads off disputes among the owners.

Taken together, all of these filings and requirements make up the legal, formal structure of your new business entity. Anything not addressed in these documents will be covered by a set of default statutory laws instituted by the state. You'll need to be aware of these specifics, as well as other unique drafting issues.

Warning

 A defectively formed LLC or corporation will be deemed a sole proprietorship if there is one owner, or a general partnership if there are two or more owners (as discussed in Chapter 6). In either case, the owner or owners will have unlimited, personal liability for all of the entity's debts and for the acts of the business's employees.

Therefore, because of the possible consequences, professional guidance is always a good idea when forming a business entity.

Articles of Organization

To start, each business form must be created by filing articles of organization with the state in which the owner has decided to form the business. The business owner is free to form the entity in any state, and not merely in the state in which he will be doing business. Delaware and, to a lesser extent, Nevada have emerged as popular sites for business formation (see Chapter 9 for choice of state issues).

When forming an LLC, a formal document known as the articles of organization must be filed with the state. In the case of the corporation, the articles of organization are usually termed "articles of incorporation."

When a corporation (as opposed to an LLC) is being formed, a statutory close corporation usually will be a better choice than a conventional corporation. The statutory close corporation must be formed by way of specialized articles of organization. These specialized articles specifically use the language required by the particular state's close corporation statute. Not all states permit the formation of a statutory close corporation (see Chapter 6 for a discussion of the statutory close corporation).

The entity legally comes into existence when the articles are accepted by the state. Thus, it is important to be able to prove, if necessary, that the articles were filed. The state will return a stamped copy of the articles. The stamp will note the effective date of the formation of the entity. For an additional fee, the state will return a certified copy of the articles.

A Records Kit can be purchased with pre-printed ownership certificates. One copy of the stamped (or certified) articles should be kept in the entity's Records Kit. Another copy of the articles should be kept in a separate secure location.

The entity should issue ownership certificates to the owners and record the issuance, including the consideration received in return, in its Records Kit and its accounting records.

Standard forms for the articles of organization (for an LLC, statutory close corporation or conventional corporation) are available from each state. The business owner can fill in the necessary information on the form.

Ideally, however, the articles of organization for an LLC or a corporation will be tailored to the business owner's specific requirements. No two situations are identical. A Sample Articles of Organization is included in the Appendices of this book. While each filing is unique to itself, there are a number of common elements that, at a *minimum*, make up standard articles of organization:

- name of the business

- principal location of the business

- purpose of the business

- agent for service of process

- classes of ownership interests

- initial managers and owners

Plan Smart

Generally, only articles of organization are necessary by law to create an LLC or a corporation. However, the small business owner should not be misled into thinking that these are the only documents necessary to form a sound business venture.

The small business owner operating an LLC or a statutory close corporation should also have an operating agreement, which includes a buy-sell agreement.

In a conventional corporation, bylaws take the place of an operating agreement, and the buy-sell agreement will be a separate document from the bylaws. Although in a closely held corporation, a shareholder agreement, which includes a buy-sell agreement, typically is used, along with the bylaws.

These documents, which allow the business owner to control such things as voting, management, division of profits and disposition of ownership interests, are discussed later.

Note that only the articles of organization are filed with the state. For this reason, many small business owners never adopt an operating agreement, bylaws or a buy-sell agreement. This is a mistake because, absent an operating agreement, the opportunity to control voting, management structure, profit sharing, etc., is lost.

In addition, this may be an even more dangerous mistake from an asset protection perspective. State law generally requires that a conventional corporation adopt bylaws after it is formed. However, no penalty is prescribed for failure to adopt bylaws. In many cases, because the bylaws are not filed with the state, the failure will not be discovered.

Nevertheless, if the failure is discovered, it may be at the most inopportune time (i.e., when the corporation faces a financial crisis). A plaintiff could use this failure to prove that the entity is defective or to pierce the veil of limited liability. In either case, the end result for the owners could be unlimited, personal liability for the business's debts.

By implication, a statutory close corporation must adopt an operating agreement, because the operating agreement takes the place of the bylaws. (A statutory close corporation also can employ bylaws in conjunction with an operating agreement, although this is usually unnecessary).

Thus, in the case of a statutory close corporation, a failure to adopt an operating agreement may have the same unfortunate consequences as a failure to adopt bylaws in a conventional corporation.

Moreover, as discussed below in more detail, articles of organization for a statutory close corporation must make the ownership interests subject to a buy-sell agreement. This condition usually is satisfied by incorporating a buy-sell agreement into the operating agreement. Thus, a lack of an operating agreement could mean that the statutory close corporation is invalid.

The majority of states do not require an LLC to adopt an operating agreement. This is consistent with the informal operating rules that apply to the LLC. Nevertheless, an LLC operating agreement provides the owners with formal guidance on issues such as voting, management and division of profits. Without this guidance, it is much more likely that disputes among the owners will arise and that piercing of the veil of limited liability will be applied by the courts.

Name of the Business

Legal Name. States require that the legal name of an LLC use the initials "LLC," or some derivation thereof, as prescribed in the state's LLC statute. Similarly, the legal name of a corporation must use the abbreviation "Inc.," or a similar term, as prescribed by the state's corporation statute.

Assumed Name. An LLC or a corporation may operate under a different name, which is termed a "fictitious" or "assumed" name. States also have rules that govern the selection of assumed names. Usually, states prohibit the use of certain terms in an assumed name. For example, usually the terms "LLC" or "Inc.," which are required in the legal name, cannot be used in the assumed name. The use of terms that refer to a financial institution (such as "bank") usually are prohibited (unless, of course, the entity is a separately licensed financial institution). The laws in each state are unique in this regard. For this reason, the business owner should always check the statutes in the state in which the entity will be formed and the states in which it will be doing business.

Typically, the business owner must register the assumed name with the state or with the county recording office in which the entity will be doing business. States charge a separate fee for the registration of an assumed name.

Trade Name as Intellectual Property. The business owner who is sure that the legal and assumed names selected are unique may want to simply use the selected names in the articles of organization and the assumed name registration. However, the name of a business entity, which is termed a trade name, is protected as a type of intellectual property.

If there is the possibility that another entity in the area may be using an identical or similar name, the owner can, for a small fee, have the state's corporations office conduct a name search. A name also can be reserved for a limited period.

Principal Place of Business

The principal place of business is, of course, the primary city and state in which the business will conduct its operations. However, after registering this location, nothing prevents the entity from conducting operations elsewhere.

Purpose of the Business

A detailed description of the purpose of the business usually is not required. In fact, the articles of organization forms in some states have pre-printed language that covers every situation. For example, the form might state that the business will be conducted "for any lawful purpose." When a more detailed description is used, the generic or catchall phrase "any other lawful purpose" should be used in addition to the detailed description.

Agent for Service of Process

Every state requires that the business owner name a resident of that state (an individual or an entity) as an agent for service of process. The agent is named in the articles of organization. In addition, an entity that registers to do business in another state also must name a resident agent in its foreign registration certificate.

The agent serves as the company's point person in legal matters regarding the state. Having a representative of your company physically located in the state allows the state to seal its jurisdiction over your business and its operations (this subject is explored in greater detail later in this chapter).

Classes of Ownership Interests

The Corporation. In the corporation, the articles must indicate the classes of shares (e.g., voting common stock and nonvoting common stock) that exist, and the number of shares within each class that are authorized. In addition, the articles must state whether the stock has a par value.

Par value is an arbitrary amount per share representing the minimum the corporation can receive in return when it issues the stock. The amount paid in for par value stock represents what is termed the corporation's minimum or legal capital. A corporation cannot legally make a distribution to the owners based on their ownership interests (i.e., a dividend, or redemption of shares) that impairs this minimum or legal capital (as discussed in Chapter 14). Distributions can be made to the owners in ways not subject to this restriction; the most common example is a salary paid to the owners for services rendered on behalf of the entity.

Corporations are not required to issue par value common stock. In fact, small corporations usually issue no par common stock. In this case, the entire amount paid in for the shares represents the minimum or legal capital, unless the corporation sets aside a portion of the proceeds within a certain period (e.g., 60 days).

Remember, you must be able to prove that the corporation was adequately capitalized, as undercapitalization can form the basis for piercing of the veil of limited liability (see Chapter 16). For this reason, in most cases, no amount is set aside from legal capital when no par common stock is issued.

Note that par value has no relationship to fair market value. Fair market value represents the true value of the shares, which is based on the value of all of the entity's assets, less its liabilities. Par value, as described above, is an *arbitrary* amount per share selected by the owners. Its only significance relates to the concept of minimum or legal capital.

The LLC. Generally, there is *no* requirement that the LLC describe different types of ownership interests in its articles of organization. Instead, consistent with the theme of simplicity that governs LLCs, this is accomplished in the LLC's operating agreement.

The concept of par value does not exist in the LLC, although there are similar restrictions on distributions to owners of an LLC based on their ownership interests. These restrictions (which are covered in Chapter 14) also can be avoided through the payment of salary to the owners.

Plan Smart

Generally, the LLC is a simpler business form, as compared to the corporation. Thus, many arrangements, including the designation of nonvoting interests, in the LLC can be controlled by way of the operating agreement, rather than the articles of organization.

This especially simplifies the operation of the LLC because the operating agreement is not filed with the state. Thus, a modification of the operating agreement also does not have to be filed with the state.

So if you wish to restructure your business by using nonvoting ownership interests, which are desirable for estate planning purposes (see Chapter 10), the LLC form allows you to make this change more simply and easily.

By contrast, an amendment to the articles of organization (for an LLC or a corporation) must be filed with the state, along with a required fee.

Finally, while not required, it may be desirable to designate classes of ownership interests in the articles of organization for an LLC, as a form of constructive notice. Because the articles are filed with the state and constitute a public document, their contents will be presumed to be public knowledge.

This same practice also can be followed with other matters not required by LLC statutes to be designated in the articles of organization. Of course, any advantage here must be weighed against the fact that changes to the articles of organization (but not the operating agreement) will require a filing with, and payment of a fee to, the state.

Initial Managers and Owners

The Corporation. Corporate articles of organization usually require that the business owner list the initial management structure (that is, the names and addresses of the initial officers and directors), in addition to the initial owners. State corporation statutes differ as to the number of directors and officers required. The modern view allows the owner to use one director, or waive the board of directors altogether in a small corporation, and to designate such officers, if any, as desired by the owner. Delaware and Nevada follow the modern view.

States following the more traditional view sometimes require a minimum number of directors, even in a small corporation. This number usually is equal to the number of shareholders, but typically no more than three directors are *required*. These states also require a minimum of two officers (a president and a secretary). In some of these states, the two officer positions must be held by two separate individuals. In others, one individual may assume both roles. If you are forming a corporation in a state other than Delaware or Nevada, check with the state's corporations office before deciding on the management structure for the corporation.

The Statutory Close Corporation. The statutory close corporation can waive the requirement for management by a board of directors and instead assign the duties normally performed by the board to the voting shareholders (or some other group). This is desirable because, as discussed later, it simplifies the management structure of the corporation. Note that this must be accomplished in the articles of organization, although the operating agreement will reinforce this arrangement.

The state's usual rules regarding corporate officers (see above) apply to the statutory close corporation.

In addition, a statutory close corporation can forego the requirement for a board of directors, but the waiver must be included in the articles of organization.

However, the articles for a statutory close corporation *must:*

- restrict ownership of the entity to a limited number of shareholders (30 or 50, depending on the state)

- subject the ownership interests to a buy-sell agreement

- prevent the corporation from making a public offering of its stock

States offer forms for the specialized articles necessary to create a statutory close corporation. The forms include these required provisions.

The LLC. Articles of organization for an LLC usually only require the listing of the names and addresses of the initial owners of the business. Some states also require that the articles of organization for an LLC indicate its management structure (i.e., whether the LLC will be member-managed or manager-managed). In the latter case, the names and addresses of the initial managers usually must be listed. A manager-managed LLC can facilitate the use of the LLC as an estate planning device (as discussed in Chapter 10).

Plan Smart

Terminology regarding owners and managers differs in an LLC and a corporation.

In a corporation, the owners are called shareholders. A conventional corporation is managed by a board of directors and officers. The officers make all of the day-to-day management decisions.

The officers are hired by the board of directors. The board sets the compensation of the officers and oversees the officers as they perform their duties. The board also makes all of the larger financial decisions, such as whether to issue additional common stock or declare a dividend. Directors usually serve for one-year terms in a small corporation. Initial directors (and officers) usually are named in the articles of organization. Subsequently, directors are elected by the shareholders.

Directors and officers also differ in another important respect. Officers are individual agents of the corporation, while directors must act as a group, through majority vote, at a duly constituted meeting or through a unanimously signed written waiver (see below).

In the statutory close corporation, usually there is no board of directors, and the voting shareholders assume the role of the board.

By contrast, in an LLC, the owners are termed "members." In the event no election is made in the articles of organization to make the LLC manager-managed, the presumption is that the LLC is member-managed. In this case, every owner, or member, is deemed a manager, and thus an individual agent of the LLC. In this respect, the member-managed LLC resembles a general partnership.

In a manager-managed LLC, a select group of members are designated as managers. (Managers also may be selected who are not members). A manager-managed LLC is often desirable for estate planning purposes, or where certain members will be passive investors.

In a manager-managed LLC, the members who are not managers have no management authority. However, provided that they hold voting member interests, the non-manager members still can vote on a limited number of issues, including selection of the managers, amendments to the articles and operating agreement, dissolution of the LLC, etc.

Usually, the LLC can assign its managers titles traditionally associated with officers in a corporation (i.e., president, vice-president, secretary and treasurer). One manager also can be designated a representative for tax matters, as permitted under the Internal Revenue Code. All of these designations are accomplished in the operating agreement.

Plan Smart

In some states, absent a provision to the contrary in the operating agreement for manager-managed LLC, members who are not managers are still deemed to be agents of the LLC, with the power to bind the LLC to contracts. It is therefore wise to provide in the operating agreement that non-manager members are not agents of the LLC. This, of course, is one example of why an operating agreement is desirable.

Furthermore, the law is not always clear when it comes to division of authority within an entity. Some issues must be decided by the owners (i.e., shareholders or members), while other issues are within the control only of the entity's managers.

It is not uncommon for an action to be authorized by the wrong group, thus making it unauthorized. Creditors can capitalize on improper authorizations in two ways. Creditors may be able to invalidate a particular action, such as the withdrawal of funds from the entity by the owners. In addition, improper authorizations can be used to pierce the veil of limited liability.

In a member-managed LLC, every member (i.e., owner) also is a manager. Thus, if all members sign an authorization, its validity cannot be challenged on the grounds that the authorization had to be signed by the managers. The members and managers are one single group.

However, as discussed previously and in more detail in Chapter 10, it often is desirable to form a manager-managed LLC and have the LLC issue nonvoting member interests to the non-managers. The voting members should be designated as the managers. In this way, once again, there is a single group (i.e., the voting members/managers). Thus, an authorization unanimously signed by this group is beyond challenge on the grounds that it was authorized by the wrong group.

As discussed above, the articles of organization should note that the LLC is to be manager-managed. The operating agreement then reinforces this fact and divides member interests into two classes: voting and nonvoting.

Therefore, to prevent confusion, it is important in a manager-managed LLC that any non-managers hold nonvoting member interests.

If the non-managers hold voting member interests, confusion may arise because the voting members will have rights to vote on all issues, except management issues. The dividing line between management issues and non-management issues is not always clear under state LLC statutes.

However, if the owners do decide to issue voting member interests to non-managers, it is especially imperative that the state statute be scrutinized to determine the proper lines of authority between the two groups (i.e., the members and the managers).

Similarly, in a statutory close corporation, the articles of organization can create two classes of common stock, voting and nonvoting, waive a board of directors and assign management duties to the voting shareholders. In this way, there is only one group, and the issue of improper authorization should not exist when that one group unanimously signs an authorization.

Foreign Registration Certificates

Before an LLC or a corporation can do business on a regular basis in another state (a state other than the one in which it was formed), the entity must file a foreign registration certificate with the other state and pay a required fee. The foreign registration fee usually is the same amount as the fee the state charges *to form* an entity of that type in the state.

A failure to register as a foreign entity *usually* does not invalidate the entity or the entity's contracts in that state. However, in a few states, the entity or its contracts may be deemed invalid. Distinguishing states in this respect shouldn't be necessary, as the issue can be avoided simply by registering the entity as a foreign entity in every other state in which it will be doing business. Typically, an entity needn't register in another state if it will be conducting only a few isolated transactions in the state.

State Fees

Each state charges a fee for the formation of an LLC or corporation in the state. (As discussed above, each state also charges an identical fee when a foreign entity registers to do business in the state). In the case of the LLC, there is usually a flat fee.

With the corporation, the fee is usually based on the number of shares the corporation is authorized to issue. This fee, however, is subject to a minimum charge. The minimum charge corresponds to a minimum number of authorized shares. Thus, a business owner who wants to pay the minimum fee to form a corporation should also select the corresponding number of authorized shares.

Example

In Delaware, the formation fee for a corporation is $0.01 for the first 20,000 shares of no par stock that is authorized, with a minimum fee of $50.

If the small business owner wants to pay the minimum fee, he will have 5,000 shares authorized (5,000 shares x $0.01 per share = $50)

With an LLC, the state formation fees are not based on the number of ownership interests. Instead, states usually charge a flat fee. This flat fee *typically* is lower than the minimum fee that states charge to form a corporation (see Chapter 6).

Warning

A few states (New York, Pennsylvania and Arizona) require that the articles of organization (or a foreign registration) for an LLC be published in a newspaper. New York, for example, requires that the articles, or foreign registration, be filed each week, for six weeks, in two different newspapers.

Fees for publication can be extreme. In some cases, publication fees can amount to $1,000-$2,000. If you will be forming an entity in one of these states, or registering to do business there, first obtain an estimate on the cost of publication, and consider using a statutory close corporation in lieu of an LLC (see Chapter 6 for a detailed discussion).

A corporation does not have to *issue* all of its *authorized* shares, but you should carefully consider how many to authorize, because any changes require that an amended articles of organization—and a fee—must be submitted to the state. Follow these guidelines, in deciding how many shares to issue:

- Don't issue too few shares (e.g., one share) because this could make the subsequent raising of capital problematic. For example, in a one-owner corporation, one share or 1,000 shares would both represent 100 percent ownership. However, if only one share were issued, and the original owner subsequently sought to raise additional capital from others, he would be forced to purchase some of the additional shares, or perhaps lose control of his corporation.

- On the other hand, don't issue all of the authorized shares. Otherwise, if the original owner subsequently sought to raise additional capital from others, he would be forced to draft and file an amendment to the articles of organization with the state of formation, along with a required fee.

Thus, for example, in Delaware, if 5,000 shares were authorized, in a one-owner corporation, an issuance of 1,000 shares to the owner would represent a sound choice. (Note that 1,000 shares may be represented by a single stock certificate).

In the LLC, while the concept of authorized shares does not exist, a similar strategy can be employed. It is advisable to divide LLC ownership interests into "shares." The original owner could receive, say, 1,000 shares for his investment. Subsequently, to raise capital from others, he could issue additional ownership shares, without significantly diluting his ownership interest.

Finally, as discussed below, a resident agent for service of process will be necessary when a business entity is formed. This involves an ongoing annual fee that averages about $75.

Agent for Service of Process

Every state requires that the business owner name a resident of that state (an individual or an entity) as an agent for service of process. The agent is named in the articles of organization. In addition, an entity that registers to do business in another state also must name a resident agent in its foreign registration certificate.

Service of process refers to the delivery of a summons and complaint, which is the required way of initiating a lawsuit. Generally, a state will have personal jurisdiction over a party only if the party is served with the summons and complaint within the geographical boundaries of the state.

By naming a resident agent in the state, the entity is, in effect, consenting, in advance, to the state's assertion of personal jurisdiction over the entity, in the event of a lawsuit in that state. To sue the entity in the state, a plaintiff merely has the summons and complaint served *on the resident agent,* who then mails a copy to the entity. Of course, if the entity will not be doing business in that state, it is unlikely it will be sued there.

If the owner is a resident of the state in which the entity is formed (or will be doing business, in the case of the registration of a foreign entity), usually the entity can simply name *the individual owner* as the agent for service of process.

Where the entity will be formed, or will be doing business outside of the owner's home state, a resident agent will have to be located. In states that are popular for business formation, including Delaware, numerous organizations exist that provide this service. Typically, resident agent fees average about $75 per year. In addition, in some states (e.g., New York), the owner can name the secretary of state's office as the resident agent.

Operating Agreements

The small business owner is most likely to form either an LLC or a statutory close corporation. In either case, it is, at the very least, prudent to have an operating agreement. As was suggested above, in the case of the statutory close corporation, an operating agreement may be legally required. In the case of a corporation, the operating agreement is usually called a "shareholder agreement."

When there are two or more owners of the entity, an operating agreement is especially desirable, because it can eliminate misunderstandings among the owners.

In addition, the operating agreement, in conjunction with the articles of organization, can be used to control voting, management structure and authority, division of profits, resolution of disputes, disposition of ownership interests and many other issues.

Plan Smart

Each owner of the entity should sign the operating agreement in front of two witnesses.

In addition, as long as they will cooperate, the spouses of the owners also should sign the agreement. This is important because, in the event of a divorce, a spouse of an owner could take over the owner's property rights, including, perhaps, the owner's interests in the business entity.

The LLC enjoys the advantage in this respect because the spouse could not become a member without the other owners' consent. Nevertheless, in any situation, the spouse's signature would mean that the spouse was bound by the agreement, irrespective of the particular rights that the spouse acquired.

Default Statutory Rules

In certain cases, absent contrary provisions in the articles of organization or operating agreement, state statutes apply default rules. As you may imagine, these default rules are not always desirable.

By default, an LLC is member-managed, and a statutory close corporation is managed by a board of directors. Similarly, the presumption, in both cases, is that all of the owners hold voting interests and divide profits and losses according to their relative ownership interests.

It is often desirable to modify each of these default rules and incorporate them into your articles of organization or operating agreement.

Similarly, in many cases, the state statute simply will provide no rule whatsoever. This invites disputes among the owners and slipshod management of the entity, which could lead to piercing of the veil of limited liability (see Chapter 16).

For example, state LLC statutes do not cover an extremely important issue—disposition of ownership interests. It usually is desirable to prevent an owner from selling his interest to an outsider.

However, absent a buy-sell agreement, which should be part of the operating agreement, an LLC owner is free to dispose of his interest as he sees fit. While the transferee of an LLC interest cannot become a full-fledged owner with voting rights without the other owners' consent (see Chapter 6), a transfer to an outsider can still disrupt the entity's operations.

Conversely, in the statutory close corporation, the transferee, in fact, becomes a full-fledged owner *without* the consent of the other owners (see Chapter 6). While the statutory close corporation is compelled by state statute to adopt a buy-sell agreement, the actual agreement can take different forms. The owners of the entity control how this is actually executed.

In addition, absent a provision in the operating agreement to the contrary, the parties are free to resolve disputes among themselves by way of a court proceeding. Mediation and arbitration usually are better alternatives to a court proceeding because they are much less expensive and less time consuming (as discussed in Chapter 17). However, mediation and arbitration are consensual. In other words, the parties to the dispute must agree to use mediation and arbitration, in lieu of a court proceeding. The best place to do this is in the operating agreement, which is executed before disputes arise.

Also, state statutes generally *allow* an LLC or a corporation to indemnify the entity's managers for losses that they incur while carrying out the entity's business. Indemnification is an important adjunct to the use of insurance (as discussed in Chapter 18). The statutes merely authorize the entity to include an indemnification provision in its operating agreement. The operating agreement (or bylaws in a conventional corporation) must take advantage of this opportunity and actually provide for indemnification.

Other issues may be adequately addressed in state statutes, but often it is advantageous to repeat the statutory language in the operating agreement. So, if a state statute is later amended, but the previous statute is written into the agreement, the owners do not have to be concerned that a new, and perhaps unknown, rule now governs the business's affairs. The existing rule in the operating agreement would remain valid.

For example, default rules usually mandate that a conventional corporation hold, at a minimum, annual meetings of shareholders and directors. A waiver of a board of directors in the statutory close corporation, of course, eliminates the need for annual meetings of the board of directors.

LLC statutes are more informal, mandating that certain actions need to be approved by the voting members, and that management decisions be approved by the voting members or the voting managers in a manager-managed LLC. However, usually LLC statutes are silent on the issue as to how frequently either group must meet.

Both the LLC and statutory close corporation (as well as a conventional corporation) can, according to state statutes, take action without formal meetings. Any action that would have been taken at a formal meeting may, instead, be accomplished through the execution of a written document, which is unanimously signed by the particular group that had authority over the issue (e.g., the shareholders or members). The notice requirement for meetings also is automatically waived, simply by way of execution of the document.

Plan Smart

Though this type of waiver is authorized by state statutes, the language from the particular state's statute should be incorporated into the entity's operating agreement. This should eliminate problems that might arise should the statute be amended. The owners of an entity certainly don't want to discover, in the midst of a financial crisis for example, that they were operating under older statutory provisions that had been replaced.

In addition, the incorporation of statutory provisions into an operating agreement gives the owners firm guidance on the rules that govern the entity. As questions arise, the owners are far more likely to refer to the operating agreement, as opposed to the state statute.

Other Formation Issues

Before drafting articles of organization or an operating agreement, the small business owner should always read the state statute that will govern the entity. State statutes can differ significantly. Remember that the statute for the state in which the entity will be formed will govern the entity's internal affairs.

Professional guidance is always recommended. Unfortunately, many small business owners seek legal guidance only after they have created an entity through the filing of articles of organization, perhaps at a point where they are considering an operating agreement. However, as discussed above, certain provisions must be created in the articles of organization, as opposed to the operating agreement (e.g., waiver of a board of directors in a statutory close corporation). Thus, legal guidance should be sought before the articles of organization are drafted, unless the small business owner has read the applicable state statute and is *absolutely sure* that he has incorporated any desirable provisions into the articles.

THE BUY-SELL AGREEMENT

State statutes governing the statutory close corporation actually mandate that the owners enter into a buy-sell agreement. Moreover, sound business planning dictates that a buy-sell agreement also be used in an LLC or conventional corporation, especially when there are two or more owners.

The buy-sell agreement prevents an owner from selling his interests to an outsider without the consent of the other owners. The agreement usually takes one of three forms:

- **Cross-Purchase Agreement** — In this form, a withdrawing owner agrees to sell his interest to the remaining owners. This is the simplest form of the buy-sell agreement. It is suitable especially for the small business with only a few owners. As the number of owners increase, this form can become unwieldy. In a larger business, an entity-purchase agreement may be more suitable.

- **Entity-Purchase Agreement** — In this form of the buy-sell agreement, the withdrawing owner agrees to sell his interest to the entity, which then retires the ownership interest.

- **Hybrid Agreement** — This form is a combination of the first two. Typically, the withdrawing owner must first offer his ownership interest to the entity. If the entity declines or is unable to make the purchase, then the shares must be offered to the other owners.

Ownership certificates must be endorsed with notice of the restriction on transfer created by the buy-sell agreement. In many cases, state statutes require that precise language be used in the ownership certificates. Thus, it is important to examine the particular state's statute and incorporate the exact required language into all ownership certificates.

Warning

The Appendices contain a Sample Operating Agreement, including a buy-sell agreement, for a Delaware LLC. An operating agreement should be professionally drafted and tailored to the needs of the particular owners and the business's operations. The sample operating agreement is for illustration purposes only!

A proper buy-sell agreement not only describes how an interest will be sold, but for how much as well. The agreement spells out how interests will be valued when they are sold, so as to avoid these kinds of disagreements.

Moreover, events may arise that could necessitate the selling of an ownership interest. Specifically, what if an owner goes bankrupt or is forced to liquidate or, worse yet, dies or becomes incapacitated? Insurance policies are often bought by owners to cover these circumstances.

Valuing the Interest

It is said that in the world of commerce, everything has a price. The problem is, most people have a hard time agreeing on that price. What is valuable to one person may have little value to another.

In addition, a business is comprised of any number of variables, each possessing its own values. As with any major purchase, a deal usually has to be negotiated to reach the final price.

To simplify the buy-sell process and ensure fairness for all owners, the buy-sell agreement should specify how the owners' interests are to be valued. Essentially, there are three choices:

- book value

- fair market value

- formula approach

Warning

Caution must be used in the selection of any formula because of its finality. If the parties have agreed to the formula, it is extremely unlikely that a challenge of its result will be successful.

Book Value

Book value represents the allocated amount of the particular interest, *as recorded in the entity's accounting records*. Thus, the amount is already determined. Accordingly, book value has the advantage that a costly appraisal is unnecessary.

On the other hand, book value should never be confused with fair market value (see below). When an interest is being purchased at book value, the seller is not receiving the fair market value of his interest. Typically, but not always, book value will be lower than fair market value. Thus, purchase at book value is simple, but can be inherently unfair to the withdrawing owner.

Plan Smart

The book value of a business is the amount recorded in the entity's accounting records for the owners' equity in the business. The book value of the business is also equal to the recorded "net assets" of the entity (i.e., the recorded amount for the assets, minus the recorded amount for the liabilities).

Book value is likely to be significantly lower than fair market value, especially in a thriving business, for two reasons. Under conventional accounting practices, one very valuable asset is not even recorded in the entity's accounting records—the business's internally generated goodwill. In many small businesses, this will be the entity's most valuable asset, one that, in fact, would represent a significant portion of the purchase price if the business were sold to an outsider. Because goodwill is not recorded, book value automatically excludes goodwill.

In addition, conventional accounting practice is still largely based on the historical cost principle. This principle dictates that, generally, with the exception of certain investments, assets remain in the entity's books at historical cost. In particular, subject to this narrow exception, while assets are written off or depreciated as they expire or, in some cases, when they suffer a decline in value, the recorded amount for assets is never increased for increases in the assets' fair value.

In short, the amounts for assets in the entity's accounting records (i.e., the book value) do not reflect fair market value, but instead reflect the original cost or a lower amount. In fact, with buildings, the discrepancy between book value and fair market value can be extreme. As buildings age, they are written off, through a process termed "depreciation." Yet, in reality, buildings usually appreciate in value. Thus, over time, the two amounts actually move in opposite directions, making the discrepancy larger.

Fair Market Value

Purchase at fair market value requires that the value of the entity's goodwill be included and that the entity's recorded assets be restated to fair market value. Both of these adjustments usually require an appraisal.

Clearly, purchase at fair market value is more equitable to the withdrawing owner. Purchase at book value deprives the seller of his share of the entity's goodwill and the appreciation in the value of the entity's recorded assets.

On the other hand, appraisals can be very expensive and, in certain cases, time-consuming. For this reason, when purchase at fair market value is desired, it is wise to provide in the buy-sell agreement that the parties may agree on "fair market value" informally, and that an appraisal is to be used only in the absence of an informal agreement among the parties as to the fair market value.

In addition, mediation and arbitration clauses in the operating agreement should also apply to any disputes that arise as to the valuation of an interest. This, in itself, may significantly reduce the cost (and time) that will be involved in assessing fair market value (see Chapter 17 for a discussion of mediation and arbitration).

Formula Approach

Because of the inherent unfairness of a purchase at book value, and the additional cost, time and complexity involved in a purchase at fair market value, some business owners rely on a formula approach designed to approximate fair market value without a formal appraisal.

One option is a purchase at book value, plus an arbitrary percentage (e.g. 5 percent). The arbitrary percentage is supposed to approximate the withdrawing owner's share of the entity's goodwill and of the appreciation in the entity's recorded assets.

Similarly, capitalization of earnings at a fixed percentage is sometimes used to approximate the fair market value of the withdrawing owner's interest. In this method, the entity's average annual net earnings for a period (e.g., the prior three years) are divided by the stated percentage to yield the presumed fair market value for *all* of the entity's assets, including its goodwill. By subtracting the entity's liabilities from this amount, the fair market value of the entity is derived

For example, if the annual earnings have averaged $90,000, and the capitalization rate is 10 percent, the presumed value of the assets is $900,000. If the liabilities total $600,000, the value of the entity is presumed to be $300,000.

A new business is unlikely to generate significant goodwill or appreciation of its recorded assets in its first year of operations. Further, during the first year of operations, relationships among the owners could be especially unstable.

Thus, if fair market value is to be used, one approach is to specify that, during the one-year period after the buy-sell agreement is signed, fair market value is presumed to be equal to book value.

This eliminates the expense of an appraisal, which in any event would probably yield a result that approximated book value.

Finally, the buy-sell agreement can apply different methods to fix the purchase price, depending on the circumstances. For example, the agreement might fix a lower amount (e.g., book value) as the price if the owner files a personal bankruptcy action, but a higher value (e.g., book value plus 5 percent, or appraised fair market value) in other circumstances.

The strategy in this example is designed to prevent a significant payout to a bankrupt owner (which would only pass to the owner's creditors) or to convince the bankruptcy trustee to abandon the owner's property interest in the business. This strategy is open to challenge, so advanced strategies, such as this one, should only be employed with the advice of an attorney.

Using Life Insurance

Sufficient cash may not be available to the entity, or to its owners, to make it feasible for the purchase of a withdrawing owner's interest. Usually, if the owners and/or the entity, as the case may be, are unwilling or unable to make the purchase, the buy-sell agreement provides that the withdrawing owner is free to sell his interest to an outsider.

Clearly, this defeats the very purpose of the buy-sell agreement. For this reason, life insurance, on the withdrawing owner's life, is frequently used to the finance the purchase of the interest.

When something called a cross-purchase agreement is used, owners take out life insurance polices on each other's lives. With the use of an entity-purchase agreement, *the entity* takes out polices on the lives of its owners, with the entity named as the beneficiary of the policies. The cross-purchase agreement is more commonly used in practice.

Obviously, life insurance can only be used to fund a purchase made on account of an owner's death. Funding the purchase of a withdrawing owner's interest, in other cases, can be controlled in several other ways.

The operating agreement may provide that an owner may not withdraw, except upon unanimous consent or subject to other enumerated conditions.

For example, the operating agreement might allow withdrawal by an owner who suffers a permanent disability. "Permanent disability" could be defined as a disability that prevents the owner from working in the business for six consecutive months. Disability insurance might be used, in the same way life insurance is used, to facilitate the purchase of the interest.

In addition, the buy-sell agreement may provide that, in certain cases (e.g., a voluntary withdrawal) the interest is to be valued at a lower amount (e.g., book value). Moreover, the buy-sell agreement may provide that the interest is to be purchased in installments, over a fixed period (e.g., five or 10 years). Any of these options can make it more practical to purchase the interest.

OTHER CONSIDERATIONS

After forming the business entity, the owner will have to apply to the Internal Revenue Service for an employer identification number (EIN). This is the identification number the business will use on all of its bank accounts, as well as on all of its income and employment tax filings.

In addition, in each state in which the entity will be doing business, you will have to apply to the state's tax department for a sales tax identification number and register with the state's labor department.

Other legal issues also should be considered. In particular, the owner should determine whether he needs a license to conduct the business, whether the business can be operated at its intended location under local planning and zoning laws (especially important if it is a home-based business), and whether contracts with consumers must take a particular written form.

Consumer contracts are likely to be the subject of special state legislation where an area has been marked by past abuse (e.g., home improvement contracts). Where applicable, to be valid, the contract may have to be in writing, contain certain disclosures, and be voidable by the consumer for a fixed period (typically three days).

However, state laws vary widely in these respects. The state's consumer protection department or a professional organization (e.g., a contractors' association) usually can provide information on any special requirements that must be met for consumer contracts.

For the actual process of forming the business entity, adequate record keeping is essential if the owner is to avoid the piercing of the veil of limited liability. Proper recordkeeping should begin even before the entity is formed (Chapter 16 covers these issues). Moreover, the formation of a business entity involves important estate planning and securities law issues (addressed in Chapter 10 and 11). Plus, strategies can be employed in structuring and funding the business enterprise, so as to limit personal and business liability (see Chapter 8).

Finally, the importance of a sound business plan cannot be overlooked. The business plan should include projections related to the market and competition, sales, expenses, breakeven point and required resources.

Clearly, the business can be adequately and carefully funded only if projections are made of the required resources. These types of projections also are essential if the entity is to avoid an accusation that asset transfers from the business to the owners were fraudulent (as discussed in Chapter 4). Similarly, these projections are important in defeating allegations that the entity was fraudulently capitalized (as discussed in Chapter 16).

The *Toolkit*™ book, *Business Plans That Work for Your Small Business, Second Edition*, can be used in developing a business plan. Useful information also can be found on CCH's extensive web site for small business owners, the *Business Owner's Toolkit*™ at http://www.toolkit.cch.com. Finally, any number of computer software programs can be used to develop a business plan that includes financial projections.

Part **III**

Avoiding Day-to-Day Liability Risks

Traditionally, business owners have relied on how-to guides that offer instruction *limited to the process of forming the business entity.*

Unfortunately, the *mere formation* of an LLC or a corporation is *not*, in itself, a sufficient asset protection strategy. Asset protection planning requires that the business be *structured and funded* to eliminate personal and business liability. These issues are addressed in Part II of this book.

However, the formation of an LLC or a corporation is *not* a sufficient asset protection strategy, *even when the entity is structured and funded to avoid personal and business liability.* The entity must also be *operated* in ways that preserve the owner's limited liability and, thus, protect the owner's personal assets outside of the entity as well as the business's assets (the owner's investment in the business). All of this is achievable with the strategies developed in Part III of this book.

Chapter 14: Withdrawing Funds from the Business is, in essence, a complement to the structuring and funding strategies presented in

---

Chapter 8. The business entity must be structured and funded strategically, to minimize the amount of vulnerable capital invested within the business form. In this way, the business's assets, which face the highest risk of loss, are protected, along with the owner's personal assets outside of the business form.

The withdrawal strategies developed in Chapter 14 ensure that vulnerable funds are withdrawn from the business entity as they are generated. Without withdrawal strategies, vulnerable funds would accumulate in the business entity, defeating the very purpose of the structuring and funding strategies implemented in accordance with Chapter 8.

This chapter presents the advantages and disadvantages of alternative withdrawal strategies, including distributions of earnings and payments to the owners for salary, loans and leases, with a special emphasis on the effect that fraudulent transfer restrictions and the self-employment tax have on these withdrawal methods. The chapter also examines the interrelationship between the fraudulent transfer restrictions imposed by state LLC and corporation statutes, and the restrictions imposed under the Uniform Fraudulent Transfers Act.

Finally, this chapter underscores the importance of authorizations and documentation when withdrawing funds from the business entity.

Chapter 15: Limiting Liability for Contracts and Torts explains the significant exceptions to the limited liability for owners of an LLC or a corporation, with respect to the business entity's debts. If an exception applies, unlimited personal liability for the business entity's debts is imposed on the owners. When this occurs, the very purpose for which an LLC or a corporation is created—limited liability—is lost.

Because business owners, typically, are unaware of these exceptions, the objective of this chapter is identification of the specific exceptions, both in terms of the entity's contracts and any torts (e.g., negligence) committed by the entity's employees. With this knowledge, and the strategies presented in this chapter, business owners can avoid these exceptions and, thus, preserve their limited liability for the business's debts.

Chapter 16: Piercing the Veil of Limited Liability examines another important exception to limited liability—the concept of creditors "piercing the veil of limited liability" through what are termed the alter ego theory or the undercapitalization theory.

Clearly, if either theory is applicable, the owners of the business will suffer unlimited personal liability for the business's debts, and the very essence of the LLC or corporation (limited liability) will be destroyed. This chapter examines the nature of these two theories and the strategies that can ensure neither theory will be applied to the business.

Chapter 17: Navigating the Court System identifies aspects of the court system, itself, that are significant risk factors for business owners. Yet, through an understanding of how the court system heightens the risk of loss, and how to use the strategies presented in this chapter, business owners can control the court system and, thus, significantly reduce their overall exposure to liability.

Chapter 18: Insurance—The Protection of Last Resort explains the ins and outs of your last line of defense in asset protection. Ideally, the small business owner will structure his financial affairs so that claims will not be made or, if claims occur, the claimants will be unable to satisfy their claims from the business owner's personal or business assets. The asset protection strategies advocated throughout this book are based on these principles.

Occasionally, however, claims will be made. Some of these claims may penetrate the layers of protection set up by the business owner. If this occurs, one last layer of protection still should be ready to defend the business owner—insurance.

This chapter describes the nature of liability and property insurance in general, and the specific types of individual liability and property polices appropriate for business owners. Emphasis is placed on understanding and planning for coverage and exclusion issues that arise in each type of policy. This chapter also covers important points that arise when business owners deal with insurance companies on claims, including notification rules, the duty to defend clause and the use of bad faith claims against insurance companies.

Chapter 14

Withdrawing Funds from the Business

As we now know, an owner of an LLC or a corporation enjoys limited liability for the business's debts. In other words, the owner's liability is limited to the amount he invested (or promised to invest) in the business entity. This is explained in detail in Chapters 6 and 7.

In contrast, the entity itself has *unlimited, personal liability* for all of its debts. Further, because of the inherent risks associated with the operation of a business entity, generally the assets invested within the business form are more vulnerable than the owner's personal assets outside of the business form.

Thus, owners should strive to minimize the amount of vulnerable capital invested within the business form. In strategically funding a business entity, the owner can accomplish this goal in several different ways, including initially investing a minimum amount in the entity; capitalizing the entity with debt (i.e., loans and leases); and using equity to encumber the entity's assets with liens that run in favor of the owner (or a separate entity controlled by the owner), and which result from extensions of credit (e.g., loans, unpaid salary, etc.) from the owner to the entity (see Chapter 8 for a discussion of protecting capital through separate holding and operating companies).

However, to be effective on a continuous basis, the strategy of minimizing the amount of vulnerable capital invested within the business form must be coupled with a strategy calling for *regular withdrawals* of vulnerable funds from the business as these funds are generated.

Funds generated by the business entity, but left within the business form, are in essence invested in the entity, as if they were invested from an outside source, but in a way that leaves them vulnerable to the claims of the business's creditors. A continual withdrawal of funds, as they are generated, guarantees that vulnerable funds will not accumulate within the business entity.

To efficiently accomplish this goal, you'll need an understanding of the restrictions on withdrawals, before you then can review the withdrawal methods available to you. Once your plan to minimize vulnerable capital is in place, you'll need proper authorization and documentation to secure the withdrawals from a creditor's challenge.

Plan Smart

Clearly, a business planning a major expansion, requiring a significant amount of capital, may want to accumulate assets within the business form. Assets can be safely accumulated, provided that the owners employ other asset protection strategies in lieu of continuous withdrawals, in particular the use of liens that run in favor of the owners (see Chapter 8 for details on structuring and funding decisions). The best strategy in this case, of course, would be to accumulate the funds in the holding entity.

Alternatively, these funds may be withdrawn, in accordance with a regular withdrawal policy, as discussed in this chapter, and then reinvested when necessary.

RESTRICTIONS ON WITHDRAWALS

Before deciding on the best withdrawal strategy, small business owners must be aware of the different restrictions on withdrawals in every state's statutes governing LLCs and corporations, as well as the general restrictions imposed by the Uniform Fraudulent Transfers Act (UFTA).

The UFTA outlaws two different types of fraudulent transfers: constructive fraud and actual fraud (Chapter 4 details restrictions on asset transfers, in general, imposed by the Uniform Fraudulent Transfers Act).

As discussed below, the UFTA's *actual fraud* provisions will apply to withdrawals from a business entity. Further, the separate provisions imposed by the LLC and corporation statutes are based on the UFTA's *constructive fraud* provisions, although, the corporation statutes, in particular, usually impose more significant restrictions than the UFTA.

Actual Fraud Restrictions

The actual fraud restrictions, under the UFTA, *will apply* to *all transfers from a business entity to the owners*, including distributions to owners on account of their ownership interest (i.e., dividends and ownership reductions), as well as payments for salary, loans and leases.

Actual fraud exists only when it can be proven that the transferor *intended* to defraud creditors through the transfer. Under this test, a transfer is not automatically deemed fraudulent simply because certain conditions are met.

Instead, courts use a number of criteria to determine the transferor's intent, including:

- an assessment of the transferor's motive

- the timing of the transfer

- the solvency of the transferor at the time of the transfer

- whether the transfer was concealed from the creditor

- whether the business received adequate consideration in return for the transfer

- whether at the time the transfer occurred the debtor had incurred a substantial debt

- whether the transfer was made up of all or substantially all of the debtor's assets

- whether the transfer was to an insider (i.e., family member or controlled entity)

- whether the debtor absconded or tried to hide assets

- whether the debtor transferred assets to a lien holder, who then transferred the assets to an insider of the debtor

As described above, actual fraud requires that a creditor prove that the transferor's *actual intent* in making the transfer was to defraud creditors. This can be a very difficult burden, absent specific circumstances from which this intent can be clearly inferred.

Constructive Fraud Restrictions

Under the UFTA, constructive fraud arises when both:

1. the transferor receives nothing (or less than full value) in return for a transfer

2. the transferor is insolvent at the time of, or because of, the transfer, under either a cash flow test (unable to pay debts as they come due) or a balance sheet test (liabilities exceed assets)

When *both* of these two conditions apply, the transfer *is automatically deemed to be fraudulent, irrespective of the transferor's intent.* Fortunately, with respect to transfers from the business entity to its owners, constructive fraud is easy to avoid because transfers to the owners *for return value* take the transfers out of the reach of the definition of constructive fraud. Thus, payments to the owners for salary, loans and leases do not come within the purview of the constructive fraud restrictions. (For more information on the UFTA in general, see Chapter 4.)

But in most cases, the UFTA's constructive fraud provisions are supplanted by provisions in the state LLC and corporation statutes.

Statutory Fraud Limits on the LLC

In the case of LLCs, restrictions imposed by state LLC statutes are usually identical to the UFTA's constructive fraud restrictions. This is consistent with the theme of simplicity that applies to the LLC.

Thus, in the LLC, distributions to owners on account of their ownership interests (i.e., distributions of LLC income or redemption of an owner's interest) will automatically be deemed fraudulent if both:

1. the LLC receives nothing (or less than full value) in return for a transfer

2. the LLC is insolvent at the time of, or because of, the transfer under either a cash flow test (unable to pay debts as they come due) or a balance sheet test (liabilities exceed assets).

The constructive fraud restrictions imposed by the LLC statutes are *limited to* distributions of LLC income or redemptions of an owner's interest, and thus do *not* apply to payments by the LLC to the owners for salary, loans and leases. So in this way, they differ from the UFTA's constructive fraud provisions.

Note that, by definition, a distribution of LLC income or the redemption of an owner's interest will be for *no return consideration.* Thus, the first criterion under the constructive fraud test is really irrelevant, and the only issue involves the solvency of the LLC under the cash flow test and the balance sheet test (see Chapter 4 for more on these tests).

Statutory Fraud Limits on the Corporation

For corporations, state laws usually impose the same types of constructive fraud provisions on transfers. First, a transfer is fraudulent if the corporation receives nothing (or less than full value) in return.

Second, solvency is determined by imposing a cash flow test and a balance sheet test to prove the legality of distributions to owners on the basis of their ownership interests (i.e., distributions of earnings or dividends and stock redemptions). However, while these statutes impose the *standard* cash flow test (inability to pay debts as they come due), they usually apply a *more restrictive* balance sheet test than that used by the UFTA (see Chapter 4 for more on these tests).

WITHDRAWAL METHODS

A small business owner should always seek to keep at a minimum the amount of funds within the business entity vulnerable to a creditor. Formal and regular withdrawals, backed in writing, are one of the best ways to do this. Funds can be withdrawn thorough:

- distributions of earnings to the owners (i.e., dividends)

- payments of salary to the owners for services rendered

- payments to the owners for loans and leases that the owners have extended to the entity

- the contractual obligation of guaranteed payments

- sales of accounts receivable

Each of these alternatives is analyzed in detail later in this chapter.

In general, the UFTA's constructive fraud provisions can cause significant problems for small business owners, because if certain conditions are met, transfers are *automatically* deemed to be fraudulent, irrespective of the transferor's intent. Similarly, the restrictions imposed by state LLC and corporation statutes on distributions to owners on account of their ownership interests can cause these same problems because these restrictions are based on the UFTA's constructive fraud concept. Further, as addressed below, the balance sheet version of the constructive fraud test as applied by these statutes is even more severe than the UFTA's balance sheet test.

However, distributions to owners *for salary, loans and leases* avoid this problem, as the constructive fraud provisions under the UFTA or the state corporation and LLC statutes do not apply to these distributions. In particular, because these distributions are for return value, the UFTA's constructive fraud does not apply. Also, because the distributions are made to the owners, *other than on* account of their ownership interests, the restrictions imposed by state LLC and corporation statutes also do not apply.

In short, distributions for salary, loan and lease payments, as opposed to distributions of earnings, are much more likely to be valid, especially when the entity is experiencing a financial crisis. Only the

UFTA's actual fraud concept will apply as a restriction in making these distributions.

The impact of self-employment tax may affect the choice of withdrawal methods (i.e., whether the withdrawals are structured as distributions of earnings, salary, or payments for loans and leases). This tax (discussed in detail in Chapter 7) is the Social Security and Medicare tax imposed on earnings from self-employment. Essentially, the tax is comprised of the rate that, outside of self-employment, employees pay *plus* the matching rate that employers pay, for a total of 15.3 percent.

Clearly, the self-employment tax is significant. How the self-employment tax affects the choice of withdrawal methods depends on whether the entity is a corporation or an LLC.

In general, *all of the earnings* of the LLC are subject to the self-employment tax, *irrespective of whether or how these earnings are distributed.* (One exception may be payments from loans and leases, as discussed below).

Current proposed IRS regulations would exempt distributions (other than for salary) to owners who work for the LLC fewer than 500 hours per year. However, the proposal has faced opposition, and its enactment is in doubt. In short, the self-employment tax represents one of the few situations where the corporation may enjoy an advantage over the LLC.

Dividend Distributions

By definition, a distribution of a corporation's income (i.e., a dividend) or in redemption of an owner's interest (i.e., a stock redemption) will be for *no return consideration*. Thus, the first criterion under the constructive fraud test again really is irrelevant, and the only issue involves the solvency of the corporation, under the cash flow test and the balance sheet test.

The cash flow test, under the corporation statutes, is identical to the cash flow test under the UFTA. Thus, if a distribution to an owner on account of his ownership interest is made when a corporation is unable to pay its debts as they come due, the distribution *automatically* is deemed to be fraudulent.

State corporation statutes also impose a balance sheet test. However, as described below, the balance sheet test under the *corporation* statutes, which is limited to distributions of earnings (i.e., dividends) and stock redemptions, is much more restrictive than the balance sheet test imposed by the UFTA.

The actual balance sheet test applied to dividends and stock redemptions varies, to a certain degree, from state to state, and is based on the capital structure of the corporation.

Finally, distributions for dividends and stock redemptions by a corporation also will be restricted by the earned surplus test (described below).

Balance Sheet and Earned Surplus Tests for Dividends

Most states restrict distributions to the owners in the form of dividends or stock redemptions to the corporation's "earned surplus." This account will always be *less than the corporation's assets minus its liabilities,* and thus is a more restrictive test than the balance sheet version imposed by the UFTA.

The laws vary from state to state. Corporation statutes in some states may apply the *standard* balance sheet test (liabilities exceed assets) rather than the more restrictive earned surplus version of this test, along with the cash flow test.

Even LLC statutes, which usually apply the standard balance sheet test, as well as the standard cash flow, can vary from state to state.

To determine the exact restrictions that will apply to these distributions, it always is wise to check the statute in the particular state in which the business entity was formed and consult a legal advisor regarding the interpretation of this statute.

Finally, some state corporation statutes apply a less restrictive version of the earned surplus test. This test, in terms of restrictions, is somewhere between the standard balance sheet test and the earned surplus test. This version underscores the variability among the states with respect to these restrictions. This less restrictive test, which applies in Delaware and Nevada (among other states), is described later.

Plan Smart

Because of the nature of the earned surplus test, it is important that small business owners have a basic understanding of a corporation's financial structure and the terminology used to describe the elements that comprise this structure.

A corporation's financial structure can be represented by what accountants term the accounting equation: assets = liability + owner's equity. The liabilities (i.e., debts) and the owner's equity (i.e., the owner's investment) represent the two ways that the owners of the corporation can finance the corporation's acquisition of assets.

The owner's equity is subdivided into two categories, which represent the two ways that owners can make contributions to the corporation:

- *Contributed capital, which includes the contributions to the corporation in return for common stock*

- *Earned surplus, (also called retained earnings) which is comprised of the corporation's cumulative earnings, less distributions of those earnings (i.e., dividends)*

The concept that an owner can make an investment to a corporation in two ways can be understood by an analogy to a savings account. Let's say an individual deposits $100 into a new savings account that earns 4 percent interest. At the end of the first year, the account has earned $4 of interest, which the depositor leaves in the account. His initial investment, or contributed capital, is $100. At the end of the year, the retained earnings or earned surplus in the account amounts to $4. At the end of the year, the total investment, or the owner's equity, in the account is $104. Really, the $4 contribution, in the form of earned surplus (retained earnings), is no different than a withdrawal of the $4 of interest, which is then followed by a deposit of $4.

The contributed capital (common stock) is further divided into the *minimum or stated capital* (amount paid in for par value or, absent a special allocation, the total amount paid in for no par stock) and the *capital surplus* (amount paid in above minimum, or stated capital).

When par value common stock is issued, the minimum or stated capital will be equal to the amount paid in for the par value. The amount paid in above par value is the capital surplus.

When no par value common stock is issued, the entire amount paid in will be minimum or stated capital, unless within a fixed period (e.g., 60 days) the corporation makes a special allocation of a portion of these proceeds to capital surplus (see Chapter 13 for a discussion of par value and no par stock). Usually, no allocation is made, as an allocation could possibly open the corporation to a piercing of the veil of limited liability argument, based on the undercapitalization theory (as described in Chapter 16).

As noted above, the owner's equity component of the accounting equation can be divided into these basic constituents:

Owner's Equity:

- Contributed Capital (Common Stock):

  — Minimum or Stated Capital (amount paid in for par value or, absent a special allocation, total amount paid in for no par stock)

  — Capital Surplus (amount paid in above minimum or stated capital)

- Earned Surplus or Retained Earnings (cumulative income minus dividends paid)

The common state corporate earned surplus version of the balance sheet test, as applied to dividends, is illustrated in the following example.

Example

Let's say a corporation's financial structure is depicted by the following equation:

$$assets = liabilities + owner's\ equity$$

$$\$100,000 = \$60,000 + \$40,000$$

Let's say the owner contributed $25,000 of owner's equity, through the purchase of common stock, that the common stock has no par value, and that the corporation has not allocated any portion of the $25,000 to capital surplus. Thus, the corporation's minimum or stated capital is $25,000. This also is the total amount of the corporation's contributed capital.

The remaining balance of owner's equity, $15,000, is the corporation's earned surplus or retained earnings. This amount represents the corporation's cumulative earnings, less any distributions of these earnings to the owners (i.e., dividends).

Under the constructive fraud balance sheet test applied in most states, distributions of dividends and for stock redemptions must be limited to the amount of earned surplus. Thus, the corporation can distribute a maximum of $15,000 to the owners on account of their ownership interests.

Because dividends, by definition, are a distribution of earnings, limiting dividends to available earned surplus or retained earnings is logical.

However, the earned surplus version of the balance sheet test usually applies to *both* distributions of earnings (i.e., dividends) *and* to stock redemptions. Application of this restriction to *stock redemptions* really doesn't seem to make sense, because stock redemptions are not paid out of earned surplus, but instead come out of capital stock.

This extension came about as states broadened the definition of the term "distribution" beyond dividends, so as to include *all distributions on account of an ownership interest,* including stock redemptions. Logical or not, the earned surplus restriction applies to stock redemptions as well as dividends in most states.

Plan Smart

Stock redemptions and redemptions of LLC interests can qualify for favorable capital gains treatment. Before redeeming or selling an interest in a corporation or an LLC, small business owners should consult a tax advisor.

More Liberal Dividend Tests

Delaware and Nevada (among other states) apply a less restrictive earned surplus test in determining the legality of distributions of earnings and stock redemptions. The less restrictive test allows the corporation to pay dividends and stock redemptions out of earned surplus or the net income of the current or prior year (i.e., capital surplus).

As previously noted, closely held corporations typically issue no-par stock and make no allocation from the amount received to capital surplus. Thus, in this case, the entire proceeds received for the stock are minimum (legal) capital. In this case, the entire amount received for the stock is minimum or stated capital, and there is no capital surplus.

The ability to pay a dividend or a stock redemption out of the current and prior year's net income is a significant improvement over the standard earned surplus test. When the corporation has no earned surplus, or a negative balance in earned surplus, the expanded test may allow the corporation to pay dividends or redeem stock.

As discussed above, the earned surplus account represents the corporation's *cumulative earnings (or loss), less distributions of earnings (i.e., dividends)*. Thus, a corporation that has generated losses or that has paid out significant dividends in past years may have no earned surplus or a negative earned surplus. Under the *standard* earned surplus test, no dividends may be distributed or stock redemptions paid in this situation. However, under the more liberal test, if the corporation has net income in the current or prior year, dividends may be distributed or stock redemptions paid, *even though the net income for these periods is not sufficient to erase the deficit in earned surplus*.

Clearly, this more liberal test is especially important to startup companies, which may generate large losses for several years before turning a profit.

Example

Now let's say the financial structure of the corporation in the prior example, after two years of operation, is depicted by the following accounting equation:

assets = liabilities + owner's equity.

$30,000 = $20,000 + $10,000

In the prior example, the owners contributed $25,000 of owner's equity through the purchase of common stock. This $25,000 is the corporation's total contributed capital, and the minimum or stated capital, as the stock is no par and no allocation was made to capital surplus.

Now the owner's equity is $10,000 because the corporation has a negative balance of -$15,000 in earned surplus or retained earnings. Contributed capital of $25,000, net of the negative balance of -$15,000 in earned surplus or retained earnings, yields the total owner's equity of $10,000.

Finally, the corporation earns net income of $4,000 in year three, and another $4,000 in year four. Under the standard earned surplus test, no dividend (or stock redemption) may be paid in any of the years, because even after the net income for years three and four is added to earned surplus, the earned surplus is still -$7,000 (-$15,000 deficit after year two, offset by $8,000 of total earnings for years three and four).

However, under the more liberal test applied in Delaware, Nevada and some other states, the corporation may pay dividends (or stock redemptions) of $8,000 out of the year three and four earnings.

The cash flow test will still apply, *as a separate constructive fraud test,* even in states that apply more liberal versions of the earned surplus version of the balance sheet test. Thus, in the last example, if the corporation were unable to pay its debts as they came due, the corporation would not be able to pay dividends or stock redemptions, despite the earnings in years three and four.

In addition, as noted above, while the specific constructive fraud tests in state corporation and LLC statutes replace the UFTA's constructive fraud test, the UFTA's *actual fraud* provisions apply to *all transfers.* Thus, the UFTA's actual fraud provisions will apply *as a separate limitation* to distributions on account of an ownership interest (i.e., distributions of earnings and redemptions of ownership interests).

Plan Smart

As was discussed above, state LLC statutes usually apply the standard cash flow test and the standard balance sheet test in the same way that these two tests apply under the UFTA's constructive fraud provisions. The LLC statutes also apply only with respect to distributions to owners on account of their ownership interests.

However, in Nevada, an LLC can waive application of the balance sheet test. A waiver of the balance sheet test leaves only the cash flow test as a constructive fraud restriction, and thus allows the LLC a greater opportunity to make distribution of earnings and for ownership redemptions. This waiver, which is recommended, must be accomplished in the articles of organization for the LLC.

More liberal restrictions on distributions of earnings by corporations help explain why Delaware and Nevada are popular choices for business formation, and why small business owners should consider forming the business entity in one of these states (see Chapter 9 for a discussion of choice of state issues).

Payments for Salary

Salary payments are the most common form of withdrawal for small business owners. IRS rules limit payments to reasonable compensation, and the courts have consistently allowed rather high salaries to the owners of small businesses.

In addition, constructive fraud provisions do not limit the payment of salaries because this income is by definition in exchange for return value (i.e., time spent working for the business). However, the UFTA's actual fraud provisions, and the financial tests associated with them, still apply to these types of withdrawals from the business.

The important thing to remember about salary payments, when it comes to these fraud provisions, is to make these withdrawals regular and in writing. Good recordkeeping will go a long way toward proving the validity of these withdrawals.

Generally, for salary payments, there is an important tax situation to consider. All the earnings of an LLC are subject to the self-employment tax, as opposed to a corporation where the tax is imposed only on salary paid to the owners. This difference can affect how you structure the withdrawals from your business based on the form you do business in.

Salary Tax Issues for the Corporation

In the corporation, the self-employment tax is imposed *only on actual salary paid to the owners*. Thus, the self-employment tax may be avoided by simply distributing earnings (i.e., dividends) to the owners rather than paying salary for services rendered. Moreover, because small business owners who operate a corporation usually will elect subchapter S corporation tax status, there will be no double tax on dividends (see Chapter 7 for a discussion of avoiding the double tax on dividends).

The advantage of paying dividends (i.e., avoiding the self-employment tax) must be weighed against the disadvantage of distributing earnings, as opposed to paying salary, which is discussed above. In particular, payment of salary avoids the constructive fraud provisions in the UFTA and the stringent state corporation statutes imposed on distributions of earnings.

In addition, salary earned or accrued is exempt under many state post-judgment exemptions, as well as under federal bankruptcy exemptions, subject to certain limits (as discussed in Chapter 3). Distributions of earnings or dividends will not normally meet the definition of "wages" or "salary," and therefore will not be exempt. Thus, from an asset protection viewpoint, payment of salary offers advantages over mere distributions of earnings.

Of course, elimination of taxes is a form of asset protection (as discussed in Chapters 5, 6 and 10). Thus, small business owners must weigh the relative benefits of each form of asset protection.

As a general rule, in the early years of a business, when the entity is likely to be *technically* insolvent, or have no net income, and thus no earned surplus or retained earnings if it is a corporation, it may be wise to pay salary, so that the constructive fraud provisions under the UFTA or the state's corporation statute will not apply. It also qualifies the distributions under the state and federal exemption provisions in the event the business fails, resulting in litigation or, possibly, a bankruptcy filing.

As the business grows, and thrives, producing regular and substantial income, withdrawals in the form of distributions of earnings may be a better alternative than payment of salary, because these payments avoid the self-employment tax. In addition, the constructive fraud provisions will not be a real issue due to the business's sound financial position.

Overall, a better, more complementary approach, that works in both the early and more productive years of a business entity, is withdrawal of funds as loan and lease payments.

Salary Tax Issues for the LLC

Generally, the earnings of the LLC will be subject to the self-employment tax, irrespective of whether or how these earnings are distributed.

Therefore, there is no self-employment tax advantage to distributing earnings as opposed to paying salary. In other words, there is *no disadvantage*, as far as self-employment taxes are concerned, to paying salary as opposed to distributing earnings. However, because the state LLC statutes usually impose the same constructive fraud test as the UFTA, the paying of salary in the LLC also does not confer any advantage.

In contrast, as discussed above, the state corporation statutes impose more stringent balance sheet tests than what is imposed by the UFTA. Thus, in the case of the corporation, the payment of salary confers a benefit, because salary is not paid on account of an ownership interest, and thus helps you to avoid the state corporation statutes' more stringent balance sheet tests.

Nevertheless, similar to the corporation, an LLC's payment of salary, as opposed to distribution of earnings, does qualify the distribution under the state and federal asset exemption provisions. Thus, especially because there are no self-employment tax disadvantages, overall, payment of salary is the better alternative in the LLC.

Finally, an effort should be made to structure the LLC's payments of salary as "guaranteed payments." The advantages are explained in detail later.

Payments for Loans and Leases

Using loans and leases has multiple advantages for the small business owner. From an asset protection standpoint, physical property secured by loans and leases running to the owner will not be lost to a creditor when the business owner is also a secured creditor for the property (as explained in Chapter 8). When creditors line up, the business owner will be among the first in line.

Moreover, courts have consistently held that payments for loans and leases are legitimate expenses. These expenses allow the owner to withdraw vulnerable funds from the operation, instead of allowing them to accrue and making them a target.

In addition, payments from corporations for loans and leases are exempt from the self-employment tax if the recipient is not in the regular business of extending loans or leasing property. The LLC enjoys the same self-employment tax advantage as a corporation when it makes payments for leases and loans, but only in specific circumstances.

Loan/Lease Tax Issues for the Corporation

Self-employment tax regulations exempt payment for loans and leases, where the recipient is not in the regular business of extending loans or leasing property. Small business owners should always check with a tax advisor before assuming this will be the outcome under the particular circumstances.

In addition, because these distributions are for return value (similar to payments for salary), they are not subject to the UFTA's constructive fraud provisions. Moreover, these distributions are not made to owners on account of their ownership interests (again, similar to salary). Thus, the distributions also are not subject to the constructive fraud restrictions imposed by state corporation and LLC statutes. However, in contrast to payments for salary, these distributions also avoid the self-employment tax.

In short, this alternative offers the ability to withdraw funds in a way that avoids *both* the self-employment tax *and* the onerous constructive fraud restrictions. Further, as discussed in Chapter 8, funding the business entity with loans and leases is a significant asset protection strategy. The use of this type of debt funding ensures that assets contributed by owners to the entity will not be vulnerable to the claims of the business's creditors. Thus, the use of loans and leases should be a first-line withdrawal strategy.

Loan/Lease Tax Issues for the LLC

As discussed previously, for the corporation, withdrawing funds as payments for loans and leases offers significant advantages and should ordinarily be a first-line choice for withdrawing funds.

Overall, the same advantages apply in the case of the LLC. However, in the one-owner LLC, the self-employment tax advantage with respect to loans and leases is not as clear.

While, essentially, the tax treatment of a one-owner LLC and a multi-owner LLC is identical, the tax classification in each situation is somewhat different. For tax purposes, a multi-owner LLC is classified as a partnership. (Note that this classification is *only for tax purposes* and does not affect the limited liability of the owners of the LLC). Thus, the multi-owner LLC files an information return with the IRS, which reports the LLC's income and the allocation of this income to the individual owners. The owners then report their share of the income on their personal income tax returns.

The multi-owner LLC should enjoy the same exact self-employment tax advantage with respect to payments for loans and leases that owners of a corporation enjoy. Thus, the payments should not be subject to the self-employment tax if the recipients are not in the regular business of extending loans or leasing property. In this case, owners would pay self-employment tax only on their share of LLC earnings, plus payments received for salary.

Further, funding an LLC with debts (i.e., loans and leases) offers the same distinct asset protection advantages, which are described above for the corporation. Thus, in the case of the multi-owner LLC, withdrawals as payments for loans and leases also should be a first-line strategy.

In the case of the one-owner LLC, the situation is somewhat less clear, because the one-owner LLC, technically, is classified as a "disregarded entity" for tax purposes, similar to a sole proprietorship. (Once again, this classification is *only for tax purposes* and does not affect the limited liability of the owner). Because the entity technically does not exist for tax purposes, it files *no form at all* with the IRS. The owner simply reports the LLC's income on his personal income tax return. This greatly simplifies the payment of income taxes and is consistent with the theme of simplicity that applies to LLCs.

However, this also means that payments by the LLC to the owner for loans and leases will not be recognized on the tax return, because *for tax purposes* the entity and the owner are one in the same. Due to this fact, these payments may not escape the self-employment tax. Conceivably, having the LLC make these payments to a separately owned LLC will fall to the same argument, as the other LLC also will be "disregarded" for tax purposes.

Of course, if even one other person (i.e., another family member) were an owner, irrespective of how nominal the ownership interest, then the LLC would be a multi-owner LLC and should come under the partnership version of the rules, which are described above (absent the application of any aggregation rules, which might, for example, count all of the family's interests as one interest).

As described in Chapter 10, conveying ownership interests to family members also can be a very effective estate planning, and thus asset protection, strategy. In short, qualifying the LLC as multi-owner *may* allow the LLC to avoid the self-employment tax with respect to payments for loans and leases. However, because this area of law is still currently developing, it is especially wise to check with a tax advisor to determine the self-employment tax consequences of particular withdrawal strategies in an LLC.

Finally, the use of "guaranteed payments," which is explained in detail later, should be considered when operating a multi-owner LLC.

Plan Smart

Withdrawing funds as salary and for loans and leases offers advantages over mere distributions of earnings.

In summary, in the case of both the corporation and the LLC, consideration should be given to making payments for loans and leases as a first-line withdrawal method. In the early years of a corporation, and in the LLC in general, salary also is a sound choice. In later years, when a corporation is thriving, distributions of earnings (i.e., dividends), coupled with payments for loans and leases, may be the better alternative, as these distributions will avoid the self-employment tax.

Guaranteed Payments and the Multi-Owner LLC

The small business owner should be familiar with the tax code concept of "guaranteed payments" and how it applies to the multi-owner LLC. Whether payments for salary, loans and leases constitute guaranteed payments will affect the tax basis of each owner, and exactly how the information return of the LLC will report the payments.

Specifically, payments to an owner, on account of his ownership interest, reduce the owner's tax basis in the LLC. In contrast, payments to an owner for guaranteed payments do *not* cause a reduction in tax basis, because these payments are made to an owner *other than in his capacity as an owner* (i.e., as an employee, lender or lessor).

A lower tax basis will mean higher taxable gain when the equity interest is later sold. Thus, usually, it is better to structure salary, loan and lease payments as guaranteed payments.

In addition, guaranteed payments are deducted, along with other expenses, on the LLC's information return filed with the IRS. When payments are not guaranteed payments, they are not deducted on the information return and, instead, are disclosed as part of the allocation of net income to each owner. The owners receive the same amounts in either case, but the reporting is different.

Generally, guaranteed payments are payments made to the owners other than in their capacity as owners and without reference to the LLC's earnings. Thus, usually, payments for salary, loans and leases should qualify as guaranteed payments.

However, when a salary is stated simply as a percentage of profits, this may appear to be just a way of dividing income. Thus, in this case, the salary may not qualify as a guaranteed payment. For example, if an agreement provided that one owner in a two-owner LLC was to receive a "salary" of 50 percent of the LLC's earnings, with the other 50 percent allocated to the other owner, this "salary" would be unlikely to constitute a guaranteed payment.

Example

John and his partner each own half of an LLC. John receives a salary of $100,000 from his LLC. The LLC's income, before deducting this payment, is $400,000.

Let's say John's $100,000 salary is a guaranteed payment. On its information return filed with the IRS, the LLC reports income of $300,000 ($400,000 less the $100,000), of which $150,000 is allocated to each owner.

Thus, John has income from the LLC of $250,000 ($100,000 plus $150,000), while his partner's share is $150,000. John would separately report the salary of $100,000 as wage income and the $150,000 as his share of the LLC's income. He would pay self-employment tax on the total received, $250,000, as generally all of an owner's share of the LLC's earnings, whether an allocated share of income or a guaranteed payment, is subject to self-employment tax. (As noted above, payments for loans and leases may avoid the self-employment tax).

John must reduce the tax basis of his equity interest in the LLC only by the amount of his share of the distributed earnings, or $150,000, rather than the $250,000 he received, because the $100,000 is salary and not a distribution on account of an ownership interest.

If the salary were not classified as a guaranteed payment, John and his partner still would still receive the same $250,000 and $150,000, respectively. However, now each partner would reduce the tax basis of his equity interest by the full amount received, because all of the payments would be on account of their ownership interests. Thus, John would reduce his tax basis by $250,000, rather than $150,000.

In addition, now the $100,000 would not be reported as a deduction for salary on the LLC's information return. Instead, the information return would show income of $400,000, with $250,000 allocated to John, and the remaining $150,000 allocated to his partner.

Sales of Accounts Receivable

Still another strategy exists for businesses that generate a large volume of accounts receivable. This strategy is based, in part, on a concept termed "securitization."

The strategy involves the sale of receivables by the operating entity to the holding entity (or to the owner, personally, if no holding entity is used). Cash is paid into the operating entity for the purchase of its accounts receivables, and then quickly withdrawn by the owner as payments for salary, leases, loans, operating expenses, etc. In this way, vulnerable assets (i.e., the accounts receivable) are not left for any appreciable time within the form of the operating entity, where they would be vulnerable to the claims of the operating entity's creditors (these strategies are discussed in more detail in Chapter 8).

AUTHORIZATION AND DOCUMENTATION

Chapter 16 discusses in detail the concept of piercing the veil of limited liability, in which creditors of the business entity seek to have a court impose unlimited, personal liability on the owners of the entity. As discussed in that chapter, one of the two theories that can form the basis for piercing of the veil is the "alter ego theory."

Under the alter ego theory, creditors must demonstrate that the owners of the entity have operated the business *not* as if it were a true separate legal entity, but instead as if it were merely another side (i.e., the "alter ego") of the owners. Thus, if applied, the theory means that the business will not be recognized as being separate from the owners, and accordingly the owners will have unlimited, personal liability for all of the business's debts.

The primary way to avoid this outcome is through proper recordkeeping and, in particular, by ensuring that all transactions between the owners and their business entity are authorized and documented (see Chapter 16 for details).

Thus, all arrangements for salary should be based on a written salary arrangement, which is authorized and signed by the entity's management. Similarly, loan arrangements should be based on written promissory notes and security agreements, and lease arrangements should be based on written lease contracts. In the case of loans and leases, once again the agreements should be authorized and signed by the entity's management.

One final point should be made with respect to the issue of actual fraud and withdrawals from a business entity. As discussed above, the UFTA's actual fraud provisions will apply to all transfers from a business entity to its owners. As also noted above, actual fraud, as opposed to constructive fraud, requires that creditors prove the transferor *intended* to defraud the creditors through the transfer. Thus, actual fraud is not automatic, but instead depends on the court's inferring intent from the circumstances of the particular case (the factors from which a court will draw these inferences are discussed below and in more detail in Chapter 4).

Regular Withdrawals

One of the factors that can indicate actual fraud involves the *timing* of the transfers. Transfers (for salary, loans, leases or distributions of earnings) that occur suddenly, when the business entity experiences financial difficulty, indicate that the motive for the transfers was avoidance of creditor's claims. Thus, fraudulent intent may be inferred from this type of conduct.

Accordingly, withdrawals should be made on a regular basis. If the business entity subsequently experiences financial difficulties and withdrawals continue, *in accordance with a long established pattern*, a court is much less likely to infer fraudulent intent. Thus, a pattern of regular withdrawals can work to defeat a finding of actual fraud, even as the withdrawals continue.

Note that if the withdrawals are for return value and not on account of the owner's interests, constructive fraud provisions under the UFTA and the state corporation and LLC statutes will not apply to the withdrawals. Thus, in particular, a regular pattern of withdrawals in the form of payments for salary, loans and leases usually will be the most effective strategy.

Amount of Withdrawals

Creditors may sometimes argue that *large* withdrawals (e.g., for salary) are indicative of fraudulent intent. However, *provided these withdrawals are authorized, documented and occur on a regular basis*, creditors will have a difficult burden in establishing intent, based on the size of withdrawals.

In particular, tax cases involving regular or C corporations frequently involve the issue as to whether salary is reasonable, because a corporation can deduct only "reasonable" salaries. Due to the time and effort an entrepreneur devotes to his business, courts in these cases deem as "reasonable" extremely large salaries taken by owners. This same reasoning also should extend to actual fraud cases.

Example

 In one case, the tax court found "reasonable" compensation of almost $900,000 for one year paid by a corporation to its only owner. This compensation consisted of a $200,000 salary, a $400,000 bonus, and a $296,000 lump sum retirement benefit.

The tax court relied on five factors in deciding whether the compensation was reasonable:

- *the employee's role in the business*

- *a comparison of the compensation with what is paid to similar employees by other companies*

- *the character and condition of the business*

- *whether, in a regular C corporation, the compensation is really a "disguised dividend" intended to avoid the double tax on dividends (see Chapter 7)*

- *whether the compensation was consistently paid under a structured and formal arrangement*

The fourth factor underscores why these tax cases arise. A regular or C corporation is a separate tax-paying entity. Dividends paid by a C corporation are subject to a double tax, because they are not deductible by the corporation and thus are taxed at the corporate level. Dividends also are taxed a second time, at the individual tax rates when they are received by the owner (see Chapter 7). C corporations sometimes attempt to disguise a dividend as salary, in an attempt at avoiding the tax at the corporate level, as the salary is deductible by the corporation. The salary is considered to be a disguised dividend, only to the extent the salary is deemed to be unreasonable.

While the same tax issue does not arise in the case of the subchapter S corporation or the LLC, the reasoning should extend to actual fraud cases. Payment of a reasonable salary is not indicative of fraudulent intent.

Note, too, that the fifth factor formally recognizes authorization and documentation as important factors in determining the reasonableness of the salary.

Between payments for salary, loans and leases, and other withdrawal strategies, it will seldom be a problem for small business owners to withdraw all of the vulnerable funds from the business in a manner that is "reasonable," and thus not found to be fraudulent.

Chapter 15

Limiting Liability for Contracts and Torts

The mere *formation* of an LLC or a corporation is not a sufficient asset protection strategy. As discussed in Part II of this book, the entity must be *structured and funded* properly to limit exposure to liability.

Moreover, even properly structuring and funding the LLC or corporation is not sufficient, because some assets remain vulnerable within the business entity itself. The LLC or corporation must be *operated* properly, in ways that preserve limited liability granted by law.

Specifically, significant exceptions to limited liability exist, in terms of both contract and tort liability. When an exception applies, limited liability is lost, and the owners of the business have unlimited, personal liability for the business's debts. Yet, most times, with proper planning, these exceptions successfully can be avoided. The first step is understanding the nature of contract law.

Warning

The unfortunate truth is that most small business owners operate their business blissfully unaware that they have a tremendous exposure to liability through contracts or torts (acts or actions whose outcome produces a lawsuit or settlement forcing payment of monetary damages). Perhaps they are under the illusion that the LLC or corporation they formed will protect them from liability. Of course, reality sets in when a financial disaster strikes, such as a major lawsuit. By this time, it usually is too late to take corrective measures.

So by avoiding the exceptions to limited liability for contacts and torts, the small business owner will preserve his legally guaranteed protections, thus securing his personal assets outside of the business.

Further, the small business owner can take actions to limit this limited liability, and thus protect the business's assets as well. A careful understanding and application of authority under contract law, and the pitfalls that can result from contracts and torts, will go a long way toward ensuring maximum asset protection for you and your business.

AUTHORITY UNDER CONTRACT LAW

Ordinarily, an agent of the business must have actual authority to form a contract for a principal of the business. Usually, this will be *express* authority—permission from the principal given verbally or in writing. Obviously, written authority is preferable, as it is difficult to substantiate verbal authority. In a corporation, common sources of written express authority include bylaws and resolutions from directors' meetings. In an LLC, common sources include an operating agreement and resolutions from managers' meetings (or members' meetings, in a member-managed LLC).

Actual authority also may be *implied*. Specifically, someone who is implied to automatically have all the authority necessary *to carry out the express authority*. For example, if an agent representing a Connecticut company is expressly authorized to sign a contract in California, and he must travel there to accomplish this, he is also (most likely) impliedly authorized to contract for travel and lodging, as an agent of the company, because this is necessary if he is to accomplish his express authority and sign the contract in California.

Clearly, implied authority can present problems, because it is neither in writing nor verbal. It is simply understood. Remember, though, that implied authority stems from express authority. By specifically addressing express authority, problems with implied authority can be avoided.

The bigger problem for the small business owner is *apparent* authority. If apparent authority exists, an agent or employee can bind the business to a contract, *even though the agent or employee has no actual authority to act for the business.* Apparent authority can represent a significant source of liability for the business.

If it reasonably appears to a creditor that an agent has actual authority to represent a principal on a contract, then the principal is legally bound to the contract, based on the apparent authority theory, even though the agent had no actual authority at all to represent the principal.

This is frequently a problem when an employee is fired or the scope of his authority is curtailed, and creditors of the business are not properly notified of this fact. Clearly, this can especially be a problem when the agent had significant authority (e.g., an officer in a corporation, a manager in an LLC or an employee such as a purchasing agent).

The Problem with Apparent Authority

In most cases, apparent authority arises when there has been what is termed a "past course of dealing" with a creditor. In this situation, the agent, *acting with actual authority*, has on many prior occasions contracted with this particular creditor on behalf of the principal. In each of these cases, a bill was sent to the principal, and the bill was paid.

Subsequently, the employee's authority is revoked or curtailed. It is easy to see that, because of the past course of dealing, the creditor can reasonably believe that the agent is still authorized to represent the principal, if the creditor is not notified otherwise. Thus, if the agent subsequently forms a contract with the creditor, while representing that he is acting for the principal, the principal is liable on the contract because of apparent authority. *In short, an employee may be fired, or a partner may withdraw from a business, and still bind the business to contracts.*

Here, it is the LLC or corporation that will be the principal held liable—provided, of course, that the owner has properly taken the precautions to separate the owner from the business's liabilities.

By eliminating apparent authority, the small business owner can protect his investment in the business. The key to this comes down to one word—notice. Specifically, if apparent authority is to be eliminated, notice that the agent no longer has authority to act for the principal must be provided to creditors.

There are two types of notice:

- actual individual notice

- constructive notice

The law requires that the principal provide actual individual notice to all creditors with whom the business and the agent have established a past course of dealing. It also requires that the principal prove the creditor *actually received* the notice.

A telephone call, for its immediacy, and a letter should satisfy this requirement. The business owner should always document the date and time of telephone calls, and the name of the individual who took the message. Where immediacy is not an important issue, the business owner may want to bypass the telephone call.

A copy of the letter should be retained. Moreover, if a serious question of possible wrongdoing by an agent exists or exposure to liability is particularly high for some other reason, a certified letter, return receipt requested, is recommended.

Of course, it is not possible to make a telephone call or send a letter to a creditor with whom the business has not yet established a relationship. Here, the law provides that *constructive notice* is sufficient. This type of notice is best represented by a newspaper advertisement, in a newspaper that circulates in all the areas the company has done business. Here, there is no requirement that the principal prove the notice was actually received.

Note that constructive notice is ineffective against creditors with whom the principal and agent have a past course of dealing (unless the principal is able to prove the creditor actually read the advertisement, which is usually impossible).

The best course is for the small business owner to use both actual individual notice to known creditors and constructive notice to cover all future potential creditors.

Warning

Agents can bind a principal to a contract based on express authority, implied authority or apparent authority.

Apparent authority can represent a significant source of liability for a business. If apparent authority exists, an agent or employee can bind the business to a contract, even though the agent or employee has no actual authority to act for the business.

This is likely to be a problem when an employee's authority is curtailed, an employee is fired, or a partner withdraws from a business. The business owner must terminate apparent authority by providing notice to creditors that the agent no longer has authority to act for the principal, in accordance with the rules discussed above.

When notifying creditors to terminate apparent authority by letter or newspaper advertisement, the small business owner must be careful to avoid saying anything regarding the agent that might be actionable as defamation. (See Chapter 17 for a discussion of defamation). No explanation should normally be given. A simple report that John Jones no longer is an employee or agent (or partner) of the company is appropriate.

CONTRACT EXCEPTIONS TO LIMITED LIABILITY

The small business owner must have a basic understanding of the law of principal and agent, because agency law is one of the keys to understanding the exceptions to limited liability.

An agent is a representative of the principal. As a general rule, whatever the principal could do himself, he can instead hire an agent to do on his behalf. The employer/employee relationship represents an example of a principal and an agent.

An LLC or corporation is recognized as a "person" or separate entity from the owners. However, the LLC or corporation can accomplish nothing at all *on its own*—the LLC or corporation obviously is inanimate.

More importantly, because the LLC and corporation are, in fact, inanimate, they must *always* act through agents. In the LLC, these agents will primarily be the managers in a manager-managed LLC, or all of the members in a member-managed LLC. In a corporation, these agents will primarily be the officers and the directors. However, in both cases, employees also are agents who act on behalf of the entity.

In striving to preserve limited liability, the small business owner must always ensure that he acts as an *agent* of the entity, and not in his personal capacity. Further, he must also always ensure that all other agents, including employees, act as representatives of the LLC or corporation, rather than as representatives of the owner personally (i.e., that the *principal* on whose behalf an agent acts is *the entity*—the LLC or corporation—and not the small business owner personally).

With proper planning, the small business owner can accomplish these objectives and thereby preserve limited liability for contracts as well as torts.

The small business owner operating in the LLC or corporate form will still have unlimited, personal liability for a contract in these four situations:

- the owner forms a contract before the LLC or corporation legally comes into existence (a pre-formation contract)

- the owner fails to identify the principal (i.e., the LLC or corporation) in the contract

- the owner identifies the principal, but fails to disclose that he represents the principal on the contract (his representational capacity)

- the owner personally guarantees the entity's contract

The first three exceptions can be avoided in all cases by using careful business sense. The last exception can be avoided in many cases. In addition, many other precautions (discussed at the end of this chapter) can be taken so that the entity does not unnecessarily incur contract liability.

By avoiding the four exceptions, the small business owner will enjoy limited liability for any contract entered into on behalf of the business. Thus, the most he can lose on any business contract will be his investment in the business (i.e., the business's assets—to the extent these assets are left vulnerable). Personal assets are protected.

By also taking precautions against the entity unnecessarily incurring contract liability, he will protect his business's assets. Why rely on limited liability, when there can be no liability at all?

Pre-Formation Contracts

Ideally, the small business owner will sign a contract solely as an *agent* of his LLC or corporation. If an agent does this properly (as discussed below), *only the principal is liable on the contract*. The agent will have no liability at all on the contract. Thus, if the owner of a business properly signs a contract as an agent of the LLC or corporation, *only* the principal (i.e., the LLC or corporation) will be liable on the contract.

The most the owner could lose on the contract will be what the LLC or corporation can lose. This amounts to the owner's investment in the business (the business's assets to the extent they are vulnerable). In other words, the owner will enjoy limited liability for the contract.

One exception to this outcome involves a pre-formation contract (i.e., a contract formed by the owner before his LLC or corporation legally came into existence). An individual can act as an agent only if there is a principal. With a pre-formation contract, there is no principal, as the entity has yet to legally come into existence. Thus, with a pre-formation contract, the owner is acting *in his personal capacity*. Accordingly, he has unlimited, personal liability on the contract.

The way to avoid this outcome is simple: The business owner should avoid forming any contracts until *after* the LLC or corporation legally comes into existence. Each entity is created formally under state law, by filing articles of organization with the state along with the appropriate fee. The state will approve the articles and send back a written acknowledgment indicating the date the entity came into existence. Only after this date can the owner act as an agent for the entity.

Plan Smart

When the owner mistakenly signs a pre-formation contract (without a novation clause), the owner has two choices:

- *The owner should first attempt to have the creditor sign a novation, which will release the owner from personal liability, and substitute the LLC or corporation in his place.*

- *Failing this, he should carefully consider an indemnification agreement from the LLC or corporation. This agreement allows the owner to seek reimbursement from the LLC or corporation, in the event the owner is called on personally to honor the contract. However, this agreement has disadvantages: this agreement does not actually release the owner from personal liability as it is not signed by the creditor, and the agreement will make the LLC or corporation liable on the contract and, thus, expose the business's assets to liability, in addition to the owner's personal assets.*

Again, the best course, obviously, is to avoid signing any pre-formation contracts.

In short, it is wise to wait until this written acknowledgment is received before forming any business contracts. Unfortunately, many small business owners form business contracts first and then form the business entity. It is easy to understand how this can happen. As the owner surveys the market for his business, many times contracts are signed to lease space, buy equipment and furniture, hire employees, etc. Somewhere in the middle or at the end of this process, the entity is formed.

Of course, it does make sense to *survey the market* before the entity is formed. A well-researched business plan is an essential ingredient in any new business's success. The business plan will include projected costs of doing business. Obviously, this requires that the business owner survey the market to document these projected costs.

The business plan will allow the owner to determine whether the idea is feasible. Thus, usually the owner should create the business plan and, accordingly, survey the market for the costs of doing business *before* forming the business entity. After all, why form an LLC or corporation first, and then find out that the idea for the business will not work?

However, the owner should *make inquiries* about the costs of leasing space, purchasing equipment and furniture, hiring employees, etc., *just do not execute any contracts until after the entity is formed.*

Plan Smart

A business plan is an important tool in forming a business. CCH, as part of its Business Owner's Toolkit™ series, has published two excellent books that provide detailed guidance on the process of preparing a business plan: Business Plans that Work for Your Small Business, second edition *and* Start, Run and Grow a Successful Small Business, fourth edition.

Indemnification Agreements

Many business owners harbor a misconception concerning pre-formation contracts. Commonly, when a pre-formation contract exists, the entity, upon coming into being legally, will agree to adopt the contract and release the owner from personal liability on the contract. Unfortunately, this "release" does *not* actually release the owner from liability.

This type of agreement, commonly called an indemnification agreement, makes the entity liable on the contract *in addition to the owner personally.* In a small business, the owner who has made the mistake of signing a pre-formation contract may actually be better off if he does not use this type of agreement. Why now make the business *also* liable on the contract and expose the business's assets to liability, in addition to the owner's personal assets?

However, this type of agreement may have some value, especially in a larger business with multiple owners. While the agreement does not release the owner from liability, it does mean that, if the owner is called on to personally honor the contract, the owner then can seek reimbursement from the business. In a larger, more complex business, this advantage probably outweighs the cost of exposing the business's assets to liability, at least from the perspective of the individual owner in question.

Novations

It is possible for a creditor to actually release the owner from liability on a pre-formation contract, through an agreement termed a novation. Do not confuse the novation with the indemnification agreement, described above. In a novation, *the creditor on the contact* signs the release.

This is the key to the novation. Only the creditor, and not the owner's entity, can release the owner from liability. Think about it: Wouldn't it be nice if everyone could form an entity, which would then release him or her from liability on a home mortgage? Obviously, only the bank (i.e., the creditor) can release the homeowner from liability for a mortgage.

More specifically, the novation, signed by the creditor, releases the owner from liability and substitutes the entity in his place. Technically, a novation can take place only after the entity is formed. If there is a pre-formation contract, the owner can approach the creditor and request that the creditor sign a novation, releasing the owner from personal liability and substituting the entity in his place. However, with a newly formed entity that is not exactly overflowing with vulnerable assets, the owner should not usually expect a positive response.

Ultimately, the owner, in anticipation of forming his business entity, can insert a clause in a pre-formation contract wherein the creditor agrees to a novation upon the creation of the entity. Clearly, this is the approach that should be taken.

This may occur, for example, when the owner discovers an unusual bargain that he would like to capitalize on during the exploratory stage of his business formation. Once again, however, the creditor would have to be willing to sign off on this clause. In addition, if the entity, in fact, is not actually created, as sometimes happens with new businesses, the owner will retain personal liability on the contract.

Clearly, the best approach is to avoid a pre-formation contract, and thus the need for an indemnification agreement or a novation.

In one case, an individual, in anticipation of creating a corporation, signed a contract with a large accounting firm for $10,000 of accounting and tax services for the prospective business. Though the corporation was legally created only one month later, the owner had unlimited, personal liability on the contract, because the principal (i.e., the corporation) did not exist at the time the contract was formed.

In addition, the owner argued that he should have no personal liability because the accounting firm knew he intended to create the corporation. However, the court ruled against the owner, because he did not insert a novation clause in the pre-formation contract.

Failure to Identify the Principal

As a rule, the party to a business contract should always be the principal (i.e., the LLC or corporation). So it is surprising that many business owners form an LLC or corporation, but then sign contracts in their own name.

Sometimes this happens because the creditor (e.g., a supplier) fills in a form contract with the owner's name, and the owner simply signs the bottom of contract with his own name. It also happens frequently when a business converts to an LLC or corporation. Many times the owner will continue to use checks, stationery and pre-printed forms in the owner's personal name, doing business as (d.b.a.) the name of the business. Here, the owner will usually face personal liability for transactions.

If the principal's name is not disclosed, the law is clear: The *owner* is the party to the contract. Accordingly, he has unlimited, personal liability on the contract. The solution is simple—where the names of the parties to the contract appear, the name of the LLC or corporation, and *not* the name of the individual owner, should be inserted. Of course, the entity itself cannot sign the contract. The next step in preventing personal liability is for the owner to properly *sign* the contract, *solely as an agent of the entity*.

All contracts, checks, stationery and pre-printed forms, should be in the name of the LLC or corporation. When a business is converted to the LLC or corporate form, do not continue to use forms that are in the personal name of the individual owner.

Failure to Sign Properly as an Agent of the Principal

Inserting the name of the entity as the party to the contract is necessary to avoid personal liability, but it is not sufficient by itself. The owner must then properly sign the contract as the agent, or representative, of the principal (the entity). This is referred to as the agent disclosing his "representational capacity." If it is not clear that the owner signed *as an agent or representative of the principal*, he has failed to disclose his representational capacity. To the law, the owner has thus signed *in his personal capacity* and, accordingly, has personal liability on the contract.

There are many ways to properly disclose representational capacity when signing a contract as an agent. The classic way is to use the word "by" before the owner's individual name. The owner's title (e.g., manager, president, etc.) should appear after the owner's name. Of course, this *alone* would induce personal liability. Remember that the principal's name must appear above the owner's signature as well.

Case Study — Properly Signing Contracts, part 1

John Smith is the owner of ABC, LLC, and wants to sign a contract with a supplier, XYZ Supplies, Inc. Smith should execute the contract as follows:

Parties to the contract:

Seller: <u>XYZ Supply, Inc</u>

Buyer: <u>ABC, LLC</u>

* * *

Signed: <u>ABC, LLC</u>

By: <u>John Smith, Manager</u>

John Smith, Manager

(Of course, the contract would also be signed, similarly, by an agent of XYZ Supplies, Inc.)

Because the name of the entity, ABC, LLC, appears at the top of the contract, it would be acceptable to omit repeating the name of the principal a second time above John's signature, as follows:

Signed: By: <u>John Smith, Manager</u>

John Smith, Manager

Note that it is customary to print a name under a signature (if the name is not printed elsewhere in the contract) so that the party's name can be clearly identified.

Other variations are acceptable, as long as it is clear that the owner is signing as agent of the entity. The following alternative should work, although it is more cumbersome and less reliable: "Signed, John Smith, Manager for ABC, LLC." The best approach, however, is to use the time-proven "by" as described above.

When signing checks, however, a mere signature, along with the owner's title, will be sufficient, without the word "by," provided of course the pre-printed name at the top of the checks is the name of the LLC or corporation, and not the individual name of the owner. Here, it is understood that the owner is signing as an agent of the entity.

Similarly, in ordinary correspondences, name and title for the signature, without the word "by," will suffice, provided, of course, the name on the letterhead is the name of the LLC or corporation, and not the owner's individual name. However, if the correspondence involves an offer or acceptance, or any other type of contractual promise, the word "by" should be used.

Finally, it helps to use the correct titles. In the LLC, the owner will be either a manager or simply a member. In a corporation, the traditional titles of president, vice president, secretary and treasurer are appropriate.

Personally Guaranteeing the Business's Contracts

In practice, personally guaranteeing the business's contracts will be an exception that the small business owner will not be able to avoid in some cases.

Simply put, creditors often will insist that the owner of a small business personally guarantee the entity's contract because the creditor is unwilling to rely on the credit of the entity itself (usually for good reason, either because the entity has been structured properly for asset protection, or because the business is not successfully generating any wealth). It would be unheard of, for example, for a commercial lender, such as a bank, to make a loan to a small LLC or corporation without insisting on a personal guarantee.

With a personal guarantee, the owner will sign the contract twice, as illustrated in the following example.

Case Study — Properly Signing Contracts, part 2

Refer back to the prior case study, but now assume that XYZ Supplies, Inc. insists on a personal guarantee in the contract from John Smith, the owner of ABC, LLC. The contract will look like this:

Parties to the contract:

Seller: XYZ Supply, Inc

Buyer: ABC, LLC

* * *

Signed: ABC, LLC

By: John Smith, Manager

John Smith, Manager

Signed: John Smith

John Smith

The second signature makes Smith personally liable on the contract.

Usually, language regarding the personal guarantee will appear before the second signature. This language may make the owner primarily liable, along with his entity, so that the creditor can call on either immediately to pay the debt: "The undersigned hereby personally agrees to perform all of the obligations in this contract." Or, the language may make the owner a surety, or guarantor, who agrees to pay the debt only if it is not first paid by the entity: "The undersigned hereby personally agrees to perform all of the obligations in this contract in the event ABC, LLC does not perform these obligations."

With a one-owner business, the two alternatives will probably produce no difference in outcome. However, with a multiple-owner business, the individual owner usually will prefer to act as a surety, rather than a co-primary party.

While commercial lenders and many other providers of credit will commonly request a personal guarantee, it is also true that many creditors will *not* make such a request. For example, in practice, it is common for some suppliers to request a personal guarantee, while others providing the same materials and quantities will not make such a request.

Here is one rule for the small business owner to follow: If they don't ask for a personal guarantee, don't volunteer it. Of course, as previously described, care must also be taken in executing the contract to ensure that the party to the contract is the entity, and that the owner signs properly only as an agent of the entity.

In many cases, a pre-printed form contract from a supplier will already have a guarantee clause in it. Business owners will find that, in this situation, they can sometimes sign only as an agent of the business entity and leave the signature line for the guarantee clause blank, without objection from the supplier. Other times, the clause will be absent, or the supplier will allow the small business owner to open an account informally with a pre-printed form that merely serves as a collection vehicle for information about the business. This form is not actually a contract and usually will not contain a personal guarantee clause.

Clearly where no form is used at all, there is no personal guarantee. Here, it is especially important, however, to make sure the account is opened only in the name of the entity, all invoices are billed solely in the name of the entity, and that the invoices are paid with checks that, at the top, contain only the name of the entity.

In summary, even this exception to limited liability can be avoided in many cases.

Plan Smart

The personal guarantee exception to limited liability for contracts can be used to illustrate another rule in asset projection planning—it's a two-way street.

The strategies that the small business owner employs when he is the debtor should be considered, in an opposite way, when he is a creditor. For example, the small business owner will always try to avoid providing a personal guarantee when he is the debtor, but he should always insist on a personal guarantee when he is the creditor.

Finally, despite having a business entity such as an LLC or corporation, some business owners mistakenly sign contracts in their own name only. This is the most egregious example of failing to sign a contract properly and inadvertently personally guaranteeing a contract. Fortunately, it's also the easiest mistake to avoid.

TORT EXCEPTIONS TO LIMITED LIABILITY

Once again, agency law is a key to understanding the exceptions to limited liability with respect to torts committed in the business. As a brief definition, tort law is really personal injury law. The best example of a tort, perhaps, is negligence (i.e., carelessly causing injury to a person or damage to property).

When an individual commits a tort, he is legally liable to the aggrieved party. The aggrieved party can bring a lawsuit for monetary damages against the party who commits the tort. This is true even when the individual committing the tort is acting as an agent for a principal at the time he commits the tort. Simply put, the individual is always responsible for his or her actions, whether working or not.

Unfortunately, many individuals mistakenly believe that if they commit a tort while acting as an agent for a principal (e.g., while an employee is carrying out duties for the employer), they have no liability. This mistaken belief may arise for two reasons: insurance and the fact that the principal (the employer) also will be liable in this situation.

The employer, or more specifically the insurance policy carried by the employer, will pay off on the liability. However, *the employee or agent has personal liability in this situation.* The fact that the principal or employer has liability does not relieve the agent or employee from his or her personal liability. This is important to understand especially because there will not always be insurance that covers every situation or has sufficient face value to cover all of the damages involved. This is when the agent or employee is likely to be called on to pay the damages, discovering the belief of no liability was mistaken.

Warning

The small business owner must remember that he will be acting as an agent or employee of his business entity. Therefore, the owner is doubly exposed to liability when committing a tort, because the entity and the owner personally are responsible. This is potentially a very damaging exception to your efforts to limit liability inside and outside of your business.

If an agent commits a tort while carrying out the principal's business (or "acting within the scope of the business" as some courts put it), the principal is *automatically* also liable for the agent's torts under a doctrine called respondeat superior, or the master-servant rule. This type of automatic liability, which is termed vicarious liability, also applies in other areas of law. It means that no wrongdoing by the principal *at all* needs to be proven.

The principal could have acted carefully and reasonably, but it makes no difference when it comes to defending against a lawsuit. When an agent commits a tort, the only real defense that may be offered by the principal is the argument that the agent was, in fact, not carrying out the principal's business at the time he committed the tort.

Example

John Jones, a purchasing agent for XYZ Materials, Inc., negligently hits a pedestrian while picking up a load of supplies in XYZ's truck. Both Jones and XYZ are liable.

Jones is personally liable because he committed the tort. XYZ is liable because Jones was acting as its agent at the time he committed the tort.

For the owner of the entity, three exceptions exist to limited liability for torts committed in the business. The *owner* will have unlimited, personal liability for torts when the owner:

- personally commits a tort, which is especially possible in a personal service business

- is guilty of negligent hiring or supervision of employees

- hires agents or employees, or sells goods, in his personal capacity rather than as an agent of the LLC or corporation

Many times, all of these exceptions can be avoided. The last exception can be avoided in every case.

Plan Smart

An employer also may be able to avoid liability for its agents or employees through the use of independent contractors (as discussed at the end of this chapter).

Personal Commission of a Tort

Remember, as previously discussed, if an individual personally commits a tort, that person is liable to the injured party. This is true irrespective of whether the individual was acting as an agent for another party at the time he or she committed a tort.

Consistent with this general rule, if the small business owner commits a tort while acting as an agent for his LLC or corporation, the owner is liable to the injured party. The fact that his LLC or corporation *also* will be liable is not relevant to the owner's personal liability.

Many states codify this exception in their statutes governing professional corporations (PCs). All states incorporate this exception into their statutes that govern professionals (doctors, lawyers, architects, electricians, etc.) operating in the form of LLCs (or LLPs). Even when the provision is not statutory, however, the rule is universally applied by the courts, as a matter of common law.

This exception can be encountered even in a business that sells goods and provides no services. This is especially true in a business that involves risk of injury to the customer (e.g., operation of a lumberyard). An owner who personally stacks the store shelves or loads a customer's car in a careless manner will have personal liability for his negligence. An auto accident caused by the owner of the business represents another commonly encountered example of this exception. This, of course, can occur in almost any business.

Nevertheless, this exception to limited liability will represent perhaps the most significant exposure to liability for the small business owner who operates a personal service business.

Warning

Operation of the business in the form of an LLC or corporation will not save the owner from unlimited, personal liability in this instance.

The exception to limited tort liability underscores why it is dangerous to rely on one asset protection strategy (e.g., formation of an LLC or corporation). Here, the owner will have to rely on other asset protection strategies, such as exemption planning, asset protection trusts, insurance, etc.

Despite this exception, however, the LLC or corporation still offers significant advantages to the small business owner in terms of limited liability protection from torts committed by *co-owners* and *other employees* of the business, as illustrated in the following example.

Case Study — Tort Liability in an LLC, part 1

Smith, Jones, and White are all physicians and operate a medical practice, which is organized as an LLC.

Let's say Smith commits an act of malpractice. Smith has unlimited, personal liability for this tort because he committed it. The LLC also has unlimited, personal liability automatically because of the respondeat superior doctrine.

The other two co-owners, Jones and White, have limited liability. *The most they can lose is what they have invested, at the time, in the LLC* (i.e., they have no personal liability for this tort).

Now let's say the practice (specifically the LLC) hires another physician who is not a partner in the business. This doctor commits an act of malpractice. Assuming there has not been an independent *act of negligence by one of the partners (as discussed below), liability will be as follows: this physician will have personal liability because he committed the tort and the LLC will have personal liability under the respondeat superior doctrine.*

All three owners will have only limited liability, and no personal liability, for this tort.

Negligent Hiring or Supervision

It is possible for a business owner to be *personally* liable when an agent of the business commits a tort, *if the owner committed a separate tort, such as a separate act of negligence.* Here, *three* parties are liable:

- the agent or employee who commits the tort—because he or she committed it

- the entity—under respondeat superior

- the owner—for his or her own independent tort

Really, two separate torts are committed: one by the employee and the second by the owner. Most likely, this independent tort will be in the form of negligent hiring or supervision of an employee of the entity.

Plan Smart

This exception is really just a specific example of the first exception—namely, personal commission of a tort. Here, personal liability is predicated on the fact that the owner has personally committed a tort (i.e., the improper hiring or supervision of the employee) that is separate from, and in addition to, the tort committed by employee.

In addition, while this exception, too, is usually incorporated in state statutes governing PCs, LLCs and LLPs operated by professionals, it will apply in all states as a matter of common law and will apply to all businesses, not simply to those businesses providing professional services.

The small business owner will want to avoid application of this exception by taking measures to ensure that he acts reasonably in hiring and supervising employees. Many strategies here involve time, costs and philosophical questions related to employee's privacy. The business owner must weigh these factors against the likelihood that the employee will commit a tort causing personal injury or property damage. This, in turn, will depend on the nature of the business and the employee's particular job.

For example, a criminal background check would be especially important in hiring employees at a day care center or in a business where the employees will handle large sums of cash. Drug testing would be appropriate in hiring bus drivers or where employees will operate machinery, such as construction equipment.

Case Study — Tort Liability in an LLC, part 2

Refer to the prior case study, where the fourth doctor, as an employee, but not as a co-owner, commits an act of malpractice.

If it can be proven that the three co-owners committed negligence in failing to properly train and supervise this employee, the three co-owners will have unlimited, personally liability for their tort and, effectively, for the employee's tort.

Technically, the three co-owners are not liable because of the act of malpractice committed by this employee. Nor are they liable because of the doctrine of respondeat superior. They are liable for their own independent act of negligence. This is consistent with the general rule that an individual is liable when he personally commits a tort.

The same result would occur if the three co-owners were negligent in hiring the employee. This could happen, for example, where the owners failed to conduct a background check to verify the employee's credentials, arrest records, credit rating, work history, etc., and one or more of these failings were a factor in the employee's malpractice.

In terms of hiring new employees, the small business owner may want to consider:

- **Background checks** — including verification of prior employment, academic transcripts, licenses, professional affiliations, credit history, and arrest history

- **Drug testing** — generally, state laws allow mandatory testing for all applicants, and then periodic random testing of employees, where the business involves safety risks

In terms of supervising employees, the small business owner may want to consider:

- a mentoring process, whereby a new employee is instructed and supervised by a senior-level employee for a prescribed period

- a system of checks and approvals before work is sent to clients, patients or customers

- case/job tracking systems

- regularly scheduled meetings where case/job status is discussed

- training sessions (in-house or outside seminars) for employees

Many other recommendations can be found at the *CCH Business Owner's Toolkit*™ web site at http://www.toolkit.cch.com.

Example

Smith & Jones, LLC, a law office, hires a new attorney, Stevens, as an employee. Smith does all of the hiring for the firm. He interviews Stevens twice before hiring him. Smith makes sure that the LLC hires Stevens, so that the LLC, rather than Smith or Jones personally, will be the principal in any transactions initiated by Stevens.

Let's say that, ten months later, Stevens commits an act of malpractice, costing a client $400,000 in losses. Then, as it turns out, Stevens actually had dropped out of law school in his first year. This fact was never discovered by the firm, as Smith found him knowledgeable concerning the law during the two interviews and never conducted a background check.

It is likely that Smith will be sued personally for this loss due to negligent hiring.

Jones should have no personal liability for negligent hiring, because he did not personally participate in the hiring of Stevens. However, both Smith and Jones may face personal liability because it is likely that they each will have committed yet another personal tort—negligent supervision of Stevens.

In addition, of course, Stevens will be personally liable for his act of malpractice, and the LLC itself will be liable under the doctrine of respondeat superior. Nevertheless, the greatest concern to Smith and Jones will be the fact that all of their personal assets outside the business will now be exposed to liability for this tort.

Had Smith conducted a proper background check, he would have avoided this liability. Let's say he did and finds that Stevens' background passes muster. In addition, assume the firm had instituted reasonable measures to train and supervise Stevens. Here, Smith and Jones should face no personal liability for malpractice committed by Stevens, because they will not have personally committed a separate act of negligence and because the LLC is Stevens' principal.

Of course, with a proper background check and proper supervision, the likelihood that Stevens will commit a tort is significantly reduced in any event.

Selling or Hiring in a Personal Capacity

A small business owner acts as an agent or employee for the LLC or corporation when selling goods or hiring agents or employees for the business. Acting in that capacity generally affords the owner personal liability protection for torts committed in the business.

However, there is an exception to this general rule. When the business owner forms a contract to sell goods in his own name or hires an employee or agent in his own name, he will have unlimited, personal liability for any resulting torts. Note that this can only occur as a result of a serious mistake on the part of the business owner.

The use of independent contractors, rather than employees or agents, can help a small business owner avoid the outcome from a tort committed by someone the owner personally hired.

Sale of Goods Contracts

Where the business owner forms contracts for the sale of goods in his own name, rather than as an agent of his LLC or corporation, he may be personally liable for injuries caused by the goods sold.

If a consumer is injured by the product, the tort of strict liability may apply. Strict liability basically means that if you sold the product that caused the injury, you are liable. Here, the seller of the product (i.e., the owner personally), if this happens, will be liable for this tort.

On the other hand, if the sales contract is in the name of the LLC or corporation only, then the seller is the entity, and the owner has limited liability—which, if the entity has been structured and funded properly, may amount to no liability at all.

Plan Smart

A sale of goods contract can have tort implications if the product ends up injuring a consumer. It is important that the LLC or corporation, and not the owner himself, be the party to the sale. This can be accomplished by making sure all contracts for the sale of goods and all invoices, advertisements, etc., are in the name of the LLC or corporation only, and that the owner signs documents solely as agent for the entity.

Of course, as stressed throughout this chapter, this should be the procedure with respect to any business contract formed by the owner.

Employment Contracts

As previously discussed, the business owner must ensure that all business contracts are formed in the name of the LLC or corporation, and that he signs these contracts solely as an agent of the LLC or corporation. This is necessary if the owner is to escape personal liability for the contracts.

However, there is another reason to ensure this outcome. If an employee is hired personally by the owner, then the owner and not the LLC or corporation will be the principal. In this case, if the employee commits a tort, then his principal (i.e., *the owner personally*) will have unlimited, personal liability, in accordance with the doctrine of respondeat superior.

This could result when there is a written employment agreement that has been improperly executed in the name of the individual owner, or where there is no written employment agreement and the owner pays the employee from a checking account in the owner's personal name. In both cases, the business owner will be the employer/principal.

Plan Smart

The small business owner must avoid being deemed the personal employer/principal of employees. The LLC or corporation must be the employer.

A written employment agreement is advisable in all cases. The agreement must clearly identify the employer as the LLC or corporation, and the owner must properly sign solely as an agent of the LLC or corporation.

The written agreement can be simple, specifying job description, rate of pay, and that the relationship is employment at will, for example, if that is desired. In employment at will, the employee may be terminated without providing a reason and without advance notice (and the employee may quit without giving a reason or any advance notice).

A written agreement also can be used to specify that the worker has been hired as an independent contractor (see below for a discussion of how the use of independent contractors can significantly reduce exposure to tort liability).

An informal relationship with employees (i.e., where no written employment agreements exist) can still be used, but this offers less protection. In this case, paychecks in the name of the LLC or corporation only can be used to establish that the LLC or corporation is the employer.

Independent Contractors

When someone performs services for a business, he may be deemed an employee or an independent contractor. The differences between the two are highly significant, as explained below.

The small business owner should use independent contractors, rather than employees, whenever possible. The use of independent contractors, rather than employees, is one of the most effective asset protection tools because the employer:

- is *not* liable for torts committed by an independent contractor he employs, as the doctrine of respondeat superior does not apply to independent contractors; this fact is in stark contrast to the law that applies to torts committed by employees, and makes the use of independent contractors a singularly effective tool in eliminating tort liability that otherwise would apply against the LLC or corporation

- is *not* required to pay employment taxes (Social Security and Medicare tax as well as unemployment tax) or worker's compensation insurance on the wages paid to independent contractors and, similarly, is not required to withhold federal income taxes for the wages paid; the employer only pays the independent contractor his gross wages and, at the end of the year for each independent contractor paid $600 or more, sends the independent contractor and the IRS a Form 1099-MISC showing the gross wages paid

An additional benefit is that the law does not require that independent contractors participate in any retirement plan offered by the employer. In contrast, anti-discrimination rules usually mean *all employees* must be covered by an employer-sponsored retirement plan.

Plan Smart

Nothing prevents a business from voluntarily including independent contractors in a retirement plan.

While doing this will involve additional costs, it also may sufficiently appease workers enough to avoid worker challenges to their independent contractor status. The employment tax and tort liability savings may outweigh the costs of including these workers in the retirement plan. Of course, as discussed below, a misclassification can come to light in other ways, such as during an IRS audit.

The employment tax savings alone warrant the use of independent contractors. When the employer uses employees, rather than independent contractors, the Social Security and Medicare taxes paid by the employer amount to 7.65 percent of wages paid. Federal and state unemployment taxes typically average 0.8 percent of wages. This, of course, is in addition to unemployment insurance, which can be quite costly in many businesses.

In addition, recordkeeping is simplified, because no withholding from wages or employer tax reports are necessary. As a result, the small business owner normally will not need a payroll service, which will produce still more savings.

Nevertheless, the tax savings pale in comparison to the elimination of the business's tort liability.

Warning

Independent contractors are self-employed. In essence, they are operating their own business (usually as sole proprietors). Accordingly, they report their wages on Schedule C of IRS Form 1040, pay their own Social Security and Medicare taxes (termed a self-employment tax), and file their own estimated taxes in quarterly reports. The self-employment tax, before any reductions, amounts to 15.3 percent (as discussed in Chapter 7).

Because of the steep self-employment tax and the additional recordkeeping that will be required, many workers will object to independent contractor status and insist on being deemed employees.

Workers also may object to independent contractor status because they want to participate in the business's retirement plan.

A small business owner can choose to use independent contractors, but their ultimate classification as such is not up to the employer. Strict rules must be followed so workers are properly deemed as independent contractors. A good place to start is with a written employment agreement, which clearly labels the worker as an independent contractor.

However, labels will not control the outcome. The law (both tax law and agency law) has developed elaborate rules that control whether a particular worker is properly classified as an independent contractor. If the worker does not meet these tests, the label will mean nothing. The worker will be re-classified by the courts or the IRS as an employee. If this happens, the small business owner can expect a bill for back employment taxes, with interest and penalties, or an unfavorable outcome in a tort lawsuit.

Warning

Be careful about mislabeling workers. Because of the significant payroll tax advantages to using independent contractors, the IRS targets misclassifications when it audits small businesses.

Another instance when a misclassification may come to light is when a worker commits a tort and the injured party seeks to sue the LLC or corporation under the doctrine of respondeat superior. Here, the misclassification is at least worth a try. If the suit is lost, the result is no worse than if the worker had been properly classified in the first place.

Overall, however, the risks associated with an IRS audit may outweigh the benefits realized here.

Independent Contractor Legal Guidelines. Over the years, the courts have developed approximately 20 factors in testing whether workers are properly classified as independent contractors. For the most part, the IRS follows the same guidelines. Many of these factors can be condensed into one factor—control. What follows is a comparison of the two forms of employment, in terms of this factor.

Who Controls Them?

Independent Contractors	Employees
Control themselves. They determine their own fees and their own working hours, and provide their own tools. Fee usually set as bid per job. Usually work for multiple employers. Leave one employer when the job there is finished.	*Controlled by the employer. The employer determines the wages, paid (as an hourly wage or annual salary), and the working hours. The employer also provides all the tools of the trade. Usually work for one employer on a more or less permanent basis.*

Unfortunately, cases will usually turn on the peculiar facts of each particular employment situation.

Examples

The following three examples were taken from actual tax court cases:

- *Bicycle assembly workers were deemed employees even though they brought their own tools to work, furnished their own transportation to sites, and were largely unsupervised at sites because the employer had absolute control over the workers in terms of directing their rate of pay, working hours, assignments, etc., and prohibiting them from working for competitors.*

- *Telephone company solicitors who worked on the premises of the telephone company were deemed employees, but solicitors who worked at home were deemed independent contractors because they provided their own "tools of the trade."*

- *Associate physicians at a hospital were deemed employees because the hospital could fire them if they did not meet hospital standards, thus indicating that the hospital had control over the physicians.*

Following is the IRS 20-Factor Test. It was developed by the IRS for use in employer tax cases, but it also provides excellent general guidance as well. Be sure to check all 20 factors before attempting to use independent contractors. If there's any doubt, consult a legal professional.

IRS 20-Factor Test

These 20 factors are used to determine whether a worker is an independent contractor or employee.

1. **Instructions.** *A worker who is required to comply with other persons' instructions about when, where, and how he or she is to work is ordinarily an employee. This control factor is present if the person or persons for whom the services are performed have the right to require compliance with instructions.*

2. **Training.** *Training a worker by requiring an experienced employee to work with the worker, by corresponding with the worker, by requiring the worker to attend meetings, or by using other methods, indicates that the person or persons for whom the services are performed want the services performed in a particular method or manner.*

3. **Integration.** *Integration of the worker's services into the business operations generally shows that the worker is subject to direction and control. When the success or continuation of a business depends to an appreciable degree upon the performance of certain services, the workers who perform those services must necessarily be subject to a certain amount of control by the owner of the business.*

4. **Services Rendered Personally.** *If the services must be rendered personally, presumably the person or persons for whom the services are performed are interested in the methods used to accomplish the work as well as in the results.*

5. ***Hiring, Supervising and Paying Assistants.*** *If the person or persons for whom the services are performed hire, supervise, and pay assistants, that factor generally shows control over the workers on the job. However, if one worker hires, supervises, and pays the other assistants pursuant to a contract under which the worker agrees to provide materials and labor and under which the worker is responsible only for the attainment of a result, this factor indicates an independent contractor status.*

6. ***Continuing Relationship.*** *A continuing relationship between the worker and the person or persons for whom the services are performed indicates that an employer-employee relationship exists. A continuing relationship may exist where work is performed at frequently recurring although irregular intervals.*

7. ***Set Hours of Work.*** *The establishment of set hours of work by the person or persons for whom the services are performed is a factor indicating control.*

8. ***Full Time Required.*** *If the worker must devote substantially full time to the business of the person or persons for whom the services are performed, such person or persons have control over the amount of time the worker spends working and impliedly restrict the worker from doing other gainful work. An independent contractor, on the other hand, is free to work when and for whom he or she chooses.*

9. ***Doing Work on Employer's Premises.*** *If the work is performed on the premises of the person or persons for whom the services are performed, that factor suggests control over the worker, especially if the work could be done elsewhere. Work done off the premises of the person or persons receiving the services, such as at the office of the worker, indicates some freedom from control. However, this fact by itself does not mean that the worker is not an employee. The importance of this factor depends on the nature of the service involved and the extent to which an employer generally would require that employees perform such services on the employer's premises. Control over the place of work is indicated when the person or persons for whom the services are performed have the right to compel the worker to travel a designated route, to canvass a territory within a certain time, or to work at specific places as required.*

10. ***Order or Sequence Set.*** *If a worker must perform services in the order or sequence set by the person or persons for whom the services are performed, that factor shows that the worker is not free to follow the worker's own pattern of work but must follow the established routines and schedules of the person or persons for whom the services are performed. Often, because of the nature of an occupation, the person or persons for whom the services are performed do not set the order of the services or set the order infrequently. It is sufficient to show control, however, if such person or persons retain the right to do so.*

11. ***Oral or Written Reports.*** *A requirement that the worker submit regular or written reports to the person or persons for whom the services are performed indicates a degree of control.*

12. **Payment by Hour, Week, Month.** *Payment by the hour, week, or month generally points to an employer-employee relationship, provided that this method of payment is not just a convenient way of paying a lump sum agreed upon as the cost of a job. Payment made by the job or on a straight commission generally indicates that the worker is an independent contractor.*

13. **Payment of Business and/or Traveling Expenses.** *If the person or persons for whom the services are performed ordinarily pay the worker's business and/or traveling expenses, the worker is ordinarily an employee. An employer, to be able to control expenses, generally retains the right to regulate and direct the worker's business activities.*

14. **Furnishing of Tools and Materials.** *The fact that the person or persons for whom the services are performed furnish significant tools, materials, and other equipment tends to show the existence of an employer-employee relationship.*

15. **Significant Investment.** *If the worker invests in facilities that are used by the worker in performing services and are not typically maintained by employees (such as the maintenance of an office rented at fair value from an unrelated party), that factor tends to indicate that the worker is an independent contractor. On the other hand, lack of investment in facilities indicates dependence on the person or persons for whom the services are performed for such facilities and, accordingly, the existence of an employer-employee relationship. Special scrutiny is required with respect to certain types of facilities, such as home offices.*

16. **Realization of Profit or Loss.** *A worker who can realize a profit or suffer a loss as a result of the worker's services (in addition to the profit or loss ordinarily realized by employees) is generally an independent contractor, but the worker who cannot is an employee. For example, if the worker is subject to a real risk of economic loss due to significant investments or a bona fide liability for expenses, such as salary payments to unrelated employees, that factor indicates that the worker is an independent contractor. The risk that a worker will not receive payment for his or her services, however, is common to both independent contractors and employees and thus does not constitute a sufficient economic risk to support treatment as an independent contractor.*

17. **Working for More Than One Firm at a Time.** *If a worker performs more than de minimis services for a multiple of unrelated persons or firms at the same time, that factor generally indicates that the worker is an independent contractor. However, a worker who performs services for more than one person may be an employee of each of the persons, especially where such persons are part of the same service arrangement.*

18. **Making Service Available to General Public.** *The fact that a worker makes his or her services available to the general public on a regular and consistent basis indicates an independent contractor relationship.*

19. **Right to Discharge.** *The right to discharge a worker is a factor indicating that the worker is an employee and the person possessing the right is an employer. An employer exercises control through the threat of dismissal, which causes the worker to obey the employer's instructions. An independent contractor, on the other hand, cannot be fired so long as the independent contractor produces a result that meets the contract specifications.*

20. **Right to Terminate.** *If the worker has the right to end his or her relationship with the person for whom the services are performed at any time he or she wishes without incurring liability, that factor indicates an employer-employee relationship.*

IRS Section 530 Independent Contractor Safe Harbor Rule. In 1978, the Internal Revenue Code was amended to provide a so-called safe harbor for employers interested in using independent contractors. Note that this safe harbor will apply only in tax cases and should have no bearing in a tort case where the plaintiff is seeking to hold the employer accountable under respondeat superior. Further, under the rule, employers remain liable to contribute to retirement plans and are still required to withhold income tax and Social Security tax from employees' wages.

Plan Smart

The small business owner should attempt to fit his use of independent contractors into the confines of the IRS Section 530 safe harbor. To do so, the employer must prove two things, that the owner:

- *did not, ever, classify this worker, or any similar workers, as employees*

- *had a reasonable basis for classifying the worker as an independent contractor, either because of the common law tests or because a significant segment of the industry (usually 20 percent, but perhaps as low as 18 percent) has treated workers of this type as independent contractors for a long period of time (generally, at least 10 years).*

Section 530 is not available when the worker provides services as an engineer, designer, drafter, computer programmer, system analyst, or any similar line of work.

In 1996, the Section 530 safe harbor was amended to allow business owners to shift the burden of proof in cases to the IRS. Effective January 1, 1997, the employer, by showing any reasonable grounds were relied on in classifying the worker, can shift the burden to the IRS to disprove independent contractor status. Unless the IRS can do this, the classification is presumed to be valid. This modification was designed to codify an earlier court ruling. It is regarded as establishing a relatively low burden of proof for employers.

Until recently, the use of "temps" from an employment agency was considered another type of safe harbor. It was thought these workers could always be classified as independent contractors. However, in 1998 and 1999, court decisions clearly established that this is not a safe harbor.

In many cases, temporary workers are considered employees of the temp agencies that hire them. It also was thought that workers could only have one employer and that, accordingly, if temp workers were employees of the temp agency, then they could not be employees of the companies to which they were assigned. Thus, they must necessarily be independent contractors at the companies where they actually work. In these cases, the courts rejected this argument.

According to the courts, for tax purposes, workers may have two employers and be considered employees of both the temp agency and the company to which they are assigned.

In short, with respect to temp agency workers, the regular common law 20-factor test or the Section 530 safe harbor rules will apply.

Independent Contractor Exceptions. In tort cases, contrary to the general rule, courts may hold an employer liable for the acts of his independent contractor when:

- the employer has a legal duty that may not be delegated to another (such as the duty of an apartment building owner to maintain the premises in a safe condition)

- the activities involved are abnormally dangerous (such as using dynamite)

- the employer was negligent in hiring the independent contractor and, thus, committed a separate tort (as discussed previously)

Further, in contrast to the safe harbor rules, the IRS has special exceptions that govern independent contractor status for certain workers. These workers are *automatically, for tax purposes only*, deemed to be statutory employees.

These rules include an employer's workers who are:

- independent drivers who deliver beverages (other than milk), meats, vegetables, fruits, bakery products, or laundry or dry cleaning

- sales workers who call on hotels and restaurants

- home workers who perform work in their own home or the homes of others and are paid more than $100 during the year

- full-time life insurance salespersons

The employer, in each case, must withhold and match the required Social Security and Medicare taxes, as would be done for any other employee, but is not required to withhold income taxes from the employee's wages. Finally, except for full-time life insurance

salespersons, statutory employees—like independent contractors—
may be excluded from employee retirement plans.

Warning

As discussed in Part II, the Delaware LLC statute provides for the opportunity to create holding and operating entities within a single LLC. The advantages of this statute are significant. However, caution must be exercised so as to separate liability among the different separate entities. The first place this begins is in the articles of organization and the operating agreement.

Beyond this, however, in forming contracts, including the hiring of employees, the small business owner must ensure that the contracts are signed solely as an agent for a particular entity and not the LLC at large. Though there is only one LLC, each unit should be given a specific designation (as discussed in Chapter 13). The owner should then sign contracts as an agent of that particular named unit of the LLC.

Moreover, many states afford owners of a limited liability partnership (LLP) only a limited shield version of limited liability (as discussed in Chapter 6). This is a very significantly reduced form of limited liability. In these states, the owners of the LLP have limited liability only for the torts committed by co-owners of the LLP. In every other case, the owners have unlimited, personal liability. Thus, for example, the owners of an LLP in these states will have unlimited, personal liability for the acts of employees (contracts formed by employees and torts committed by employees), rather than the limited liability enjoyed by the owners of an LLC or a corporation.

This amounts to an almost wholesale exception to limited liability. This is why the small business owner should not confuse the LLP with the LLC, and why the LLP should not ordinarily be considered as a choice of business form, at least in those states that offer only the limited shield form of limited liability (see Chapter 6 for a detailed discussion of the limited shield of liability).

Chapter 16

Piercing the Veil of Limited Liability

A small business owner must pay close attention to recordkeeping and initial capitalization to avoid the doctrine of "piercing the veil" of limited liability. The veil is the shield of limited liability that stands between the owner of an LLC or corporation, and the business's creditors. Ordinarily, because of this valuable legal shield created when you formed your business entity, the business's creditors can only seek payment out of the business's assets.

When this veil is pierced, the business's creditors can reach the owner's personal assets outside of the business. In short, limited liability, perhaps the most important attribute of an LLC or a corporation, is lost.

This is a complete exception to limited liability. Unlike the financial withdrawal and transaction exceptions discussed in the Chapter 15, this exception does not apply to a *particular* business debt. It applies to all of the business's debts, if it applies at all.

However, this exception will arise in a lawsuit by a *particular creditor* of the business, who is seeking in a complaint to impose personal liability on the owner of the business. In other words, the creditor must sue the business owner personally, plead the doctrine of piercing of the veil of limited liability in his complaint, and then prove to the court that the doctrine should be applied to that particular case.

Of course, this type of lawsuit is even more likely in a business that has little capital within the business form, where the debt in question is unlikely to be satisfied from the business's assets. In fact, piercing of the veil of limited liability is regarded as one of the most frequently litigated issues involving small businesses.

The courts will apply this doctrine if the creditor can prove either one of two legal theories:

- **Alter Ego Theory** — The creditor must establish that the business owner failed to separate his financial affairs from the entity's financial affairs, and/or observe statutory formalities regarding division of authority within the entity, required meetings, and recordkeeping.

- **Undercapitalization Theory** — The creditor must prove that the owner *intentionally* underfunded the entity, when it was formed, to defraud the business's creditors.

Warning

There are circumstances where the piercing of the veil will automatically apply, and thus the owners of the business will automatically lose their limited liability.

LLCs and corporations must renew their status annually by filing a report with, and paying a fee to, the state in which they were formed. Failure to file the report and pay the fee will result in the automatic dissolution of the entity.

If this happens and the owner continues to operate the business, the owner is then operating a sole proprietorship if there is one owner, or a general partnership if there are two or more owners. Either way, the owners have unlimited, personal liability for all of the business's debts.

Other events can trigger dissolution of the business and produce a similar result. However, these events can be controlled in an entity's articles of organization and operating agreement, or bylaws (this topic is covered in Chapter 13).

Finally, don't confuse a failure to renew the entity annually or biannually, which triggers an automatic dissolution, with failure of an LLC or a corporation to register as a foreign entity when it does business in a state other than the state in which it was formed. Here, the failure, in most states, does not trigger dissolution, and the foreign entity's contracts and limited liability remain intact. In some states, however, this failure, too, can cause dissolution (see Chapter 13 for details).

ALTER EGO THEORY

Under the alter ego theory, the creditor must prove that the owner did not operate his LLC or corporation as if it were a separate legal entity.

It is this "separateness" that forms the basis for limited liability. Ordinarily, the LLC and corporation are recognized as separate legal entities, and each is responsible for its own debts. The owner, as a separate person, has no personal liability for the business entity's debts.

Accordingly, as long as the owner respects this separateness, the business entity will continue to be recognized as a separate entity, and the business entity itself (and not the owner, who is a separate person) will be responsible for the business's debts. The most the owner can lose will be what has been invested into the business entity. In other words, the owner will have limited liability for the business's debts.

Conversely, if this separateness is not apparent in the way the business owner operates the LLC or corporation, there is no basis for limited liability. In short, if the owner acts as if the LLC or corporation is not a separate legal entity, but instead just another side of the owner (i.e., his alter ego), the court may rule that the owner and the entity are one and the same. Thus, the owner will, out of necessity, have *unlimited, personal liability for all of the business's debts.*

In general, avoiding the alter ego theory means operating the business entities in ways that steer clear of the factual patterns wherein courts have applied the theory. As was suggested above, the owner should form an LLC or statutory close corporation, and then must separate and document ownership of assets. Further, the formalities regarding division of authority within the entity, required meetings and recordkeeping must be observed. Finally, the owner must separate his or her financial affairs from the entity's financial affairs, as well as separating the financial affairs among all operating entities.

Form an LLC or a Statutory Close Corporation

The management structure and operating rules for the LLC and statutory close corporation are extremely flexible. There are only a few rules imposed on these entities by statute. This can be a real advantage in terms of asset protection. The failure to follow mandatory rules imposed on business entities makes up one of the main bases courts use in invoking the alter ego theory. A lack of mandatory rules should, *to a certain extent*, immunize the LLC and statutory close corporation from the application of this theory.

In contrast, a conventional corporation is governed by what are sometimes termed the "corporate formalities." The management structure and operating rules for a conventional corporation are imposed by statute. These mandatory statutory rules dictate that the corporation be governed by three classes: shareholders, directors and officers. The rules divide authority among these three groups. The rules also require shareholders and directors to hold meetings, at least on an annual basis. The rules define notice and quorum requirements for meetings, and provide strict procedures for waiver of meetings. Adequate records must be kept of all meetings.

It is not difficult to run astray of these rules. Salary, lease and loan agreements might be authorized by the wrong group, or not authorized at all. Scheduled meetings may not be held or formally waived. These failures are prime ingredients that may allow a creditor to make a claim based on the alter ego theory.

On the other hand, one group can manage the LLC and statutory close corporation: the owners (or a select number of owners). The management form is selected in the articles of organization (note that, in the case of the statutory close corporation, the necessity of a board of directors would have to be waived in the articles of organization). This eliminates the confusion that can arise when authority is divided among three groups (shareholders, directors and officers), each with its own specific authority.

Further, the LLC is not required, by statute, to hold any meetings. In the statutory close corporation, generally the articles can waive the necessity of a shareholder's meeting.

In each case, the entity is managed by an operating agreement signed by all of the owners. The absence of the division of authority among separate groups, and the absence of mandatory meeting requirements, should make it difficult for a creditor to prove a claim based on the alter ego theory.

Plan Smart

Nearly all of the cases in which courts have applied the alter ego theory have involved conventional corporations.

Planners know that this theory will also apply to LLCs, but exactly how it will apply involves some degree of speculation. The argument advanced above, that the theory is less likely to apply to LLCs and statutory close corporations, because of a lack of statutory formalities, is not yet tested. In short, while this argument is likely to prove out in practice, there is no guarantee that every court will accept this argument.

Note too, that as discussed below, courts can invoke this theory in other ways that will apply to LLCs and statutory close corporations.

Separate and Document Ownership of Assets

As previously mentioned, the owner can fund the business entity as an owner and as a creditor with debt such as leases and loans (as discussed in Chapter 8). In order to avoid application of the alter ego theory by the courts when an outside creditor seeks to pierce the veil of limited liability, assets must be associated with a particular entity.

So when assets are transferred to a business entity in exchange for an ownership interest, care must be taken to ensure that legal title is effectively transferred. Transfer of real estate and motor vehicles requires that a formal document of title, that takes a certain form, be executed and recorded. In other cases, a written document, that is more flexible in its form, should be used to transfer title (see Chapter 4 for a further discussion of transfer issues).

In short, the business entity should hold title to the assets it owns. Similarly, bank accounts and credit cards should be established in the entity's name.

Frequently, the small business owner will continue to use an existing checking account, stationery or legal forms that were established in the owner's personal name or the old business's name. Doing this can trigger a piercing of the veil of limited liability, because the new business will, in effect, be using assets that it does not own, or have the right to use, under a written agreement.

Close old bank accounts and credit card accounts. Discard unused checks. Open new accounts and credit cards in the new entity's name. Discard old stationery and legal forms. Have stationery and legal forms printed in the new entity's name.

The cost of doing this is minimal, especially in comparison to the risk of loss that is eliminated.

In addition, when leases and loans are used in funding the business entity, written agreements must be recorded. These agreements also should be formally authorized by the entity if the management structure requires such authorization (e.g., by a majority of the LLC managers).

Co-Mingling

Co-mingling of assets involves the owner using business resources for personal purposes, or the business using the owner's personal resources for business purposes. Co-mingling is also a primary basis upon which courts apply the alter ego theory. When the above rules regarding separation and documentation are followed, co-mingling of assets should not occur.

Especially in the case of the small business owner, co-mingling can occur in other instances, because assets and expenses can have mixed (part business, part personal) uses. Adequate documentation of the business purpose of a transaction can ensure that no co-mingling will occur.

In one case, a court refused to pierce the veil of a corporation, even though the owner had used corporate funds to pay what appeared to be personal expenses, including travel, dry cleaning, telephone, and even housing expenses of the owner.

The court found that these expenses could be considered legitimate business expenses. The court based this conclusion on the fact that the owner meticulously maintained separate corporate records and accounts that clearly identified the business purpose of the expenditures. Thus, no co-mingling of business and personal resources occurred, as the expenses paid by the business were business expenses and not personal expenses of the owner.

In contrast, this same court did pierce the veil of a corporation where the corporation paid unauthorized *salary advances and* unauthorized *loan payments on the owner's personal car. Here, the lack of records and authorizations meant that the expenses were not legitimate business expenses, but instead personal expenses of the owner. Thus, co-mingling (paying personal expenses from business resources) occurred.*

The small business owner should be aware of a fact pattern that afflicts many small business owners, one that can prove fatal from an asset protection perspective. Many times, there will be insufficient cash available in the business's accounts to pay the business's bills, or in the owner's personal accounts to pay the owner's personal bills. Be aware that this is the situation most likely to result in a co-mingling of resources.

Unfortunately, it is also likely that, in this situation, the business will be experiencing financial difficulties. This makes it more likely that the business will undergo scrutiny from creditors who are not being paid. This scrutiny may take the form of a lawsuit, wherein the creditors attempt to prove that the alter ego theory should be applied to the owner and the entity.

A business entity should *never* directly pay what are clearly personal expenses of the owner.

Example

 Let's say a business owner needs a new roof on his personal residence, which will cost $4,000, but the owner does not have sufficient funds in his personal accounts to cover this cost. He does, however, have sufficient funds in his business entity's accounts. This cost cannot be justified as a business expense, at least if the owner conducts his operations outside of the home.

It would be a mistake to have the entity issue a check on the business account payable to the roofing company. This would represent a co-mingling of resources and could open the owner to a piercing of the veil argument.

Instead, the entity should authorize, in writing, and then pay the owner a salary, pursuant to a written salary agreement between the owner and the entity. A check from the business account would be issued to the owner, and recorded on the entity's books as salary expense. The owner would deposit the check in his personal account and then write a personal check to the roofer.

This ensures that the required separateness exists. It is advisable to pay an amount of salary that does not exactly match the owner's personal expense. It also is advisable to pay salary on a regular basis. Following these two strategies can prevent a court from "collapsing" the separate transactions into a single transaction, wherein the court would conclude that the business paid the owner's personal expenses. Note, too, that regular payments from the entity to the owner for leases and loaned assets also accomplish the same goal as a payment of salary.

Similarly, the business owner should never *personally* pay what are clearly business expenses from his personal accounts.

Example

Say the business entity's telephone bill, for $400, is due, but this business lacks the required funds in its accounts to pay the bill. It would be a mistake for the owner to pay this bill with a personal check or credit card. Instead, the owner could lend the cash to the entity, under a written loan agreement. *It is not necessary that a new loan agreement be executed each time. Instead, an open-end agreement can be used (see Chapter 14 for details). The entity could use the loaned funds to pay the bill directly from its business checking account.*

Mixed-Use Assets

Further, in some instances, the small business owner will personally own mixed-use assets, used for both personal and business purposes. Good examples are a home where the owner has a home-based business, a computer and an automobile.

Plan Smart

A personal residence should never *be transferred to a business entity (as discussed in Chapter 3). Doing so will result in the loss of the homestead exemption.*

Further, the small business owner should consider personally owning certain "tools of the trade," including a personal automobile, office equipment and furniture, and then leasing these assets to the business entity (as discussed in Chapters 3 and 8). This also ensures that the exemption for this category of assets will continue to be available to the owner. Of course, such arrangements must be properly authorized by the entity, and in the form of a written agreement between the owner and the entity.

With assets that are personally owned, but have mixed uses, the best approach is as follows:

- The owner should pay the general expenses associated with the asset from his personal accounts. The entity should then, pursuant to a written agreement between the entity and the owner, reimburse the owner for the business portion of these expenses. Records must be kept of the business usage. For a home, the relative square footage of the business office can be used. For a computer, a log evidencing hours of business usage and personal usage is appropriate. For an automobile, a record of business miles and total mileage driven is required.

- Where a particular expense can be directly attributed in its entirety to the business, this expense should be paid from the business account.

Example

 John Smith, sole owner an LLC, uses his personally owned automobile for both personal and business purposes. He records the automobile's mileage at the beginning and end of the year. In one year, he drives 18,000 miles. His log shows he drove 12,000 business miles. This represents two-thirds of the automobile's total usage.

Smith should pay the general operating costs for the vehicle from his personal accounts, because he owns the vehicle personally. Smith should form a written agreement with the LLC, wherein the LLC will reimburse Smith for two-thirds of all operating expenses associated with the vehicle. This can be done on a weekly, biweekly or monthly basis.

If Smith incurs an expense solely attributable to business usage (e.g., a parking fee or toll on a business trip), this expense should be paid directly from the business's accounts.

Note that the objective here is the separation of the owner's and the entity's financial affairs, so as to prevent an application of the alter ego theory. However, keep in mind that, although tax planning is not the objective here, for tax purposes, a one-owner LLC is a "disregarded entity" (see Chapter 14). Thus, for tax purposes, *reimbursement from the entity serves no purpose.* For tax purposes, *the owner and the entity are one and the same.*

Emphasize Proper Recordkeeping

The small business owner should purchase an LLC or a corporate Records Kit. This can be done at any office supply store. The kit represents a centralized place to keep the entity's articles of organization, operating agreement (or bylaws), resolutions and minutes from meetings, lease and loan agreements, and ownership certificates.

It is important that the owner use ownership certificates when an equity interest is received in return for a contribution of property to the entity. A kit can be ordered that will contain ownership certificates that are pre-printed with the entity's name. Or a kit can be purchased with blank certificates and then filled in by the owner with the entity's name.

It also is essential that the entity have its own accounting system. If this is not done, it will prove impossible to separate the owner's and the entity's financial affairs. Popular accounting software packages, which are generally affordable and useful, include Quickbooks, Peachtree and One-Write Plus.

Plan Smart

Don't try to start a new business and learn a new accounting system at the same time. Doing so will often mean that recordkeeping will fail, and the business owner will become vulnerable to a piercing of the veil attack by a creditor.

Owners of new businesses will be preoccupied with many issues. With perhaps 60 or 70 hours per week spent on marketing and management issues alone, many small business owners will neglect the business's accounting system.

Ideally, the small business owner should hire a bookkeeper familiar with the software package selected. Admittedly, this may not be realistic in many small businesses, where the budget will not allow this alternative.

In this situation, the small business owner should consider purchasing software and learning how to use it, before starting operations. *Many community colleges offer courses or seminars on many popular accounting software packages.*

All arrangements between the owner and the entity should be documented. This means that all salary, lease and loan arrangements should be reduced to the form of written agreements between the owner and the entity. While this may seem to border on the absurd in a one-owner business, establishing such a formal relationship with the entity is significant evidence that the owner is treating the entity as separate from himself. Authorization may require a meeting, or that a waiver form be executed by the business's owners.

Hold Regularly Scheduled Meetings

Both the LLC and the statutory close corporation can negate the need for meetings. However, a conventional corporation is required by statute to hold, at a minimum, annual meetings of shareholders and directors. These meetings are governed by statutory rules regarding required notice, quorums, voting, etc. Care must be taken that all of these requirements are followed. The meetings can be waived, if the waiver is in writing and unanimous. Business is then transacted in the written waiver form.

A failure to hold required meetings or execute written waivers has been used to pierce the veil of limited liability in numerous cases.

Sometimes the operating agreement for an LLC or a statutory close corporation may require meetings of the management. This may be desirable, for example, in a large, multi-owner organization, to prevent any one individual from carrying out activities without the knowledge and authorization of the other owners. Where meetings are required by the operating agreement, there may be less of a likelihood that piercing of the veil of limited liability would be applied due to a failure to hold meetings, as the meetings are not mandated by statute. Nevertheless, in this situation, it would be wise to follow the previous advice regarding meetings in the conventional corporation.

In a one-owner entity, or an entity with just a few owners, it may be advisable in the operating agreement to dispense with the need for meetings altogether and instead delegate authority to particular owners to carry out the business's operations. This eliminates a frequent avenue of attack under the alter ego theory.

Separate the Financial Affairs for Each Entity

Previously, we advocated the strategy of using a holding entity and an operating entity (see Chapter 8). In addition, the small business owner also may want to consider forming multiple operating entities, one for each distinct area of the business. Court decisions have made it clear that the entities will be recognized as separate from each other, and from the owner, even when there is one common owner who manages each entity. However, care must be taken to ensure that the principles described above are applied *separately* to *each* entity.

Thus, each entity should hold title to its own assets. These assets should be contributed to the entity in exchange for an ownership interest. The contributor should take back ownership certificates in his/her or its name (as discussed in Chapter 8, the holding entity may be the contributor, and thus the owner, of the operating entities). Each entity should also have separate bank accounts and credit cards in its own name, its own Records Kit, and its own accounting system.

Note that a single accounting software package can be used for multiple separate entities. Each entity is simply accounted for as a separate file within the system.

Where ownership and management overlaps among the entities, the owner also must ensure that he acts individually for each separate entity. Separate recordkeeping systems and separate documentation can help ensure that this is the case.

Under the Delaware LLC statute, when multiple entities are created under a single LLC, special care must be taken to ensure that each entity is recognized as separate and distinct. Each unit should be designated with a name in the articles of organization, and this name should be used in all of the transactions affecting that unit. The unit should be operated in the same way it would be had it been established as an unrelated LLC.

UNDERCAPITALIZATION THEORY

The undercapitalization theory requires that the creditor prove the business owner *intentionally* underfunded the entity when it was initially organized to defraud the business's creditors.

Because an owner's liability for the business's entity's debts is limited to the investment in the entity, the business owner should invest as little vulnerable capital as possible within the business form (as suggested in Chapter 8). Further, this strategy will continue to be effective only if there also is in place a plan to withdraw vulnerable funds as they are generated by the business entity.

These strategies may seem incompatible with the undercapitalization theory. However, with proper planning, the small business owner can minimize his investment of vulnerable capital within the business form *and* avoid the application of this theory.

Specifically, to avoid the undercapitalization theory, the business owner should avoid doing anything that might result in application of the alter ego theory and focus on the initial capitalization of the operating entities.

Avoid the Alter Ego Theory in Undercapitalization

In almost every case where courts have pierced the veil of limited liability based on the undercapitalization theory, the courts were influenced, in large part, by a finding that ingredients also were present to pierce the veil based on the alter ego theory. Thus, avoiding the alter ego theory, as previously discussed, can be a major component in avoiding the undercapitalization theory as well.

Example

In one case, a court pierced the veil of limited liability and held the owner of a corporation personally liable for his corporation's debt, which amounted to over $100,000. The court applied both piercing of the veil theories. It found that the corporation in whose name the debt existed:

- *never held a corporate meeting and kept no corporate records*

- *owned* no *assets at all (except one checking account) and instead used* without any written agreements or formal arrangement *assets owned by a second corporation*

- *used its only asset, the checking account, to pay the owner's salary in the second corporation*

- *paid personal expenses of the owner, including his golf dues and the cost of landscaping his yard, without establishing that these were in any way business expenses.*

The court also pierced the veil in the second corporation, which was owned by the same individual. The end result was that the individual owner and the two corporations, which he controlled, were all held personally liable for a significant debt only in the name of one corporation. The court found that the second corporation:

- *also never held corporate meetings and kept no corporate records*

- *owned vehicles that carried the name and logo of the first corporation*

- *owned a vehicle which was used by the owner as his* personal *vehicle, once again,* without any written agreement or formal authorization

This case presents a classic example of co-mingling of assets, a failure to follow formalities in operating the business, and an inadequate capitalization due to the lack of formally authorized and documented arrangements between the owner and the two corporations. All of this could have been avoided. The owner's mistakes cost him $100,000!

Focus on the Initial Capitalization

Courts examine the capitalization of the business *at the time it was formed*. Thus, the *initial capitalization* also should be the focus of the business owner. Further, because the holding entity will have no direct operating activities, the focus here should be on the entities exposed to liability—namely, the *operating entities*.

Court decisions establish that if an entity subsequently becomes underfunded because of events unanticipated at the time it was formed, the undercapitalization theory will not apply. This is due to the fact that, in this theory, the creditor must prove fraudulent intent on the part of the owner. This will be lacking when the initial capitalization was reasonable, in relation to the entity's anticipated capital and operating needs.

Thus, before forming the business or beginning operations, the small business owner should prepare a capital budget that projects the business's need for equipment, furniture, supplies and other capital assets. The owner also should prepare a forecast of anticipated operating revenue and operating expenses for the first year, on a quarterly basis. Consideration should be given to financing any anticipated shortfall in this operating budget, along with the capital needs of the business.

Adequately financing the entity means supplying the entity with capital that does not fall significantly short of its anticipated needs. Financing the entity adequately does *not* mean contributing the anticipated capital and operating shortfall in return for an ownership interest in the entity. Court decisions have established that funding the entity with debt (i.e., leases and loans) is a legitimate business practice. In fact, in most cases in which the undercapitalization theory has been invoked, there has been a complete failure to adequately capitalize the entity with equity or debt.

Nevertheless, it would be a mistake to finance the entity entirely with debt. The owner must take back an ownership interest (in funding the business, the small business owner should follow the guidelines outlined in Chapter 8).

There, a mixture of equity and debt financing is recommended. The debt component can represent 30 through 70 percent of the capital contributed. A higher debt component may be justifiable, but unnecessary. Assets contributed for the equity interest can subsequently be encumbered with liens that run to the holding entity or the owner (as discussed in Chapter 8). These liens will adequately protect the asset contributed in return for an ownership interest.

In short, it is important to adequately fund the entity to meet its anticipated capital and operating needs. This can be done with a combination of equity and debt financing. The assets contributed for the debt portion through leases and loans will not be vulnerable because the owner (or the holding entity) will assume the role of a creditor. The assets contributed for the equity interest will be encumbered with liens that run in favor of the owner or the holding entity. These assets will be protected as well.

Thus, adequately financing the entity does *not* mean the capital contributed has to be vulnerable to the claims of the business's creditors.

Courts have specifically approved of the use of a holding entity, which owns most of the business's assets, and a separate operating entity, which conducts the business's activities and is funded primarily through leases and loans.

Example

In one case, a court refused to pierce the veil of an operating corporation under the undercapitalization theory, even though most of the business's assets were owned by a separate holding entity. At stake was liability for a series of promissory notes in default.

The court reached this conclusion even though the owner personally testified that the operating entity was grossly undercapitalized, and that the operating entity depended entirely on the resources of the holding entity.

The court ruled that the plaintiffs misconstrued the owner's testimony. The court found that there was a legitimate business purpose behind the arrangement. Because the holding company owned the assets, creditors could rely on the credit of the holding entity through personal guarantees from the holding entity, for example. Thus, it was unnecessary to place ownership of most of the capital within the operating entity. In short, there was nothing fraudulent about the arrangement. Absent any fraud, the undercapitalization theory will not apply.

Of course, all arrangements between the holding entity and the operating entity, including the establishment of the equity interest in the operating entity, and lease and loans arrangements, should be authorized and in written form.

In addition, the focus on the initial capitalization also means that unanticipated capital needs, operating expenses, or losses in revenue should not invoke the undercapitalization theory—even if future capital becomes inadequate, and the owner continues to receive payments for salary, leases and loans made to the entity.

Example

In one case involving a car dealership, the court refused to pierce the veil of a corporation, even though the business's growth meant that the entity became *significantly undercapitalized. The court ruled that the capitalization,* at the time the business was formed, *was the relevant consideration. The court found that, at the time the business was formed, it was adequately funded. Subsequently, due to significant growth, unanticipated at the time the business was formed, additional capital became necessary. A failure to provide this additional capital was not fraudulent. Thus, the undercapitalization theory was inapplicable.*

The court also ruled, consistent with the general rule discussed above, that withdrawals of assets for legitimate business purposes by the owner (here, a withdrawal of $250,000 occurred) are not fraudulent, under the undercapitalization theory, even though they leave the business undercapitalized.

This ruling was made even though the owner testified that he withdraw the $250,000 to cover operating expenses in another entity he owned, because that entity was experiencing financial difficulties. The court concluded that the withdrawal was motivated by a legitimate business purpose, and not by an intent to defraud the car dealership's creditors.

The same conclusion could have been reached had the payments been made to the owner for salary, leases and loans, especially if these were ongoing payments, made pursuant to authorized and written agreements.

Note that, as previously discussed under the alter ego theory, all *arrangements between the owner and the entity (or between entities) should be authorized in the form of written agreements.*

In making withdrawals from the business, the owner must be cognizant of the rules imposed by the Uniform Fraudulent Transfers Act (UFTA). The small business owner must also be aware of separate rules in state LLC and corporation statutes that regulate payments to the owner on account of his ownership interest, such as distributions of earnings, dividends or ownership redemptions (these rules are covered in Chapter 14).

Plan Smart

Remember that roles can be reversed. At times, the small business owner may be a creditor who is owed a significant sum of money by a debtor who has defaulted.

The small business owner should rely on principles presented in this chapter (as well as in Chapter 15) when acting in the role of creditor.

Thus, the small business owner should be protected in this instance because he will have required the other party to personally guarantee his entity's debts (as discussed in Chapter 15).

In addition, the small business owner, armed with the information in this chapter, may be able to pierce the veil of limited liability, in the event there has been no personal guarantee, and in this way hold the debtor personally liable for the debt.

In summary, by using all of the strategies outlined above, the business owner can minimize his investment of vulnerable capital within the business form *and* avoid both the alter ego theory and the undercapitalization theory.

When combining this strategy with the advice on limiting liability for contracts and torts (see Chapter 15), the small business owner can avoid all, or almost all, of the exceptions to limited liability and thus preserve this valuable legal shield.

Warning

It is probably not an exaggeration the say that, in the majority of cases, small business owners operate their businesses in ways that mean piercing of the veil of limited liability could easily apply.

In addition, studies have shown that piercing of the veil is one of the most frequently litigated issues involving closely held businesses.

Be aware: these two facts can combine to destroy a business and an owner's personal wealth.

By preserving limited liability, the owner will have protected his personal wealth outside of the business. Chapter 17 discusses ways in which the small business owner can use the civil litigation system to protect both personal wealth and business's assets.

Chapter 17

Navigating the Court System

Most Americans understand that we live in a litigious society. For example, new physicians usually are taught that they should *expect* to be sued for malpractice. The results of being sued can be both financially and psychologically devastating.

In many cases, even a defendant who wins a lawsuit still loses financially, because the cost of defending against the suit generally will not be reimbursed, even when the defendant prevails. Even preparing for the *possibility* of being sued can be financially devastating.

Warning

Physicians in many specialty areas pay over $50,000 per year for malpractice insurance. Insurance companies justify such extreme premiums by underscoring the significant likelihood that the insured party will be sued, and that the plaintiff will be awarded substantial monetary damages.

Extreme malpractice premiums have caused some physicians to forego malpractice insurance, and many states, in turn, mandate that they carry such insurance.

Litigation also can have significant psychological consequences. In some cases, those who render professional services may begin to question their competency. Defendants, in general, may be extremely anxious and concerned, in particular, that they may lose their reputation and their home, bank accounts, or other personal property, acquired through years of hard work.

As discussed below, not all of these concerns are misplaced, as most defendants do not know how to control a court system that significantly heightens the risk of loss, and then they complicate matters by also not having a comprehensive asset protection plan in place.

The significant risk of being sued, of course, is not limited to physicians or even to professionals in general. The small business owner who will be performing personal services must be especially cognizant of the risks of being sued. Personal commission of a tort, such as negligence or malpractice, represents a significant exception to the limited liability that otherwise applies in an LLC or a corporation (as discussed in Chapter 15). Thus, the consequence of personally committing a tort will not only be a risk of loss of the business's assets, *but of the owner's personal assets, outside of the business, as well.*

Moreover, a successful business will employ many other people who may commit negligence while carrying out the entity's business. Liability for negligence committed by employees generally will run to the entity, thus exposing the business's assets to a risk of loss (as described in Chapter 15). Further, when the business entity sells goods that could cause injury, there is a significant risk that the purchaser, members of that household and, possibly, subsequent transferees will sue the business based on what is termed "product liability."

Of course, the small business owner also will face a significant risk of litigation due to the many contracts the business entity forms. Further, if the entity and its contracts (including sales and employment contracts) are not properly structured, liability may run *to the owner personally*. In addition, if the owner has guaranteed the entity's contracts, liability will extend to the owner's *personal assets* (as discussed in Chapter 15).

For these reasons and more, it is imperative to have an understanding of the risk factors inherent in litigation, as well as the ways you can better control the risk factors of the court system to your advantage.

RISK FACTORS INHERENT IN LITIGATION

As previously discussed, risk of loss from contract and tort liability can be significant for small business owners because the operation of a business naturally involves exposures to liability. Further, limited liability will not protect the owner of a personal service business (e.g., an accounting firm) who personally commits a tort.

However, the civil litigation system *itself* also represents a significant risk, because many factors make it more likely that an unjust lawsuit will be filed and, as a consequence, the defendant will be forced to pay significant monetary damages to the plaintiff—either to settle the case or as the result of a jury assessment. On the flip side, a plaintiff with a just but relatively small claim will be forced to forego making the claim for economic reasons that discourage litigation. By understanding these risk factors, and controlling them, the small business owner can significantly reduce his overall exposure to liability.

Many factors in civil litigation make exposure to liability, and thus risk of loss, so extreme:

- the combination of contingent fee arrangements for plaintiffs, hourly rates for defendants and the lack of a "loser pays" system makes litigation economically disadvantageous to a business owner being sued

- a business owner filing suit also faces economic disadvantages because of the lack of a loser pays system, and he or she usually cannot take advantage of getting legal help on contingency, but must pay upfront for hourly services, further discouraging action

- low burden of proof needed to win civil cases

- expert witnesses for hire

- liberal availability of pre-trial discovery

- right to a jury trial

- exclusion of evidence from trial

- ease of proving negligence

- ease of proving monetary damages for negligence

- impact of the government as a plaintiff

Economic Disadvantages When Being Sued

The combination of three components of our civil litigation system presents a real threat to small business owners who one day may find themselves at the receiving end of a lawsuit:

- Attorneys for plaintiffs (the person or entity suing) handle many damage-type cases on a contingency basis. In other words, the plaintiff doesn't have to lay out any money to sue and the attorney only gets paid if his client prevails.

- While the person suing may not have to put any money down, the defendant (the person being sued) is paying an attorney an hourly rate to defend himself against the lawsuit. As you can imagine, these hourly rates are substantial and can really add up.

- In our civil litigation system, if someone sues you and they lose, as a general rule, they do not have to reimburse you for your cost of defending yourself against their suit. The United States does not have, for lack of a better phrase, a "loser pays" system.

Warning

At this point you may be asking yourself what happens if you're the plaintiff in a civil litigation suit? If a small business owner wants to sue a customer who defaulted on an account, or maybe the owner has a claim against another business, chances are the attorney's fee is still going to be paid on an hourly basis. Attorneys typically take cases on contingency only if there is a great likelihood that the damage award will be large enough to justify the services they provide.

So no matter which side you're on, as a small business owner, there's a serious economic downside to being involved in a lawsuit.

Contingent Fees for Plaintiffs

Typically, attorneys for plaintiffs will handle personal injury and other cases on a contingent fee basis, where there is a substantial likelihood of both a win and a large award of damages. Usually, the attorney will collect, as a fee, one-third of the amount of monetary damages secured by way of a judgment or a settlement, although some states limit such fees when damages are very large. With a contingent fee arrangement, if the attorney secures a $180,000 settlement, the fee for this one case is $60,000. However, of course, if he is unable to secure a settlement or judgment, he collects no fee at all.

A contingent fee arrangement also means that a plaintiff can bring or threaten an action without spending any financial resources whatsoever. Even the other costs of bringing the action (e.g., sheriff's fees, court fees, and fees for experts) are usually advanced by the attorney.

The availability of a contingent fee arrangement for plaintiffs is considered to be justifiable, from a social point of view, because it allows individuals without financial resources to seek redress for losses.

Of course, in practice, plaintiff's attorneys often will not accept a contingent fee arrangement unless there is both a substantial likelihood of a win *and* a large monetary settlement or judgment. However, many cases that are worthwhile from a societal viewpoint, or as a matter of principal, do not involve either of these possibilities and, thus, are not accepted by attorneys on a contingent fee basis.

When being sued, you're at a serious economic disadvantage because the plaintiff often has the services of an attorney motivated by the rewards a contingent fee can bring. Unfortunately, you will probably not be able to offer the same economic incentive to your legal team.

Hourly Rates for Defendants

Contingent fee arrangements are not generally available to defendants, who usually are not attempting to collect damages. Thus, if you're sued, you must hire an attorney on an hourly fee basis, at rates usually in the range of $150 to $250 *per hour*. A retainer, or "down payment," typically in the range of $1,000 to $5,000, will be required upfront.

A defendant who does not have significant financial resources will not be able to hire an attorney and, thus, will not be able to effectively defend against the claim. This is in stark contrast to the plaintiff who will bring the claim.

So before you even get your day in court, economic factors put two strikes against you when preparing for the suit.

The Lack of a Loser Pays System

On top of the economic disadvantages of defending a suit with limited resources against an opponent who is not similarly limited, the outcome—win or lose—produces a third financial setback. The legal system does not allow for you to recoup your costs, even if you're right.

In a "loser pays" litigation system, the loser of the action is compelled to reimburse the other party for attorney's fees and related costs. This means that, if the plaintiff wins, he is awarded his regular monetary damages, *plus* his attorney's fees and other costs. If the defendant wins, he pays no damages to the plaintiff, *and* he is reimbursed by the plaintiff for his (the defendant's) attorney's fees and costs. Reimbursement does not result in any gain to the defendant. Instead, it just means that the defendant will not suffer any loss.

This outcome seems to make sense. For this reason, many people are surprised to learn that the United States does *not* have a "loser pays" system. In the United States, as a general rule, a plaintiff who wins collects only his compensatory damages. He must compensate his attorney at his expense, perhaps from the proceeds of the case. If the defendant wins, he must still pay his own attorney's fees and related costs. Despite the court victory, this is a loss in itself.

The system used in the United States is known as the American Rule. The theory behind the American Rule is that a risk of reimbursement might dissuade plaintiffs from bringing legitimate claims, thus causing losses not only to the plaintiffs themselves, but to society as well.

Warning

The lack of a loser pays system has serious implications.

In a contingent fee case, even the defendant with significant financial resources faces a serious dilemma. He must pay his attorney $150 to $250 per hour (or more), while the plaintiff's attorney will cost him nothing out of pocket.

A full trial, in a simple case, might cost the defendant $10,000 or more in attorney's fees. Even if the defendant wins the case, he does not get reimbursed for his attorney's fees, and thus loses $10,000. So, whether you win or lose the case, you ultimately lose in the long run.

This system provides a strong incentive for defendants to settle cases by offering to pay plaintiffs monetary damages, even when defendants are sure they will prevail at trial. If a defendant offers to pay the plaintiff $6,000 to settle the case, the defendant will actually save $4,000, as compared to "winning" the case at trial and paying his own attorney $10,000.

The combination of contingent fees for plaintiffs, hourly fees for defendants, and the lack of a loser pays system works to allow a type of legal extortion. Plaintiffs with frivolous claims can threaten to sue, unless they are given financial compensation. Faced with this type of threat, defendants have a strong financial incentive to meet the plaintiff's demands.

Of course, this combination also means that plaintiffs can sue (or threaten to sue) *without risking anything whatsoever.* If the suit is not successful, the loss will have cost the plaintiff nothing. This fact makes the use of such threats even more pervasive.

Economic Disadvantages When Filing Suit

Ironically, the same legal system that makes it easy for a business owner to be sued also makes it hard for a business owner to bring a suit of his own.

Of course, business owners also are involved in the civil litigation system as plaintiffs. Unfortunately, in these types of cases, the services of an attorney usually cannot be secured by way of a contingent fee. Where the likelihood of either a win or a substantial award of damages is small, plaintiffs will be forced to hire an attorney on an hourly basis.

Moreover, the lack of a loser pays system can adversely affect plaintiffs who have to pay an attorney on an hourly basis. In this situation, plaintiffs face a dilemma: Why bring a claim that may result in, say, $10,000 in attorney's fees, when nothing or less than $10,000 is likely to be collected?

In short, the combination of an hourly fee for plaintiffs and a lack of a loser pays system gives plaintiffs with legitimate claims a direct financial incentive to forego the claims. Thus, for example, small business owners may find it more economical to simply write-off claims against customers that default on their accounts or other commercial parties in breach of contract, instead of filing suit.

Low Burden of Proof in a Civil Case

The standard a plaintiff must meet to win a civil case (e.g., a claim based on negligence or breach of contract) is "preponderance of the evidence." This standard is fairly low and easy to meet. This can make the civil litigation system a serious risk factor for small business owners who find themselves defendants in actions, especially in light of other related risk factors discussed later (i.e., expert witnesses for hire, pre-trial discovery and right to a jury trial).

Under the preponderance of the evidence standard, the plaintiff needs only to establish a more-than-50-percent probability that the allegations are true. Thus, if a jury concluded that there was a 51 percent probability the plaintiff's claim was justified and a 49 percent probability that the defendant's assertions were true, the plaintiff would win, even though, essentially, the case is evenly split between the two parties.

In contrast, in criminal cases, the plaintiff (i.e., the government) must prove its case "beyond a reasonable doubt." This standard—which equates to the plaintiff establishing a more-than-90-percent probability that the allegations are true—is designed to prevent the conviction of innocent persons. It offers significant protection to innocent defendants. Unfortunately, this standard, and its protection, applies only in criminal cases.

Expert Witness for Hire

In reality, it is often not difficult for plaintiffs to present enough evidence to get over the 50-percent mark in a civil case. This especially is true because "expert" witnesses readily offer their services to plaintiffs. It is quite amazing to see "experts" line up on either side of a case, and then offer their "expert" opinions, which are exactly opposite to each other. For example, it is not uncommon to see a physician hired by the plaintiff testify that the plaintiff has a 15 percent permanent disability to his back, while a similar expert hired by the defense testifies that the disability is actually 5 percent, or simply nonexistent. Obviously, in every case, so-called experts are wrong 50 percent of the time.

In fact, studies have questioned the validity of experts' opinions. They point out that the wide divergence of expert testimony in a particular case conclusively proves that "experts," in many cases anyway, merely are offering their personal opinions, which may be based on conjecture, their own perception of their skills, their personality, and the payment of their fee. Sadly, this is true in criminal, as well as civil, cases.

Nevertheless, in our legal system, if an expert has the credentials, the testimony may be accepted as if it were a simple incontrovertible mathematical formula. That the plaintiff can use an expert in this way may allow the lawsuit to meet the relatively low burden of proof in the case, even when the defendant attempts to counter this testimony with his own expert. The fact that the defendant will have to personally pay the expert's fee may put the defendant at a disadvantage, since the plaintiff's lawyer is likely covering the cost of their expert in return for a contingent fee.

Finally, as discussed below, experts also play a significant role in convincing juries that the plaintiff suffered significant monetary damages.

Liberal Availability of Pre-Trial Discovery

The liberal availability of pre-trial discovery can work against either party to a case, but particularly against a defendant in a civil action.

Through the use of the specific tools of pre-trial discovery, you can be forced to answer an opponent's questions under oath and to provide copies of all relevant documents in your possession, or under your control, even when this evidence is extremely damaging to your case. Defenses to pre-trial discovery are scarce.

The consequences of pre-trial discovery are two-fold. While pre-trial discovery is more often likely to harm a defendant's case—because the claim is being made against and monetary damages are being sought from the defendant—it also can undermine a plaintiff's case, because the plaintiff, too, can be forced to provide information that undermines his claim.

The Tools of Pre-Trial Discovery

The specific tools of pre-trial discovery include interrogatories, depositions and requests for documents.

- **Interrogatories** — These consist of written questions mailed to the opposing party. The opposing party then generally has a set period (usually 30 days) to return written answers signed under oath.

- **Depositions** — With a deposition, the deposed party is directed to appear, with an attorney, most commonly at the office of the opponent's attorney or less often at another location. At the deposition, the opponent's attorney will ask verbal questions of the deposed party, and the deposed party will provide verbal answers, while a stenographer records the exchange, so that a written transcript can be prepared. Before answering the questions, the deposed party will take an oath to answer the questions truthfully.

- **Requests for Documents** — These requests also are a frequent tool of pre-trial discovery. A party can be forced to turn over copies of all relevant documents in his possession or under his control. Generally, once a party can reasonably anticipate future litigation, and certainly after the action has commenced, it is illegal, and thus too late, to destroy damaging documents.

Plan Smart

While the usual tools of pre-trial discovery include interrogatories, depositions and requests for documents, other pre-trial discovery tools exist. For example, in a case in which the plaintiff alleges he suffered personal injuries, the defendant could have his own physician examine the plaintiff.

Consequences of Pre-Trial Discovery

Generally, through any of these discovery tools, a party can be forced to disclose anything that may be relevant to the case. Failure to comply with such requests can result in a loss of the case, through the entering of a default judgment by the court, the imposition of a monetary sanction by the court or something far worse—a jail term. For example, should a party fail to show up for a deposition, the court might, at the request of the other party, order the deposed party to appear. Failure to comply, at that point, might result in a criminal contempt citation and a jail term of six months.

Further, because of the liberal nature of discovery, a plaintiff can use requests for documents to overwhelm a defendant. The cost and time involved in complying with such requests can be tremendous. This is not always a mere side effect. It is sometimes the very intent of a strategic decision by the plaintiff's counsel.

The intent of pre-trial discovery is to force the parties to reveal weaknesses in their cases and, thus, to encourage the parties to settle the case, or at the very least narrow the issues for trial. While there are a few defenses that will allow a party to refuse to answer questions or turn over documents (see below), discovery is broadly construed, and thus the defenses are relatively rare. The end result of pre-trial discovery may be that a defendant will be forced to answer questions or turn over incriminating documents that will provide the very evidence necessary for the plaintiff to win the case.

Limited Defenses to Pre-Trial Discovery

Defenses to pre-trial discovery (i.e., legal means that can be used to justify a refusal to comply) are very limited. The U.S. Constitution's right against self-incrimination allows defendants in *criminal* cases to refuse to testify in pre-trial discovery or in the trial itself. However, the right against self-incrimination simply does not extend to a private civil action.

On the other hand, if something is truly irrelevant and could not lead to other relevant information, a party could refuse to answer a question or turn over a copy of a document. Nevertheless, this defense rarely applies, partly because the courts broadly construe relevance in itself.

In addition, attorney-client privilege will represent a solid defense, if it applies at all. It will apply to private, confidential communications between an attorney and client. Neither the attorney nor the client can be compelled to reveal such communications. Protected communications can take the form of person-to-person communications, telephone calls, letters, etc.

Be cautious, however. The law limits this privilege to *private, confidential* communications. The privilege may be lost, for example, where the communication is made in an open area within the hearing of other people, or in a private area within the presence of other persons not connected to the case.

For instance, if in a deposition a party was asked the nature of his discussions with his attorney, the party could refuse to answer the question. Of course, in most cases, the other party, aware of the privilege, will steer clear of these types of questions.

In short, the courts broadly construe the right to pre-trial discovery, while defenses are narrowly construed. As a result, a party may be forced to reveal the very evidence necessary for the other party to secure a win.

Right to a Jury Trial

Most people are aware of remarkable cases wherein juries have awarded millions of dollars to plaintiffs who appeared to have injured themselves or, perhaps, suffered only relatively minor injuries. The media is quick to report such cases, precisely because the results are so astounding.

In theory, frivolous cases should be dismissed before the trial ever begins. For example, parties can make motions for "judgment on the pleadings" and for "summary judgment" before a jury is even convened. However, in practice, there is an *extremely* strong presumption that a plaintiff should be allowed to present a case to the jury, as the jurors are the triers of fact. In other words, usually such motions will fail, and the case will reach the jury.

This can present a problem for a defendant. Many times, juries decide cases based on their emotional response to the situation presented, irrespective of the legal issues involved. A defendant may have a solid defense that proves he did not cause the plaintiff's injuries, but a plaintiff who nonetheless suffered serious injuries may invoke sympathy from the jury. This sympathy can easily result in a substantial judgment for the plaintiff. This is why the jury selection process is of the utmost importance in preparing for a trial.

These days, it is generally understood by trial attorneys that the make-up of the jurors represents the most important factor in the outcome of many cases. In fact, an entirely new profession has recently developed: the jury consultant. Prior to the trial, jury consultants, who usually are psychologists or sociologists, will stage mock jury trials, conduct surveys, etc., and then prepare a profile of the "ideal" juror. This profile will be based on factors such as age, race, ethnicity, gender, religion, political party affiliation, etc. Studies have shown that such profiles play a very important role in the outcome of a case.

Specifically, based on this profile, attorneys can use peremptory challenges to eliminate potential jurors who do not fit the profile during voir dire, or the choosing of the jury. While limited in number, the peremptory challenges offer an important advantage—the attorney needn't offer any explanation to justify the elimination of a potential juror.

Once a case reaches the jury, any result is possible. When it comes to juries, the sympathy factor cannot be overlooked, especially because the jury may be intentionally skewed by a party to respond to this factor.

Case Study — Jury Trial Judgments, part 1

In a recent Connecticut case, a jury awarded a plaintiff over $500,000 in monetary damages in a case based on an auto accident. According to news reports, the defendant, a New York Supreme Court judge, admitted he caused the accident. However, he testified that the accident was minor and did not require either an ambulance or a tow truck.

How, then, could such a judgment be justified? The basis of the plaintiff's claim for damages was that the accident triggered memories of severe child abuse. The jury apparently believed that the plaintiff suffered these memories, and that the defendant should be held accountable for these memories because he caused the auto accident.

It is, of course, impossible to uncover the exact basis for the jury's decision. However, certain factors may have played a role in the jury's decision.

Severe child abuse, of course, would warrant substantial damages. When the actual culprit cannot be held accountable, jurors may be inclined to hold someone else accountable, because the victim clearly is deserving of compensation. Moreover, in a case such as this, much of the testimony would have to center on the nature of the memories and, thus, the severe abuse suffered by the plaintiff. Evidence of severe child abuse would be expected to evoke extreme sympathy and, thus, might form the basis for an emotional conclusion by a jury not based on reason.

Moreover, a defendant's wealth also can play a role in large and seemingly unwarranted awards of monetary damages. In this case, is it possible that the defendant's status as a New York Supreme Court judge also played a role? (The judge also had been nominated to become a federal judge). While it is not clear whether the jury was informed of this fact in court, in many cases jurors become aware of this type of information either in court or from outside sources. Such status, if known to a jury, might be equated with wealth and, thus, the presumed ability of the defendant to pay a substantial judgment without significantly impairing his wealth. In other words, in the jury's mind such a decision may be fair to both parties.

Perhaps, in one sense, though, the defendant in this case should be thankful. The plaintiff had asked for over $6 million in damages. However, before the defendant can celebrate a $500,000 judgment against him, it must be noted that the plaintiff plans to appeal the case. The plaintiff's attorneys announced that they were very disappointed by the "low" ($500,000) damage award.

Most of the damage award was for "pain and suffering," a very subjective determination made by the jury designed to compensate the plaintiff for the emotional trauma suffered. The breakdown of the damage award, in this case, is discussed in more detail later.

The facts in this case are unique, but the results, unfortunately, are shared with many other cases. In reality, many factors, including the personal make-up and emotional reactions of individual jurors, will influence a jury's decision. The result may be a decision by the jury that defies reason.

In this case, clearly the defendant was not responsible for the severe abuse suffered by the plaintiff when she was a child. Further, the defendant established that, as could be expected, the plaintiff had suffered severe emotional problems prior to the auto accident. Moreover, there was no way, of course, that the defendant could have foreseen that an automobile accident with that plaintiff would trigger her memories of severe child abuse.

Few people, thinking objectively, would conclude that defendants should be held accountable for harm that is primarily the result of someone else's conduct, or harm that they could not foresee would result from their conduct. Don't count on this result in an actual jury trial, even when the law prescribes it.

When the small business owner or the employees drive the business's vehicles, the owner should recall the results in this case. In addition, it also is important to remember that these results are not limited to automobile accident cases.

Finally, note, too, that this case illustrates a separate risk factor. It is highly likely that the plaintiff hired her attorney on a contingent fee basis, and thus it cost her nothing out-of-pocket, while the defendant hired his attorney on an hourly basis. With a full trial and an appeal, the defendant will have paid out a very significant sum of money to his attorney to cover these fees. Even if the defendant prevailed on appeal, these fees would not be reimbursed.

In short, a case that is not voluntarily settled usually will reach a jury. The jury may be configured to favor a particular outcome and may decide the case on an emotional basis. These facts do not bode well for the defendant. The result may be exacerbated by the fact that the judge may, in effect, not allow significant evidence to be heard by the jury.

Exclusion of Evidence from Trial

During a trial, the judge will rule on what evidence is admissible and what evidence is to be excluded, and thus hidden from the jury. Antiquated rules of evidence, which emanate from ancient England, often ensure that significant evidence never reaches the jury. And with significant evidence hidden from the jury, the jury's conclusions may not produce a just result.

Example

Recently, a jury awarded two individuals approximately $2 million in damages against a Miami hotel. The two plaintiffs were shot while staying as guests at the hotel. They sued the hotel for negligence, on the grounds that the hotel failed to provide reasonable security.

At first glance, a finding of negligence doesn't seem to be that outrageous. However, the jury was unaware of one key fact: The police concluded that the two plaintiffs were shot when they were involved in a drug deal that went awry. The jury was never aware of this fact, as the judge ruled that this evidence was inadmissible.

The judge invoked a commonly used rule of evidence that dictates evidence is inadmissible when the "prejudicial effect" of the evidence outweighs its "probative value." The "prejudicial effect" refers to the likelihood that a jury would act emotionally and seize on this one piece of evidence to decide the case, while ignoring all of the other evidence. The "probative value" refers to the extent that the evidence actually proves an essential element in the case. The presumption really is that juries lack the intelligence to be able to properly weigh evidence, which of course is a logical inconsistency.

Apparently, in this case, the judge believed that upon hearing this evidence the jury would have immediately found that the defendant was not negligent, based solely on this one piece of evidence. Of course, virtually everyone (aside from the plaintiffs and, perhaps, the judge in the case) realize that this would have been the right result. Certainly, hotels should not be charged with the duty of providing security for drug dealers. That the jury was prevented from hearing this evidence meant that a result occurred that few people would find was reasonable.

How can a sound, reasonable result be expected when important evidence is hidden from the jury? This result is because the rules of evidence are the product of an English tradition that has no place in today's society. Specifically, the rules came from ancient England, when uneducated "commoners" or peasants served on juries. Judges, the product of the noble class, had little or no respect for jurors. They believed that jurors were incapable of higher reasoning and, thus, unable to sift through and weigh all of the evidence. This had to be done by the judge, who would screen the evidence for the lowly jurors.

While jurors today can be influenced by emotions, as discussed above, they typically are educated and capable of hearing and weighing *all* of the relevant evidence. While antiquated, the rules of evidence persist today in the United States only because of another hallmark of the English system: tradition.

In fact, as discussed below, arbitration cases have discarded these rules of evidence. In arbitration, these rules simply do not apply, and thus the arbitrator is able to hear and weigh *all* of the evidence. The results usually are more reasonable, offering proof that elimination of these rules is possible and desirable. In a jury trial, as in an arbitration hearing, all of the relevant evidence could be admitted. The judge's role could be limited to simply reminding the jury that a particular piece of evidence is just one piece of the puzzle and must be weighed along with all of the other evidence.

Nevertheless, the rules *do* apply in jury trials. Because of the emphasis placed on tradition, it is unlikely that this will change in the near future. The fact that the jury is precluded from hearing key pieces of evidence raises the distinct possibility that an unreasonable, and unjust, result will occur in a trial.

Ease of Proving Negligence

Negligence is one of the most common causes of action that will be brought against a small business owner, potentially exposing you to significant liability issues (breach of contract represents another common cause of action and significant exposure to liability).

The essence of negligence can be reduced to one word—carelessness. Unfortunately, it is not hard to find something that, at the very least, resembles carelessness in most cases. Hardly anyone acts flawlessly in all situations. The law clearly establishes that individuals should not be held accountable for all mistakes. Technically, a defendant is supposed to be held accountable in a negligence action only if his conduct fell short of what a "reasonable person" would have done under the same circumstances.

However, this is not what happens in reality. When the defendant makes a mistake that injures the plaintiff, most juries will already be inclined to hold the defendant accountable. With the addition of the testimony by experts who are hired by the plaintiff, the case against the defendant may be sealed. It is a small wonder, then, that television today is full of advertisements by attorneys seeking personal injury cases that they will handle on a contingent fee basis.

Ease of Proving Monetary Damages for Negligence

In many cases, the existence of a cause of action, such as negligence, may not be a real issue. For example, it would be unlikely that any question would exist as to whether a driver was negligent if he crashed his car into the rear of a car at a stoplight. The only real issue, in many cases, is the amount of monetary damages that should be awarded to the plaintiff.

In theory, compensatory damages, in a tort action such as negligence, are supposed to merely make the plaintiff whole. This is not usually what happens in practice. People who are severely injured will never be made whole and, thus, are under-compensated. People who exaggerate or simply fake their injuries, and rely on "experts" to bolster their claims, are frequently over-compensated.

The calculation of monetary damages in a tort case lends itself to malfeasance. Usually, the largest components in a damage award will be subjective and not verifiable in any substantial way. The award consists of reimbursement for past medical bills and past lost wages; an estimate of future medical bills and lost wages; and an estimate of past, present and future pain suffering.

Only *past* medical bills and *past* lost wages are objective and verifiable. Of course, exaggerating or faking injuries can produce even these items. *Future* medical bills and *future* lost wages necessarily are the product of *estimates,* and thus more subjective. "Experts," who are hired by the plaintiff, can easily exaggerate these estimates (see the previous discussion).

The last element in the formula, namely "pain and suffering," is the most subjective of all and, *in many cases, is the largest component in the award of damages.* The jury, of course, is the ultimate group that will decide on the amount of the award. Unfortunately, expert testimony, along with emotional appeals to the jurors, are likely to be the most successful in terms of the pain and suffering component of the award.

Case Study — Jury Trial Judgments, part 2

In the first part of this case study, the plaintiff alleged in a negligence action that an auto accident had triggered memories of severe child abuse. The jury awarded the plaintiff $523,175 in damages.

The $523,175 in damages was divided among the following individual components in the formula:

- *$25,000 for medical bills*

- *$198,175 for lost wages (the plaintiff alleged she could not work due to the auto accident)*

- *$300,000 for pain and suffering*

This result is consistent with the results in many other cases, in that the award for pain and suffering is the largest component in the formula.

Unfortunately, the pain and suffering component also is the most subjective element in the formula, as previously mentioned. While the award for pain and suffering can be expected to be a function of the amount of past medical bills and lost wages, in reality there is no formula that calls for this result. In fact, there is no mathematical formula used to compute the award for pain and suffering. It is within the complete discretion of the jury, although some states limit this component in certain cases, such as medical malpractice actions.

Note that the plaintiff had sought $6 million in damages. Presumably, most of this $6 million that the plaintiff had sought would be attributable to compensation for pain and suffering, although some amount could be attributable to future medical bills and lost wages.

Impact of the Government as a Plaintiff

In a civil case, if the plaintiff can enlist the help of the government, the defendant will be at a significant disadvantage. The resources available to the government can be staggering. Plaintiffs may find that it is difficult to motivate a government agency, such as a state's attorney general's office, to bring or join a case. However, when there are allegations of fraud, and especially when there are multiple allegations by different parties, the defendant may find that the entire weight of the state or federal government is brought to bear against him. When this occurs, even the wealthiest of defendants will be at a significant disadvantage.

One of the most common ways this can occur is though the Federal Trade Commission (FTC) Act, or one of the state statutes based on the federal act. The FTC Act outlaws "unfair and deceptive" business practices, a term extremely broad in scope. In fact, the courts so broadly interpret the term that it extends to *any type* of business activity that might be construed as unfair. Further, each state has its own version of the FTC Act. Finally, the FTC and 15 states also regulate franchises.

Under these acts, the federal and state governments have the power to investigate complaints, levy civil fines and initiate lawsuits. In addition, as discussed later, unlike the FTC Act itself, the state versions of the FTC Act also authorize individuals to file private lawsuits. When an action is brought under the state statutes, successful plaintiffs may recover reimbursement of attorney's fees, court costs and *punitive damages,* in addition to compensatory damages.

The Racketeer Influenced and Corrupt Organizations Act (RICO) also is an effective way to involve the federal government in a case. RICO authorizes the government to investigate complaints, levy civil fines and initiate lawsuits, *and* similar to the state versions of the FTC Act, it authorizes private individuals to file suits in which they may seek reimbursement of attorney's fees, court costs and *punitive damages,* in addition to compensatory damages.

The FTC Act, its state counterparts, and RICO are discussed in detail later. Claims under any of these acts can significantly increase the risks a defendant faces in a lawsuit.

CONTROLLING THE RISK FACTORS IN LITIGATION

The civil litigation system *itself* represents a significant risk factor, because it makes it more likely that a lawsuit will be filed and that significant damages will be awarded to the plaintiff. However, by understanding these risk factors and controlling them, the small business owner can significantly reduce overall exposure to liability.

The previous discussion was dedicated to understanding these risk factors. What follows are the significant opportunities available to the small business owner to control these factors and, thus, reduce exposure to liability:

- elect mediation and arbitration

- file in small claims court

- make the loser pay

- seek punitive damages

- file a counterclaim

- plan for pre-trial discovery

- use choice of law clauses

- consider exculpatory clauses

- enact disclaimers

- enlist state or federal government assistance

- apply leverage

- choose liability insurance effectively

- engage in asset protection planning

Certain strategies primarily benefit small business owners who may be defendants in litigation or the targets of a claim. Other strategies primarily benefit small business owners who are plaintiffs or have a claim against another party. However, most strategies benefit small business owners in either capacity.

Elect Mediation and Arbitration

As discussed above, the civil litigation system itself represents a significant risk factor and exposure to liability. By using mediation and arbitration as an alternative to the court system, the small business owner can mitigate, or completely avoid, many of the risk factors found in the civil litigation system, including the leverage created by the lack of a loser pays system, the exclusion of significant evidence from the trial and the emotional (and sometimes unreasonable) conclusions reached by jurors.

This strategy primarily benefits small business owners who may be defendants in a civil action. However, the strategy also may benefit small business owners who are plaintiffs, when claims are fairly small, and when the lack of a loser pays system will preclude reimbursement of attorney's fees and related costs (see below for exceptions that will allow such reimbursement).

- **Mediation** involves the parties hiring a mediator, who makes *recommendations* to the parties on a resolution of their dispute. A mediator (in contrast to an arbitrator) cannot, without consent from both parties, make a decision binding on the parties. A mediator's role is limited to bringing the two parties together to discuss the issues, acting as an intermediary in these discussions and making recommendations to the parties. For this reason, parties who are unable to resolve their dispute through mediation usually agree to proceed to arbitration.

- **Arbitration** is a way to resolve a dispute, in which the parties waive their rights to sue in court and, instead, agree to have their dispute *decided privately, outside of the court system,* by an arbitrator. After a hearing (as opposed to a trial), the arbitrator will render a decision, called an award (as opposed to a judgment) if the plaintiff prevails, and it is binding on the parties.

While state laws differ, usually the grounds upon which an appeal may be taken to a court after an arbitration decision are severely limited. Thus, it usually is best to consider that arbitration will likely be the final step in the resolution of the dispute.

Usually, a single arbitrator will hear the case, at an office if he or she is an area attorney, or at a conference room at an area hotel. The hearing is much more informal and usually much less costly than a court trial. Normally, there is no stenographer, no jury and no rules of evidence. While a trial might take one or two *years* to schedule, arbitration hearing usually will be scheduled in two or three *months*.

For these reasons, attorney's fees and related costs usually are much lower in an arbitration proceeding.

Further, *voir dire*, or the choosing of a jury, can be used to stack a jury with sympathetic jurors who are already inclined to side with one party (as discussed above). Because there is no jury in an arbitration hearing, there is no significant ability to manipulate the make-up of the body that will decide the case.

The complex rules of evidence, which can prevent significant evidence from reaching a jury, and thus may distort the outcome of a trial, simply do not apply in an arbitration hearing. The arbitrator will hear and weigh *all* of the relevant evidence and, thus, render a much more reasonable decision than would a jury prevented from hearing important pieces of evidence.

Mediation and Arbitration Clauses

Mediation and arbitration are consensual. This means that *both* parties must agree to mediate or arbitrate the dispute. Usually, this is done *before* the dispute arises, in a contract between the two parties, although it is possible to agree to mediation or arbitration after a dispute arises.

Mediation and arbitration clauses can be used in agreements for the sale of goods and services to consumers, or between two business parties, or in operating agreements that govern the relations among a business entity's owners.

Usually, the agreement requires that the parties split the fee of the mediator or arbitrator. Typically, both a mediation and arbitration clause specifies that the two parties will select a single mediator or arbitrator. However, an arbitration clause also may specify that three arbitrators will hear the case. In this situation, each party will choose an arbitrator, and these two arbitrators will select the third arbitrator.

The clause may specify that the dispute is to be mediated or arbitrated by a particular organization, such as the American Arbitration Association (AAA).

While courts tend to disfavor exculpatory clauses (see below), *exactly the opposite is true with respect to mediation and arbitration clauses.* There is a strong presumption in favor of the validity of such clauses, because the courts encourage parties to resolve their disputes outside of the court system.

Example

The U.S. Supreme Court recently held that an employer could have a job applicant sign an agreement to arbitrate any disputes that arise by virtue of his employment. The Court held that signing the agreement could be a condition of hire and, once the agreement was signed, the employee had no recourse in the courts.

In fact, arbitration clauses between business owners and consumers have been upheld by the courts even when the clauses were disclosed in the instructions enclosed with a product, and even when the clauses were printed on the outside of the *box* that contained the product. In these situations, to better ensure that the clause will be upheld, it may be advisable to allow the consumer a certain period (e.g., 60 days) to void the arbitration clause, by notifying the business in writing of this decision. Professional legal guidance should always be sought in using arbitration clauses, especially in consumer contracts.

Example

In 1997, a U.S. Court of Appeals upheld an arbitration clause that was included in the packaging materials that Gateway shipped along with its computers. The clause could be voided by consumers within a fixed period, but became binding after that period had expired. The plaintiff, who had purchased a Gateway computer, had sought to invalidate the clause after this period had expired and sue Gateway in court.

The Court ruled that the clause was valid and binding, and that, accordingly, the consumer's only remedy was through an arbitration hearing.

Ultimately, mediation and arbitration hearings involve low costs, no jury and no complex rules of evidence. Accordingly, mediation and arbitration can mitigate or eliminate significant risk factors inherent in the civil litigation system.

Therefore, mediation and arbitration clauses should be used in agreements for the sale of goods and services to consumers, and in contracts between two business parties, as well as in operating agreements that govern the relationship among a business entity's owners.

Because mediation is more informal, and usually less costly, consideration should be given to including a mediation clause in addition to an arbitration clause. In this situation, the mediation clause would provide that, if mediation failed to resolve the dispute, the matter would proceed to arbitration. Mediation and arbitration clauses should be professionally drafted.

File in Small Claims Court

As previously discussed, the lack of a loser pays system can work against a plaintiff, as well as a defendant. If a plaintiff has a relatively small claim, the cost of bringing the claim in court may exceed the recovery. Because attorney's fees and related costs *generally* will not be reimbursed, even when the plaintiff is successful, it may be more economical to forego the claim and simply write it off as a loss. Of course, this happens frequently in practice, especially among larger businesses.

However, the small business owner can significantly lower the cost of bringing a court action and, thus, make recovery of the claim more economical by filing in the small claims court.

Parties may proceed "pro se," or without an attorney, in a lawsuit. Doing so, however, usually puts a party at a significant disadvantage, because of the complexity of the trial system. Even attorneys who are personally involved in litigation usually hire legal counsel, especially when operating outside their area of expertise.

One exception may be a small claims proceeding. The rules that govern a small claims action are very relaxed. The pleadings are simplified. While, in many states, plaintiffs must know how to draft a formal civil complaint according to criteria specified in the state's practice book, in a small claims case the complaint form almost always is a pre-printed form obtained at the court house.

Similarly, while service of process (i.e., the delivery of the complaint and summons to the defendant) in a regular action requires hiring a sheriff, who hand-delivers the complaint and summons to the defendant, in a small claims action service usually is by way of a certified letter. This simplifies and lowers the cost of the service of process in a small claims action. In addition, the court entry fee usually is significantly lower in a small claims action.

Simplified procedures also govern the actual trial process. Rules of evidence are relaxed in the small claims case, which makes it much easier to proceed pro se. There is no jury in a small claims case, which eliminates a complex and time-consuming aspect of a regular action—choosing of the jury.

In short, the costs and complexity of bringing a small claims action are much reduced compared to regular litigation, thus allowing the plaintiff to proceed pro se, avoid attorney's fees altogether, and bring an action that otherwise would be too uneconomical to file on the regular court docket.

However, a small claims action only can be brought when the amount of the claim is "small." While the jurisdictional limit of small claims courts differs among the states, the limit is usually in the range of $2,000 to $5,000. So, obviously the small claims alternative will not be appropriate in all cases.

In addition, a small claims case is argued before a judge or attorney who is termed a "magistrate." When the small business owner believes he would benefit by an emotional appeal to the trier of fact, a court action on the regular docket with a jury may be in order. Moreover, usually a small claims decision is final, with few rights of appeal. Thus, the finality of a small claims action should be carefully weighed against the benefits of bringing the case to small claims court.

Finally, as is true with any case in general, the small business owner also must consider whether he will be able to *collect* the judgment if he wins. A judgment against a defendant with no resources will still be uneconomical, even if secured in a small claims action.

Make the Loser Pay

Generally, the United States lacks a loser pays system (as previously discussed). However, two exceptions exist: the contract exception and the statutory exception. With either of these two exceptions, the loser in the court action will have to reimburse the winner for his attorney's fees and related costs.

However, caution must be exercised here, as the exceptions do not always apply to *both* parties to the court action. Typically, the exceptions authorize reimbursement *only to the plaintiff*, when the plaintiff wins the action.

With careful planning, the small business owner may be able to use the contract exception to provide for reimbursement in the event he or she is the defendant and prevails in the action. Further, in some situations, a statute may provide an exception that authorizes reimbursement to the defendant when he or she prevails in the action.

Contract Reimbursement Clauses

Simply put, the parties to a contract may agree in writing that the loser in a legal dispute must reimburse the other party for his attorney's fees and related costs.

In practice, this is a standard clause used by large commercial parties in many types of contracts. *However, here the clause is almost always one-sided.* Specifically, the clause usually will provide that, if the large commercial party brings an action to enforce the contract, the other party (i.e., a small business party or a consumer) will reimburse the large commercial party for its attorney's fees and related costs.

For example, a franchise agreement almost certainly will provide for this result, if the franchisor has to enforce the agreement against the franchisee. However, the law clearly allows the parties to contract for a more equitable arrangement. Thus, a more complete clause might provide simply that the loser in a legal dispute must reimburse the other party for his attorney's fees and related courts. This would mean that either party, as either a plaintiff or as a defendant, would be awarded reimbursement, if he or she prevailed in the action. For example, this type of clause would mean a franchisee would be awarded reimbursement if he brought a successful claim against the franchisor, or if the franchisee successfully defended a claim brought by the franchisor.

The clause also could be expanded beyond a standard one-sided clause, but still made more limited than a complete clause. For example, the clause might authorize reimbursement to either party who successfully *brought* a claim, but *not* authorize reimbursement to either party who successfully *defended against* a claim.

The real point is that the law allows the parties to control the reimbursement clause. In practice, the nature of the clause will be limited by two factors—the relative bargaining power of the parties and legal limitations that may apply to contracts between a business entity and consumers.

For instance, a franchisee may not have sufficient bargaining power to force a franchisor to include a complete or an expanded clause in a franchise agreement. With respect to consumer contracts, courts normally uphold a one-sided clause that authorizes reimbursement *only to the business party who successfully brings a claim*. However, a broader one-sided clause that *also* authorizes reimbursement to the business party who successfully defends against a claim, but further provides for no reimbursement to the consumer in any situation, may be deemed unfair and, therefore, invalid, as a violation of public policy.

In general, the small business owner should consider whether he or she is likely to be a plaintiff or a defendant, with respect to the agreement, and draft the reimbursement clause accordingly. The small business owner should always seek professional guidance when drafting or reviewing contracts in general, and in drafting the reimbursement clause in particular.

Statutory Reimbursement Exceptions

A party may bring a court action based on a "common law" right to sue or a right to sue authorized by statute. The courts originally developed common law causes of action, which include almost all tort (i.e., personal injury) actions, as well as breach of contract cases. The general rule that governs a common law cause of action is that, absent a contract clause to the contrary (see above), the winner of the action will not be reimbursed by the loser for attorney's fees and related costs.

However, a second exception exists when a cause of action is based on a statute that specifically authorizes reimbursement. Note that not every statute that authorizes a private cause of action also authorizes reimbursement. Moreover, the statutes that do authorize reimbursement typically work in a very narrow way, sanctioning reimbursement *only to the plaintiff when he prevails in the action.*

State Versions of the FTC Act. The small business owner who is a plaintiff will be at a distinct advantage if he can base his claim on a statute that authorizes reimbursement of attorney's fees and related costs. Perhaps the most common statute used for this purpose will be the state's version of the Federal Trade Commission (FTC) Act.

As previously discussed, the FTC Act itself does not authorize private causes of actions. However, every state has a version of the FTC Act that does authorize the filing of private actions. While consumers who believe they have been the victims of "unfair and deceptive" business practices typically use the statutes, the statutes are not limited to protecting consumers. Small business owners can file actions against other commercial parties under these statutes. The term "unfair and deceptive" business practices is interpreted very broadly by the courts. Thus, it usually is not too difficult to fit most claims under these statutes.

State Franchise Acts. The FTC also extensively regulates franchise agreements (see below). A violation of the FTC's franchise rules automatically is deemed to be an unfair and deceptive business practice, and thus a violation of the FTC Act. However, because the FTC Act does not authorize private actions, this relationship also means that a franchisee cannot sue under the federal statute for a violation of the FTC's franchise regulations.

Plan Smart

Fifteen states have franchise laws based on the FTC's franchise regulations. These states include:

California	North Dakota
Hawaii	Oregon
Illinois	Rhode Island
Indiana	South Dakota
Massachusetts	Virginia
Michigan	Washington
Minnesota	Wisconsin
New York	

Each of these state statutes authorizes a private cause of action and reimbursement to the plaintiff for attorney's fees and related costs, if the plaintiff prevails in the action. The acts also authorize awards of punitive damages (discussed later). Because of the extensive disclosures required by these statutes, it often is not difficult to find a violation by a franchisor. Because many small business owners will operate franchises, and disputes frequently occur between franchisors and franchisees, these state statutes can offer small business owners a distinct advantage in litigating the dispute (franchise regulations are discussed in more detail below).

RICO. The Racketeering Influenced and Corrupt Organizations (RICO) Act is the federal statute originally enacted to combat organized crime. It is perhaps best known for its criminal provisions.

However, RICO also authorizes the filing of private civil causes of actions by parties who suffer losses due to "racketeering." The statute also authorizes reimbursement of attorney's fees and related costs to a plaintiff who prevails in the action.

Ordinarily, small business owners would not have reason to sue an organized crime syndicate. Thus, it may initially seem that RICO would be of little use to small business owners. However, as is true with many other areas in the law (e.g., the definition of unfair and deceptive trade practices, as described above), the term "racketeering" has been very broadly construed by the courts, so as to extend well beyond organized crime syndicates.

Specifically, RICO is violated if an organization carries on a pattern of illegal activities. A business entity can meet the legal definition of an organization, which usually is defined simply as a group comprised of two or more individuals. A pattern of illegal activities exists if a party repeats the illegal activity as little as two different times. Further, the illegal activities do not have to be criminal in nature, but instead can be in the nature of unfair or fraudulent business practices that may or may not result in a monetary loss to another party.

An action may be based on RICO in many situations that arise in ordinary business relationships. For example, a franchise relationship could form the basis for a RICO cause of action by the franchisee against the franchisor, if the franchisor had committed a series of fraudulent or deceptive acts.

In fact, successful civil actions under RICO have been brought against banks, insurance companies, brokerage houses and even protestors. In general, if the small business owner is the victim of any type of fraudulent scheme carried out by another party, a RICO action may be available.

Statutes Providing Reimbursement to Either Party. Finally, certain statutes apply a broader rule, authorizing reimbursement to *either* party who prevails in the action. For example, a federal statute that outlaws copyright infringement also authorizes a private cause of action. This statute allows the court to order reimbursement of attorney's fees and related costs *to either party, including the defendant*, when that party prevails in the action.

These types of statutes are relatively unusual, as most statutes merely authorize reimbursement to *plaintiffs* who prevail in the action.

Seek Punitive Damages

The two main exceptions that allow for reimbursement of attorney's fees and costs to the party who prevails in a lawsuit are statutory and contractual, as previously discussed. When one of the exceptions does not apply, a party may seek punitive damages, as an *alternative way* to *effectively* recover attorney's fees and related costs. Punitive damages can allow a plaintiff to bring an action that otherwise would not be economically justified. Punitive damages can more than offset a plaintiff's outlay for attorney's fees and related costs.

Example

In a case involving misrepresentation in the purchase of insurance, an appellate court awarded each of the two plaintiffs approximately $1,500 in compensatory damages and $175,000 in punitive damages. The court specifically termed the plaintiffs' litigation costs as a significant factor in assessing the amount of punitive damages to award the plaintiffs.

The $175,000 in punitive damages awarded to each plaintiff, in all likelihood, more than offset the plaintiffs' attorney's fees and court costs, thus effectively reimbursing them for these fees and costs.

Punitive damages generally are available in any action—except one based solely on breach of contract—when it is proven that the defendant acted willfully and maliciously. Small business owners who suffer losses due to fraud usually will be able to seek punitive damages under common law actions for fraud or under statutory actions based on the states' versions of the FTC Act and the federal RICO statute.

Further, a defendant can seek punitive damages against a plaintiff by way of a counterclaim (as discussed below). Thus, a defendant also can use a recovery of punitive damages to offset his attorney's fees and related costs.

Case Study — Punitive Damages

 *Until 1996, punitive damages represented more of a risk factor, rather than an opportunity, for small business owners. Specifically, during the 20-year period leading up to 1996, business owners suffered extremely large punitive damages awards. These awards, in many cases involving larger businesses, amounted to tens of millions of dollars, and some awards exceeded $100 million dollars. In 1996, however, the U.S. Supreme Court established guidelines for punitive damages awards that have significantly reduced the size of awards since that time.*

In a case against BMW, a trial court awarded the plaintiff $2 million in punitive damages, in addition to $25,000 of compensatory damages. The plaintiff proved that BMW had failed to disclose that a new car he had purchased had been re-painted.

In 1996, the U. S. Supreme Court ruled that the punitive damages award was grossly excessive. Upon remand, the lower court reduced the punitive damage award to $50,000. Importantly, the Court also established guidelines that courts must apply in awarding punitive damages. Courts now primarily examine three factors in determining the amount of punitive damages:

- *The degree to which the defendant's conduct was reprehensible.*

- *The ratio of the punitive damages to the compensatory damages.*

- *The amount of civil and criminal fines that could be levied against the defendant by the government.*

In the case against BMW, the defendant's conduct was not especially outrageous. Further, the ratio of punitive damages to compensatory damages, based on the original award, at 80:1, appeared extreme. The ratio, based on the revised award, at 12.5:1 seems more reasonable and in line with the U.S. Supreme Court's guidelines. Finally, the comparable civil penalty that could have been levied by the government amounted only to $2,000. This fact, too, suggested a much lower punitive damage award.

Post-1996 cases have resulted in much lower punitive awards. For instance, in the insurance misrepresentation case described in the prior example, the trial court *originally awarded each of the plaintiffs* $7.5 million in punitive damages. *The appellate court reduced these awards to approximately $175,000 for each plaintiff, based on the BMW criteria. The final award of punitive damages was consistent with the BMW criteria, as the defendant's conduct was not especially outrageous, each plaintiff suffered only approximately $1,500 in compensatory damages, and the comparable civil penalty was only $1,000.*

Today, because of the U.S. Supreme Court's 1996 decision, punitive damages probably represent more of an opportunity than a risk for small business owners who operate their businesses in a reputable manner. Punitive damages represent an important way for a plaintiff—and perhaps a defendant though a counterclaim—to effectively recover attorney's fees and costs.

Nevertheless, large punitive damage awards are still a distinct possibility, when a defendant's conduct is especially outrageous, as outrageous conduct will trigger the first criterion under the BMW test. Further, extremely outrageous conduct will likely produce a large amount of compensatory damages and thus trigger the second factor in the equation. Therefore, at least two of the three factors will be skewed in favor of a large punitive damage award.

For example, in a product liability case brought against a manufacturer of an asbestos product, an appellate court awarded the plaintiff $1.5 million in punitive damages. The court concluded that the defendant's conduct was especially reprehensible, given the extreme health damage caused by exposure to asbestos. Thus, the first factor under the BMW test indicated in favor of a large punitive damage award.

Further, the extreme risk inherent in exposure to asbestos, along with the defendant's lack of regard for the public's safety, meant that the plaintiff's compensatory damages, at $2 million, were especially large. The level of the compensatory damages, in turn, also justified a large punitive damage award under the second BMW factor.

The small business owner can avoid this outcome, and thus avoid making punitive damages a significant risk factor, by operating the business in a reputable manner.

Many states now have statutes that limit punitive damage awards, although the nature of the limits varies widely from state to state.

In some states, the limits apply only to certain causes of action (e.g., Connecticut's $250,000 limit in product liability actions). In some states, the limits apply to all causes of action (e.g., Virginia's limit of $350,000). In still other states, the limits apply to all causes of action, but are subject to exceptions (e.g., Florida's limit of three times the amount of compensatory damages, unless the party can show by clear and convincing evidence that a greater award is not excessive).

Plan Smart

States with limits on punitive damage awards, as of 2002, include:

Alabama	*Kansas*
Colorado	*Nevada*
Connecticut	*New Jersey*
Florida	*Oklahoma*
Georgia	*Texas*
Indiana	*Virginia*

These limitations generally favor the small business owner, by reducing the possibility that he will suffer an unreasonably large and unjustified award of punitive damages. At the same time, the option of punitive damages means that, when reimbursement of attorney's fees and related costs is not possible, the small business owner can seek punitive damages as a substitute way of recovering these fees and costs. This strategy might be used, for example, against another commercial party in a suit based on fraud.

File Counterclaims

A counterclaim can represent an indirect way for a defendant to recover his attorney's fees and related costs, in the absence of a contract or statutory exception that otherwise allows it. In fact, a successful counterclaim will result in the defendant being awarded damages that will be *more than sufficient* to compensate for these fees and costs. In addition, a counterclaim can be used as significant leverage to convince the plaintiff to drop the lawsuit (as discussed below).

The defendant can assert a counterclaim against the plaintiff in answer to the complaint. In the counterclaim, the defendant goes on the offensive, reversing the roles of the two parties. In essence, the defendant seeks monetary damages from the plaintiff. Clearly, for this to be effective, the defendant must have a sound cause of action against the plaintiff. In many suits between business parties, this is a real possibility, especially in light of the court's expansive definitions for the terms "unfair and deceptive" business practices and "racketeering," as well as the complex provisions imposed by many laws (e.g., the FTC Act and state laws that govern franchisors).

Ideally, the defendant will be in a position where he or she also can seek punitive damages in his counterclaim. The same standards and limitations that govern punitive damage awards to plaintiffs (see above) also would apply to the defendants in a counterclaim.

Finally, in a counterclaim, the defendant is essentially acting as a plaintiff. Thus, a one-sided provision in a statute or a contract that authorizes reimbursement only to a successful party who brings the claim *would fully apply to a counterclaim*. So, a defendant may be able to base his counterclaim on a cause of action that authorizes reimbursement of attorney's fees and related costs, such as a state's version of the FTC Act, RICO, or a provision in a contract between the parties. Here, the reimbursement would be for the attorney's fees and related costs incurred in bringing the counterclaim. However, this reimbursement, of course, would be in addition to the compensatory (and possibly punitive) damages that would be awarded to the defendant for the counterclaim itself.

Clearly, a counterclaim based on a provision that authorizes such reimbursement *and* one that seeks punitive damages would be especially likely to provoke a favorable outcome. The party who brought the suit would then face a triple-threat from the defendant:

- the possibility of an award of compensatory damages for the counterclaim itself

- reimbursement to the defendant of his attorney's fees and related costs incurred in bringing the counterclaim

- a separate award for punitive damages

Even a plaintiff who is a big risk taker may decide to drop the claim when faced with these risks (see below for more on the strategy of "leverage" in a lawsuit).

Plan Smart

The plaintiff begins a lawsuit by having a summons and complaint served on the defendant (usually by a sheriff). The defendant will then respond by filing an appearance and an answer.

The plaintiff's complaint must both:

- *recite the material facts of the case, so as to establish a cause of action or legal right to sue*

- *request a remedy, which usually will be monetary damages*

The defendant's answer will contain:

- *point-by-point responses to the statements made in the plaintiff's complaint; these responses will be comprised of admissions, denials or statements that the defendant doesn't know whether or not an allegation is true*

The defendant's answer also may contain:

- *an affirmative defense to the cause of action*

- *a counterclaim, wherein the defendant asserts a cause of action against, and seeks monetary damages from, the plaintiff*

Plan for Pre-Trial Discovery

Pre-trial discovery represents a significant risk factor for business owners, because you can be forced to answer an opponent's questions under oath and to provide copies of all relevant documents in your possession or under your control, even when this evidence is extremely damaging to your case.

While pre-trial discovery is more often likely to harm a defendant's case, because the plaintiff is pressing the claim, it also can undermine a plaintiff's case, because the plaintiff, too, can be forced to provide damaging information.

Strategies exist that can significantly reduce the risks associated with pre-trial discovery. A system must be in place for document retention and destruction. In addition, if called to answer a deposition, you must carefully prepare your appearance. However, planning and implementation of these strategies must begin well before litigation arises.

Document Retention and Destruction

Traditionally, attorneys have underscored the importance of maintaining written records. Written records can be used to conclusively prove certain facts, when verbal representations would be of little use. Further, without receipts, tax deductions will be met with skepticism and, thus, usually disallowed by the IRS. Similarly, there will be no proof a warranty claim was filed in a timely manner, when the claim is made over the telephone, while a letter (especially a certified letter) would be significant proof that the claim was filed within the warranty period.

Innumerable cases, in virtually every area of law, have proved the principle that documentation can make the difference in winning or losing a case. In addition, the law requires that certain records, including tax and employment records for example, be maintained for a fixed period.

Recently, however, advice has taken a different direction—business owners should *avoid* creating certain written records, or *shred* the written records immediately after they are reviewed. This advice, of course, is limited to records that might be damaging to a company should they be disclosed, for example through pre-trial discovery. This advice has arisen from experience: Requests for documents, during pre-trial discovery, can result in the defendant producing the very evidence that the plaintiff needs to win the case.

Example

In numerous personal injury cases, involving many different types of products—including cars, heart valves, silicone breast implants and cigarettes, among others—plaintiffs have used pre-trial discovery and, in particular, requests for documents to uncover from the defendant's own records the very evidence necessary to win a judgment in the case, or force a favorable settlement.

In many prominent cases, plaintiffs have uncovered studies, dated many years prior to the litigation, in which defendants apparently acknowledged the defective properties of their products, but concealed this information from the public to maximize profits.

For example, in one of the earliest cases that led to the trend toward the elimination of written records, Ford Motor Company was sued for injuries sustained by the plaintiff when his Ford Pinto automobile exploded into flames after a low-speed rear impact. The plaintiff alleged that the explosion was caused by the defective design of the Pinto.

Ford fought the lawsuit. However, during pre-trial discovery, the plaintiff uncovered from Ford a cost-benefit study that Ford had previously conducted involving the Pinto. The study examined the Pinto's tendency to explode into flames after a low-speed impact, blaming the positioning of the gas tank as the cause of this problem. In the study, it appeared that Ford engineers had calculated the costs of correcting the problem, through recalling and retrofitting existing Pintos, and re-engineering the design and manufacture of new Pintos. According to the plaintiff, in the study, Ford compared these costs, which were significant, to the costs of concealing the problem (essentially the settlement and judgment costs Ford would have to pay because the automobile, left uncorrected, would continue to kill and injure people).

The study appeared to conclude that, because the cost of correcting the problem would exceed the cost of doing nothing (i.e., the settlement and judgment costs), Ford should do nothing— that is, effectively conceal the problem from the public.

The jury awarded the plaintiff approximately $7 million, which included punitive damages.

Ford maintained that the study had been misinterpreted. However, even if this were true, the disclosure *of the study to the jury would likely invoke outrage at Ford and sympathy for the plaintiff. In short, the forced disclosure of the study to the jury was probably the determining factor in the case, both in terms of the jury returning a judgment in favor of the plaintiff and the actual amount of damages awarded to the plaintiff.*

Today, the results of this type study would likely be verbally *reported and the data for the study destroyed, well in advance of any notice of litigation.*

Today, a sound practice is to verbally report any findings that may be damaging to the business, in the event of future litigation. Any written records (including computer records) generated should be destroyed, before any issues arise.

As discussed below, the small business owner must take into account the fact that records may exist not only in paper form, but also in paperless form, on a computer's hard drive or disks.

Special care must be taken with respect to e-mail and computer files, in general. The small business owner also should avoid creating these records, or be sure they are effectively destroyed (see below).

This emphasis on verbal reporting and document destruction should not be interpreted too broadly. It should be confined to those situations where the underlying information would be damaging to the business, if disclosed.

In particular, several warnings are in order concerning verbal reporting and document destruction:

- Documentation of transactions between the owners and their business entity represents an important asset protection strategy (as discussed in Chapters 15 and 16). It forms an important basis that can prevent piercing of the veil of limited liability.

  Further, as noted above, federal and state statutes require that certain records, such as employment records, be maintained for a fixed period. Guidelines for record retention related to employee records can be found on the Internet in *CCH Business Owner's Toolkit*™ at http://www.toolkit.cch.com. In addition, prudence dictates that other records (e.g., tax receipts) be maintained. Documentation is essential for tax purposes to sustain a deduction or to prove that certain receipts were from nontaxable sources.

  In many cases, the law is silent on the period of time for which records must be retained, but in the absence of a fixed statutory period, the recommended period should coincide with the expiration of the statute of limitations. For example, income tax records should be retained indefinitely, as an IRS allegation of fraud has no statute of limitations.

- Document destruction that occurs after notice of a lawsuit is received, or even after an event (e.g., an accident) occurs, may be a criminal offense. Verbal reporting and document destruction should be an ongoing asset protection policy. As is true with asset protection strategies in general, planning in advance of a crisis is required.

- Technically, in a civil action, a party could be subpoenaed to testify about a study, record or report. This testimony might include questions concerning information from a verbal report or a written record that was destroyed. Clearly, a party with this information has a legal obligation to testify truthfully. In practice, however, where a record or report was generated many years before the litigation, the parties involved in the record or report may be unavailable, or their memories related to the record or report may not be so clear. Thus, truthful testimony may not be damaging.

- The small business owner should be aware that records might be stored on computer hard drives, floppy disks, zip drives and other data storage devices. These records may include data damaging to the business, in the event of litigation.

Even when this data is "deleted," computer specialists can sometimes retrieve the data. Mere deletion usually does not actually eliminate the data. Instead, when files are deleted, the computer's operating system no longer maintains an association with the data, and considers the space it occupies as available for new data. However, after "deletion," the data remains on the storage device.

Formatting a storage device, such as hard drive or floppy disk, should eliminate the data. Further, software exists that purportedly eliminates all remnants of data.

In addition, when a computer is discarded, the hard drive should be physically destroyed to prevent recovery of data. Of course, when a computer is to be sold or traded, this is not possible. In this situation, the recommendations discussed above should be followed.

Of course, with respect to information that may harm a company, the simplest and most effective strategy is to avoid creating a computer record in the first place.

Preparing for Depositions

Defendants frequently make mistakes when verbally answering questions during a deposition. In contrast, similar errors are not common when submitting written answers to interrogatories. Because a party must, more or less, spontaneously answer questions during a deposition, there is the distinct possibility that the deposed party will make a damaging statement.

In contrast, with interrogatories, a party usually has 30 days to return written answers. Thus, in this case, the party can carefully craft answers, going through many different drafts, until a final and favorable version is derived.

A deposition involves a face-to-face meeting, in which the opposing attorney will ask verbal questions, and the deposed party will give answers, after taking an oath that the responses will be truthful. A stenographer will record the proceeding, so that a written transcript can be made.

Usually, the deposition will take place at the *opposing attorney's office*. The nature of the face-to-face questioning and the location of the deposition can unnerve the deposed party. Most importantly, of course, the deposed party will not have 30 days to draft the responses. When asked a question, he will be required, more or less, to provide an immediate verbal answer. While the deposed party's attorney also will attend the deposition, he cannot answer the questions, at least not directly.

In reality, the deposed party's attorney should, *in effect*, be answering every question. Adequate preparation is the key to making a deposition neutral, or even turning around its effect, so that the evidence it produces works against the party conducting the deposition.

Effective preparation requires that the deposed party anticipate every question that will be asked in the deposition. A skilled attorney should be able to do this, as an attorney should be aware of all of the legal issues and facts that must be proved in the case. The deposed party's attorney should ask these questions of his client, well in advance of the deposition, and help the party craft his answers. Note that, while a party cannot lie in a deposition, choice of wording can have significant implications.

Plan Smart

Specifically, a deposed party should:

- *Anticipate every question that will be asked and craft narrow answers to these questions in advance of the deposition. This really is not a difficult task. For example, in an automobile accident case, the plaintiff's attorney will attempt, through the deposition, to prove the deposed party was negligent. Thus, he will ask questions that may prove carelessness on the part of the deposed party (e.g., the speed of his vehicle, the distance between his vehicle and the other driver's vehicle, his activities at the time the accident, etc.). The deposed party also should be prepared to explain how he knows these facts (see below).*

- *Rehearse and craft answers in the same way that rough drafts of written answers would be used, if the party were faced with interrogatories. Essentially, then, the deposed party should treat the deposition no differently than if it were a set of interrogatories. This practice defeats what otherwise represents the main advantage of the deposition to the other party—that in the absence of preparation, the deposed party usually will provide spontaneous and, thus, damaging statements.*

For example, there is a significant difference between a deposed party saying he glanced at his speedometer "just before the accident" (which implies he caused the accident due to his inattention to the road) and saying he knew he wasn't speeding because he "glanced at his speedometer a block before the accident." Note the importance of the exact choice of wording. If the deposed party says he glanced at his speedometer "several blocks" before the accident, this fact may be irrelevant because during the intervening period the speed of his vehicle may have changed. Wording is everything.

Note, too, that preparation requires a general understanding of the facts surrounding the case. A deposed party who guesses that the speed of his vehicle was about 40 m.p.h. probably should have guessed another number, if the speed limit in the area was 25 m.p.h.

In short, nothing in a deposition should be spontaneous.

- *Do not volunteer answers to questions that are not asked when these answers would damage the deposed party's case. Thus, a party who caused an automobile accident does not have to volunteer that he was not wearing his prescription glasses, if this question is not asked.*

- *Do volunteer answers to questions that are not asked, when these answers will help the deposed party's case. Thus, if the deposed party saw that the other party had no brake lights or failed to use a turn signal, these facts should be worked into answers, even when questions do not directly address these issues. Through this technique, a deposed party actually can take an aggressive or offensive stand in a deposition, and thus turn the deposition into a weapon that can be used against the other party. Preparation, again, is the key, if this is to be done.*

Use Choice of Law Clauses

The cost of litigation can be extreme. Due to the lack of a loser pays system, these costs can force defendants to pay settlements for unjustified claims or plaintiffs to forego legitimate claims.

Litigation in a foreign jurisdiction (i.e., a different state) can only make these costs more expensive, exacerbating these problems. Travel and hotel costs, time lost from work, and the difficulty of finding an attorney in a different state can cause a party to forfeit making a claim or defending against a claim.

A choice of law clause can eliminate these possibilities because it controls two issues: the choice of the state in which the action must be filed and the choice of which state's laws will be applied.

A choice of law clause is especially appropriate when parties reside in two different states. Usually, the clause would specify the state in which the action must be filed and designate that this state's laws also will govern the dispute. The small business owner should use a choice of law clause in purchase agreements with out-of-state vendors or in sales agreements with out-of-state consumers. Here, the clause normally would specify that disputes must be brought in the state in which the small business owner operates, and that this state's laws would apply in the case. Note, too, that the choice of law clause should apply not only to actual court actions, but mediation and arbitration actions as well.

The courts do not always uphold choices of law clauses. There must be sufficient connections to a state for the state to have authority to decide the case or for its laws to apply in a case. If a small business owner designates the state in which he operates, this should not be a real issue. However, when a party or an action has sufficient connections to *more than one state*, the courts may reject the clause and allow an action in the other state, or apply the other state's laws. When a small business owner confines his activities to a single state, this too should not represent a significant issue.

Warning

The small business owner should be aware that it is common for franchise agreements to provide that any disputes between the franchisee and franchisor must be brought in the franchisor's home state, and that this state's laws will govern the dispute. This may be a serious problem to a franchisee who would like to sue the franchisor, especially because the franchisor may be located in many states and far from the franchise. A potential franchisee should demand that this clause be changed to allow the franchisee to file an action in the state in which he will operate the franchise.

As is true with contract negotiations, in general, nothing can compel the franchisor to accept this demand. If the franchisor refuses to change the clause, the franchisee must consider assuming the risks of signing the agreement with the existing clause or simply moving on to a different opportunity.

Finally, it may be desirable to designate that the action must be filed in one state, but that a different state's laws will govern the agreement. For example, owners who will *operate* their LLC in Connecticut may form the LLC in Delaware to take advantage of Delaware's favorable LLC statute (see Chapter 8). An operating agreement for a business entity, such as an LLC, should always have a choice of law clause. In this situation, the operating agreement may specify that any litigation among the owners must take place in Connecticut, but that Delaware law will control the agreement, the relationships between the parties and the internal operations of the entity. In this way, the litigation will take place in a convenient forum, but a more desirable set of laws will govern the outcome.

Consider Exculpatory Clauses

An exculpatory clause is a waiver of a right to sue. Clearly, if a small business owner uses such a clause, *and, if challenged later, the court deems the clause enforceable,* then the small business owner will have completely avoided liability.

Unfortunately, the law is not quite that simple. The courts tend to disfavor exculpatory clauses and, in fact, frequently deem these clauses invalid, as against public policy, especially when consumer contracts are involved. Further, when intentional, reckless or criminal conduct is involved, the clause is almost assuredly invalid.

Nevertheless, in the right context, the courts will enforce the clause. An exculpatory clause is *much more likely* to be enforced if some combination of the following conditions apply in the case:

- The contract is between two business parties, especially if the parties have approximately equal bargaining power.

- The clause is limited in scope (e.g., to negligent acts) and, by its own terms, does not apply when intentional, reckless or criminal conduct is involved.

- The clause is prominently disclosed in the contract.

- The contract language is negotiated, and not merely a form or "adhesion" contract, which was offered by the party with superior bargaining power (e.g., the commercial party in a consumer contract) on a "take it or leave it" basis.

- The party that agrees to the waiver was not vulnerable due to advanced age, illness, inability to understand the English language, etc.

- The waiver does not involve release of the right to sue for negligence in the rendering of professional services (e.g., a physician, accountant, etc.)

- The context of the waiver makes the waiver fair and reasonable. For example, courts have upheld waivers in consumer contracts that involved diving, skiing and parachuting instruction, and that met the other conditions described above. Similarly, a waiver of a right to sue for injuries that an employee sustains while using a company's fitness equipment probably would be upheld.

While limited in scope, exculpatory clauses are at least worth considering, because, when valid, they do result in a complete elimination of liability. In practice, the validity of an exculpatory clause will depend on the unique circumstances of the particular business. Legal guidance should be sought in determining the extent to which exculpatory clauses can be used in the particular business, and in drafting the language for these clauses.

Enact Disclaimers

Disclaimers are closely related to exculpatory clauses. Disclaimers, in fact, are essentially a *more limited* waiver of a right to sue. The waiver may apply only to a narrow cause of action or to a particular type of damages. In general, the courts will apply the same exculpatory clause guidelines (see above) to test the validity of disclaimers. But disclaimers are more likely to be upheld by the courts, because they are narrower in scope than exculpatory clauses.

Disclaimers of the implied-in-law warranties of merchantability and fitness for a particular purpose are frequently used in consumer contracts.

Unless disclaimed, the implied-in-law warranty of merchantability *automatically* applies to any sale of goods by a merchant. The warranty, which arises automatically by way of statute, and not through any written or verbal representations by the merchant, means that the merchant is guaranteeing to the consumer that the product will perform the general purpose for which it was intended.

Moreover, unless disclaimed, the implied-in-law warranty of fitness for a particular purpose will apply whenever a consumer makes known to the merchant the unique purpose for which he will use the product, and then relies on the merchant's recommendation of a product. Thus, while this warranty, too, arises automatically by way of statute, the circumstances in which it applies are somewhat narrower than those involved in the implied warranty of merchantability.

Disclaimer of each of these warranties means the consumer, of course, does not receive these guarantees. In other words, the disclaimer means that the consumer will have waived his right to sue based on these warranties.

The disclaimer of these warranties should mention the warranties by name and be prominently displayed in the contract. *Statutes—which dictate the exact parameters that the language and disclosure must take to be valid—differ slightly among these states.* Thus, it is wise to obtain legal advice on the exact wording required in the particular state. In general, however, if the disclaimer meets the statutory requirements, it will be valid, even though the contract is a form or "adhesion" contract.

Warning

A business owner must be cautious when disclaiming the implied warranties of merchantability and fitness for a particular purpose, while also granting an express warranty.

An express warranty is granted through actual language in the agreement between the parties. When the implied-in-law warranties are disclaimed in the same agreement in which an express warranty is granted, the disclaimer may be deemed an unfair business practice, on the grounds that the consumer is actually receiving less of a warranty than if the agreement contained no express warranty and also no disclaimer of the implied-in-law warranties.

Usually, the prominent display of the disclaimer, in the same portion of the agreement that contains the express warranty, will eliminate this possibility. However, especially when using this combination, legal advice should be sought in drafting the actual agreement.

In addition, disclaimers in which a party waives the right to sue for "consequential damages" and "incidental damages" also are frequently used in practice, in both consumer contracts and contracts between business parties.

- **Consequential Damages** — reasonably foreseeable *additional* damages caused by a breach of contract (between business parties, the most common form of consequential damages would be the lost profits a business may suffer because it was unable to operate due to the breach of contract)

- **Incidental Damages** — the out-of-pocket expenses the party suffers in trying to compensate for the breach

In consumer contracts, disclaimers of liability for *personal injuries* are not valid. Disclaimers of liability for consequential and incidental damages to *property* may be valid. Some states may further limit the rights of businesses to disclaim consequential and incidental damages. Thus, as discussed above, it is wise to obtain legal advice on how these disclaimers may be used in the particular state.

Plan Smart

Disclaimers can be valuable in consumer contracts. As discussed above, businesses may not disclaim liability for personal injuries in consumer contracts. However, disclaimers can limit liability for property damages in consumer contracts, by limiting consumers to a particular remedy.

For example, in its agreement with its customers, a photo processing business will almost certainly limit the consumers' remedy, in the event of a breach of contract, to a replacement roll of film (and thus eliminate the pain and suffering, etc., that might arise because film that was lost, damaged or destroyed).

Limitations on consumers' remedies, in the event of warranty claims, also can significantly reduce a business's liability for these claims. Commonly, when an express warranty is granted, the agreement will limit consumers' rights to obtaining repair or replacement of the products at the business's discretion, and disclaim liability for incidental and consequential damages. This limitation allows the business to choose the most economical route to satisfy warranty claims (i.e., repair or replacement) and eliminates the rights of consumers to claim a cash refund, or consequential or incidental damages.

When the seller grants no express warranty, but one is granted by the manufacturer of the product, the agreement commonly will limit the consumers' rights to making claims against the manufacturer based on its warranty. Thus, the agreement might state that no express warranty is being granted by the retailer and also disclaim liability for the implied-in-law warranties of merchantability and fitness for a particular purpose, and for consequential and incidental damages, in the event of a breach of contract.

In contracts between business parties, the courts routinely uphold declaimers of liability for consequential and incidental damages. In fact, these disclaimers are especially valuable in a contract between two business parties.

Example

In one case, IBM sold a computer to a transportation company that operated a fleet of over 3,000 temperature-controlled trailers.

One year later, the computer failed and the transportation company sued IBM for breach of contract. As a result of the downtime, the transportation company lost $470,000 in profits and sued for this amount as consequential damages. The company also spent $4,500 to restore the company's lost data and sought to recover this amount as incidental damages.

The transportation company lost on both issues, because it had signed a contract with IBM that contained a disclaimer of liability for consequential damages and incidental damages. The appellate court upheld the disclaimer. Thus, the disclaimer saved IBM almost $500,000 in damages.

Note that consequential damages and incidental damages are additional damages that a party may recover. If it did prove that IBM breached the contract, the transportation company in this case still might recover its basic measure of compensatory damages, which would be the cost to repair the computer hardware.

Enlist State or Federal Government Assistance

Usually, *consumers* enlist the assistance of the government in claims made *against* small business owners. Thus, as discussed above, the potential for government involvement in a case usually amounts to a serious risk factor for small business owners.

However, involving the government in an action is not limited to the protection of consumers. Small business owners who suffer losses due to fraud or unfair business practices in dealings with other commercial parties should always consider filing a complaint with the government and requesting that the government take action against the other party.

Even a small business owner who is a *defendant* in an action brought by another commercial party may be able to use this strategy, through the assertion of a counterclaim (see the previous discussion).

Filing a complaint with the federal or state government can be an extremely effective strategy for small business owners. If the government pursues the matter, then the government will bear the full cost of the claim. Thus, the small business owner, in effect, will have hired a large, qualified law firm free of charge and with minimal effort (i.e., the filing of a letter of complaint).

Further, the government has immense resources that usually cannot be matched by the other party. This puts the other party at a significant strategic disadvantage and, in many cases, will force the other party to settle the case. The settlement normally would require full restitution to the aggrieved party (in this case, the small business owner).

Common ways that small business owners, as plaintiffs, can enlist the assistance of the federal or state government are when there are violations of the FTC Act, the state counterparts to the FTC Act, the FTC's franchise regulations, the state franchise laws and the RICO Act.

In addition, these statutes, with the exception of the FTC's provisions, also authorize private causes of action and, if the party is successful, reimbursement of attorney's fees and related costs, as well as punitive damages. Thus, small business owners may also consider this option, especially if the government fails to take action.

FTC Act

The FTC Act—which prohibits unfair, deceptive and fraudulent business practices—represents a common route that small business owners can use to involve the federal government in a lawsuit against another party, especially because the term "unfair and deceptive" business practices is so broadly interpreted by the courts. Each state has its own version of the FTC Act, which can similarly be used to involve the state government in the action.

Usually, these laws represent a significant risk factor for small business owners, as consumers most commonly use the acts to file suit. However, the protection offered by the acts also extends to business owners.

If the government takes action, then the small business owner will benefit significantly, because the government will bear the full cost of the claim and has immense resources that usually cannot be matched by the other party.

Because, the term "unfair and deceptive" trade practice is defined so broadly by the courts, small business owners who suffer losses in dealings with other commercial parties have a better chance of fitting the other party's conduct under the state acts.

Moreover, as discussed above, in contrast to the FTC act, the state acts also authorize a private party to file an action and recover attorney's fees and related costs, in addition to compensatory and, possibly, punitive damages.

The small business owner operating a franchise also can use the FTC Act to enlist the government's assistance. The FTC franchise regulations require that franchisors provide perspective franchisees with a pre-sale disclosure statement, known as "offering circular."

The disclosure statement contains *very* extensive and detailed financial and management information concerning the franchisor and its existing franchises. A franchisor who fails to provide the disclosure statement, or who provides a statement that contains errors or omissions, is deemed to have committed an unfair trade practice under the FTC Act.

Because the disclosures are so extensive and detailed, there are many instances where a franchiser can run afoul of the rules. These types of mistakes can represent effective ways for the small business owner to engage the government's assistance, when a dispute arises with a franchisor.

Of course, many actions of a franchisor may amount to unfair and deceptive trade practices under the FTC Act itself. Thus, the franchise regulations represent an *additional* way to engage the federal government in the action.

As previously mentioned in this chapter, several states also have franchise laws based on the FTC regulations. Of these 15 states, all except Michigan and Oregon require that the franchisor deliver to each perspective franchisee a pre-sale disclosure document, which is similar to the disclosure document required by FTC's franchise regulations. Michigan and Oregon do not require a filing of a pre-disclosure statement. In Oregon, no filing of any type is required. However, in Michigan, a notice of the sale must be filed with the state.

Importantly, *all of these 15 states,* including Michigan and Oregon, grant franchisees the right to file a complaint with the state, which may result in the state taking action against the franchisor. In addition, in contrast to the FTC franchise regulations, *all these states* grant franchisees the right to bring a private cause of action against franchisers. This statutory cause of action offers many advantages over a common law cause of action, because the franchisee can recover attorney's fees and related costs, as well as punitive damages, under these statutes. Thus, the statutory cause of action usually will result in a larger monetary damage award and is more likely to bring about a favorable settlement before trial.

Finally, where the other party has engaged in a pattern of illegal activity, the small business owner may be able to engage the assistance of the federal government through (and file an action under) the RICO Act, the federal anti-racketeering statute. RICO also authorizes the filing of private causes of action with recovery of attorney's fees and punitive damages. The RICO Act is discussed in more detail above.

Apply Leverage

Small business owners can use leverage to force a favorable settlement of a dispute. Leverage forces the other party to settle the case out of fear that a resolution of the case through the court system would produce a worse outcome.

Leverage can be used by plaintiffs or defendants. For example, plaintiffs with weak personal injury cases can, nevertheless, many times force defendants to pay settlements. This form of leverage is effective because plaintiffs are able to hire attorneys on a contingent fee basis (i.e., at no out-of-pocket cost), while defendants, who have to hire attorneys on an hourly fee basis, realize that the costs of defending against the claims (which ordinarily will not be reimbursed due to the lack of a loser pays system) will be more than the cost of paying a settlement (this form of leverage is covered in the discussion of risk factors).

The FTC Act, its state counterparts, the FTC's franchise regulations, the state franchise acts, and RICO also can be used as effective leverage to induce favorable settlements, because parties can enlist the assistance of the federal or state governments, and thus the government's significant resources and power.

In addition, as discussed above, the state acts and RICO also authorize the filing of private civil actions. This is significant, in terms of leverage, because the acts authorize reimbursement of attorney's fees and related costs, as well as punitive damages if the other party's actions were willful and wanton. When a party faces the possibility of paying these costs, in addition to compensatory damages, the party is more likely to settle the case. When the government joins a private suit as a plaintiff, the case is especially grim for the other party.

Example

Recently, tobacco companies settled suits that had been filed against them for a staggering $200 billion. The tobacco companies had been accused of racketeering under RICO, and unfair and deceptive business practices under the FTC Act and the related state acts. The tobacco companies faced suits filed by the federal government, numerous state governments and private parties. All of the plaintiffs sought reimbursement of attorney's fees and related costs, as well as punitive damages, in addition to compensatory damages.

Prior to these suits, the tobacco companies had been very successful in defeating plaintiff's claims. However, up against the federal government, many state governments, and private parties represented by large law firms, the powerful and seemingly invincible tobacco companies seemed small and overmatched by comparison. The tobacco companies faced the real possibility of being overwhelmed with legal expenses in defending against the claims, as well as the real possibility of losing the cases and paying substantial judgments.

This realization apparently convinced the tobacco companies that $200 billion was a "reasonable" settlement.

As discussed above, while these acts usually benefit consumers against business parties, small business owners who suffer losses due to fraud, or unfair and deceptive business practices, committed by other commercial parties also can use these acts to achieve favorable results, although, of course, not on the scale of the tobacco settlement.

Moreover, *any* claim based on an exception that allows for reimbursement of attorney's fees and related costs (e.g., a contract provision), or for punitive damages, can represent an effective form of leverage (see the previous discussion for details on the exceptions that allow for reimbursement of attorney's fees and related costs, and the circumstances under which punitive damages may be available).

While plaintiffs frequently use leverage, it also can be used by defendants through the assertion of counterclaims. In fact, a solid counterclaim can be very effective in forcing the plaintiff into dropping the claim or settling the case for a relatively nominal amount. Plaintiffs, especially in cases where they have hired their attorneys on a contingent fee basis and thus paid nothing out-of-pocket, usually can simply wait for a settlement check.

However, with the assertion of a counterclaim, the plaintiff's attorney now will have to inform the plaintiff that not only might he collect nothing in the case, but he may also end up *paying damages to the defendant*. This can cause a rift between the plaintiff and his attorney, which is ideal for the defendant from a strategic perspective. It may also cause the plaintiff to consider, for the first time, that he faces significant risks in continuing the lawsuit. Many plaintiffs faced with these prospects will accept a smaller settlement or simply withdraw the suit.

Warning

 The threat of a civil action to induce a settlement is permissible, provided that the party making the threat has a good-faith claim against the other party.

In contrast, the threat of criminal prosecution or, more precisely, the threat that a criminal complaint will be filed if the other party does not settle the case is never permissible. In fact, this type of threat is a crime itself, termed extortion or blackmail.

Nevertheless, when fraud is involved, a crime may have been committed. The actual filing of a criminal complaint, under these circumstances, also can force a settlement of the civil dispute.

The other party may settle the civil case quickly, in the belief that this will result in a favorable outcome to the criminal complaint. Further, civil restitution may be part of any resolution of the criminal complaint.

Finally, skilled attorneys can, many times, subtly make sure that the other party is aware of the criminal implications of his conduct. However, this strategy is best left to an attorney, because of the possible implications noted above.

Choose Liability Insurance Effectively

Insurance can be considered a protection of last resort in that it will cover a loss in the event that other measures have failed. Clearly, if liability insurance fully covers a claim, the business owner will suffer no loss (except, of course, with respect to higher future premiums).

Whether the policy will cover the loss will depend on the policy's limits, as well as the scope of its coverage and exclusions. Strategies involving coverage and exclusions are covered in detail in Chapter 18.

Chapter 18 also examines other strategies involving insurance, outside of coverage and exclusions issues, which can provide significant benefits to small business owners. For example, a liability policy should have a duty to defend clause. When a claim is made against the insured, this clause requires the insurance company to defend the insured against the claim. In particular, the insurance company must hire an attorney for the insured, and pay the attorney's fees and related costs of litigation. The clause is especially important because the costs of defending against a claim, which can be significant, generally will not be reimbursed, even in the event the defendant prevails in the case.

In addition, as discussed in the next chapter, the small business owner may be able to rely on other people's insurance. Here, a contract would require *another party* to secure and pay for a liability policy that also insures the small business owner. The arrangement might be used, for example, where a small business owner with superior bargaining power enters into a joint venture with another party. In this instance, the small business owners enjoy all of the benefits of the policy, but at no cost.

Finally, the small business owner may be able to compel reimbursement of his litigation losses through an indemnification agreement. This type of agreement compels another party to reimburse the small business owner for any litigation losses he suffers. Indemnification may offer less security, as compared to relying on other people's insurance, because an individual's ability to cover the losses will almost never equal the ability of an insurance company to cover the losses. However, in practice, indemnification clauses are frequently used in conjunction with other people's insurance. When both strategies are used together, indemnification adds a second layer of protection.

Engage in Asset Protection Planning

Finally, of course, small business owners should adopt a comprehensive asset protection plan, based on the strategies advocated in this book (e.g., exemption planning, asset projection trusts, strategic structuring and funding of the business entities, avoiding exceptions to limited liability, etc.).

These strategies are designed to place both personal and business assets outside of the reach of creditors, and to reduce the possibility that claims against the business owner, in his personal capacity or against his business entity, will be made or will be successful.

In short, a comprehensive asset procession plan can help ensure that if monetary damages are awarded, your assets will not be reachable by the plaintiff—making you judgment-proof.

Chapter 18

Insurance—The Protection of Last Resort

Ideally, the small business owner will structure his financial affairs so that claims will not be made or, if claims occur, the claimants will be unable to satisfy their claims from the business owner's personal or business assets. The asset protection strategies advocated throughout this book are based on these principles.

Occasionally, however, claims will be made. And some of these claims may penetrate the multiple layers of protection set up by the business owner. If this occurs, the business owner should have one final layer of protection—insurance.

There are two basic types of insurance:

- **Liability Insurance** covers damages that the insured causes to *other* persons, both personal injuries and property damage. Thus, a liability insurance policy will have separate provisions, including separate limits, for personal injury and property damage caused to other persons.

- **Property Insurance** covers damages *to the insured's own property*. Property coverage will be addressed separately in an insurance policy. Thus, property coverage should not be confused with liability coverage for property damage that the insured causes to another person's property.

Each basic type of insurance is subdivided into specific types of liability and property insurance policies. The small business owner should have a comprehensive liability and property insurance policy, *and* specialized forms of liability and property coverage, which will cover the risks inherent in the specific business. This chapter addresses both comprehensive and specialized forms of insurance.

Plan Smart

The business owner is likely to have multiple insurance policies. Accordingly, if a claim apparently is not covered (or not fully covered) under one policy, don't overlook the possibility that the claim may be covered by other policies. In a business setting, overlapping insurance coverage is very common.

In fact, overlapping coverage and, in particular, the extent of each insurance company's duty to contribute toward the loss is one of the most frequently litigated issues in business insurance claims. In this litigation, insurance companies are pitted against each other, with the insured as an adversary of each company. As is true with respect to any insurance claim (see below), don't expect any insurance company to voluntarily admit that it has a duty to contribute or that, in general, the claim is covered under its policy.

In some instances (e.g., auto insurance or in some states, professional liability insurance for certain professions), liability coverage is mandatory. Where insurance is mandatory, coverage at the minimum policy limits required by state law may be insufficient (as with automobile liability insurance addressed later).

In most cases, insurance is optional. This raises the issue as to whether or not to obtain insurance coverage. In certain cases, the small business owner may wish to forego insurance and instead rely on other asset protection strategies because premiums are cost-prohibitive (see, e.g., long-term care insurance, which is discussed at the end of this chapter). This can be a risky strategy in many cases. In a close case, choosing insurance will be the better decision.

But in order to make sound decisions regarding the types and levels of liability and property insurance needed for your particular business situation, you'll need an understanding of the basics of insurance coverage and terminology.

UNDERSTANDING INSURANCE COVERAGE

Insurance companies earn a profit in two ways:

- through the spread (the difference between insurance premiums charged and the payments made to insured parties for claims)

- thorough investment income (interest derived from investing the premiums received)

If an insurance company can deny a claim, the spread and, therefore, its profits will be higher.

Similarly, the longer an insurance company can delay paying a claim, the longer the premiums will continue to earn income. This form of income cannot be overlooked because, in practice, it represents a significant source of profits since insurance companies collect billions of dollars in premiums. For example, $1 billion of premiums earning interest at 8 percent for an extra six months will yield an additional $40 million in profits.

Why should this be an important issue for the small business owner? When making a claim on a policy, the business owner should expect the insurance company to deny the claim or to delay paying the claim. The insurance company has a strong financial incentive to do both.

In fact, what most people don't understand is that denial of a claim begins well before a claim is made. It begins with the carefully selected wording in an insurance policy. The actual language in the policy, subject to court interpretation, will delineate the scope of the coverage and exclusions from coverage.

Certain issues run across lines of coverage. The small business owner should follow the general guidelines discussed below with respect to *any* type of insurance coverage.

Compare Premiums and Policies Beforehand

Consider obtaining an unexecuted copy of the policy *before* agreeing to coverage. It is well known that premiums for exactly the same coverage can vary significantly among insurance companies. However, what is less known is the fact that policy provisions (i.e., coverage and exclusions) can also very widely from company to company.

Insurance policies are form (or adhesion) contracts. Don't expect the insurance company to negotiate the language of various clauses. The insurance company is making a "take it or leave it" offer for coverage. Obtain an unexecuted copy of the policy, read it thoroughly, and if the coverage is too narrow or the exclusions tóo wide—"leave it!"

Comparison shopping is ideal. However, don't limit this to a comparison of premiums and don't accept the insurance company's (or an agent's) word as to the policy's coverage and exclusions. Request policies from several companies and compare the policies, in terms of coverage and exclusions, as well as premiums. If there is no existing policy, this is best done well in advance of the time coverage is needed.

Retain Insurance Policies Indefinitely

Most policies insure against any covered loss that occurred during the policy period. Thus, even though a policy expires, claims can still be made that will be covered under the policy.

Don't expect the insurance company to willingly provide you with a copy of a policy in effect for an earlier period in which a covered event occurred, or even admit that you were covered during that period.

Be prepared to prove that you were insured during the period in which the claim arose and be able to produce a copy of the policy in effect for that period. Remember that policies are amended from time to time. A current policy may not be identical to the policy that was in effect when the claim arose.

Generally, insurance policies should be retained indefinitely. This is especially true with respect to liability policies. At the very least, liability policies should be retained until all of the statutes of limitations for all possible causes of action have expired.

Generally, tort actions must be filed within two or three years of the event that gave rise to the damages. However, laws vary from state to state, and in certain instances (e.g., personal injuries due to exposure to asbestos), states have significantly lengthened the statute of limitations. The best practice is to retain insurance policies indefinitely.

Plan Smart

Ideally, the actual policy should be kept in a secure location, such as a bank safety deposit box. A copy should be kept in a separate location, in a fireproof box, with a note attached to it that indicates the location of the original policy. This in fact is a sound practice with respect to all important legal documents.

Give Prompt Verbal and Written Notice of a Claim

Generally, all insurance policies have a clause that requires the insured to give prompt notice of a claim. This is best done immediately by way of a telephone call, which is always followed by written notice in the form of a letter.

This telephone call *and* letter should be recorded in a log. The date, time and name of the other party should be recorded when any verbal communication occurs.

Policies may contain very specific requirements for giving notice. For example, if a summons and complaint were received, the insured will usually be required to forward a copy to the insurance company. Failure to follow these exact requirements may result in the notice being deemed defective.

Where notice is not given or is defective, the insurance company may deny the claim. However, in all states except a few (see below for the specific states), for the insurance company to legally deny the claim, it must be able to prove that it was prejudiced by the failure to give adequate notice.

Example

If an insured party was sued and a default judgment was entered against the insured because he never responded to the suit (and never notified the insurance company of the claim), the insurance company might be able to deny coverage.

On the other hand, most failures to give adequate notice are harmless. In this case, in almost all states, the insurance company cannot deny coverage. The District of Columbia, New York and Illinois, however, follow an older rule, which allows the insurance company to automatically deny coverage when adequate notice was not given, even though the insurance company was not prejudiced in any way.

Giving prompt verbal and written notice eliminates these issues.

Enforce the Duty To Defend Clause

A standard clause used in various types of liability insurance policies requires the insurance company to supply an attorney, at its cost, to defend against a lawsuit filed against the insured. The duty to defend clause also extends to covering all of the related costs involved in defending against the suit, including for example, the cost of expert testimony, depositions, etc.

Clearly this additional coverage can be significant. In many cases, hiring an attorney at a rate of $150 to $300 *per hour* may preclude the defendant from obtaining representation or induce him to settle a case on unfavorable terms (as discussed in Chapter 17).

Accordingly, where litigation costs will be extensive, the small business owner should realize the insurance company will have an extra financial incentive to deny coverage. Where the claim is not covered, the duty to defend, of course, does not apply.

The small business owner should determine if the proposed policy has a duty to defend clause. If it doesn't contain this clause, or the clause contains too many exclusions, the business owner may want to consider a different policy. This is yet another reason to obtain an unexecuted copy of the policy before agreeing to its terms.

When the insurance company denies the claim or provides inadequate representation, the insured may be able to force the company to reconsider its position through the threat of a "bad-faith" claim.

Plan Smart

 As discussed in Chapter 17, when a lawsuit is filed, the plaintiff alleges a certain cause of action (e.g., negligence) in his complaint. Multiple causes of action may be alleged and each is identified in the complaint as a "count."

Where multiple causes of action are alleged, but one of the causes of action is excluded from coverage, insurance companies sometimes attempt to deny coverage or deny their duty to defend against the action. This is improper. The courts have ruled that if one cause of action is covered, the claim is covered and the duty to defend applies.

In addition, where there is a duty to defend clause, the insured still can hire separate legal counsel. The private legal counsel can ensure that the insurance company provides adequate representation, assist in developing strategies, and document any evidence that may be the basis of a bad-faith claim against the insurance company (see the discussion of bad faith below).

Because the insurance company will provide, at its expense, the lead counsel on the case, the cost of hiring private legal counsel should be less expensive.

Use the Threat of a Bad-Faith Claim

"Bad faith" is a tort cause of action that can be used against an insurance company that has denied a claim, provided inadequate representation under its duty to defend or engaged in other wrongful conduct.

Bad faith can be a serious form of leverage used against an insurance company. Many times, the mere mention of "bad faith" causes an insurance company to change its position. A successful bad-faith claim will result in the insurance company being held liable to pay the claim, along with defense costs (if there is a duty to defend clause) and, in many cases, punitive damages as well.

A common form of bad faith involves an insurance company's refusal to settle a case for the policy limits, which is based on a reasonable offer from the injured party.

Insurance companies have a financial incentive to behave in this way. For example, assume the policy limit on an automobile insurance policy is $100,000. Assume the plaintiff, who has damages that equal or exceed $100,000, offers to settle the case for the policy limit.

The worst-case scenario, *for the insurance company,* is paying the policy limit. Its liability, of course, cannot exceed this limit. Thus, in this situation, the insurance company may conclude that it has nothing to lose by refusing to settle these case and going to trial. If, after a trial, the judgment is $400,000, the insurance company still only pays $100,000, the policy limit.

Thus, by refusing to settle the case and going to trial, the insurance company is gambling that the jury might award less than the policy limit, thus producing savings for the insurance company. In engaging in this gambling, however, the insurance company is taking no risk at all. *Instead, all the risk is on the insured.* Essentially, the insurance company is gambling with the insured's money. In this case, for example, the additional $300,000 in damages would have to be paid entirely by the insured.

If it can be shown that the injured party's offer to settle the case, at the policy limit, was reasonable, but the insurance company refused the offer and went to trial, the insurance company may be held liable on a bad-faith tort claim brought by the insured. The result of a successful bad-faith claim in this case will be that the insurance company will be ordered to pay *the entire judgment. In other words, the insurance company's liability will not be limited to the policy limit.* In this case, continuing our example, a successful bad-faith claim would mean that the insurance company would be required to pay the entire $400,000 of damages.

Clearly, insurance companies have plenty of incentive to dispute and delay claims up to the point in engaging in bad faith.

Plan Smart

The insured also would be taking a risk if he actually files a bad-faith claim against his insurance company. The risk, of course, is the possibility of losing the action.

As stated above, many times the mere mention of the possibility of a bad-faith claim is sufficient to cause an insurance company to change its position. Thus, if the insured believes his insurance company is guilty of bad faith, the best strategy would be to send a carefully worded letter to the company that subtly mentions the possibility of a bad-faith claim. This letter ought to be drafted by an attorney. The insurance company will understand the implications of the letter.

The threat of a bad-faith claim also can be coupled with another effective strategy. As discussed in Chapter 17, involving the government in a lawsuit or dispute can be very effective in inducing a favorable settlement. The government has immense resources and, in certain cases (e.g., disputes with insurance companies), the power to levy civil fines. Involving the government is the equivalent of hiring a large law firm free of cost.

Every state has an insurance department. The threat of a complaint to the insurance department can, many times, force an insurance company to act reasonably. However, as is true with any threat, if the threat does not produce results, it should be followed by the actual filing of a complaint.

Rely on Another Party's Insurance

Banks are fully insured for damages (from fire, etc.) that occur to a home on which they carry a mortgage. In fact, a bank will be named as an insured party on a hazard insurance policy. Yet, the insurance costs the bank nothing. The homeowner is required, by contract, to obtain and pay for the coverage.

The small business owner can do the same thing and rely on another person's insurance coverage. The business owner who lends money, by way of a mortgage, or in any other case where collateral supports the loan, can require that the other party obtain liability and property coverage, which specifically names the business owner as an insured party, in the same way that a bank requires this coverage. In the case of a mortgage or other collateral loan, do not limit yourself to property coverage. Liability for environmental pollution, for example, has sometimes been extended by the courts to banks holding a mortgage on the affected property.

Further, the small business owner can also rely on another party's insurance when he leases property to, or engages in a joint venture with, another party. Here, again, care should generally be taken to ensure that the other party obtains adequate property *and* liability coverage.

Reliance on other person's insurance, in practice, is usually limited to situations where the other party will be carrying out all, or nearly all, of the activities. A mortgagee and lessee, for example, will have exclusive possession and use of the property. Thus, it is reasonable in both cases to require these parties to secure insurance coverage. Similarly, in the case of the joint venture, where the small business owner's role is only secondary to the venture (e.g., limited to putting up capital or devising a business plan), it would be reasonable to require that the primary party (i.e., the other party) obtain and pay for insurance coverage.

The small business owner should always obtain a copy of the policy, rather than rely on word from the other party that the coverage has been secured. Where the small business owner is named as an insured party, the insurance company will provide him with a copy of the policy, as well as copies of notices, including cancellation notices, related to the policy.

Indemnification by Other Parties

The small business owner should consider coupling a requirement that the other party obtain insurance with a requirement that the other party indemnify the small business owner. This indemnification, or "hold harmless" provision as it is frequently called, requires that the other party reimburse the small business owner for any loss he suffers in the transaction or relationship. In this way, the small business owner adds an extra layer of protection.

An indemnification clause may seem to be superfluous given the insurance protection. However, insurance policies, of course, have many exclusions from coverage. The indemnification clause will apply when the insurance does not cover the liability.

Risk managers for large corporations and municipalities, for example, typically require both insurance coverage *and* indemnification.

Factor Liability Insurance into Insolvency Tests

Insurance can offer protection beyond the scope of its apparent coverage. As discussed in detail in Chapter 4, the Uniform Fraudulent Transfers Act (UFTA) outlaws transfers consummated thorough constructive fraud *or* actual fraud.

Constructive fraud exists when a transfer is made that makes the transferor insolvent, *and* the transferor receives less that full value in return. "Insolvent" means either that the transferor's liabilities exceed his assets (the balance sheet test) or that the transferor is unable to pay his debts as they come due (the cash flow test). If the two conditions apply, the transfer is *automatically* deemed fraudulent.

With actual fraud, the transfer's intent is the key issue. It must be proved that the transferor intended to defraud creditors through the transfer. However, even here insolvency is important, as it is one factor bearing on intent.

Moreover, distributions from an LLC or a corporation to an owner on account of his ownership interest (i.e., distributions of earnings or dividends, or ownership redemptions) are also subject to a constructive fraud test (as discussed in Chapter 15). Generally, these distributions are deemed fraudulent if they are made at a time that the business entity is insolvent.

How do insurance liability limits relate to insolvency? The limits of a liability insurance policy can be deemed to be an "asset" under the balance sheet test and a future receipt of capital in the cash flow test. The result then can be that the transferor has a positive balance sheet (assets exceed liabilities) and a positive cash flow (cash receipts exceed cash payments) position, and thus is not insolvent. Accordingly, the transfer would not be deemed fraudulent.

One important catch, though: The insurance liability limits will be factored in only if the creditor challenging the transfer as fraudulent is someone who could benefit from the policy.

Example

Let's say a physician, a sole proprietor, is successfully sued for malpractice and a judgment of $100,000 is rendered. The physician, upon receiving notice of the lawsuit, transfers $800,000 to his children as a gift.

The transfer leaves the physician with assets of $20,000 and liabilities (including the court judgment) of $400,000.

The physician is insolvent under the balance sheet test ($400,000 of liabilities exceeds $20,000 of assets). Thus, the $800,000 transfer to the children would be deemed fraudulent.

Now, however, let's say the physician carried an E&O (Error & Omission) policy, which is a type of liability insurance for professionals (explained later), with a policy limit of $800,000. The physician is solvent before and after the transfer (assets of $20,000 plus $800,000, or $820,000, exceed liabilities of $400,000). Therefore, the transfer of $800,000 to the children is valid.

Court Interpretation of Coverage and Exclusions

All insurance policies contain language that can be ambiguous in certain situations. The ambiguities may relate to the scope of coverage or to specific exclusions from coverage.

In dealing with an insurance company on coverage and exclusion issues, the small business owner should be aware that the courts almost uniformly have held that *coverage is to be liberally construed*, while *exclusions from coverage are to be narrowly construed*. Don't expect the insurance company to tell you this or even to assume you know this, but where coverage is an issue, generally there is a strong presumption in favor of coverage.

Warning

Don't be misled by this presumption. If there are no ambiguities concerning a lack of coverage or a specific exclusion from coverage, the presumption in favor of coverage will not apply and the insurance will not cover the situation.

Ideally, as discussed above, the small business owner will obtain an unexecuted copy of the policy and determine the scope of coverage and exclusions before purchasing the policy.

GENERAL AND SPECIALIZED LIABILITY POLICIES

The small business owner should become familiar with coverage issues involved in a comprehensive general liability insurance policy, as well as with specialized liability policies. These issues are addressed below.

Specific forms of liability insurance (or endorsements, discussed below) are necessary to cover exclusions from a standard comprehensive general liability policy. Also, the small business owner may be compelled to purchase certain specialized liability insurance in some cases (e.g., errors and omissions liability insurance, discussed below), depending on the particular circumstances.

Comprehensive General Liability Insurance

As previously discussed, liability insurance covers damages in the form of *personal injuries and property damage* that the insured causes *to other persons*. Importantly, liability coverage does not protect property owned by the insured.

Comprehensive general liability insurance is designed to provide broad coverage for liability to other persons. Generally, it covers all liability for personal injuries or property damage caused to other persons, *unless specifically excluded*. Thus, in a comprehensive general liability insurance policy, it is very important to read and understand all of the exclusions, and compare your options, before purchasing the policy.

Common Elements and Exclusions

Before deciding on the type of coverage you'll purchase, you'll need to understand some basic information.

Endorsements. Specialized forms of liability insurance are more restricted in scope and are, in fact, specifically designed to cover situations excluded in a comprehensive general liability insurance policy. Sometimes, rather than purchase a separate specialized policy, an insured may be able to pay an additional premium for an "endorsement"—an amendment to a comprehensive general liability insurance policy that will cover a standard exclusion.

This may be possible, for example, where the insured party wants protection for liability that arises from damage caused to another person's computer data, but where the standard form of the policy excludes data from the definition of "property" (see below for a discussion of this issue). When liability relates to a unique risk (e.g., professional services by an accountant), a specialized policy will be required (e.g., an errors and omissions, or E&O, policy), in addition to a comprehensive general liability insurance policy.

Plan Smart

 An endorsement to an insurance policy can end up saving the day for a small business owner. For example, today, liability for cleanup and related costs for a polluted site can easily run into the millions of dollars, even in a seemingly small case. Further, liability for these costs can be imposed on an innocent *party who currently owns or operates the affected property, even though the pollution was caused by another party many years earlier.*

Where liability for environmental pollution is a possibility, check the policy in advance for coverage. A standard policy will usually contain an exclusion for this type of coverage. Consider adding an endorsement to the policy that will cover liability for environmental pollution, if liability is a possibility and the endorsement is not cost-prohibitive.

Moreover, as mentioned, this type of liability can be imposed on an innocent party. One simple strategy can be used to eliminate this possibility—namely, an environmental inspection. The contract for the purchase of the property would contain a clause mandating that such an inspection be conducted, and conditioning the obligation to purchase on the results of the inspection being favorable to the buyer.

When an endorsement is to be issued that will cover liability for environmental pollution, an environmental inspection may be required by the insurance company, as a condition of writing the endorsement.

Note that standard inspections mandated in real estate contracts do not *include an environmental inspection. Standard inspections include testing for structural integrity, the proper functioning of mechanical systems, pests (e.g., termites), and environmental hazards (including lead-based paint, asbestos, radon gas, and urea formaldehyde insulation).*

These environmental hazards, which are usually included in a standard real estate contract, are potential dangers to the property owner himself. In contrast, an environmental inspection is designed to uncover pollution on the property that may harm surrounding properties and their owners. *An environmental inspection would include a review of the property's history, soil and water samples, etc.*

An environmental inspection generally must be done by an environmental engineering company and can be very expensive as compared to standard inspections. However, this type of inspection may be mandatory if an endorsement on the policy is requested. In any event, where the possibility of pollution is suggested by the history of the property or by the current owner or operator, the cost of the inspection must be weighed against the potential savings it may produce. The potential savings could be significant because, generally, liability will not be imposed on an innocent party who obtained a favorable environmental inspection before he purchased the property. Under these circumstances, the cost of the inspection will usually pale in comparison to the potential savings.

Coverage of Occurrences. The comprehensive general liability policy will cover liability for any "occurrence" during the policy period—that is, the policy will cover liability for personal injuries or property damage that the insured caused to another party while the policy was in effect. A lapse in insurance coverage opens a window of vulnerability.

Expected or Intended Damages. Damages that were subjectively "expected or intended" by the insured will be excluded from coverage. Courts have ruled that to deny a claim, it is not sufficient for the insurance company to prove that a "reasonable person" would have expected the outcome (i.e., what the law terms "objective intent" is not sufficient). Rather, the insurance company must prove what the insured party was actually thinking at the time, which is a more difficult burden to meet.

Intellectual Property, Advertising, etc. Coverage for personal injuries to other persons—as a result of libel; slander; defamation; invasion of privacy; copyright, patent, trade name and trademark infringement; and unfair business practices—*traditionally* has been included in a comprehensive general liability policy. This type of liability can arise from advertising, publications on web sites, or general business practices.

Recently, however, insurance companies have begun adding exclusions from coverage for copyright, patent, trade name and trademark infringement (intellectual property rights), as well as more narrowly defining "advertising," for purposes of denying coverage for libel, slander and infringement of intellectual property rights.

Accordingly, the small business owner should examine any proposed comprehensive general liability policy for this type of coverage. If coverage is too narrowly drawn or the exclusions too significant, the small business owner should consider requesting an endorsement to the policy that will include this coverage or purchasing a specialized "cyberspace" insurance policy (explained later), especially if the company maintains a large presence on the Internet.

Data as Property. Outside of the area of intellectual property, coverage for damages to another person's property only may apply if the property is "tangible," or the damage "physical." Issues arise here as to whether computer data is "tangible," or capable of "physical" harm. Thus, a company that provides computer hardware, software, or programming services should determine whether the standard policy includes this coverage. If it does not include the desired coverage, the party should request an endorsement that includes this coverage or consider purchasing a separate, specialized liability policy (see the cyberspace insurance discussion later).

Property Insurance Distinguished. A *single policy* may provide for comprehensive general liability coverage (for damages caused to other persons in the form of personal injuries and property loss) *and separate* coverage for damage to property owned by the insured. However, remember that comprehensive general liability coverage *alone* does *not* offer protection for damage to property owned by the insured. Property insurance must be included in the policy for the insured's property to be covered.

Specialized Liability Policies

The small business owner may need specialized forms of liability insurance that will cover exclusions from a standard comprehensive general liability policy. The small business owner also may be compelled to purchase specialized liability insurance in some cases. The various specialized liability policies discussed below include:

- Errors and omissions liability policies

- Directors and officers liability policies

- Cyberspace liability insurance policies

- Automobile liability insurance

E&O Liability Insurance

An errors and omissions, or E&O, liability policy covers liability for negligent acts, errors and omissions committed by professionals, including physicians, accountants, lawyers, etc.

An E&O liability policy may be mandatory. State law sometimes requires that certain professionals maintain an E&O policy with a certain minimum amount of liability coverage. The requirement may only extend to certain professionals (e.g., physicians). In some cases, the obligation applies to anyone practicing in the profession, irrespective of the business form in which they operate. In other cases, the obligation may be imposed by the state's code that empowers professionals to form professional corporations, limited liability partnerships, or possibly limited liability companies. In this case, professionals operating outside of these business forms may not be compelled to obtain liability coverage. State laws differ significantly in these respects, so make sure you check your state's particular laws.

State licensing boards and professional organizations in each state are good sources for information on liability insurance requirements imposed on particular professions.

Where E&O liability coverage is optional, the professional must weigh the risk of being self-insured against the costs of insurance. In doing so, the professional must remember that the personal commission of a tort, such as malpractice, represents a significant exception to the limited liability that otherwise applies in an LLC or a corporation (see Chapter 15 for a discussion of this exception).

To protect against other forms of liability, the professional will have to undertake other asset protection measures described in this book, including strategically structuring and funding the business entity, exemption planning, the use of asset protection trusts, etc.

When the cost of insurance is especially significant (e.g., some physicians pay annual premiums of $50,000 or more for E&O liability insurance) *and* an effective asset protection plan is in place, consideration may be given to foregoing insurance, if this is an option in your particular state. Clearly, this decision should only be made after very careful deliberation.

Negligent Acts v. Errors and Omissions. An E&O policy will cover both "negligent" acts *and* errors and omissions that result in loss to another person. Thus, coverage should extend to all causes of action that arise from the insured's professional services and not merely a cause of action based on negligence.

Insurance companies sometimes attempt to limit coverage to a cause of action based on negligence, arguing that only *negligent* errors and omissions are covered. The courts generally have rejected this argument from insurance companies.

Definition of Professional Services. An E&O policy will only cover liability arising out of "professional services." Insurance companies sometimes attempt to disclaim coverage on the grounds that the insured's activities did not amount to professional services.

As previously discussed, the courts generally have ruled that any ambiguity must be construed in a way that favors coverage. Thus, a definition of professional services will be broadly construed. Courts have ruled that any activity that requires mental or intellectual skill meets the definition of "professional services."

Claims-Made Basis v. Occurrence Basis. An E&O liability insurance policy will usually be issued as a "claims-made" policy. This is not the standard form of coverage with which most people are familiar.

Rather than coverage applying to any "occurrence" during the policy period, coverage instead applies to any claim made during the policy period.

Thus, in a claims-made policy, coverage will *not* continue after the policy period has expired. So if something happens while covered, but a claim isn't made until sometime after the policy period, the claim isn't valid. By contrast, in a comprehensive general liability policy that covers occurrences arising during the policy period, claims made after the expiration of the policy period, but based on events that occurred during the effective period of the insurance, are covered by the policy.

On the surface, it may appear that a claims-made policy enjoys an advantage with respect to events that took place *prior to* the effective date of the policy. A comprehensive general liability policy will not apply to these claims. However, a claims-made policy also will not apply to these claims, even when the claims are made during the policy period. This apparent contradiction is explained by the fact that the claims-made policy will exclude from coverage any claims based on an event that occurred before the effective date of the policy.

In short, a claims-made policy usually offers less effective coverage, but accordingly is less expensive for an insurance company to issue. This savings may result, in theory anyway, in lower premiums for the insured party.

Nevertheless, because of the superior protection generally offered by an occurrence-based policy, the small business owner should inquire as to whether an occurrence-based, as opposed to a claims-made, E&O policy is available. If such coverage is available and the premium is not cost-prohibitive, the small business owner should consider paying the additional premiums and purchasing the occurrence-based E&O policy.

Plan Smart

In determining the policy limits of an E&O policy, the small business owner should remember that a professional will be personally liable for malpractice (i.e., negligence) he commits while providing professional services irrespective of the business form in which he is operating. This represents a significant departure from the limited liability that otherwise exists in the LLC or corporation.

An LLC or corporation offers protection from personal liability for malpractice committed by other owners and other employees of the business entity, provided of course that arrangements among the owners and with the employees are properly structured (see Chapter 15 for a detailed discussion of these arrangements).

However, a professional who negligently hires or supervises an employee may be held personally liable if the employee commits an act of malpractice or some other act of negligence (as discussed in Chapter 15). Here, the professional is not being held liable for the employee's act of negligence, but instead for his own separate act of negligence, in failing to reasonably hire or supervise the employee.

Of course, the nature of the professional's specific activities will dictate the exact extent of the exposure to personal liability and, thus, the recommended dollar amount for the policy's limits. In short, however, in deciding on the policy's limits, the professional must consider the fact that despite operating in the form of an LLC or a corporation, he may still have significant exposure to unlimited, personal liability.

Directors and Officers Liability Insurance

Corporations frequently purchase directors and officers, or D&O, liability insurance. These policies have very specific provisions relating to coverage. A careful advance reading of a D&O liability policy is always in order.

In addition, the small business owner should be aware that an LLC will require a specialized policy that applies to "managers" of the LLC, rather than to directors who manage a conventional corporation.

Similarly, a statutory close corporation, which is usually managed by the shareholders rather than by a board of directors, will require a specialized policy that covers the shareholders while acting in their capacity as managers of the entity.

Both the LLC and statutory close corporation also may have officers who are selected from among the managers. It is important that coverage is extended to these officers while they are carrying out their specialized roles.

A D&O liability policy usually is a claims-made policy. As discussed above, a policy that covers any occurrence during the policy period usually is the best type of coverage, but it may only be offered at a higher premium, or not at all. Where an occurrence-based policy is available and it is not cost-prohibitive, the occurrence-based policy usually will be the better choice (see the discussion of claims-made vs. occurrence-based policies in the context of E&O insurance).

A D&O liability policy normally will be *limited to the individuals* who are named in the policy. Thus, caution must be exercised to ensure that each director, officer or manager is properly listed, and that new parties are added or deleted when there is a change in the management of the business.

The entity itself, its managers, subsidiary entities, and managers of subsidiaries usually can be listed as covered parties under the same policy. Of course, a separate entity may alternatively decide to take out a separate D&O liability policy. This usually makes sense only when management of the entities is not overlapping or the insurance company requires separate policies. If a single policy is used, it is always wise to review the policy in advance to ensure that each entity and its managers are covered.

Indemnification of Officers, Directors and Managers. An operating agreement for an LLC or statutory close corporation (or bylaws for a conventional corporation) generally should include an indemnification clause that requires the entity to reimburse the managers for any liability they personally incur while carrying out their management duties. Generally, state laws allow indemnification, except to the extent that the manager's conduct was a willful violation of the law. Business-friendly states, such as Delaware, allow for extremely broad indemnification of owners.

The clause will add an extra layer of projection for managers, in addition to the D&O liability policy. Of course, when an indemnification clause is triggered, the entity itself pays the damages. The D&O liability policy will mean that the loss will not have to be borne by the entity, provided of course, that the entity is a named party on the policy.

D&O Policy Exclusions. Exclusions in a D&O liability policy can be significant. Therefore, read the proposed policy thoroughly. Common exceptions include:

- bodily or personal injuries

- intentional or criminal violation of laws

- "ultra vires" acts (i.e., acts outside of the scope of the manager's authority)

- liability assessed by a regulatory agency

Each business is unique. In some highly regulated businesses, for example, managers may face their greatest exposure to liability from actions taken by state or federal agencies. If a significant form of exposure to liability is excluded (e.g., liability assessed by a regulatory agency), request that the policy include an endorsement adding coverage. Clearly, the cost of the endorsement must be weighed against the cost engendered by the risk itself.

Finally, D&O liability polices sometimes exclude defense costs from coverage. The duty to defend (as discussed above) is important. Therefore, make sure that the policy includes a duty to defend clause.

Cyberspace Liability Insurance

Cyberspace liability insurance covers Internet and computer-related losses caused to other parties. These losses may be covered in a comprehensive general liability insurance policy. However, as previously discussed, many companies have been changing policy language in comprehensive general liability insurance polices to exclude coverage of violations of intellectual property rights, as well as for certain advertising activities. A careful reading of the comprehensive general liability insurance policy and an endorsement to the policy, if necessary, can ensure coverage for these types of liability.

Alternatively, a party that does a regular amount of business on the Internet (or perhaps a regular amount of advertising) should consider purchasing a specialized cyberspace liability insurance policy. This type of policy is relatively new and is not offered by all insurance companies.

A cyberspace liability insurance policy should cover liability for violations of intellectual property rights, invasions of privacy, libel, slander, and property damage, in the form of lost data.

In addition to liability coverage, cyberspace insurance also may have a property insurance component, and thus cover damages to computer hardware, software and data *owned by the insured*.

Finally, an E&O component may be available in a cyberspace insurance policy. This insures against liability incurred due to the negligent acts or errors and omissions of the insured's computer professionals who provide services to others.

A cyberspace insurance policy would be especially appropriate for a computer consulting business, an Internet service provider, a web site developer, or any company involved in e-commerce. Before a cyberspace insurance policy is purchased, however, the small business owner should examine its comprehensive general liability, E&O *and* property insurance policies for possible coverage overlap. To the extent the company's activities are not covered under one of these policies, a cyberspace insurance policy may be needed.

Automobile Liability Insurance

States generally mandate that drivers carry automobile *liability* insurance, subject to minimum policy limits, but this mandate does *not* extend to automobile *property* insurance covering damage to the insured's own vehicle. In short, states are concerned only about drivers having insurance to cover damages caused to *other* persons and their vehicles, and not coverage for their *own* personal and property damages resulting from an automobile accident.

Typically, the minimum policy limit is stated in terms of the *liability for personal injuries caused to other persons*, but the small business owner also should remember that separate limits in a liability policy will apply to property damage caused to another party. Usually, states impose a smaller minimum liability limit for property damage, although some states may have no minimum requirement at all for this type of liability coverage.

In particular, the small business owner should consider the following issues when purchasing an automobile liability policy:

Split-Limit v. Single-Limit Policy. Automobile liability coverage for personal injuries may be issued on either a split-limit or single-limit basis. The split-limit policy provides for two separate limits: one that applies to each *individual* injured and a second overall limit that applies to each accident. In contrast, a single-limit policy, as the term implies, has one limit per accident. The single limit may be recovered entirely by one individual or divided among all of the injured parties. Generally, a single-limit policy offers better protection.

Example

For example, a $20,000/$40,000 split-limit policy would pay a maximum of $40,000 for personal injuries, per accident, with each injured individual entitled to collect a maximum of $20,000.

A $40,000 single-limit policy would pay a maximum of $40,000 for that same accident, with any one individual entitled to collect the entire policy limit.

Generally, a single-limit policy is superior to a split-limit policy, provided the single limit is equal to, or greater than, the maximum limit per occurrence in a split-limit policy. In this example, if there is a single-limit policy ($40,000) and an individual suffered $40,000 of damages, the policy would pay all of the damages.

By contrast, if there is a split limit policy ($20,000/$40,000), the injured individual could collect only $20,000 of his damages from the policy, and the responsible driver (i.e., the insured party) would have to personally pay the remaining $20,000 of the damages.

State-Mandated Minimum Liability Coverage. Personal injury lawyers all agree: Minimum liability coverage, as mandated by state law, is woefully inadequate. While this may seem self-serving, virtually every defense lawyer would agree that state-mandated minimum liability coverage for automobile insurance is insufficient. Simply put, seemingly small cases can result in judgments of several hundred thousand dollars.

Generally, in negligence cases, the civil litigation system works against defendants, making it much more likely that a negligence lawsuit will be successful and that monetary damages will be significant (as discussed in Chapter 17).

As a rule, the small business owner should consider a single-limit policy with a *minimum* limit of $300,000. A split-limit policy should have a minimum limit of $300,000, *per individual, and thus a higher overall limit.*

Plan Smart

Remember, although you may be tempted, don't drive with only the state-mandated minimum amount of liability coverage for personal injuries caused to others. Get yourself a single limit policy with a minimum policy limit of $300,000.

Uninsured/Underinsured Motorist Coverage. Many other drivers are uninsured in violation of state law or underinsured (i.e., they carry liability insurance, but with an inadequate policy limit such as the state-mandated minimum).

Uninsured/underinsured motorist coverage allows the insured to make a claim *for his own personal injuries, against his own policy,* in the event that the responsible driver is uninsured or underinsured. Thus, this type of coverage is *not* concerned with liability to *other* parties. It also is limited to damages for personal injuries and thus is not concerned with liability for property damage.

The best time for the small business owner to consider the policy limits for uninsured/underinsured motorist coverage is when he is considering the limits for his liability coverage. After all, both liability coverage and uninsured/underinsured motorist coverage will pay for personal injuries. The question then really is the same: What is the dollar amount of damages for personal injuries that could result from an accident?

Thus, as a general rule, the small business owner should purchase uninsured/underinsured motorist coverage in the same amount as his liability coverage. Thus, a policy with a single limit of $300,000 should also contain uninsured/underinsured motorist coverage in the amount of $300,000.

States differ as to when and exactly how underinsured motorist coverage applies. Generally, the insured must first recover the entire policy limit from the responsible driver before he can make an underinsured motorist claim against his policy. Thus, if such an underinsured motorist claim were being considered, it would be a mistake to accept less than the full policy limit of the other driver's policy as a settlement.

In some states, the amount of the underinsured motorist coverage is the stated policy limit for this coverage, *less the other driver's policy limit.* Thus, a driver with $300,000 of uninsured/underinsured motorist coverage, really only has $280,000 of coverage when the responsible driver has a policy limit of $20,000. In other states, the limit for this type of coverage is the stated limit, without subtraction for the responsible driver's liability coverage.

Finally, in some states, it is possible to aggregate all uninsured/underinsured motorists coverage for all of your vehicles. Usually, where this feature is available, it requires the payment of an additional premium.

Plan Smart

Don't neglect uninsured/underinsured motorist coverage. Too many other drivers are either uninsured or carry only the minimum amount of liability coverage for personal injuries that is mandated by state law.

A victim of a serious auto accident may legitimately suffer personal injuries that amount to hundreds of thousands of dollars of damages. Thus, at a minimum, the small business owner should carry uninsured/underinsured motorist coverage in an amount equal to his liability coverage.

Again, this type of coverage is limited to personal injuries that the injured person sustains and does not apply to property damage.

Note that generally, insurance companies will not raise a driver's rates for making an uninsured/underinsured motorist claim, because the insured is not the party who is responsible for the accident.

Automobile Liability Coverage for Property Damage. As is the case with respect to liability policies in general, *separate policy limits* for property damage will apply in an automobile liability policy.

Too often, liability limits for property damage are not the product of careful deliberation because the primary attention is focused on liability coverage for personal injuries. The result usually will be inadequate liability coverage for property damage.

Consider that many vehicles today cost $30,000 to $50,000 (or more). In addition, as a result of an automobile accident, extensive and costly property damage may be caused to public and other forms of private property, including buildings, utility poles and lines, traffic lights, etc. Thus, the small business owner should purchase an automobile liability policy with a *minimum* limit of $50,000 for property damages.

Automobile insurance is an example of a single policy capable of providing both *liability* coverage (for personal injuries and property damages caused to other parties) and *property* coverage (for damages to the insured's own vehicles). The small business owner definitely should also protect his own vehicles against loss by obtaining property coverage in the form of collision *and* comprehensive protection (see our discussion of property insurance later in this chapter). The business owner with no health insurance should consider adding medical coverage for his own injuries.

Plan Smart

An automobile liability and property policy will cover the named insured and other drivers who do not drive the vehicle on a regular basis.

Thus, if the owner of a vehicle (and the named insured under the policy) lends the vehicle to a friend in an isolated instance, the policy would continue to apply. In other words, the friend would be driving under the owner's policy.

Where someone will be driving the vehicle on a regular basis, they will have to be added to the policy as an insured party. If this is not done, insurance coverage will not apply.

Insurance coverage and liability for the accident are two different issues. Insurance coverage is controlled by the insurance contract and is described above.

Personal liability is controlled by tort law, which has been developed by the courts and supplemented by state statutes. Generally, a business entity will be held liable for an accident caused by one of its employees, because the doctrine of respondeat superior will apply (see Chapter 15 for a discussion of this doctrine). In contrast, an insured party will not have liability for negligence committed by another driver, who is also insured to drive the same vehicle, if the responsible driver is not the employee or agent of that party. *Thus, technically, a husband would have no personal liability for the negligence of his wife while she was driving a vehicle for which they share insurance (although, of course, the joint nature of their assets would present a problem).*

Similarly, an individual who lends his vehicle to friend, in an isolated instance, will not be held liable for the friend's negligence, as there is no employment or agency relation between the two parties. Thus, in this case the owner's insurance would cover the accident in accordance with the insurance contract, but the owner of the vehicle would have no personal liability for the loss due to the absence of an employer-employee or agency relationship.

Finally, it must be noted that if the owner commits an act of negligence that was separate from the accident itself *(e.g., allowing his friend to take the vehicle even though he was intoxicated or otherwise unqualified to drive the vehicle),* the owner may be held liable for his own act of negligence.

GENERAL AND SPECIALIZED PROPERTY POLICIES

As discussed above, care should be taken to distinguish *liability coverage*, which protects against losses that arise from damages to another person's property, and *property insurance*, which protects against losses that arise from damages to property owned by the insured. This is especially important because a single comprehensive policy may include both types of coverage, but with each subject to separate limitations.

Most property insurance policies are issued on an "all-risk" basis. This means the policy covers all damages to property subject to the specific exclusions in the policy. Where the insured desires coverage for what is an excluded occurrence under a standard policy, an endorsement, or a separate specialized policy, must be purchased.

In contrast, a property insurance policy may be issued on a "named-peril" basis. This form insures only against the specific risks listed. Any risk not specifically listed is automatically excluded.

Hazard/fire insurance and automobile insurance represent two common examples that will offer protection for the insured's property. Other specialized types of property insurance that also deserve attention are fidelity insurance, long-term care insurance, and various types of mortgage insurance.

Automobile Property Insurance

An automobile insurance policy is issued as a single comprehensive policy that offers both liability and property protection.

Property coverage in an automobile policy is subdivided between two types of coverage: collision (which covers losses due to a collision, where the insured is at fault) and comprehensive (which covers losses from fire, and other acts of nature, theft and vandalism).

Automobile insurance property coverage is issued on a named-peril basis. Thus, a failure to mention in the policy one form of coverage (e.g., comprehensive) acts as an automatic exclusion of this form of coverage.

Plan Smart

Both forms of property coverage in an automobile policy (i.e., collision and comprehensive) will be subject to deductibles. One way to reduce premium costs is to raise the deductible on the policy. For example, many advisors recommend a $500 deductible for collision coverage. The savings in premium costs can be significant.

Fire/Hazard Property Insurance

Hazard insurance, or fire insurance as it is frequently called, covers losses caused by acts of nature or accidents. Typically, a single comprehensive policy is issued offering both liability and property protection. Property protection in a hazard insurance policy covering a building will apply to the real property (i.e., the building) and to the personal property associated with the real property (i.e., the building's contents). The real property and personal property coverage will be subject to separate limits and exclusions.

Property coverage in a hazard insurance policy usually is issued on an all-risk basis. A universal exclusion from property coverage involves losses (to the building and its contents) due to flooding. To obtain property coverage for thus type of loss, a separate specialized flood insurance policy, which is underwritten by the federal government, must be purchased.

General property coverage comes in all shapes and sizes, and comparing policies can sometimes be similar to comparing apples and oranges. But a number of common variables should be considered before making a decision on a policy:

- coverage for data as property

- coverage for defective property

- business interruption coverage

- guaranteed replacement value

- deductibles

- co-insurance clauses

- proof of loss

Warning

Don't confuse hazard insurance with title insurance, personal mortgage insurance (PMI), or mortgage life insurance. Each is a form of property insurance associated with real property (see discussion below). However, each form insures against very specific and unique risks. Hazard or fire insurance is the form of property insurance familiar to almost all homeowners.

Coverage for Data as Property

Loss of the insured's data on its computers should be covered by the general property policy. However, insurance companies sometimes attempt to deny this type of coverage on the grounds that data does not meet the definition of "tangible" property that can suffer a "physical" loss. (This is the same argument that insurance companies have made with respect to liability coverage for damages caused to other person's data.) The courts, however, have rejected this argument.

Nevertheless, prudence dictates that the small business owner carefully reviews the definitions of "property" and "physical" loss, along with exclusions, in any proposed property insurance policy to determine if the proposed policy specifically excludes data from coverage. A specific and clear-cut exclusion in a policy will be enforced. In this event, an endorsement including this coverage should be considered.

Coverage for Defective Property

Insurance companies sometimes attempt to deny property insurance coverage for repair and replacement of a defective product, or the attendant decrease in value of the defective product, on the grounds that such losses are not the result of a "physical" loss, similar to their arguments against data as property. The small business owner should be aware that generally, insurance companies have also lost this argument in court.

However, property insurance policies may exclude coverage for this type of loss under a clause that applies to "defective design," "faulty workmanship," or "manufacturing error" exclusion.

This type of clause will be enforced. The insured's main argument would have to be that the terms of the clause were not met (i.e., that the product was not defectively designed, etc.). Of course, in any of these situations, the insured may have recourse against the party from whom it bought the defective product.

Business Interruption Coverage

Property insurance, for the business owner, should include business interruption coverage. This covers the losses associated with a business being unable to operate normally (e.g., due to a fire, a loss of electricity, etc.)—namely, the lost profits, additional extraordinary operating expenses incurred (e.g., rent of temporary space), and the cost of re-starting the business.

Generally, the same exclusions that apply to the property coverage (e.g., design defects) also will apply to the business interruption coverage. In addition, *some policies* may offer business interruption *only if the business cannot operate at all*. A policy that covers even a partial shutdown of the business is superior to no coverage at all. Whether the coverage requires a complete or only a partial shutdown of the business usually will depend on the language in the policy. A careful reading of the policy's provisions governing business interruption coverage is required.

Guaranteed Replacement Value

The small business owner should, when available, obtain guaranteed replacement value property coverage. This may be standard, but usually requires an endorsement. With guaranteed replacement value, the insured is able to replace each item of covered property, at the current replacement cost, under the policy.

If the policy does not provide for guaranteed replacement value, the insured will recover only the depreciated value of the property, which, many times, will be only a fraction of the replacement cost.

Guaranteed replacement cost usually is available in a hazard/fire insurance policy, but unfortunately it's almost never available in an automobile insurance policy.

Plan Smart

Hazard/fire insurance, with liability and property coverage, should always be maintained on real property. When there is a mortgage on the property, the mortgage agreement typically will require the mortgagor/owner to purchase property coverage, and name the mortgagee/lender in the policy as a co-insured.

Generally, the policy limits need to cover only the value of the building, and not the land since it usually cannot be lost to hazards, such as fire. Thus, ordinarily it is not necessary to obtain property coverage equal to the full purchase price of the property. Rather, property coverage should be purchased at the appraised value of the building itself, excluding the value of the land.

Property coverage for a building should always be at guaranteed replacement cost. Generally, guaranteed replacement cost will be available, by way of an endorsement, provided the insured purchases coverage for the building at the building's current value, as of the date of the policy. (Insurance companies use formulas to determine this value).

Deductibles

Property insurance may contain a deductible. This amount of a loss is borne by the insured. A deductible is designed to make the insured person self-insured for relatively small losses.

Various deductibles should be compared. A higher deductible frequently is a way for the insured to obtain coverage at a significantly lower premium cost. At the same time, the insured is still covered for any large or catastrophic loss.

For example, as previously discussed, a $500 deductible for collision coverage on an automobile property policy can yield significant premium savings, in comparison to, say a $250 or $100 deductible. The same holds true for virtually any property insurance policy.

Co-Insurance Clauses

A property insurance policy may contain a "co-insurance" clause. This clause *reduces the apparent amount* of insurance when it is triggered, making the insured a "co-insurer" for his own loss.

Generally, the co-insurance clause, which is expressed as a percentage (80 percent is common), will be triggered when the policy limit for the insurance is less than the fair market value of the property multiplied by the co-insurance percentage. In short, the result derived by multiplying the fair market value of the property by the co-insurance percentage represents the *minimum* amount of insurance that must be carried if the insured is to receive a full recovery for his loss.

Example

Let's say John Smith owns a commercial building with a value of $800,000. In an attempt to save on the premium cost for the policy, Smith insures the building for only $600,000. His theory is that it would be unlikely the building would suffer a total loss, so in effect, he is fully insured.

The policy contains an 80 percent co-insurance clause, and then the building suffers fire damage in the amount of $600,000. Smith feels confident that the loss will be fully covered as the loss equals his policy's limit.

Smith is mistaken. When there is a co-insurance clause, the insured will not receive a full recovery if the amount of the insurance is less than the fair market value of the property multiplied by the co-insurance percentage.

In this situation, the amount received will equal:

The amount of the insurance divided by the co-insurance percentage multiplied by the value of the property and then multiplied by the amount of the loss.

In this example, $600,000 ÷ (80 percent x $800,000 = $640,000) = .9375. Then, .9375 x $600,000 = $562,500.

Smith is a co-insurer (along with the insurance company) for the loss. Specifically, Smith's share of the loss is $37,500 ($600,000 less $562,500).

Note that there will be a full recovery (subject to the policy limit, of course), if the amount of the insurance is equal to, or higher than, the fair market value of the property multiplied by the co-insurance percentage. Thus, in this example, Smith would have received a full recovery for his loss ($600,000), had he insured the building for at least 80 percent of its fair market value ($800,000 x 80% = $640,000).

In general, when there is a co-insurance clause, the insured will recover the lowest of the policy limit, the value of the loss or the amount derived from the co-insurance calculation.

Proof of Loss

The small business owner must be ready to prove a loss occurred, as well as the amount of the loss. Essential for these purposes are an inventory of all property owned, along with records evidencing ownership and value, including receipts, documents of title and appraisals, if available. Photographs or videotape are sometimes used to establish the existence, physical condition and, thus, the value of the property.

Ideally, these records will be maintained in a bank safe deposit box (they may be needed after a catastrophe, such as a fire), or at the very least in a fireproof box, with a duplicate set of records maintained in a separate location.

Of course, the small business owner's accounting system will contain a record of all of the property owned by the business entity. However, the small business owner also should maintain a *separate* inventory of property personally owned, to facilitate claims under the owner's personal property insurance policy.

Title, Personal Mortgage and Mortgage Life Insurance

A number of specialized property policies should be considered when seeking to protect your real property assets. Some people often confuse these policies with one another or mistakenly believe that their general property policies cover these situations. They do not.

Title insurance. This protects *the title to the property*. It does *not* protect against loss due to fire or any other hazard. It protects against the possibility that a purchaser of real property (land and buildings) has obtained an invalid legal title. The policy pays off if the owner loses *ownership of the property* because his title to the property turns out to be defective.

A title search (i.e., an examination of the chain of title, as it appears on the land records) should always be done before real property is purchased. Most states require that an unbroken chain of title go back 40 or 60 years.

The title searcher will determine that the seller's signature appeared on each deed, that it was properly witnessed and acknowledged, and that the legal description of the property is identical in each deed.

Why is title insurance necessary if a title search is completed? A title search cannot absolutely ensure that the title is valid. For example, there is no way of determining, through a title search, that every signature on a deed is genuine. If one signature anywhere in the chain of title was forged, the chain is broken and the current owner holds an invalid title. A holder of an invalid title cannot, as a general rule, make a transfer to a buyer.

When the real property is collateral for a loan, the mortgagee (the lender) usually will require that the purchaser obtain a mortgagee title insurance policy.

Plan Smart

The small business owner should also be sure to purchase an owner's title insurance policy. The mortgagee title policy, which will be issued in the amount of the mortgage, only pays off to the mortgagee in the event of a covered loss. Thus, a mortgagee title policy protects the lender's property interest in the real property.

However, a mortgagee title policy also protects the owner. If the owner loses title to the property, the mortgage title insurance policy ensures that the owner will not have to continue to make payments on property he no longer owns.

Ultimately, a mortgagee title insurance policy alone is not sufficient protection. An owner's title policy will protect the owner's equity in the property and will pay off to the owner if a covered loss occurs.

Unlike virtually every other form of insurance, title insurance requires only the payment of a single, lump-sum premium, which is due upon the purchase of the property, as opposed to ongoing monthly premiums. Usually, the owner's policy will contain an inflation endorsement that automatically raises the policy limit each year, in accordance with a prescribed formula.

Personal Mortgage Insurance (PMI). PMI is entirely different from title insurance in that it offers protection *only for the lender*. This insurance pays off the lender in the event the borrower defaults on the mortgage. Lenders generally require PMI whenever the down payment on a purchase is less that 20 percent of the purchase price. PMI premiums can be expensive. Usually, advance payment of the first year's premium is due, in one lump sum, upon purchase. A monthly premium is then added to the mortgage payment.

PMI can be terminated when the equity in the property reaches 20 percent due to payments of mortgage principal, appreciation in the value of the property, or both. Lenders require an appraisal to establish that the 20 percent threshold has been reached.

Note that hazard insurance, title insurance and PMI represent examples of the principle of relying on another person's insurance, discussed previously. The *owner* of the property will be compelled by the lender to pay for the insurance, even though the *lender* will be a beneficiary of the insurance.

Mortgage life insurance. An *owner* of real property, who has taken out a mortgage on the property, can purchase mortgage life insurance. This form of insurance pays off the mortgage upon the death of the mortgagor/owner. While this may seem desirable, the high-cost premiums are not usually justified by the benefit. Premiums remain level, even as the policy's benefit (i.e., the mortgage balance) decreases.

Plan Smart

Usually, a separate term life insurance policy, with the party who will inherit the real property named as the beneficiary, will represent a better use of your insurance funds than mortgage life insurance.

Fidelity Insurance

Fidelity insurance covers loss of property due to an employee's dishonesty, as well as a suspicious loss of property that cannot be directly attributed to a particular employee. Coverage usually extends to losses of property due to theft, embezzlement, forgery and computer crimes.

Generally, the policy will cover the loss of property while on the business's premises, as well as while the property is in transit or otherwise temporarily in another location. Because policies differ in these respects, and because employee dishonesty can take many forms, a thorough reading of the proposed policy, in advance, is required, to determine the scope of any exclusions.

If you only want to cover your business's funds and the people who have access to them, you may be able to save on insurance premiums by buying a fidelity bond. This less expensive, but more specific and narrow, form of fidelity insurance is limited to the individual, or individuals, who are named in the policy.

Usually, a business's treasurer and other persons who have access to the entity's cash (and other vulnerable assets, such as securities) and accounting records are bonded. Because a fidelity bond is limited to particular individuals, premiums generally are lower, compared to fidelity insurance, which protects against losses due to employee dishonesty in general.

Long-Term Care Insurance

Long-term care insurance pays for nursing home costs, thus it is a type of property insurance. Here, the insurance is protecting the property you own from nursing home costs.

Medicare, which is part of the Social Security system, pays only for the first 100 days of nursing home care. After this period expires, the individual must personally pay the cost of the nursing home or qualify for Medicaid, which is a government entitlement program available only to persons who have extremely limited resources.

Plan Smart

Qualifying for Medicaid is extremely complex, especially for individuals who are not indigent. Planning strategies may have to be not only implemented but completed several years prior to the point when you actually may need long-term care. Chapter 4 contains a discussion of the transferring of assets to qualify for Medicaid. Be sure to consult with one of the many professionals who specialize in this area if you are looking to have Medicaid provide for your long-term care needs.

So with nursing home costs averaging about $70,000 *per year,* long-term care insurance seems, at first glance, to be a sound choice. Such high costs per year can quickly deplete a family's resources. Even the family home, in some instances, may have to be sold to pay for the costs of the nursing home.

However, many advisors recommend *against* purchasing long-term care insurance. Simply put, premiums for long-term care insurance can be extreme. Despite government efforts at marketing this type of insurance, it has not proved popular, probably due the premium cost.

Long-term care insurance is fairly new. It is possible that premium cost will be reduced, especially if demand continues to be lackluster. However, it is likely that premiums will always be significant, simply because of the extreme costs that the insurance covers.

Other asset protection strategies, including asset transfers, can provide effective protection, but without the premium cost (Chapter 4 details planning for nursing home costs and, in particular, the use of asset transfers as a means of qualifying for Medicaid, which will cover the full cost of the nursing home). Although the transferor must give up title to the assets transferred to family members, the transfers are cost-free *to the family.* Further, as discussed in Chapter 4, in certain instances, assets simply are exempt and need not be transferred to gain protection.

The small business owner should investigate the cost of long-term care insurance, review Chapter 4, and compare other strategies to the cost of long-term care insurance. The premium cost must be weighed against the possible benefits.

Further, it must be considered that after paying very substantial premiums for long-term care insurance, a policyholder may very well never have to take advantage of the policy. In short, long-term care insurance may represent (at this time anyway) one instance where the small business owner may want to rely on other asset protection strategies rather than purchase insurance.

THE UMBRELLA POLICY

Finally, consideration should be given to purchasing an umbrella policy. This type of policy is designed to provide *supplemental* comprehensive liability and property coverage (subject, as always, to exclusions).

An umbrella policy is always purchased as an adjunct to the coverage offered under standard policies. It pays off on a covered matter only *after* the primary insurance is exhausted. Premiums typically are affordable because the risk to the insurance company that the policy will be activated usually is low, due to the existence of the primary insurance.

Because it offers *comprehensive* secondary coverage, an umbrella policy can cover losses due to very divergent causes, such as losses associated with a building or losses due to an automobile accident. As always, a careful advance reading of the policy is recommended to determine the breadth of coverage.

Part IV

Appendices

Federal and State Asset Exemptions

As discussed in Chapter 2, when filing a bankruptcy action in certain states, you have the option to choose either the allowable federal exemptions or the applicable state's exemptions. Arkansas, Connecticut, District of Columbia, Hawaii, Massachusetts, Michigan, Minnesota, New Jersey, New Mexico, Pennsylvania, Rhode Island, South Carolina, Texas, Vermont, Washington and Wisconsin all allow this flexibility. In all other states, you must choose the applicable state exemptions. In a *state* court proceeding (e.g., execution of a judgment lien), of course, only the applicable state's exemptions will be available.

Exemption planning can represent a significant asset protection strategy. However, effective exemption planning requires an understanding of many issues, including the role liens play in limiting or, in some cases, preserving exemptions, as well as the strategies that can be adopted to defeat creditor challenges to asset transfers. Thus, for example, small business owners must understand that certain liens or claims may legally impair an exemption, thus rendering the exemption worthless. This understanding cannot be gleaned from an examination of the tables alone. These issues are discussed in detail in Chapters 1-4.

In evaluating available exemptions, keep in mind that, because exemptions are available only to natural persons, certain assets (e.g., a personal residence) should never be transferred to a business entity, while consideration should be given to personally owning, and leasing to the entity, other assets (e.g., certain tools of the trade). Mistakes in these respects can lead to a loss of the exemption.

Also, remember that exemptions for "partnership property" or property owned by a different business entity (e.g., an LLC) can be misleading. The exemption only means that a partner's *personal creditors* cannot *directly* attach the business's assets. However, *creditors of the business may freely attach these assets.* Further, personal creditors of the partners can, nevertheless, attach the partners' interests in the business (which are a type of intangible personal property) and, in the case of the general partnership (although not the LLC in many states), subsequently foreclose on the attached interests and force a liquidation of the business. Generally, there is *no specific exemption for an owner's interest in a business.* Typically, the interest must be protected by a "wild card" exemption, which does not exist or is severely limited in many states. See Chapters 1-4 for details on these issues.

The following tables include exemptions available under federal and state statutes. However, a very significant exempt category, ERISA-qualified retirement assets, are, in many states, exempt only because of *federal court decisions,* and thus may not appear in the tables. This exemption is especially important given the fact that almost all retirement plans offered by larger employers are ERISA-qualified. These assets are exempt despite what state statutes provide.

IRA assets also *may* be exempt because of federal court decisions, although the law is less settled here than it is for ERISA-qualified retirement plans (see Chapter 3).

Similarly, court decisions generally provide that ownership of assets by married couples in tenancy by the entirety, in states that allow for this form of ownership, exempt the assets from the claims of the creditors of one spouse. These assets also are exempt despite what state statutes provide. See Chapters 1-4.

Moreover, as discussed in Chapter 3, many states now offer *statutory* protection for IRAs, but these statutes distinguish between various types of IRAs. Accordingly, the tables detail whether a state's statutory exemptions for IRAs extend specifically to conventional, Roth, Education, SEP and SIMPLE IRAs. This distinction can be an important factor in a small business owner's choice of a particular retirement plan (e.g., a SIMPLE IRA vs. a SIMPLE 401(k) plan). See Chapter 3 for details. In addition, Roth IRAs offer excellent tax benefits. Where a state also exempts Roth IRAs, this investment also represents an extremely valuable asset protection device.

In addition, while state exemptions for wages vary, a federal statute exempts, at a minimum, the greater of 75% of an individual's weekly disposable earnings or 30 times the federal minimum wage. This federal statute, *which supersedes state laws* (when the state law provides a lesser benefit), is not reflected in the state listings.

Some of the more valuable exemptions that demand close attention include the homestead, retirement savings, and insurance (annuity) policy exemptions. Accordingly, the tables highlight these exemptions first.

Finally, remember that exemption laws can change. For example, expect to see more states extend protection to IRA assets by statute, and additional federal efforts to limit state homestead exemptions in federal bankruptcy proceedings, while protecting IRA benefits. For this reason, it is always wise to examine the latest version of state post-judgment and federal bankruptcy exemption statutes.

FEDERAL BANKRUPTCY EXEMPTIONS

The federal bankruptcy exemptions are adjusted every three years on April 1. The following represents the most recent adjustments, made on April 1, 2001.

Married couples double the following federal exemptions.

Homestead: Real property, including co-op or mobile home, up to $17,425; unused portion of homestead up to $8,725 may be applied to any property.

Pensions and Retirement Benefits: ERISA-qualified benefits needed for support.

Insurance: Disability, illness or unemployment benefits. Life insurance payments for person you depended on, needed for support. Life insurance policy with loan value, in accrued dividends or interest up to $9,300. Unmatured life insurance contract, except credit insurance policy.

Personal Property: Animals, crops, clothing, appliances, books, furnishings, household goods and musical instruments up to $450 per item, $9,300 total. Health Aids. Jewelry up to $1,150. Lost earnings payments. Motor vehicle up to $2,775. Personal injury recoveries up to $17,425 (not to include pain and suffering or pecuniary loss). Wrongful death recoveries for person you depended on.

Tools of Trade: Implements, books and tools of trade up to $1,750.

Miscellaneous: Alimony. Child support needed for support.

Wages: None.

Public Benefits: Crime victim's compensation. Public assistance. Social Security. Unemployment compensation. Veteran's benefits.

Wild Card: $925 of any property and $8,725, less any amount of homestead exemption claimed, of any property.

FEDERAL NON-BANKRUPTCY EXEMPTIONS

The following exemptions are available in addition to your state's exemptions, but cannot be claimed if you use the federal bankruptcy exemptions.

Retirement: Funds exempt for CIA employees, civil service employees, foreign service employees, military honor roll pensions, military service employees, railroad workers. Social Security. Veteran's benefits. Veteran's medal of honor benefits.

Survivor's Benefits: Survivor's funds exempt for judges, U.S. court directors, judicial center directors, supreme court justices, child justice administrators, lighthouse workers, members of military service.

Death and Disability Benefits: Funds exempt for government employees, longshoremen and harbor workers. War risk, hazard, death or injury compensation.

Miscellaneous: Klamath Indians tribe benefits for Indians residing in Oregon. Military deposits in savings accounts while on permanent duty outside the U.S. Military group life insurance. Railroad worker's unemployment insurance. Seamen's clothing. Seamen's wages (while on a voyage) pursuant to written contract. 75% of earned but unpaid wages (bankruptcy judge may authorize more for low-income debtors).

STATE POST-JUDGMENT EXEMPTIONS

The following tables list the allowable bankruptcy exemptions, based on state law at press time. Be sure to research the latest changes in your state's laws and be sure to consult with a qualified attorney.

Alabama

Homestead: Real property or mobile home up to $5,000; husband and wife may double. Property cannot exceed 160 acres or 320 acres for a husband and wife.

Pensions and Retirement Benefits: Funds exempt for judges (only payments being received), law enforcement officers, state employees and teachers. IRA exemptions for conventional, SEP and SIMPLE plans.

Insurance: Annuity proceeds or avails to $250 per month. Disability proceeds or avails to an average of $250 per month. Fraternal society benefits. Life insurance proceeds or avails if beneficiary is insured's spouse or child. Life insurance proceeds or avails if clause prohibits proceeds from being used to pay beneficiary's creditors. Mutual aid association benefits.

Personal Property: All necessary household goods and clothing, family pictures and books. Family burial plots and church seats.

Tools of Trade: Tools personally used by and essential to debtor's business. All personally owned uniforms, arms and equipment. One motor vehicle is exempt if used by and essential to the debtor's business, subject to consensual security goods.

Wages: 75% of earned but unpaid wages; for consumer loans/leases, greater of 75% of weekly disposable earnings or 30 times the federal minimum wage.

Miscellaneous: Business partnership property.

Public Benefits: Unemployment compensation. Workers' compensation. Aid to blind, aged, disabled. AFDC (Aid to Families with Dependent Children). Coal miner's pneumoconiosis benefits. Crime victim's compensation. Southeast Asian War POWs benefits.

Wild Card: Any personal property up to $3,000, except life insurance.

Alaska

Homestead: Principal residence up to $54,000, whether single or multiple owners. Proceeds also exempt if located in Alaska for six months.

Pensions and Retirement Benefits: ERISA-qualified retirement plans are exempt to the extent contributions made more than 120 days prior to bankruptcy. Funds building up exempt for all teachers', judicial employees' and public employees' retirement plans; other retirement benefits exempt to extent wages are exempt (only payments being received). IRA exemptions for conventional, Roth, SEP and SIMPLE plans, subject to 120 day rule, above.

Insurance: Insurance proceeds for wrongful death, to extent wages are exempt. Life insurance annuity or contract loan value to $10,000. Life insurance proceeds if beneficiary is insured's spouse or dependent, to extent wages exempt. Disability benefits. Fraternal society benefits. Insurance proceeds for personal injury, to extent wages exempt (bankruptcy judge may authorize a greater amount). Medical, surgical or hospital benefits.

Personal Property: Books, musical instruments, clothing, family portraits, household goods and heirlooms up to $3,000. Building materials. Burial plot. Health aids needed. Jewelry up to $1000. Motor vehicle up to $3,000; vehicle's market value can't exceed $20,000. Personal injury recoveries, to extent wages exempt. Pets up to $1,000. Proceeds for lost, damaged or destroyed exempt property. Wrongful death recoveries to extent wages exempt.

Tools of Trade: Implements/professional books/tools up to $2,800.

Miscellaneous: Business partnership property. Alimony, to the extent wages are exempt. Child support payments made by a collection agency. Permits for limited entry into Alaska Fisheries. Certain liquor licenses and limited entry permits are exempt.

Wages: $350 of weekly net earnings or $550 per week for debtor who is sole support for household. $1,400/mo. in "liquid assets" for debtors not paid weekly/semiweekly or monthly or $2,200/mo. for debtor who is sole support of household. Court can increase exemption for disability or personal injury payments.

Public Benefits: Unemployment compensation. Workers' Compensation. Adult assistance to the elderly, blind, disabled. AFDC. Alaska longevity bonus. Crime victim's compensation. Federally exempt public benefits paid or due. General relief assistance. 45% of permanent fund dividends. Tuition credits under an advance college tuition payment contract.

Wild Card: None.

Arizona

Homestead: Real property, an apartment or mobile home occupied by the debtor, up to $100,000. Sale proceeds exempt 18 months after sale or until new home purchase, whichever occurs first. Husband and wife may not double the homestead exemption.

Pensions and Retirement Benefits: ERISA-qualified benefits deposited more than 120 days before filing bankruptcy. Funds exempt for Board of Regents members, state employees, public safety personnel, firefighters, police officers and Rangers. IRA exemptions for conventional, Roth, SEP and SIMPLE plans, subject to 120-day rule, above.

Insurance: Life insurance cash value, to $1,000 per dependent, to $25,000 total (husband and wife may double). Life insurance cash value, to $2,000 per dependent, to $10,000 total. Life insurance proceeds to $20,000 if beneficiary is spouse or child (husband and wife may double). Group life insurance policy or proceeds. Disability, health, or accident benefits. Fraternal society benefits.

Personal Property: Husband and wife may double all personal property exemptions. 2 beds and 1 living room chair per person; 1 dresser, table, lamp, bedding per bed; kitchen table; dining room table and 4 chairs (1 more per person); living room carpet or rug; couch; 3 lamps; 3 coffee or end tables; pictures, paintings, drawings created by debtor; family portraits; refrigerator; stove; TV, radio or stereo; alarm clock; washer; dryer; vacuum cleaner all up to $4,000 total. Bank deposits to $150 in any one account. Bible; bicycle; sewing machine; typewriter; burial plot; rifle, pistol or shotgun all up to $500 total.

Books to $250. Clothing to $500. Wedding and engagement rings to $1,000. Watch to $100. Pets, horses, milk cows and poultry to $500. Musical instruments to $250. Prostheses including wheelchair. Food and fuel to last 6 months. Motor vehicle up to $1,500 ($4,000 if disabled). Prepaid rent or security deposit up to $1,000 or 1½ times your rent whichever is less, in lieu of homestead. Proceeds for sold or damaged exempt property.

Tools of Trade: Arms, uniforms and accoutrements you're required to keep. Farm machinery, utensils, seed, instruments of husbandry, feed, grain, and animals up to $2,500 total (husband and wife may double the exemption amount). Teaching aids of teacher. Tools, equipment, instruments and books (except vehicle driven to work) up to $2,500.

Miscellaneous: Business partnership property. Earnings of minor child unless the debt is for child.

Wages: Greater of 75% of weekly wages or earnings in excess of 30 times the federal minimum wage; modified regarding child support claims.

Public Benefits: Unemployment compensation. Workers' compensation. Welfare benefits.

Wild Card: None.

Arkansas

Homestead: A debtor must choose either option 1 or 2.

1. For head of family; real or personal property used as residence, to an unlimited value. Property cannot exceed ¼-acre in city, town or village, or 80 acres elsewhere. If property is between ¼- to 1 acre in city, town or village, and 80 to 160 acres elsewhere, up to $2,500; no homestead may exceed 1 acre in city, town or village, or 160 acres elsewhere. Husband and wife may not double the homestead exemption.

2. Real or personal property used as residence, to $800 if single, $1,250 if married.

Pensions and Retirement Benefits: Retirement plans for firefighters, police officers and school employees. IRA exemptions for conventional, Roth, SEP and SIMPLE plans. Limit of $500, and nondeductible contributions to a non-Roth IRA are not protected.

Insurance: Annuity contract. Disability benefits. Fraternal society benefits. Group life insurance. Life insurance proceeds if clause prohibits proceeds from being used to pay beneficiary's creditors. Life insurance proceeds or avails if beneficiary isn't the insured. Life, health, accident or disability cash value or proceeds paid or due (limited to the $500 exemption provided by section 9-1 and 9-2 of the Arkansas Constitution). Mutual assessments life or disability benefits to $1,000. Stipulated insurance premiums.

Personal Property: Burial plot to 5 acres. Clothing. Motor vehicle to $1,200. Wedding bands; any diamond can't exceed ½-carat.

Tools of Trade: Implements/books/tools up to $750.

Miscellaneous: Business partnership property.

Wages: 60 days' earned but unpaid wages if debtor's personal property plus such wages do not exceed constitutional maximum exemption. Minimum of $25 per week exempt.

Public Benefits: Unemployment compensation. Workers' Compensation. Aid to blind, aged, disabled. AFDC. Crime victim's compensation unless seeking to discharge debt for treatment of injury incurred during the crime.

Wild Card: $500 of any personal property if married or head of family; or else $200.

California

A debtor must choose between Option 1 or 2.

Option 1 —

Homestead: Real or personal property you occupy including a mobile home, boat, stock cooperative, community apartment, planned development or condo, up to $50,000 if single and not disabled; $75,000 for families if no other member has a homestead. If one spouse files, he or she may exempt one-half of amount if home held as community property and all of amount if home held as tenants in common. $100,000 limit if age 65 or older, or physically or mentally disabled; $100,000 limit if 55 or older, single and earn under $15,000, or married and earn under $20,000, and creditors seek to force the sale of the home. Sale proceeds exempt for 6 months after received. Husband and wife may not double the exemption. May file a homestead declaration.

Pensions and Retirement Benefits: Funds exempt for county employees, county firefighters, county peace officers and public employees. IRA exemptions for conventional, Roth, SEP and SIMPLE plans. Limited to amount necessary for support of debtor and dependents.

Insurance: Disability or health benefits. Fraternal unemployment bonds. Life insurance proceeds or avails if clause prohibits proceeds from being used to pay beneficiary's creditors. Fidelity bonds. Homeowner's insurance proceeds for 6 months after received, to homestead exemption amount. Matured life insurance benefits needed for support. Unmatured life insurance policy loan value to $8,000; husband and wife may double to $16,000

Personal Property: Appliances, furnishings, clothing and food needed. Bank deposits from Social Security Administration up to $2,000 ($3,000 for husband and wife). Building materials up to $2,000 to repair or improve home (husband and wife may not double). Burial plot. Health aids. Jewelry, heirlooms and art up to $5,000 total (may not be doubled). Motor vehicles to $1,900 in auto insurance if vehicle(s) lost, damaged or destroyed (may not be doubled). Personal injury causes of action. Personal injury recoveries needed for support; if receiving installments, at least 75%. Wrongful death causes of action. Wrongful death recoveries needed for support; if receiving installments, at least 75%.

Tools of Trade: Tools, implements, materials, instruments, uniforms, books, furnishings, equipment, vessel, motor vehicle up to $5,000 total; up to $10,000 total if used by both spouses in same occupation (cannot claim motor vehicle under both tools of trade exemption and motor vehicle exemption).

Miscellaneous: Business partnership property. Business or professional license, except liquor license. Inmates' trust funds up to $1,000 (husband and wife may not double).

Wages: Public employees' vacation credits (if receiving installments, at least 75%). 75% of wages paid within 90 days of filing for bankruptcy.

Public Benefits: Aid to blind, aged, disabled. AFDC (Aid to Families with Dependent Children). Financial aid to students. Relocation benefits. Union benefits due to labor dispute. Unemployment benefits. Workers' compensation.

Wild Card: None.

Or Option 2 —

Homestead: Real or personal property including a co-op, used as residence up to $15,000. Unused portion of homestead may be applied to any property.

Pensions and Retirement Benefits: ERISA-qualified benefits needed for support. IRA exemptions for conventional, Roth, SEP and SIMPLE plans. Limited to amount necessary for support of debtor and dependents.

Insurance: Disability or health benefits. Life insurance proceeds or avails needed for support. Unmatured life insurance contract accrued avails to $8,000. Unmatured life insurance policy other than credit.

Personal Property: Animals, crops, appliances, furnishings, household goods, books, musical instruments and clothing up to $400 per item. Burial plot up to $15,000, in lieu of homestead. Health aids. Jewelry up to $1,000. Motor vehicle up to $2,400. Personal injury recoveries up to $15,000 (not to include pain and suffering or pecuniary loss). Wrongful death recoveries needed for support.

Tools of Trade: Implements, books and tools of trade up to $1,500.

Miscellaneous: Alimony. Child support needed for support.

Wages: None.

Public Benefits: Unemployment benefits. Crime victim's compensation. Public assistance. Social Security. Veteran's benefits.

Wild Card: $800 of any property. Unused portion of homestead or burial exemption of any property.

Colorado

Homestead: Real property, mobile home or manufactured home (mobile or manufactured home if loan incurred after 1-1-83) you occupy up to $30,000. Sale proceeds exempt 1 year after received. Spouse or child of deceased owner may claim homestead exemption House trailer or coach used as residence to $3,500. Mobile home used as residence to $6,000.

Pensions and Retirement Benefits: ERISA-qualified benefits. Funds exempt for firefighters, police officers, public employees, teachers and veterans. IRA exemptions for conventional, Roth, SEP and SIMPLE plans.

Insurance: Disability proceeds to $200 per month; if received as a lump sum, entire amount. Fraternal society benefits. Life insurance avails to $5,000. Group life insurance proceeds or policy. Homeowner's insurance proceeds for 1 year after received, to homestead exemption amount. Life insurance proceeds if clause prohibits proceeds from being used to pay beneficiary's creditors.

Personal Property: Clothing up to $750. One burial plot per person. Food and fuel up to $300. Health aids. Household goods up to $1,500. Jewelry and articles of adornment up to $500 total. Vehicles used for work up to $1,000; $3,000 to get medical care, if elderly or disabled. Personal injury recoveries, unless debt related to injury. Pictures and books up to $750. Proceeds for damaged exempt property. Security deposit. Livestock and poultry of farmer up to $3,000.

Tools of Trade: Horses, mules, wagons, carts, machinery, harness and tools of farmer up to $2,000 total. Library of professional up to $1,500 or stock in trade, supplies, fixtures, machines, tools, maps, equipment and books up to $1,500.

Miscellaneous: Business partnership property.

Wages: Minimum of 75% of earned but unpaid wages, pension payments; bankruptcy judge may authorize more for low-income debtors.

Public Benefits: Unemployment compensation. Workers' Compensation. Aid to blind, aged, disabled. AFDC (Aid to Families with Dependent Children). Crime victim's compensation. Veteran's benefits for veteran, spouse or child if veteran served in war.

Wild Card: None

Connecticut

Homestead: Real property, mobile home or manufactured home to $75,000, excluding consensual or statutory liens.

Pensions and Retirement Benefits: ERISA-qualified benefits, to the extent wages exempt. Funds exempt for municipal employees, teachers, veterans, state employees, probate judges and employees. IRA exemptions for conventional, Roth, education, SEP and SIMPLE plans.

Insurance: Fraternal society benefits. Disability benefits paid by association for its members. Life insurance proceeds if clause prohibits proceeds from being used to pay beneficiary's creditors. Health or disability benefits. Life insurance proceeds or avails. Unmatured life insurance policy loan value to $4,000.

Personal Property: Appliances, food, clothing, furniture and bedding needed. Burial plot. Health aids needed. Motor vehicle up to $1,500. Proceeds of one residence. Wedding and engagement rings.

Tools of Trade: Arms, military equipment, uniforms and musical instruments of military personnel. Tools, books, instruments and farm animals needed.

Miscellaneous: Business partnership property. Child support. Alimony to extent wages exempt. Farm partnership animals and livestock feed reasonably required to run farm where at least 50% of partners are members of same family.

Wages: Greater of 75% of earned but unpaid wages, pension payments, or excess of weekly wages over 40 times federal minimum wage; subject to court-ordered support claims.

Public Benefits: Unemployment compensation. Workers' Compensation. Aid to blind, aged, disabled. AFDC. Crime victims compensation. Veterans benefits. Social Security. Vietnam veteran's death benefits. Wages from earnings incentive program.

Wild Card: $1,000 of any property.

Delaware

Homestead: None. However, real property held by married couples as tenancy by the entirety may be exempt against debts owed by one spouse.

Pensions and Retirement Benefits: Funds exempted for various public employees. IRA exemptions for conventional, Roth, SEP and SIMPLE plans.

Insurance: Fraternal benefit society benefits. All life insurance or group and health insurance policies exempt; also $350 per month in annuities.

Personal Property: Any property up to $5,000. Clothing and jewelry; burial place; church pew, pianos and organs; sewing machines; school books; family Bible, pictures and library.

Tools of Trade: All tools, implements, fixtures necessary to carry on debtor's trade or business, up to $75 in New Castle and Sussex Counties and up to $50 in Kent County.

Miscellaneous: Business partnership property.

Wages: 85% of earned but unpaid wages exempt.

Public Benefits: Unemployment Compensation. Workers' Compensation. State public benefits and aid to the blind

Wild Card: $500 of any personal property, except tools of trade, if head of family.

District of Columbia

Homestead: None. However, real property held by married couples as tenancy by the entirety may be exempt against debts owed by one spouse.

Pensions and Retirement Benefits: Funds exempted for teachers and judges. The law is not settled for IRA exemptions, but extremely limited benefits may be protected.

Insurance: Life insurance if proceeds cannot be used to pay creditors.

Group life insurance. Life insurance proceeds payable to other than insured. Other insurance proceeds to $200 per month, maximum 2 months, for head of family; otherwise $60 per month. Fraternal society benefits. Disability benefits.

Personal Property: Cooking utensils, stoves, furniture, furnishings, radios and sewing machines up to $300. Books up to $400. Clothing up to $300. Cooperative association holdings up to $50. Residential condominium deposit. Food and fuel for 3 months.

Tools of Trade: If head of household, $200 in tools of trade and $200 in stock/materials for debtor's business. For all others, $200 in mechanic's tools or notary seal/official documents; $300 in library, office, furniture, implements of professional or artist. For head of household debtors, one horse or mule, one cart/wagon or tray and harness, or $1,500 in one motor vehicle used principally by debtor in trade/business.

Miscellaneous: Business partnership property.

Wages: Greater of 75% of weekly wages or excess of disposable wages over 30 times federal minimum hourly wage.

Public Benefits: Unemployment compensation. Workers' compensation. Aid to blind, aged, disabled. AFDC. Crime victim's compensation. General assistance.

Wild Card: None.

Florida

Homestead: Real property including mobile home to unlimited value. Property cannot exceed ½-acre in municipality or 160 contiguous acres elsewhere. Property held as tenancy by the entirety may be exempt against the debts owed by only one spouse

Pensions and Retirement Benefits: ERISA-qualified benefits. Funds exempted for various public employees' retirement systems, along with profit-sharing benefits necessary for support. IRA exemptions for conventional, Roth, SEP and SIMPLE plans.

Insurance: Annuity contract proceeds. Death benefits payable to a specific beneficiary not the deceased's estate. Disability or illness benefits. Cash surrender value of life insurance. Fraternal society benefits.

Personal Property: All prescribed health aids for debtor/dependents and $1,000 in any other personal property exempt. One motor vehicle up to $1,000.

Tools of Trade: None.

Miscellaneous: Business partnership property. Alimony. Child support. Prescribed health aids.

Wages: 100% exempt for head of household. However, head of household may sign waiver that allows garnishment of wages in excess of $500 per week. Wages of others exempt in accordance with the federal standard (see the introduction to these tables). Also exempt are 6 months of wages paid and deposited in a bank account.

Public Benefits: Workers' compensation. Unemployment compensation. Veteran's benefits. Crime victim's compensation. Public assistance. Social Security. Alimony, support and separate maintenance to extent reasonably necessary to support debtor and dependents.

Wild Card: None.

Georgia

Homestead: Real property, including co-op up to $5,000. Unused homestead may be applied to any property.

Pensions and Retirement Benefits: ERISA-qualified retirement plans, plans for public employees and non-profits, and Social Security benefits. Other pensions and retirement benefits and annuity payments (including IRA exemptions for conventional, SEP and SIMPLE plans) exempt only to extent needed. Distributions limited to amount necessary for support of debtor and dependents, but undistributed balance is fully protected. Warning: A Georgia court has held that protection does not extend to self-funded IRAs.

Insurance: Annuity and endowment benefits. Disability or health benefits to $250 per month. Fraternal society benefits. Life insurance proceeds if needed for support. Unmatured life insurance dividends, up to $2,000 in dividends, interest or loan value, if debtor or dependent is the insured.

Personal Property: Burial place. Jewelry to $500. Motor vehicles to $1,000. Personal injury recoveries to $7,500. Wrongful death recoveries. Animals, crops, clothing, books, household goods, musical instruments to $200 per item, $3,500 maximum.

Tools of Trade: Tools and implements up to $500.

Miscellaneous: Alimony. Support and separate maintenance exempt to extent needed for debtor's or dependents' support.

Wages: Minimum 75% of earned but unpaid wages for private and federal workers. State employees'/officials' salaries totally exempt from claims relating to liability incurred in scope of government employment while responding to emergency.

Appendix A: Federal and State Asset Exemptions

Public Benefits: Workers' compensation. Unemployment compensation. Veteran's benefits. Aid to blind and disabled. Crime victim's compensation. Local public assistance. Old-age assistance. Social Security.

Wild Card: $400 of any property; and unused portion of homestead exemption.

Hawaii

Homestead: Up to 1 acre of real property or land, or co-op, or condo under long-term lease, up to value of $30,000 for married debtor/head of household over 65, and $20,000 for all others. Proceeds exempt for 6 months.

Pensions and Retirement Benefits: All state and certain municipal pensions and retirement benefits exempt. ERISA-qualified plans and IRA exemptions for conventional, SEP and SIMPLE plans are limited to contributions made more than three years prior to filing.

Insurance: Annuity or endowment policy, if beneficiary is insured's spouse, child or parent. Life or health insurance policy for spouse or child of debtor, or if a clause in the policy prohibits payments to creditors. Group life insurance. Disability benefits. Fraternal society benefits. Insurance proceeds of exempt property are exempt for 6 months.

Personal Property: All necessary household clothing, books, clothing, appliances and household furnishings. Jewelry and watches up to $1,000. Down payment reserves for non-subsidized housing projects. One vehicle up to $1,000.

Tools of Trade: Only if needed for livelihood, including one motor vehicle and one commercial fishing boat.

Miscellaneous: Business partnership property.

Wages: Unpaid wages due for services of past 31 days. After 31 days, 95% of 1st $100; 90% of 2nd $100; 80% of balance. Prisoner's wages held by Dept. of Public Safety.

Public Benefits: Workers' compensation. Unemployment compensation. Unemployment work relief funds up to $60 per month. Public assistance paid by Dept. of Health Services.

Wild Card: None.

Idaho

Homestead: Real property up to $50,000 in net value, including mobile home and unimproved land for residence. Sale proceeds also exempt for 6 months.

437

Pensions and Retirement Benefits: ERISA-qualified plans and all Social Security benefits exempt. Funds exempt for public employees, police officers and firefighters. Other pensions and retirement benefits to the extent necessary for support.

Insurance: Annuity contract proceeds to $350 per month. Death or disability benefits. Fraternal society benefits. Homeowner's insurance proceeds to amount of homestead. Life insurance, if group life insurance, or beneficiary is other than insured, or if a clause in the policy prohibits payments to creditors. Medical benefits.

Personal Property: Books, furnishings, appliances, clothing, pets, musical instruments, one firearm, family portraits and heirlooms up to $500 per item, $4,000 total. Building materials. Burial place. Jewelry to $250. Motor vehicle to $1,500. Personal injury recoveries needed for support. Wrongful death recoveries. Crops up to $1,000. Water rights up to 160 inches. Equipment necessary to perform military or police work.

Tools of Trade: Tools and implements up to $1,000.

Miscellaneous: Alimony. Child support needed for support. Liquor licenses. Business partnership property.

Wages: Minimum 75% of earned but unpaid wages and pension payments.

Public Benefits: Workers' compensation. Unemployment compensation. Veteran's benefits. Aid to blind, aged or disabled. AFDC. Crime victim's compensation, unless debt is for the treatment of injury incurred during the crime. Any type of government assistance. Social Security.

Wild Card: None.

Illinois

Homestead: Real property up to $7,500 in residence, farm, lot and buildings, condo, or co-op. Co-owners cannot multiply exemption. Proceeds from sale exempt 1 year from date of sale.

Pensions and Retirement Benefits: ERISA-qualified plans exempt. Funds exempted for civil service employees, county employees, disabled firefighters, widows and children of firefighters, general assembly members, municipal employees, police officers, firefighters, state university employees and teachers. IRA exemptions for conventional, Roth, SEP and SIMPLE plans.

Insurance: Health or disability benefits. Homeowner's proceeds for destroyed home, up to $7,500. Life insurance and annuity proceeds if beneficiary is insured's child, parent, spouse or other dependent, or if a clause prohibits payments to creditors. Life insurance proceeds if cannot be used to pay beneficiary's creditors. Life insurance proceeds needed for support. Fraternal society benefits.

Personal Property: Family pictures, schoolbooks, clothing, vehicles up to $1,200. Personal injury recoveries to $7,500. Wrongful death recoveries needed for support. Exempt property proceeds.

Tools of Trade: Tools and implements up to $750.

Miscellaneous: Alimony. Child support. Business partnership property.

Wages: Minimum 85% of earned but unpaid wages.

Public Benefits: Workers' compensation. Unemployment compensation. Veteran's benefits. Aid to aged, blind and disabled. AFDC. Crime victim's compensation. Social Security.

Wild Card: $2,000 of any personal property.

Indiana

Homestead: Real property claimed as residence up to $7,500; homestead plus personal property (except health aids) can't exceed $10,000. Property held as tenancy by the entirety is exempt against debt of only one spouse.

Pensions and Retirement Benefits: Funds exempted for firefighters, police, sheriffs, public employees and state teachers. IRA exemptions for conventional, SEP and SIMPLE plans. Nondeductible contributions are not protected.

Insurance: Fraternal society benefits. Life insurance, if group term policy, or if beneficiary is insured's spouse or dependent, or if a clause in the policy prohibits payments to creditors. Accident proceeds.

Personal Property: Any intangible personal property up to $100; except money owed to debtor.

Tools of Trade: National Guard uniforms, arms and equipment.

Miscellaneous: Business partnership property. State military personnel's uniforms, arms and equipment.

Wages: Minimum 75% of earned but unpaid wages.

Public Benefits: Unemployment compensation. Workers' compensation. Crime victim's compensation unless debt is for the treatment of injury incurred during the crime.

Wild Card: $4,000 of any real property or tangible personal property.

Iowa

Homestead: Real property with unlimited value. Property cannot exceed ½-acre in town or city, 40 acres elsewhere.

Pensions and Retirement Benefits: Funds exempted for firefighters, police and public employees. Payments being received from other pensions exempt if needed for support. The law is not settled for IRA exemptions, but extremely limited benefits may be protected.

Insurance: Life insurance acquired within two years of bankruptcy filing, up to $10,000 if paid to spouse, child or other dependent. Accident, disability, health, illness or life proceeds to $15,000, if paid to spouse, child or other dependent. Employee group insurance. Fraternal society benefits.

Personal Property: Furnishings and household goods up to $2,000. Books, pictures and paintings to $1,000. Burial plot up to one acre. Clothing up to $1,000. Motor vehicle and musical instruments up to $5,000. Wedding or engagement rings received prior to marriage.

Tools of Trade: Farming equipment, livestock and feed up to $10,000. Non-farming equipment (not including car) up to $10,000.

Miscellaneous: Alimony. Child support needed for support. Liquor licenses. Business partnership property.

Wages: Exempt according to the following table:

Annual Earnings	All Wages Exempt, Except
$12,000 - $15,999	$400
$16,000 - $23,999	$800
$24,000 - $34,999	$1,000
$35,000 - $49,999	$2,000
+$50,000	10% of wages

Also, the federal exemption standard applies (see the introduction to these tables).

Public Benefits: Workers' compensation. Unemployment compensation. AFDC. Local public assistance. Veteran's benefits. Adopted child assistance. Social Security.

Wild Card: $100 of any personal property.

Kansas

Homestead: Real property with unlimited value up to 160 acres rural or 1 acre urban.

Pensions and Retirement Benefits: ERISA-qualified plans. Funds exempt for officials in cities with populations between 120,000 and 200,000, police officers, firefighters, government employees and state school employees. Federal government pension payments needed for support and paid within three months of filing a bankruptcy action. IRA exemptions for conventional, Roth, SEP and SIMPLE plans.

Insurance: Life insurance, if a clause in the policy prohibits payment to creditors. Forfeiture value of life insurance exempt if policy purchased more than one year before bankruptcy action. Fraternal society benefits.

Personal Property: Burial place. Funeral plan prepayments. Clothing. Food and fuel. Furnishings and household equipment. Jewelry to $1,000. Motor vehicle to $20,000 (no limit for vehicle equipped for handicapped persons).

Tools of Trade: Tools and implements up to $7,500.

Miscellaneous: Liquor licenses. Business partnership property.

Wages: Greater of 75% of weekly disposable earnings or excess of disposable earnings over 30 times federal minimum wage. For child support obligations, 50% of disposable earnings exempt if debtor is supporting another spouse or dependent; 40% if not. For delinquent support more than 12 weeks in arrears, only 45% or 35%, respectively is exempt.

Public Benefits: Unemployment compensation. Workers' compensation. AFDC. Crime victim's compensation. Social welfare. General assistance.

Wild Card: None.

Kentucky

Homestead: Real or personal property used as residence up to $5,000.

Pensions and Retirement Benefits: Funds exempt for firefighters, police, teachers, state employees and county government employees. Other pensions exempt if needed for support. IRA exemptions for conventional, Roth, SEP and SIMPLE plans. Limited to contributions that are made more than 120 days before bankruptcy filing.

Insurance: Annuity benefits up to $350 per month. Life insurance, if beneficiary is a married woman or not the insured, or a clause in the policy prohibits payment to creditors, or if a group policy. Health or disability contract benefits. Cooperative life or casualty insurance benefits. Fraternal society benefits.

Personal Property: Burial plot up to $5,000 in lieu of homestead exemption. Clothing, jewelry and furnishings up to $3,000 total. Payments for lost earnings needed for support. Medical expenses. Reparation benefits. Motor vehicle up to $2,500. Personal injury recoveries up to $7,500 (not to include pain and suffering). Wrongful death recoveries.

Tools of Trade: Tools up to $300, plus artisans in the business of maintaining mechanical or electrical equipment in general use, and ministers, attorneys, doctors, chiropractors, veterinarians and dentists may exempt a motor vehicle worth up to $2,500. Ministers, attorneys, doctors, chiropractors and veterinarians may also exempt up to $1,000 of professional equipment. Farmers may exempt up to $3,000 in poultry, livestock, tools and equipment.

Miscellaneous: Business partnership property. Alimony and child support.

Wages: Greater of 75% of earned but unpaid wages or excess of disposable wages over 30 times federal minimum wage.

Public Benefits: Unemployment compensation. Workers' compensation. Aid to blind, aged and disabled. AFDC. Crime victim's compensation.

Wild Card: $1,000 of any property.

Louisiana

Homestead: Real property up to $15,000. Applies to surviving spouses and dependents. Maximum homestead is 160 acres (rural or urban) in one tract, or more than one tract with a residence on one tract and a garden, field or pasture on the other tract(s). No doubling of exemption by married spouses.

Pensions and Retirement Benefits: ERISA-qualified plans, IRAs (conventional, SEP and SIMPLE), Keoghs and other qualified plans exempt to extent of tax exemption, but no exemption for contributions less than 1 year from filing.

Insurance: Life insurance policies or proceeds, limited to $35,000 if policy was purchased within 9 months of filing a bankruptcy action. Group insurance. Health, accident or disability proceeds. Fraternal society benefits.

Personal Property: Furniture. Utensils. Clothing. Family portraits. Musical instruments. Heating & cooling equipment. Pressing irons. Sewing machine. Refrigerator. Freezer. Stove. Washer and dryer. Burial place. Engagement and wedding rings up to $5,000.

Tools of Trade: All necessary tools, instruments and books, plus one truck (maximum 3 tons) or motor vehicle used primarily for trade, and a utility trailer.

Miscellaneous: Minor child's property.

Wages: Greater of 75% of weekly disposable earnings or excess of disposable wages over 30 times federal minimum wage. For child support claims, only 50% exempt.

Public Benefits: Unemployment compensation. Workers' compensation. Aid to blind, aged and disabled, AFDC. Crime victim's compensation.

Wild Card: None.

Maine

Homestead: Real or personal property including co-op up to $12,500; if living with minors up to $25,000; if debtor over 60 or physically or mentally disabled up to $60,000. Joint debtors may double.

Pensions and Retirement Benefits: ERISA-qualified plans. Funds exempt for legislators, judges and state employees. IRA exemptions for conventional, Roth, SEP and SIMPLE plans. Limited to amounts that are necessary for the support of the debtor and his dependents. *Warning:* No protection for IRAs that are established by an "insider" of the debtor. This provision could eliminate the protection otherwise offered to small business owners by SEP and SIMPLE plans.

Insurance: Annuity proceeds up to $450 per month. Life insurance policy, life insurance payments to debtor necessary for support. Life policy, accrued dividends, or cash value of person who supported debtor. Unmatured life insurance policy (except credit insurance policy). Disability benefits and pensions. Group health or life policy or proceeds. Fraternal society benefits.

Personal Property: Animals, crops, musical instruments, books, clothing, furnishings, household goods up to $200 per item. Furnaces, stoves and fuel. Jewelry up to $750. Payments for lost earnings needed for support. Motor vehicle up to $2,500. Personal injury and wrongful death recoveries up to $12,500 (excluding pain and suffering). Prescribed health aids. Food and produce for 6 months. Burial plot in lieu of homestead exemption.

Tools of Trade: Tools up to $5,000, plus one of every type of farming implement and the debtor's interest in up to a 5-ton commercial fishing boat.

Miscellaneous: Alimony and child support. Business partnership property.

Wages: For consumer credit transactions, the greater of 75% of weekly disposable earnings, or 40 times federal minimum wage.

Public Benefits: Veteran's benefits. Workers' compensation. Unemployment compensation. AFDC. Crime victim's compensation. Social Security.

Wild Card: $400 of any property. Unused homestead exemption up to $6,000 for animals, crops, musical instruments, books, clothing, furnishings, household goods, appliances, tools of the trade, and personal injury recoveries.

Maryland

Homestead: None. However, property held as tenancy by the entirety exempt against debt of only one spouse.

Pensions and Retirement Benefits: ERISA-qualified plans. Funds exempt for state employees, teachers and deceased Baltimore police officers. IRA exemptions for conventional, Roth, SEP and SIMPLE plans. Limited to tax-deductible contributions for non-Roth IRAs.

Insurance: Life insurance or annuity proceeds if beneficiary is insured's spouse, child or dependent. Medical benefits deducted from wages. Disability or health benefits. Fraternal society benefits.

Personal Property: Appliances, furnishings, household goods, books, pets and clothing up to $500. Burial place. Recovery for lost future earnings.

Tools of Trade: Clothing, books, tools, instruments and appliances necessary for any trade or profession, and not for sale, lease or barter, up to $2,500. Excludes car.

Miscellaneous: Business partnership property.

Public Benefits: Unemployment compensation. Workers' compensation. AFDC. Crime victim's compensation. General assistance.

Wages: In Caroline, Kent, Queen Anne's and Worcester counties, the greater of 75% of earned but unpaid wages or 30% of the federal minimum wage; elsewhere, the greater of $145 or 75% of wages. All withheld medical insurance payments also exempt.

Wild Card: $5500 of any property.

Massachusetts

Homestead: Real property up to $100,000; $200,000 for debtors over 65 or disabled. Co-owners cannot double. Property held as tenancy by entirety exempt against debt of only one spouse.

Pensions and Retirement Benefits: Funds exempt for ERISA-qualified retirement benefits, public employees' plans and savings bank employees' plans. IRA exemptions for conventional, Roth, SEP and SIMPLE plans. For IRAs, contributions made within the last five years are exempt only to the extent that the contributions did not exceed 7% of the individual's income over the five-year period.

Insurance: Fraternal benefit society benefits. Life or endowment policy proceeds or cash value. Group annuity policy or proceeds. Life insurance policy if beneficiary is married woman or cannot be used to pay beneficiary's creditors. Group life insurance policy. Disability benefits up to $400 per week.

Personal Property: Bank deposits up to $125. Books to $200 total. Sewing machine up to $200. Cash for fuel, heat, water or light up to $75 per month. Clothing. Cash up to $200 per month for rent. Co-op shares up to $100. Furniture up to $3,000. Motor vehicle up to $700. Trust company bank deposits up to $500. Burial places and church pew.

Tools of Trade: Tools, implements and fixtures up to $500. Stock up to $500. Fishing gear used in debtor's business up to $500.

Miscellaneous: Business partnership property.

Wages: Earned but unpaid wages up to $125 per week.

Public Benefits: Veteran's benefits. Workers' compensation. Unemployment compensation. AFDC. Aid to aged and disabled.

Wild Card: None.

Michigan

Homestead: Real estate to $3,500. Property cannot exceed 1 lot or 40 acres rural. Property held as tenancy by entirety exempt against debt of only one spouse. Spouse or child of deceased owner may claim exemption.

Pensions and Retirement Benefits: Funds exempt for ERISA-qualified plans, firefighters, police officers, legislators, public school employees and state employees. IRA exemptions for conventional, Roth, education, SEP and SIMPLE plans. IRAs limited to contributions that were made more than 120 days before filing, and limited to tax-deductible contributions for non-Roth IRAs.

Insurance: Life, endowment or annuity proceeds if cannot be used to pay beneficiary's creditors. Life or endowment proceeds if beneficiary is insured's spouse or child. Life insurance proceeds if beneficiary is married. Fraternal society benefits. Disability, mutual life or health benefits.

Personal Property: Building and loan association shares up to $1,000 par value, in lieu of homestead. Burial place, church pew, clothing, family pictures, appliances, books and household goods, up to $1,000 total. Food and fuel for 6 months.

Tools of Trade: Tools, implements, stock, motor vehicle or other items that enable the debtor to carry on his business up to $1,000.

Miscellaneous: Business partnership property.

Wages: Head of household debtors may exempt 60% of weekly wages (but not less than $15.00 per week) plus $2.00 per dependent other than spouse. Other debtors may exempt 40% of weekly wages (not less than $10.00 per week).

Public Benefits: Veteran's benefits. Workers' compensation. Unemployment compensation. AFDC. Crime victim's compensation. Social welfare benefits.

Wild Card: None.

Minnesota

Homestead: Real property up to $200,000 ($500,000 if the homestead is used primarily for agriculture), but cannot exceed 160 acres rural or ½-acre urban. Proceeds exempt for one year.

Pensions and Retirement Benefits: ERISA-qualified plans, limited to present value of $51,000. Funds exempt for public employees and state employees. IRA exemptions for conventional, Roth, SEP and SIMPLE plans, limited to present value of $51,000.

Insurance: Life insurance proceeds if beneficiary is spouse or child of insured, up to $20,000, plus $5,000 per dependent. Police and firefighter benefits. Unmatured life insurance contract, dividends interest or loan value to $6,400, if insured is debtor or someone who supports debtor. Fraternal society benefits.

Personal Property: Burial place. Church pew. Motor vehicle up to $2,000 ($20,000 if modified for disabled person). Books and musical instruments, appliances, furniture, radio, phonographs and TV up to $4,500. Clothing. Food and utensils. Personal injury and wrongful death recoveries. Proceeds for damaged exempt property.

Tools of Trade: Farm machines, livestock, crops of farmers to $13,000 total. School teacher materials. Tools, machines, instruments, furniture, stock in trade and library up to $5,000 total.

Miscellaneous: Business partnership property. Minor child's earnings.

Wages: Greater of 75% or 40 times federal minimum hourly wage/week. Wages deposited into bank accounts for 20 days. Wages of released inmates paid within 6 months of release.

Public Benefits: Veteran's benefits. Workers' compensation. Unemployment compensation. AFDC. General or supplemental assistance. Supplemental security income, Crime victim's compensation.

Wild Card: None.

Mississippi

Homestead: Real property up to $75,000, cannot exceed 160 acres. If over age 60 and married or widowed, debtor need not occupy property. Sale proceeds exempt.

Pensions and Retirement Benefits: ERISA-qualified benefits deposited over 1 year before filing. Funds exempt for firefighters, police officers, state employees and teachers. The law is not settled for IRA exemptions, but extremely limited distributions may be protected.

Insurance: Disability benefits. Homeowner's insurance up to $75,000. Life insurance if a clause prohibits payment to creditors. Fraternal society benefits.

Personal Property: Personal injury judgments if inherited by parent, spouse or child. Any tangible personal property up to $10,000 including household goods (excluding art, antiques, electronic equipment other than 1 television and 1 radio, and jewelry other than wedding rings), clothing, motor vehicles, trade implements, health aids and cash.

Tools of Trade: None.

Miscellaneous: Business partnership property.

Wages: All wages exempt for 30 days; thereafter greater of 75% of weekly disposable earnings or excess of disposable earnings over 30 times federal minimum wage. Exemptions do not apply to tax debts. For support claims, only 50% exempt; for debtor supporting other spouse or dependent, otherwise 40%.

Public Benefits: Social Security. Unemployment compensation. Workers' compensation. Aid to aged, blind and disabled.

Wild Card: None.

Missouri

Homestead: Real property to $8,000 or mobile home to $1,000. Joint owners may not double.

Pensions and Retirement Benefits: ERISA-qualified plans. Funds exempt for employees of cities with 100,000 or more people, public officers and employees, police officers, highway and transportation employees, firefighters, state employees and teachers. IRA exemptions for conventional, Roth, SEP and SIMPLE plans, but no protection for contributions that are made within three years of bankruptcy filing.

Insurance: Death, disability or illness benefits. Life insurance proceeds if owned by a woman who insures her husband, or an unmarried woman who insures her father or brother. Life insurance dividends. Any unmatured life insurance, and up to $5,000 in accrued dividends, interest, or loan value if purchased more than 6 months prior to filing. Fraternal society benefits up to $5,000 if bought more than 6 months prior to bankruptcy action.

Personal Property: Appliances, household goods, clothing, books, crops, animals and musical instruments up to $1,000. Motor vehicle up to $1,000. Jewelry up to $500. Burial plot. Health aids. Wrongful death recoveries for death of person who supported you.

Tools of Trade: Tools and implements up to $2,000 used by the debtor or a dependent.

Miscellaneous: Alimony. Child support up to $500 per month. Business partnership property.

Wages: Minimum 75% of earned but unpaid wages (90% for head of family). Wages of servant or common laborer up to $90.

Public Benefits: Social Security. Unemployment compensation. Workers' compensation. Veteran's benefits. AFDC.

Wild Card: $400 in any kind of property. Head of household debtors $1,250, plus $250 per unmarried dependent child under 18.

Montana

Homestead: Real estate or mobile home up to $60,000. Spouses or joint owners cannot double exemption amount. Proceeds also exempt for 18 months following sale. Must record homestead declaration before attempted sale.

Pensions and Retirement Benefits: ERISA-qualified benefits. Funds exempt for all public employees. IRA exemptions for conventional, Roth, SEP and SIMPLE plans. No exemption for ERISA-qualified or IRA amounts deposited within one year filing, which are in excess of 15% of income for that one year. *Warning:* No protection for IRAs that are established by an "insider" of the debtor. This provision could eliminate the protection otherwise offered to small business owners by SEP and SIMPLE plans.

Insurance: Annuity up to $350 per month. Disability or illness benefits. Medical, surgical or hospital benefits. Group life insurance. Life insurance proceeds if prohibited to be used to pay beneficiary's creditors. Life insurance proceeds if annual premiums do not exceed $500. Unmatured life insurance contracts to $4,000. Fraternal society benefits.

Personal Property: Appliances, household furnishings, goods, animals, crops, musical instruments, books, firearms, clothing and jewelry up to $600 each, $4,500 total. Cooperative association shares up to $500 value. Motor vehicle up to $1,200. Burial place. Food and provisions for 3 months. Proceeds for damaged or lost exempt property for 6 months after received.

Tools of Trade: Tools and implements up to $3,000.

Miscellaneous: Business partnership property. Alimony. Child support.

Wages: 75% of debtor's weekly disposable earnings or excess of disposable wages over 30 times federal minimum wage is exempt, subject to court ordered support claims.

Public Benefits: Social Security. Unemployment compensation. Workers' compensation. Vocational rehabilitation to the blind. Veteran's benefits. Aid to aged and disabled. AFDC. Crime victim's compensation.

Wild Card: None.

Nebraska

Homestead: Real property up to $12,500, cannot exceed 160 acres rural or two urban lots. Sale proceeds exempt for 6 months after sale.

Pensions and Retirement Benefits: ERISA-qualified plans needed for support. Funds exempt for county, state and school employees, and military disability benefits to $2,000. IRA exemptions for conventional, Roth, SEP and SIMPLE plans. No IRA protection for plans that were established within two years of bankruptcy, and limited to amounts that are reasonably necessary for support of debtor and dependents.

Insurance: Fraternal benefit society benefits to $10,000. Unmatured life insurance contract with loan or cash values up to $10,000.

Personal Property: Clothing, furniture and kitchen utensils up to $1,500. Perpetual care funds. Recovery for personal injury. Burial place. Food and fuel for 6 months.

Tools of Trade: Tools and implements up to $1,500. Married couple may double.

Miscellaneous: Business partnership property.

Wages: Minimum 85% of earned but unpaid wages or pension payments for head of family, otherwise 75%.

Public Benefits: Unemployment compensation. Workers' compensation. Aid to disabled, blind and aged. AFDC.

Wild Card: $2,500 of any personal property if homestead is not claimed. Cannot be used for wages.

Nevada

Homestead: Real property, including mobile homes, up to $125,000. Cannot double. Must record homestead exemption before filing bankruptcy action.

Pensions and Retirement Benefits: ERISA-qualified plans and IRAs (conventional, SEP and SIMPLE) up to $500,000. Funds exempt for public employees.

Insurance: Fraternal society benefits. Life insurance benefits exempt to the extent the annual premium is no more than $1,000. Group life and health. Annuity payments up to $350 per month, unless larger amount needed for support.

Personal Property: Private libraries up to $1,500. All family pictures and keepsakes. Certain prescribed health aids. Household goods up to $3,000. Motor vehicle modified for disabled dependent. One gun. A collection of metal-bearing ores, geological specimens, art curiosities or paleontological remains if catalogued for free inspection of visitors, and all property held in a spendthrift trust; excludes coin collections.

Tools of Trade: Uniforms required by law. Farm equipment, stock & supplies up to $4,500. Other trade implements up to $4,500. Mining equipment up to $4,500.

Miscellaneous: Business partnership property.

Wages: Exempt as to greater of 75% of disposable earnings or 30 times federal minimum wage.

Public Benefits: Unemployment compensation. Workers' compensation. Aid to disabled, blind and aged. AFDC. Vocational rehabilitation benefits.

Wild Card: None.

New Hampshire

Homestead: Real property or manufactured housing up to $30,000. Must own the land.

Pensions and Retirement Benefits: Funds exempt for public employees' federal pension, but only benefits accruing. Firefighters, police officers and public employees. No protection for IRAs.

Insurance: Homeowner's insurance proceeds up to $5,000. Firefighter's death and disability benefits. Fraternal society benefits.

Personal Property: Beds. Bedsteads. Bedding. Furniture. Sewing machine. Cooking utensils needed. Cooking and heating stoves. Refrigerator. Household furniture up to $3,500. Automobile up to $4,000. Bibles and books up to $800. Burial place. Clothing. Jewelry up to $500. Proceeds for lost or destroyed exempt property. Cow. 6 sheep or fleece. 4 tons of hay. Food and fuel up to $400.

Tools of Trade: Tools and implements up to $5,000. Military members uniforms, arms and equipment. Cow, yoke of oxen or horse when needed for farming.

Miscellaneous: Business partnership property. Child support. Jury and witness fees. Minor child's wages.

Wages: Up to 50 times the federal minimum weekly wage, or as determined by a court.

Public Benefits: Workers' compensation. Unemployment compensation. Aid to blind, aged and, disabled. AFDC.

Wild Card: $1,000 of any property, plus up to $7,000 for unused portion of automobiles, bibles, books, food and fuel, furniture, jewelry, and tools of the trade.

New Jersey

Homestead: None.

Pensions and Retirement Benefits: ERISA-qualified plans. Funds exempt for public employees. IRA exemptions for conventional, Roth, education, SEP and SIMPLE plans.

Insurance: Annuity contract proceeds to $500 per month. Fraternal society benefits. Military disability or death benefits. Disability, death, medical or hospital benefits for civil defense workers. Life insurance proceeds if proceeds cannot be used to pay beneficiary's creditors. Health or disability benefits. Life insurance proceeds if another insured. Group life or health policy proceeds.

Personal Property: Personal property and corporation shares up to $1,000. Clothing. Burial place. Furniture and household goods up to $1,000.

Tools of Trade: None.

Miscellaneous: Business partnership property.

Wages: 90% of earned but unpaid wages if income under $7,500. If income over $7,500, judge decides amount. Wages or allowances of military personnel.

Public Benefits: Workers' compensation. Unemployment compensation. Old-age and permanent disability assistance. Crime victim's compensation.

Wild Card: None.

New Mexico

Homestead: Real property up to $30,000. If jointly owned, can double exemption.

Pensions and Retirement Benefits: Funds exempt for public school employees. No clear exemptions for IRAs.

Insurance: Fraternal society and benevolent association benefits to $5,000. Life, accident, health or annuity benefits or proceeds, if beneficiary is a New Mexico citizen.

Personal Property: Books. Health equipment and furniture. Building supplies. Jewelry up to $2,500. Oil and gas equipment. One motor vehicle up to $4,000. Clothing. Cooperative association shares.

Tools of Trade: Tools and implements up to $1,500.

Miscellaneous: Business partnership property. Ownership interest in unincorporated association.

Wages: Exempt as to greater of 75% of wages or 40 times federal minimum wage.

Public Benefits: Workers' compensation. Unemployment compensation. AFDC. General assistance. Crime victim's compensation. Occupational disease disablement benefits.

Wild Card: $500 of any personal property, or $2,000 of any property if homestead not claimed.

New York

Homestead: Real property, including co-op, condo or mobile home, up to $10,000. Husband and wife may double the exemption.

Pensions and Retirement Benefits: ERISA-qualified benefits needed for support. Funds exempt for public retirement benefits of state employees and village police officers. IRA exemptions for conventional, Roth and SIMPLE plans, limited to contributions that are made more than 90 days before court action.

Insurance: Annuity contract benefits due or prospectively due the debtor, who paid for the contract; if purchased within 6 months of filing for bankruptcy and not tax-deferred, only $5,000. Disability or illness benefits to $400 per month. Life insurance proceeds and avails if the person effecting the policy is the spouse of the insured. Life insurance proceeds left at death with the insurance company pursuant to agreement, if clause prohibits proceeds from being used to pay beneficiary's creditors.

Personal Property: Bible. Schoolbooks. Books up to $50. Pictures. Clothing. Church pew or seat. Stoves with fuel to last 60 days. Sewing machine. Domestic animal with food to last 60 days up to $450. Food to last 60 days. Furniture. Refrigerator. TV. Radio. Wedding ring. Watch to $35. Crockery. Cooking utensils and tableware needed. Burial plot without structure to ¼-acre. Cash, the lesser of either $2,500 or an amount, that, with annuity, totals $5,000 in lieu of homestead. Health aids including animals with food. Lost earnings recoveries needed for support. Motor vehicle up to $2,400. Personal injury recoveries up to $7,500 (not to include pain and suffering). Security deposits to landlord. Utility company trust fund principal and 90% of income. Wrongful death recoveries for death of person who supported you, to the extent needed for support.

Tools of Trade: Farm machinery, team, food for 60 days, professional furniture, books and instruments to $600 total. Uniforms, medal, equipment, emblem, horse, arms and sword of military member.

Miscellaneous: Business partnership property. Alimony. Child support necessary for support.

Wages: 90% of earnings from milk sales to milk dealers. 90% of earned but unpaid wages received within 60 days of filing for bankruptcy (100% for a few militia members).

Public Benefits: Unemployment compensation. Workers compensation. Social Security. Home relief. Local public assistance.

Aid to blind, aged and disabled. AFDC. Veteran's benefits. Crime victim's compensation.

Wild Card: None

North Carolina

Homestead: Homestead real or personal property, including co-op, used as residence up to $10,000. Up to $3,500 of unused portion of homestead may be applied to any property.

Pensions and Retirement Benefits: Funds exempt for firefighters and rescue squad workers, legislators, law enforcement officers, municipal city and county employees, teachers and state employees. IRA exemptions for conventional, Roth, SEP and SIMPLE plans, but subject to statutory liens and consensual liens.

Insurance: Fraternal society benefits. Employee group life policy or proceeds.

Miscellaneous: Business partnership property.

Personal Property: Animals, crops, musical instruments, books, clothing, furnishings, household goods up to $3,500; may add $750 per dependent, up to $3,000 total additional. Burial plot up to $10,000 in lieu of homestead. Health aids. Motor vehicle up to $1,500. Personal injury and wrongful death recoveries for person who supported you.

Public Benefits: Unemployment compensation. Workers compensation. AFDC. Special adult assistance. Aid to blind. Crime victim's compensation.

Tools of Trade: Tools and implements up to $750, if not purchased within 90 days of filing.

Wages: Earned but unpaid wages received 60 days before filing for bankruptcy, needed for support.

Wild Card: $3,500 less any amount claimed for homestead or burial exemption, for any property.

North Dakota

Homestead: Real estate, house trailer or mobile home up to $80,000. Sales and insurance proceeds also exempt.

Pensions and Retirement Benefits: ERISA-qualified pensions and IRAs (conventional, Roth, SEP, SIMPLE) up to $100,000 per plan, total cannot exceed $200,000, unless reasonably necessary for support of debtor or dependents. Funds exempt for disabled veteran's benefits and public employees pensions.

Insurance: Life insurance surrender value up to $200,000 if policy is payable to surviving spouse, dependents or other relatives, and policy owned more than one year before bankruptcy action. The $200,000 limit includes ERISA-qualified retirement benefits and IRAs. Life insurance payable to insured's estate. Fraternal society benefits.

Personal Property: Books up to $100. Pictures. Clothing. Burial plots. Church pew. Cash up to $7,500, in lieu of homestead. Crops raised on debtors land not to exceed 160 acres. Motor vehicle up to $1,200. Personal injury recoveries up to $7,500 (excluding pain and suffering). Wrongful death recoveries up to $7,500. Head of household not claiming crops may claim up to $5,000 of any personal property or any of the following: library and tools of profession up to $1,000, livestock and farm implements up to $4,500, tools and stock in trade up to $1,000, furniture up to $1,000, books and musical instruments up to $1,500. Non-head of household not claiming crops may claim up to $2,500 of any personal property in addition to above.

Tools of Trade: None.

Miscellaneous: Business partnership property.

Wages: Minimum 75% of earned but unpaid wages.

Public Benefits: Unemployment compensation. Workers' compensation. AFDC. Crime victim's compensation. Social Security. Vietnam veteran's adjustment compensation.

Wild Card: None.

Ohio

Homestead: Real or personal property used as residence up to $5,000. Property held as tenancy by the entirety exempt against debt of only one spouse.

Pensions and Retirement Benefits: ERISA-qualified plans. Funds exempt for firefighters' and police officers' death benefits and pensions, public employees, state highway patrol employees and volunteer firefighters' dependents. IRA exemptions for conventional, Roth, education, SEP and SIMPLE plans.

Insurance: Group life insurance policy or proceeds. Life, endowment or annuity contracts. Life insurance proceeds for a spouse. Life insurance proceeds if proceeds cannot be used to pay beneficiary's creditors. Health and accident benefits. Disability benefits to $600 per month. Fraternal society benefits. Benevolent society benefits up to $5,000.

Personal Property: Animals, crops, books, musical instruments, clothing, appliances, household goods, furnishings, sporting equipment and firearms up to $200 per item, up to $1,500 total, $2,000 if no homestead claimed. Jewelry up to $400 for 1 item and $200 per item for all other jewelry. Cash, money due within 90 days, bank and security deposits, and tax refunds up to $400 total. Personal injury recoveries up to $5,000 (excluding pain and suffering). Motor vehicle up to $1,000. Stove and refrigerator up to $300 each. Burial place. Prescribed health aids. Wrongful death recoveries.

Tools of Trade: Tools and implements up to $750.

Miscellaneous: Business partnership property. Alimony and child support needed for support.

Wages: The greater of 30 times the current federal minimum wage or 75% of the debtor's disposable weekly earnings, which are due for up to 30 days.

Public Benefits: Unemployment compensation. Workers' compensation. AFDC. Crime victim's compensation. Vocational rehabilitation benefits. Tuition credit.

Wild Card: $400 of any property.

Oklahoma

Homestead: Real property or manufactured home to unlimited value. Property cannot exceed ¼-acre. If property in excess of ¼-acre, up to $5,000 on 1 acre in city, town or village, or 160 acres elsewhere.

Pensions and Retirement Benefits: ERISA-qualified plans. Funds exempt for law enforcement employees, public employees, teachers, county employees and disabled veterans. IRA exemptions for conventional, SEP and SIMPLE plans. IRA protection limited to tax-deductible contributions only.

Insurance: Fraternal society benefits. Funeral benefits. Group term life insurance. Limited stock insurance benefits.

Personal Property: Books. Portraits. Pictures. Burial plots. Clothing up to $4,000. Furniture. Motor vehicle up to $3,000. Claim for personal bodily injury and workers' compensation recoveries up to $50,000, exclusive of claims for punitive damages.

Tools of Trade: Tools and implements up to $5,000, if used in business or trade of debtor or dependent.

Miscellaneous: Business partnership property. Alimony. Child support.

Wages: Exempt to the extent of 75% of wages earned during 90 days prior to filing, except for support claims. Judge can increase amount available except in support cases on showing of hardship.

Public Benefits: Unemployment compensation. Workers' compensation. Social Security. AFDC. Crime victim's compensation.

Wild Card: None.

Oregon

Homestead: Real property, mobile home or houseboat the debtor occupies or intends to occupy up to $25,000 ($33,000 for joint owners); if the debtor doesn't own land mobile home is on, up to $23,000 ($30,000 joint). Property cannot exceed 1 block in town or city or 160 acres elsewhere. Sale proceeds exempt 1 year form sale, if debtor intends to purchase another home.

Pensions and Retirement Benefits: ERISA-qualified plans. Funds exempt for public employees or officers, and school district employees. IRA exemptions for conventional, Roth, SEP and SIMPLE plans.

Insurance: Annuity contract benefits to $500 per month. Fraternal society benefits. Group life insurance policy or proceeds not payable to the insured. Health or disability proceeds or avails. Life insurance proceeds or cash value if the debtor is not the insured.

Personal Property: Books, pictures and musical instruments to $600 total (husband and wife may double). Burial plots. Bank deposits up to $7,500 which are derived from exempt assets. Clothing, jewelry and other personal items up to $1,800 total (husband and wife may double). Domestic animals. Poultry with food to last 60 days to $1,000. Food and fuel to last 60 days if debtor is householder. Furniture, household items, utensils, radios and TVs up to $3,000 total. Health aids. Lost earnings payments for debtor or someone debtor depended on, to extent needed (husband and wife may double). Motor vehicle up to $1,700 (husband and wife may double). Personal injury recoveries up to $7,500, not to include pain and suffering (husband and wife may double). Pistol, rifle or shotgun if owned by person over 16, up to $1,000.

Tools of Trade: Tools and implements up to $3,000. Husband and wife may double.

Miscellaneous: Business partnership property. Alimony. Child support. Liquor licenses.

Public Benefits: Unemployment compensation. Workers' compensation. Aid to blind and disabled benefits. Crime victim's compensation (husband and wife may double). Civil defense and disaster relief. General assistance. Injured inmate's benefits. Medical assistance. Old-age assistance. Vocational rehabilitation.

Wages: Minimum of 75% of earned but unpaid wages.

Wild Card: $400 of any otherwise nonexempt personal property. Husband and wife may double.

Pennsylvania

Homestead: None. However, property held as tenancy by the entirety may be exempt against the debts owed by only one spouse.

Pensions and Retirement Benefits: ERISA-qualified plans. Funds exempt for city employees, county employees, municipal employees, police officers, public school employees and state employees. Private retirement benefits exempt if clause prohibits proceeds from being used to pay beneficiary's creditors, to extent tax-deferred, limited to $15,000 per year deposited, and no exemption for amount deposited within 1 year of filing. IRA exemptions for conventional, SEP and SIMPLE plans, subject to above limits.

Insurance: Life insurance annuity policy, cash value or proceeds if beneficiary is insured's dependent, child or spouse. Insurance policy or annuity contract payments, where insured is the beneficiary, cash value or proceeds to $100 per month. Group life insurance policy or proceeds. Life insurance proceeds if clause prohibits proceeds from being used to pay beneficiary's creditors. Accident or disability benefits. Fraternal society benefits. No-fault automobile insurance proceeds.

Personal Property: Bibles. Schoolbooks. Sewing machines. Clothing. Tangible personal property at an international exhibit sponsored by U.S. government. Uniform and accoutrements.

Tools of Trade: None.

Miscellaneous: Business partnership property.

Wages: Earned but unpaid wages.

Public Benefits: Unemployment compensation. Workers' compensation. Crime victim's compensation. Korean conflict veteran's benefits. Veteran's benefits.

Wild Card: $300 of any property.

Rhode Island

Homestead: None.

Pensions and Retirement Benefits: ERISA-qualified plans. Funds exempt for public employees. IRA exemptions for conventional, Roth, SEP and SIMPLE plans. Non-Roth IRAs limited to tax-deductible amounts.

Insurance: Life insurance if a clause prohibits payment to creditors. Fraternal society benefits. Accident and sickness insurance. Temporary liability insurance.

Personal Property: All necessary clothing. Books up to $300. Household furniture up to $1,000. One lot or right of burial for deceased person's body. Consumer cooperative association up to $50 interest. Debts secured by promissory notes.

Tools of Trade: Working tools for debtor's use up to $500. Uniforms, arms and equipment for militia members.

Miscellaneous: Business partnership property. Earnings of a minor child.

Wages: Wages of spouse. Wages due militia members. Seaman's unpaid wages. Unpaid wages to all other debtors up to $50.

Public Benefits: Unemployment compensation. Workers' compensation. AFDC. General assistance.

Wild Card: None.

South Carolina

Homestead: Real or personal property, or co-op association, up to $5,000. Joint owners may double.

Pensions and Retirement Benefits: ERISA-qualified plans. Funds exempt for Social Security and miscellaneous state and local employee retirement systems. IRA exemptions for conventional, Roth, SEP and SIMPLE plans. *Warnings:* IRAs limited to payments, and not balance in plans. Also, no protection for IRAs that are established by an "insider" of the debtor. This provision could eliminate the protection otherwise offered to small business owners by SEP and SIMPLE plans.

Insurance: Life insurance for the benefit of spouse, children or dependents, if purchased more than 2 years prior to filing. Life insurance up to $4,000 on debtor's provider. Any unmatured life insurance policy other than credit life. Proceeds of life insurance or annuity contract. Fraternal society benefits. Wrongful death and bodily injury to debtor's provider.

Personal Property: One motor vehicle up to $1,200. Household furnishings and goods, clothing, appliances, books, animals, crops, musical instruments up to $2,500. Cash up to $1,000 in lieu of homestead or burial lot, Jewelry up to $500. Health aids. One burial plot, as an alternative to the homestead exemption.

Tools of Trade: Tools and implements up to $750.

Miscellaneous: Business partnership property. Alimony. Child support.

Wages: None.

Public Benefits: Unemployment compensation. Social Security. Public assistance. Crime victim's compensation.

Wild Card: None.

South Dakota

Homestead: Real property, including mobile home larger than 240 square feet at its base and registered in state at least 6 months before filing for bankruptcy, to unlimited value; property cannot exceed 1 acre in town or 160 acres elsewhere. Sale proceeds to $30,000 or unlimited if the debtor is over the age of 70, or an unmarried widow or widower, exempt for 1 year after sale. Can't include gold or silver mill smelter or mine. Spouse or children of deceased owner may claim homestead exemption. May file homestead declaration.

Pensions and Retirement Benefits: Funds exempt for public employees and city employees. Maximum of $250,000 for all plans. IRA exemptions for conventional, SEP and SIMPLE plans, subject to above aggregate limit.

Insurance: Annuity contract proceeds to $250 per month. Endowments and life insurance policy, proceeds or cash value to $20,000. Life insurance proceeds held pursuant to agreement by insurer, if clause prohibits proceeds from being used to pay beneficiary's creditors. Life insurance proceeds to $10,000 if beneficiary is a surviving spouse or child. Fraternal society benefits. Health benefits to $20,000.

Miscellaneous: Business partnership property.

Personal Property: Bible. Books up to $200. Pictures. Burial plots. Church pew. Food and fuel to last 1 year. Clothing. Head of family may claim up to $4,000 of any personal property or books and musical instruments up to $200, 2 cows, 5 swine, 25 sheep with lambs under 6 months, wool, cloth or yarn of sheep, food for all to last 1 year, farming machinery, utensils, tackle for teams, harrow, 2 plows, sleigh, wagon up to $1,250 total, furniture, including bedsteads and bedding up to $200, library and tools of professional up to $300, tools of mechanic and stock in trade up to $200. Non-head of family may claim up to $2,000 of any personal property.

Tools of Trade: None.

Wages: Earned wages owed 60 days before filing bankruptcy, needed for support of family. Wages of prisoners in work program.

Public Benefits: Workers' compensation. Unemployment benefits. AFDC.

Wild Card: None.

Tennessee

Homestead: Real property up to $5,000, or $7,500 for joint owners; life estate; 2-15 year lease. Spouse or children of deceased owner may claim homestead exemption. Property held as tenancy by the entirety may be exempt against debts owed by only one spouse.

Pensions and Retirement Benefits: ERISA-qualified plans. Funds exempt for public employees, state and local government employees and teachers. IRA exemptions for conventional, SEP and SIMPLE plans.

Insurance: Accident, health or disability benefits. Homeowner's insurance proceeds to $5,000. Fraternal society benefits.

Personal Property: Bible. Schoolbooks. Pictures. Portraits. Clothing and storage containers. Burial plot up to 1 acre. Health aids. Lost earnings payments for you or person supported you. Personal injury recoveries up to $7,500 (excluding pain and suffering); wrongful death recoveries up to $10,000; maximum of $15,000 total for personal injury, wrongful death and crime victim's compensation.

Tools of Trade: Tools and implements up to $1,900.

Miscellaneous: Business partnership property. Alimony owed for 30 days prior to filing bankruptcy.

Wages: 75% of earned but unpaid wages, and $2.50 per week per child.

Public Benefits: Unemployment compensation. Workers' compensation. Social Security. Veteran's benefits. AFDC. Aid to blind. Aid to disabled. Crime victim's compensation up to $5,000. Local public assistance. Old-age assistance.

Wild Card: $4,000 in any personal property.

Texas

Homestead: Unlimited. However, property cannot exceed 1 acre in town, village or city, or 100 acres (200 acres for families) elsewhere. Sale proceeds exempt for 6 months after sale. Debtor need not occupy homestead if debtor does not acquire another home. May file a homestead declaration.

Pensions and Retirement Benefits: ERISA-qualified government or church benefits. Funds exempt for county and district employees, firefighters, judges (Keoghs to extent tax-deferred), law enforcement officers' survivors, municipal employees, police officers, state employees and teachers. IRA exemptions for conventional, Roth, SEP and SIMPLE plans. Except for Roth IRAs, IRAs limited to tax-deductible contributions.

Insurance: Life, health, accident or annuity benefits or monies, including policy proceeds and cash values to be paid or rendered to beneficiary or insured. Life insurance present value if beneficiary is debtor or debtor's dependent. Retired public school employees' group insurance. Texas employee uniform group insurance. Texas state college or university employee benefits. Fraternal society benefits. Church plan benefits.

Personal Property: Athletic and sporting equipment, including bicycles. 2 firearms. Home property furnishings, including family heirlooms. Food. Clothing. Jewelry (not to exceed 25% of total exemptions). One two-, three- or four-wheeled motor vehicle per member of family or single adult who holds a driver's license, or who operates vehicle for someone else who does not have a license. 2 horses, mules or donkeys and a saddle, blanket and bridle for each; 12 head of cattle; 60 head of other types of livestock; 120 fowl and pets all up to $30,000 total ($60,000 for head of family). Burial plots. Health aids. $30,000/$60,000 total is reduced by exemptions claimed for tools of trade, unpaid commissions and life insurance cash value.

Tools of Trade: Tools, equipment, apparatus (including boat), motor vehicles, and books used in trade. Farming and ranching implements.

Miscellaneous: Business partnership property.

Wages: Earned but unpaid wages; unpaid commissions up to 75%.

Public Benefits: Unemployment compensation. Workers' compensation. AFDC. Crime victim's compensation. Medical assistance.

Wild Card: None.

Utah

Homestead: Real property, mobile home or water rights up to $10,000. Joint owners may double. Proceeds from sale exempt for 1 year. Must file homestead declaration before attempted sale of home.

Pensions and Retirement Benefits: ERISA-qualified plans. Funds exempt for public employees. IRA exemptions for conventional, Roth, SEP and SIMPLE plans, for contributions made more than 1 year prior to filing.

Insurance: Life insurance policy cash surrender value to $1,500. Life insurance if beneficiary is insured's spouse or dependent as needed for support. Disability, illness, medical or hospital benefits. Fraternal society benefits.

Personal Property: Animals, books and musical instruments up to $500 total. Artwork depicting or done by family member. Bed. Bedding. Carpets. Washer and dryer. Burial plot. Clothing (excluding furs or jewelry). Food for 3 months. Furnishings and appliances up to $500. Health aids. Heirloom or other sentimental item up to $500. Refrigerator. Freezer. Stove. Sewing machine. Proceeds for damaged exempt property. Wrongful death recoveries for person who supported you.

Miscellaneous: Business partnership property. Alimony needed for support. Child support.

Tools of Trade: One motor vehicle if used for debtor's business or profession up to $2,500. Implements, professional books or tools of the debtor's trade up to $3,500. All military or National Guard property.

Wages: Minimum of 75% of earned but unpaid wages.

Public Benefits: Unemployment compensation. Workers' compensation. Veteran's benefits. AFDC. Crime victim compensation. General assistance. Occupational disease or disability benefits.

Wild Card: None.

Vermont

Homestead: Real property or mobile home up to $75,000, along with rents, issues and profits. Property held as tenancy by the entirety exempt against debt of only one spouse.

Pensions and Retirement Benefits: Municipal employees, state employees and teachers. IRA exemptions for conventional, Roth, SEP and SIMPLE plans, limited to contributions that were made more than one year before court action; except for Roth IRAs, IRA protection is limited to tax-deductible contributions; limited to $5,000 if court action is for child support.

Insurance: Annuity benefits to $350 per month. Life insurance proceeds if proceeds cannot be used to pay beneficiary's creditors. Unmatured life insurance contracts exempt, other than credit life. Group life or health benefits. Life insurance proceeds if beneficiary is not the insured. Fraternal society benefits.

Personal Property: Furnishings, clothing, books, crops, animals and musical instruments up to $2,500 total. Limited number of livestock, poultry, equipment and feed. Jewelry up to $500. Wedding ring. Motor vehicles up to $2,500. Bank deposits up to $700. Stove. Refrigerator. Water heater. Sewing machines. Wrongful death recoveries for person who supported you. Personal injury recoveries.

Tools of Trade: Professional or trade books or tools up to $5,000.

Miscellaneous: Business partnership property. Alimony. Child support needed for support.

Wages: Greater of 75% of earned but unpaid wages or 30 times federal minimum hourly wage.

Public Benefits: Unemployment compensation. Workers' compensation. Social Security. Veteran's benefits. Aid to blind, aged and disabled. AFDC. General assistance. Crime victim's compensation.

Wild Card: $7,000 less any amount of appliances, growing crops, jewelry, motor vehicle and tools of trade of any property, and $400 of any property.

Virginia

Homestead: Real property up to $5,000 plus $500 per dependent. May include rents and profits, and mobile home. Sale proceeds exempt to $5,000. Husband and wife may double. Unused portion of homestead may be applied to any personal property. Must file homestead exemption before bankruptcy filing. Property owned in tenancy by the entirety exempt against claims of one spouse.

Pensions and Retirement Benefits: ERISA-qualified plans, limited to $17,500 income per year. Funds exempt for judges and city, town, county and state employees. IRA exemptions for conventional, Roth, SEP and SIMPLE plans. IRAs subject to above total $17,500 income limitation, and no protection for contributions made during current year, and prior two years.

Insurance: Group life insurance policy or proceeds. Group life or accident insurance for government officials. Fraternal society benefits. Accident or sickness benefits. Burial society benefits. Cooperative life insurance benefits. Industrial sickness benefits.

Personal Property: Only a householder can exempt any personal property. Bible. Burial plot. Clothing up to $1,000. Family portraits and heirlooms up to $5,000 total. Health aids. Household furnishings up to $5,000. Motor vehicle up to $2,000. Personal injury causes of action and recoveries. Pets. Wedding and engagement rings.

Tools of Trade: Horses, 2 mules with gear, wagon or cart, tractor up to $3,000, 2 plows, drag, harvest cradle, pitchfork, rake, 2 iron wedges, fertilizer up to $1,000, all growing crops for farmer/householder. For other, up to $10,000 including motor vehicles of householder, military uniforms, arms and equipment.

Miscellaneous: Business partnership property.

Wages: Greater of 75% of weekly disposable earnings or excess of disposable earnings over 30 times federal minimum hourly wage. Pension payments.

Public Benefits: Unemployment benefits. Workers' compensation. Aid to blind, aged and disabled. AFDC. General relief. Crime victim's compensation unless seeking to discharge debt for treatment of injury incurred during crime.

Wild Card: Unused portion of homestead, for any personal property. $2,000 of any property for disabled veterans who are householders.

Washington

Homestead: Real property or mobile home up to $30,000. No limit if seeking to discharge debts on failure to pay a state income tax on retirement benefits that were received while a resident of Washington. Must record homestead declaration before sale of home if property unimproved or home unoccupied.

Pensions and Retirement Benefits: ERISA-qualified plans. Funds exempt for city employees, volunteer firefighters, state patrol officers and public employees. IRA exemptions for conventional, Roth, education, SEP and SIMPLE plans.

Insurance: Annuity contract proceeds to $250 per month. Group life insurance policy or proceeds. Life insurance proceeds or avails if beneficiary is not the insured. Fraternal society benefits. Disability benefits, proceeds or avails. Fire insurance proceeds for destroyed exemption.

Personal Property: Appliances, furnishings, household goods, home and yard equipment up to $2,700 total. No limit on any property located within Washington if seeking to discharge debt based on failure to pay a state income tax on retirement benefits that were received while a resident of Washington. Burial plot sold by nonprofit cemetery association. Books up to $1,500. Clothing, furs, jewelry and ornaments up to $1,000. Food and fuel for comfortable maintenance. Keepsakes and pictures. Two motor vehicles up to $2,500 total.

Tools of Trade: Farm trucks, stock, tools, seed, equipment and supplies of farmer up to $5,000 total. Library, office furniture, office equipment, and supplies of physician, surgeon, attorney, clergy or other professional up to $5,000 total. Tools and materials used in another's trade up to $5,000.

Miscellaneous: Business partnership property.

Wages: Greater of 30 times federal minimum hourly wage or 75% of debtor's weekly disposable earnings.

Public Benefits: Unemployment benefits. Industrial insurance (workers' compensation). AFDC. Crime victim's compensation. General assistance. Old-age assistance.

Wild Card: $1,000 of any personal property, with a limit of $100 for cash, bank deposits, bonds, stocks and securities.

West Virginia

Homestead: Real or personal property, including co-op, used as residence, up to $15,000.

Pensions and Retirement Benefits: ERISA-qualified plans. Funds exempt for public employees. IRA exemptions for conventional, Roth, SEP and SIMPLE plans. IRAs limited to amounts that are necessary for the support of the debtor and his dependents. *Warning:* No protection for IRAs that are established by an "insider" of the debtor. This provision could eliminate the protection otherwise offered to small business owners by SEP and SIMPLE plans.

Insurance: Life insurance payments from policy of person who supported debtor, needed for support. Unmatured life insurance if debtor owns policy and insured is debtor or person who supports debtor. Group life insurance policy or proceeds. Health or disability benefits. Fraternal society benefits.

Personal Property: Animals, crops, clothing, appliances, books, furnishings, musical instruments up to $200 per item, $1,000 total. Burial plot to $7,500, in lieu homestead. Payment for lost earnings. Motor vehicle up to $1,200. Jewelry up to $500. Personal injury recoveries up to $7,500 (excluding pain and suffering). Wrongful death recoveries needed for support.

Tools of Trade: Tools and implements up to $750.

Miscellaneous: Business partnership property. Alimony. Child support.

Wages: Greater of 80% of wages or 30 times federal minimum hourly wage.

Public Benefits: Unemployment compensation. Workers' compensation. Social Security. Veteran's benefits. Aid to blind, aged and disabled. AFDC. General assistance. Crime victim's compensation.

Wild Card: $800 of any property. Unused portion of homestead or burial exemption for any property.

Wisconsin

Homestead: Property that the debtor occupies or intends to occupy up to $40,000. Sale proceeds exempt for 2 years from sale if debtor plans to obtain another home. Husband and wife may not double.

Pensions and Retirement Benefits: Private or public retirement benefits generally exempt for certain municipal employees; firefighters and police officers who worked in city with population over 100,000; military pensions and public employees. IRA exemptions for conventional, Roth, SEP and SIMPLE plans. IRAs may be limited to amounts that are reasonably necessary for support of debtors and dependents, and are subject to many different types of liens and claims.

Insurance: Life insurance proceeds held in trust by insurer, if clause prohibits proceeds from being used to pay beneficiary's creditors. Life insurance policy or proceeds up to $5,000, if beneficiary is a married woman. Life insurance proceeds if beneficiary was a dependent of the insured, needed for support. Unmatured life insurance contract, except credit insurance contract, owned by debtor and insuring debtor, dependent of debtor or someone debtor is dependent on. Unmatured life insurance contract's accrued dividends, interest or loan value, up to $4,000 total in all contracts, if debtor owns contract and insured is debtor, dependent of debtor or someone debtor is dependent on. Fraternal society benefits. Federal disability benefits. Fire proceeds for destroyed exempt property for 2 years from receiving.

Personal Property: Deposit accounts up to $1,000. Burial provisions. Health aids. Household goods and furnishings, clothing, keepsakes, jewelry, appliances, books, musical instruments, firearms, sporting goods, animals and other tangible property held for personal, family or household use up to $5,000 total. Lost future earnings recoveries, needed for support. Motor vehicles up to $1,200.

Tools of Trade: Tools, equipment, inventory, farm products and professional books up to $7,500.

Miscellaneous: Business partnership property. Alimony. Child support needed for support.

Wages: Greater of 75% of wages earned but unpaid, or excess over 30 times the greater of state or federal minimum wage.

Public Benefits: Unemployment benefits. Workers' compensation. Veteran's benefits. AFDC and other social services payments.

Wild Card: None.

Wyoming

Homestead: Real property occupied by the debtor up to $10,000 or house trailer occupied by the debtor up to $6,000. Joint owners may double. Spouse or child of deceased owner may claim homestead exemption. Property held as tenancy by the entirety may be exempt against debts owed by only one spouse.

Pensions and Retirement Benefits: Private and public retirement funds and accounts for criminal investigators, highway officers, county employees, firefighters, police officers, public employees and game and fish wardens. For firefighters and police officers, limited to payments being received. No clear protection for IRAs.

Insurance: Annuity contract proceeds to $500 per month. Group life or disability policy or proceeds. Life insurance proceeds if clause prohibits proceeds from being used to pay beneficiary's creditors. Fraternal society benefits.

Personal Property: Bedding, furniture, household articles and food up to $2,000 per person in the home. Bible. Schoolbooks and pictures. Burial plot. Clothing and wedding rings needed, up to $1,000. Pre-paid funeral contracts. Motor vehicle to $2,000.

Tools of Trade: Library and implements of professional up to $2,000, or tools, motor vehicle, implements, team and stock in trade up to $2,000.

Miscellaneous: Business partnership property.

Wages: Greater of 75% of weekly disposable earnings or 30 times federal minimum wage. Earnings of National Guard members, and wages of inmates on work release.

Public Benefits: Unemployment compensation. Workers' compensation. AFDC. General assistance. Crime victims compensation.

Wild Card: None.

Federal, State and Private Resources

This appendix lists many of the governmental resources and private-sector businesses that can help you when setting up your business to maximize asset protection. From forming your business entity to searching for liens, from doing legal and business research to investigating unfair trade, from finding financing information to bankruptcy and estate planning, these agencies and companies may make your task easier.

BUSINESS ENTITIES AND UCC FILINGS

Typically, articles of organization, which create business entities, and foreign registrations are filed with a division of a state's secretary of state's office. A few states use a separate office for these purposes. An efficient means of locating the appropriate office is through the online source, "Corporate Housekeeper Links to Secretary of State Sites," at http://www.danvi.vi/link2.html. The appropriate office also may be located through the "Blue Pages" of a local telephone directory.

UCC financing statements, which are used to perfect liens (see Chapter 9), also typically are filed with a state's secretary of state's office. Many offices today also allow for users to search online on their web sites for existing UCC liens.

Because it often is desirable to create a business entity in Delaware or Nevada, contact information for these states also appears below:

Delaware Secretary of State Division of Corporations

Web Address
http://www.state.de.us/corp/index.htm

Mailing Addresses
State of Delaware
Division of Corporations
401 Federal Street, Suite 4
Dover, Delaware 19901

State of Delaware
Division of Corporations
P.O. Box 898
Dover, Delaware 19903

Information on contacting Delaware Registered Agents
http://www.state.de.us/corp/agents/agt2.htm

Telephone Numbers
GENERAL INFORMATION (302) 739-3073 — For general information concerning any aspect of the incorporation process or approximate filing fees via an automated touch-tone information system.

NAME RESERVATION (900) 420-8042 or (900) 555-2677 — A fee of $10 will appear on your telephone bill. A corporate name may be reserved by telephone for **30** days. You may reserve up to 3 names per call.

CORPORATE STATUS (900) 555-CORP — A fee of $10 will appear on your telephone bill. Limit 2 corporations per call. This call will provide the verbal status (i.e. good standing, dissolved, etc.) for a Delaware corporation.

SPECIAL SERVICES (302) 739-3073 — To find out more about Priority One, same-day or 24-hour services, as well as the costs involved.

UNIFORM COMMERCIAL CODE (302) 739-3073 — For information on UCC liens. This number provides fees and addresses for state filings and the address for county filings.

FRANCHISE TAX /BANKRUPTCY (302) 739-3073 — For help in figuring franchise tax, preparing the annual report, and determining any taxes owed before dissolution.

FAX SERVICE (Depository Account or Visa, Mastercard or Discover Card required): CORPORATIONS/UCC FAX (302) 739-3812; FRANCHISE TAX/BANKRUPTCY FAX (302) 739-5831.

Nevada Secretary of State Commercial Recording Division

Web Address
http://sos.state.nv.us/comm_rec/index.htm

Mailing Address, Telephone Numbers and e-mail
Secretary of State - Annex Office
202 N. Carson Street
Carson City, NV 89701-4271
Telephone: (775) 684-5708
Fax: (775) 684-5725 for Commercial Recording, New Filings,
Amendments and Status
email: sosmail@govmail.state.nv.us

State of Nevada
Secretary of State
Corporate Satellite Office
555 E. Washington Avenue, Suite 2900
Las Vegas, NV 89101
Telephone: (702) 486-2880
Fax: (702) 486-2888

Information on contacting Nevada Registered Agents
http://sos.state.nv.us/comm_rec/ralist/index.htm

Document on demand system
(800) 583-9486

LEGAL AND BUSINESS RESEARCH

Legal and business research is most efficiently done on the Internet.

CCH Business Owner's Toolkit™ (http://www.toolkit.cch.com) is an excellent site that covers many of the legal and financial issues involved in forming, operating and dissolving a business entity.

FindLaw.com (http://www.findlaw.com) is an excellent resource for the legal researcher. Among other things, this site contains links to state and federal statutes. Before forming a business entity in a particular state, it always is wise to read that state's statute governing the particular type of entity. State statutes also provide state post-judgment asset exemptions. Because these laws change, when issues concerning exemptions arise, the appropriate state's asset exemption statute should be examined for the latest version of the state's exemption schedule. The appropriate state statutes, in each of these cases, can be accessed through this site.

Local or State Law Libraries are useful for researching state and federal statutes, as well as other sources of law, such as administrative regulations. Typically, local law libraries are located in courthouses, and are open to the public. A state law library usually can be found in a state's capital. Law school libraries and some public libraries also represent another way to locate the law.

UNFAIR TRADE AND CONSUMER PROTECTION

Small business owners (in addition to consumers) may be the victims of unfair trade practices, which are committed by other small business owners, or larger businesses that have more bargaining power. Getting the government involved on your side can be an effective way of resolving a dispute (see Chapter 15).

The **Federal Trade Commission** (FTC) has an excellent web site (http://www.ftc.gov/ftc/consumer.htm) that provides information on starting and operating a business (including information on franchises), as well as information on filing an online, or paper, complaint with the agency when an unfair trade practice has occurred.

An unfair trade practice is a broad term that encompasses, among other things, fraud, privacy violations, credit reports, debt collection, false or misleading advertising, Internet/electronic commerce, investment fraud, leasing, lending, mail order, telemarketing, advertising and warranties. The FTC also can be reached at the following toll-free number: 1-877-FTC-HELP (382-4357). Its mailing address is: Federal Trade Commission, CRC-240, Washington, D.C. 20580.

State Consumer Protection Departments may be more apt to intervene on your behalf, especially when there are not a lot of complaints against the same party. State Consumer Protection Departments also can provide information on any special licensing, or special consumer contract forms, etc., that may apply to your business. This information may help small business owners avoid *committing* unfair trade practices. One easy way to locate a particular state's Consumer Protection Department is thorough the following web site, which provides links to the appropriate agency in each state: http://www.governmentguide.com/state/agency.adp?type=none.
This information also can be obtained through the "Blue Pages" of a local telephone directory.

FINANCING A BUSINESS

Securities and Exchange Commission (SEC) has a web site (http://www.sec.gov/) with information on federal securities laws, including exemptions. The SEC also maintains an online database, which is termed the EDGAR database, of all filings with the SEC. The SEC also can be contacted at the following toll free number: 1-800-SEC-0330. Each of these resources offers SEC addresses for its headquarters, as well as its many Regional and District Offices.

State Agencies have information concerning state securities laws, including exemptions. This information can be obtained by contacting the state agency in the particular state in question. Links to each state's securities administrator can be found on the Internet at http://www.governmentguide.com/state/agency.adp?type=none. This information also can be obtained through the "Blue Pages" of a local telephone directory.

Small Business Administration (SBA) has a web site (http://www.sba.gov) with information concerning small business formation, financing and counseling, including the location of local offices. You also can contact the SBA at the following toll free number: 1-800-U-ASK-SBA (827-5722).

National Venture Capital Association web site (http://www.nvca.com) has a wealth of information on venture capital financing. The NVCA also can be contacted at its headquarters: NVCA, 1655 North Fort Myer Drive, Suite 850, Arlington, Virginia 22209. Phone (703) 524-2549. Fax (703) 524-3940.

BANKRUPTCY REFORM AND EXEMPTION PLANNING

The **American Bankruptcy Institute** web site (http://www.abiworld.org) is the premier site for bankruptcy information. This site contains continual updates on the status of federal bankruptcy legislation. It is an excellent source that can be used to check on the future of bankruptcy reform legislation that is before the Congress. The site also provides a research library, including access to information and court cases concerning pre-bankruptcy exemption planning and other bankruptcy issues.

Sample Articles of Organization

(For an LLC or Statutory Close Corporation in Delaware or Nevada)

As the founding document for a business entity, articles of organization, by their nature, have serious legal consequences. For example, if there is a conflict between an entity's articles of organization and the entity's operating agreement, in many states the operating agreement, to the extent of the conflict, will be deemed invalid.

Further, to be effective, certain provisions (e.g., waiver of a board of directors for a statutory close corporation) must be stated in the articles of organization. A provision in the operating agreement alone would be ineffective. Accordingly, these forms should not be used except with the advice of an attorney.

Actual state forms for articles of organization can be obtained from the state's secretary of state's office. Secretary of state's offices typically allow the downloading of the forms directly from their web sites. They also will mail forms upon request. In particular, it may be advisable to use the actual official Nevada forms, or verify with the state that facsimiles of the official forms are acceptable, as the official forms are organized in a distinct table format.

State of Delaware
Limited Liability Company Certificate of Formation

First: *The name of the limited liability company is* _____

Second: *The address of its registered office in the State of Delaware is* _____

_____ *in the City of* _____ *The*

name of its Registered agent at such address is _____

Third: (Use this paragraph only if the company is to have a specific effective date of dissolution.)
The latest date on which the limited liability company is to dissolve is _____

Fourth: (Insert any other mailers the members determine to include herein.) _____

_____

In Witness Whereof, the undersigned have executed this Certificate of Formation of

_____ *this* _____ *day of* _____ *20__*

BY: _____

Authorized Person(s)

Type or Print NAME: _____

Note that in the following form, paragraph nine (waiver of a board of directors) does not appear as a standard clause in the state form. It is optional, but recommended, as it allows the statutory close corporation to be operated by way of a shareholder agreement (i.e., an operating agreement) in the same way that an LLC is operated. This addition simplifies the operation of the business and thus reduces the overall exposure of the owners to liability, especially in terms of piercing of the veil of limited liability.

State of Delaware Certificate of Incorporation
A Close Corporation Of _____

First: The name of this Corporation is _____.

Second: Its Registered Office in the State of Delaware is to be located at _____ Street, in the City of _____, County of _____, Zip Code _____. The registered agent in charge thereof is _____.

Third: The nature of business and the objects and purposes proposed to be transacted, promoted and carried on, are to engage in any lawful act of activity for which corporations may be organized under the General Corporation Law of Delaware.

Fourth: The amount of the total authorized capital stock of this corporation is _____Dollars ($____) divided into _____ shares of_____ Dollars ($_____) each.

Fifth: The name and mailing address of the incorporators are as follows:
Name _____
Mailing Address _____ Zip Code _____

Sixth: All of the corporation's issued stock, exclusive of treasury shares, shall be held of record by not more than thirty (30) persons.

Seventh: All of the issued stock of all classes shall be subject to one or more of the restrictions on transfer permitted by Section 202 of the General Corporation Law.

Eighth: The corporation shall make no offering of any of its stock of any class which would constitute a "public offering" within the meaning of the United States Securities Act of 1933, as it may be amended from time to time.

Ninth: There shall be no board of directors. The business of the corporation shall be managed by the stockholders, rather than by a board of directors. The stockholders may form a written agreement to regulate all phase of affairs of the corporation, including but not limited to the management of the business, or the declaration and payment of dividends or other division of profits, or the election of officers, or the employment of stockholders by the corporation, or the arbitration of disputes.

I, The Undersigned, for the purpose of forming a corporation under the laws of the State of Delaware, do make, file and record this Certificate, and do certify that the facts herein stated are true, and I have accordingly hereunto set my hand this day of_____-_____, A.D. 20 ___

BY: _____
(incorporator)

NAME: _____
(Type or Print)

Secretary of State
101 North Carson Street, Suite 3
Carson City, Nevada 89701-4786
(775) 684-5708

Limited Liability Company Articles of Organization
(Pursuant to NRS 86)

1. *Name of Limited Liability Company:* _____

2. *Resident Agent Name and Street Address:* _____

_____

3. *Dissolution Date: (if existence is not perpetual)* _____

4. *Management: Company shall be managed by* _____ *Manager(s) OR* _____ *Members*
Names and Addresses of Manager(s) or Members:

_____
_____
_____
_____

5. *Other Matters: Number of additional pages attached:* _____

6. *Names, Addresses and Signatures of Organizer(s):*

_____
_____
_____
_____

7. *Certificate of Acceptance of Appointment of Resident Agent:*
I, _____ *hereby accept appointment*
as Resident Agent for the above named limited liability company.

_____
Signature of Resident Agent

_____
Date

Note that, in the Nevada form (in contrast to the Delaware form) for a statutory close corporation, a waiver of a board of directors appears as an option in the state's standard form.

Secretary of State
101 North Carson Street, Suite 3
Carson City, Nevada 89701-4786
(775) 684-5708

Close Corporation Articles of Incorporation
(Pursuant to NRS 78A)

1. Name of Corporation: _____

2. Resident Agent Name and Street Address: _____
_____

3. Shares (number of shares corporation authorized to issue): _____
Number of shares with par value_____ Par Value _____
Number of shares without par value_____

4. Governing Board: This corporation is a close corporation operating with a board of directors
_____yes _____no

Names, Addresses and Number of Board of Directors:

The First Board of Directors shall consist of _____members whose names and addresses are as follows:

_____
_____
_____
_____

5. Purpose: (Optional)

6. Other Matters: Number of additional pages attached:_____

7. Names, Addresses and Signatures of Incorporator(s):

_____
_____
_____
_____

8. Certificate of Acceptance of Appointment of Resident Agent:

I, _____ hereby accept appointment as Resident Agent for the above named limited liability company.

_____

Signature of Resident Agent

_____

Date

Sample Operating Agreement for a Delaware LLC

This Sample Operating Agreement incorporates many of the asset protection concepts presented throughout this book. It provides for the issuance of voting capital and allows for the issuance of nonvoting capital. Using nonvoting capital can be a major component in a popular estate planning, and thus asset protection, strategy: i.e., the family LLC (see Chapter 10). The Sample Agreement provides that members who hold only nonvoting capital have no right to vote as members or to participate as managers. This eliminates control issues involving junior family members, and also should increase the estate tax savings that result from discounting of the other family member's interests.

The Sample Agreement provides that the voting members also manage the LLC. This eliminates questions of authority between members and managers, and the potential that transactions may be authorized by the wrong group, and thus unauthorized. The Sample Agreement does not provide for regular meetings, but instead allows the voting members to act informally in managing the business.

Flexibility is built into the document elsewhere. For example, the Sample Agreement allows for the voting members to appoint officers to manage the business, but allows the voting members to control these issues outside of the agreement. This arrangement also means that the LLC can be managed in a more dynamic way, without the need to continually amend the operating agreement. All of these strategies also should significantly reduce the potential for a piercing of the veil of limited liability, i.e., a loss of limited liability (see Chapter 16).

The Sample Agreement also provides for mediation and arbitration of disputes, and for reimbursement of attorney's fees and related costs to the prevailing party, as ways of controlling the court system (see Chapter 17). The Sample Agreement also incorporates buy/sell provisions, which control a member's resignation, retirement or transfer of an interest. A member may voluntarily withdraw, but only after one year. This provision achieves security for the business. During the second year, only book value is paid to the withdrawing member. This strategy eliminates the costs and potential disputes associated with determining fair market value of an interest.

Finally, of course, this Sample Agreement is based on one of the most effective, and basic, asset protection strategies, one in which the owners can achieve protection of their personal assets from the claims of the business's creditors, and protection of their business entity's assets from the claims of their personal creditors (i.e., the formation of an LLC through which the business will be operated).

Warning

Extreme caution should be exercised before this Sample Agreement is adopted for actual use. This Sample Agreement is based on the formation of the LLC in Delaware. Certain features, such as the elimination of voting rights for nonvoting members, may not be permissible in all states. Moreover, the Sample Agreement generally requires the unanimous approval of the voting members. This is especially appropriate in small businesses (e.g., a two or three voting member LLC) to prevent the vote of one voting member from being effectively eliminated. However, a majority (greater than 50%) or supermajority (at least 67%) vote may be more appropriate in a larger LLC. Paragraph 6.4, which governs involuntary transfers, may only be appropriate in a family LLC.

Many other options also exist. For example, the Sample Agreement provides that voting rights are proportional to the ownership interests in voting capital. It might be desirable, in certain cases, to provide that voting rights are per capita (one vote per voting member), as exists in a general partnership. In addition, relative ownership interests are defined in the Sample Agreement by way of a formula and are identified in an attached schedule. This practice is standard in all partnership and most LLC agreements. Alternatively, the Sample Agreement could be modified so that interests are represented by "shares," as is the case in a corporation. This alternative is simpler, but could introduce the possibility of fractional shares. It may be more appropriate where only cash is contributed by each member.

Similarly, while the Sample Agreement allows for the voluntary withdrawal of a member after one year (subject to the buy/sell provisions), the Sample Agreement could be drafted to provide that a voluntary withdrawal of the member is a violation in any year.

It also is possible to adapt this Sample Operating Agreement so that it can serve as a shareholder operating agreement for a statutory close corporation. However, all of the aforementioned decisions require professional guidance. This Sample Operating Agreement should not be used before an attorney reviews it and adapts it to the particular circumstances of the business and the owner.

Sample Operating Agreement For _____ , LLC

A Delaware Limited Liability Company

This Operating Agreement (the "Agreement") is made effective as of _____ , by and among and those Persons (the "Members") identified in Exhibit A.

In consideration of the mutual covenants and conditions herein, the Members agree as follows:

ARTICLE I

ORGANIZATION

1.1 Formation and Qualification. The Members have formed a limited liability company (the "Company") under the Delaware Limited Liability Company Act (currently Chapter 18 of Title 6 of the Delaware Code)(the "Act")by filing Articles of Organization with the Delaware Secretary of State.

1.2 Governing Law. This Agreement shall be governed by and construed and interpreted in accordance with the laws of the State of Delaware, including the Delaware Limited Liability Company Act, (the "Act") as amended from time to time, without regard to Delaware's conflicts of laws principles. The rights and liabilities of the Members shall be determined pursuant to the Act and this Agreement. To the extent that any provision of this Agreement is inconsistent with any provision of the Act, this Agreement shall govern to the extent permitted by the Act.

1.3 Name. The name of the Company shall be "_____ , LLC." The business of the Company may be conducted under that name or, on compliance with applicable laws, any other name that the Voting Members deem appropriate or advisable. The Voting Members on behalf of the Company shall file any certificates, articles, fictitious business name statements and the like, and any amendments and supplements thereto, as the Voting Members consider appropriate or advisable.

1.4 Term. The term of the Company commenced on the filing of the Articles of Organization and shall be perpetual unless dissolved as provided in this Agreement.

1.5 Office and Agent. The principal office of the Company shall be at such place or places of business within or without the State of Delaware as the Voting Members may determine. The Company shall continuously maintain a registered agent in the State of Delaware as required by the Act. The registered agent shall be as stated in the Certificate or as otherwise determined by the Voting Members.

1.6 Purpose of Company. The purpose of the Company is to engage in all lawful activities, including, but not limited to the following activities:

_____

_____

_____

ARTICLE II

MEMBERSHIP INTERTESTS, VOTING AND MANAGEMENT

Section 2.1 Initial Members. The initial Members of the Company are the Members who are identified in Exhibit A.

Section 2.2 Classification of Membership Interests. The Company shall issue Class A Voting Capital ("Voting Capital"), to the Voting Members (the "Voting Members"). The Voting Members shall have the right to vote upon all matters upon which Members have the right to vote under the Act or under this Agreement, in proportion to their respective Percentage Voting Interest ("Percentage Voting Interest") in the Company. The Percentage Voting Interest of a Voting Member shall be the percentage that is derived when the Member's Voting Capital account is divided by the total of all of the Voting Capital accounts.

The Company may issue Class B, Nonvoting Capital ("Nonvoting Capital"). Members may own interests in both Voting Capital and Nonvoting Capital. Members who own interests only in Nonvoting Capital ("Nonvoting Members") shall have no right to vote upon any matters. Notwithstanding, to the extent otherwise permitted by this agreement, a Nonvoting Member shall have the right to file or participate in a mediation or an arbitration action, and shall be bound by an amendment to this agreement only if he signs such amendment.

Section 2.3 Percentage Ownership and Voting Interests. A Member's Ownership Interest ("Ownership Interest") is the total of his interests in Voting Capital and Nonvoting Capital, together with all of the rights, as a Member or Manager of the Company, that arise from such interests. The Percentage Ownership Interest ("Percentage Ownership Interest") of a Member shall be calculated by adding together that Member's Voting Capital Account and Nonvoting Capital Account, and then dividing this sum by the total of all of the Member's Voting Capital and Nonvoting Capital Accounts.

The Members shall have the initial Ownership, Percentage Ownership and Percentage Voting Interests in the Company that are identified in Exhibit A, immediately following the making of the capital contributions set forth therein.

Section 2.4 Management by Voting Members. The Voting Members shall manage the Company and shall have the right to vote, in their capacity as Managers, upon all matters upon which Managers have the right to vote under the Act or under this Agreement, in proportion to their respective Percentage Voting Interests in the Company. Voting Members need not identify whether they are acting in their capacity as Members or Managers when they act.

The Nonvoting Members shall have no right to vote or otherwise participate in the management of the Company. No Nonvoting Member shall, without the prior written consent of all of the Voting Members, take any action on behalf of, or in the name of, the Company, or enter into any contract, agreement, commitment or obligation binding upon the Company, or perform any act in any way relating to the Company or the Company's assets.

Section 2.5 Voting. Except as otherwise provided or permitted by this Agreement, Voting Members shall in all cases, in their capacity as Members or Managers of the Company, act collectively, and, unless otherwise specified or permitted by this Agreement, unanimously. Except as otherwise provided or permitted by this Agreement, no Voting Member acting individually, in his capacity as a Member or Manager of the Company, shall have any power or authority to sign for, bind or act on behalf of the Company in any way, to pledge the Company's credit, or to render the Company liable for any purpose.

Unless the context requires otherwise, in this Agreement, the terms "Member" or "Members," without the qualifiers "Voting" or "Nonvoting," refer to the Voting and Nonvoting Members collectively; and the terms "Manager" or "Managers" refers to the Voting Members.

Section 2.6 Liability of Members. All debts, obligations and liabilities of the Company, whether arising in contract, tort or otherwise, shall be solely the debts, obligations and liabilities of the Company, and no Member shall be obligated personally for any such debt, obligation or liability of the Company solely by reason of being a Member.

Section 2.7 New Members. The Voting Members may issue additional Voting Capital or Nonvoting Capital and thereby admit a new Member or Members, as the case may be, to the Company, only if such new Member (i) is approved unanimously by the Voting Members; (ii) delivers to the Company his required capital contribution; (iii) agrees in writing to be bound by the terms of this Agreement by becoming a party hereto; and (iv) delivers such additional documentation as the Voting Members shall reasonably require to so admit such new Member to the Company.

Upon the admission of a new Member or Members, as the case may be, to the Company, the capital accounts of Members, and the calculations that are based on the capital accounts, shall be adjusted appropriately.

ARTICLE III

CAPITAL ACCOUNTS

3.1 Initial Capital Contributions. Each original Member to this Agreement shall make an initial Capital Contribution to the Company in accordance with Exhibit A, at the time of each Member's execution of this Agreement.

3.2 Capital Accounts. A separate capital account shall be maintained for each Member's ownership interest in Class A Voting Capital (the "Voting Capital Account") and Class B Nonvoting Capital (the "Nonvoting Capital Account").

The capital account of each Member shall be increased by (i) the amount of any cash and the fair market value of any property contributed to the Company by such Member (net of any liability secured by such contributed property that the Company is considered to assume or take subject to), (ii) the amount of income or profits allocated to such Member.

The capital account or accounts of each Member shall be reduced by (i) the amount of any cash and the fair market value of any property distributed to the Member by the Company (net of liabilities secured by such distributed property that the Member is considered to assume or take subject to) on account of his Ownership Interest, (ii) the amount of expenses or loss allocated to the Member. If any property other than cash is distributed to a Member, the Capital Accounts of the Members shall be adjusted as if the property had instead been sold by the Company for a price equal to its fair market value and the proceeds distributed.

Guaranteed Payments ("Guaranteed Payments") for salary, wages, fees, payments on loans, rents, etc., may be made to the Members. Guaranteed Payments shall not be deemed to be distributions to the Members on account of their Ownership Interests, and shall not be charged to the Members' capital accounts.

No Member shall be obligated to restore any negative balance in his Capital Account. No Member shall be compensated for any positive balance in his Capital Account except as otherwise expressly provided herein. The foregoing provisions and the other provisions of this Agreement relating to the maintenance of Capital Accounts are intended to comply with the provisions of Regulations Section 1.704-1(b)(2) and shall be interpreted and applied in a manner consistent with such Regulations. The Members agree that the initial Capital Accounts of the Members on the date hereof are as set forth in Exhibit A.

3.3 Additional Contributions. If, at any time or times hereafter, the Voting Members shall determine that additional capital is required by the Company, the Voting Members shall determine the amount of such additional capital and the anticipated time such additional capital will be required; whether such additional capital shall be provided by the Members by way of additional Capital Contributions or by way of loans from Members; whether additional Capital Contributions, if any, shall be of in the form of Class A Voting Capital or Class B Nonvoting Capital. No Member shall be obligated, at any time, to guarantee or otherwise assume or become liable for any obligations of the Company or to make any additional Capital Contributions advances or loans to the Company, unless such obligations are specifically accepted and agreed to by such Member.

In the event that additional Class A Voting Capital is to be issued, the Voting Members who exist immediately prior to such issuance shall be provided written notice of this intent, and shall be offered in such notice the opportunity to make additional capital contributions in Class A Voting Capital in proportion to their respective Percentage Voting Interests; provided that this right, if not exercised within ninety (90) days after such notice is received, shall expire automatically, unless this period is extended by the Voting Members. Any loans or additional capital contributions shall be voluntary.

The capital accounts of the Members, and the calculations that are based on the capital accounts, shall be adjusted appropriately to reflect any transfer of an interest in the Company, distributions, or additional capital contributions.

ARTICLE IV

MANNER OF ACTING

4.1 Officers and Agents of the Company. The Voting Members may authorize any Member or Members of the Company, or other individuals or entities, whether or not a Member, to take action on behalf of the Company, as the Voting Members deem appropriate. Any Member may lend money to and receive loans from the Company, act as an employee, independent contractor, lessee, lessor, or surety of the company, and transact any business with the Company that could be carried out by someone who is not a Member; and the Company may receive from or pay to any Member remuneration, in the form of wages, salary, fees, rent, interest, or any form that the Voting Members deem appropriate.

The Voting Members may appoint officers of the Company who, to the extent provided by the Voting Members, may have and may exercise all the powers and authority of the Members or Managers in the conduct of the business and affairs of the Company. The officers of the Company may consist of a President, a Treasurer, a Secretary, or other officers or agents as may be elected or appointed by the Voting Members. The Voting Members may provide rules for the appointment, removal, supervision and compensation of such officers, the scope of their authority, and any other matters relevant to the positions. The officers shall act in the name of the Company and shall supervise its operation, within the scope of their authority, under the direction and management of the Voting Members.

Any action taken by a duly authorized officer, pursuant to authority granted by the Voting Members in accordance with this Agreement, shall constitute the act of and serve to bind the Company, and each Member hereby agrees neither to dispute such action nor the obligation of the Company created thereby.

4.2 Meetings of Voting Members. No regular, annual, special or other meetings of Voting Members are required to be held. Any action that may be taken at a meeting of Voting Members may be taken without a meeting by written consent in accordance with the Act. Meetings of the Voting Members, for any purpose or purposes, may be called at any time by a majority of the Voting Members, or by the President of the Company, if any. The Voting Members may designate any place as the place of meeting for any meeting of the Voting Members. If no designation is made, the place of meeting shall be the principal place of business of the Company.

4.3 Notice of Meetings. In the event that a meeting of the Voting Members is called, written notice stating the place, day and hour of the meeting and the purpose or purposes for which the meeting is called shall be delivered not less than five nor more than sixty business days before the date of the meeting unless otherwise provided, either personally or by mail, by or at the direction of the Members calling the meeting, to each Voting Member. Notice of a meeting need not be given to any Voting Member who signs a waiver of notice or a consent to holding the meeting or an approval of the minutes thereof, whether before or after the meeting, or who attends the meeting without protesting, prior thereto or at its commencement, the lack of notice to such Voting Member.

4.4 Record Date. For the purpose of determining Voting Members entitled to notice of or to vote at any meeting of Voting Members or any adjournment thereof, the date on which notice of the meeting is provided shall be the record date for such determination of the Voting Members. When a determination of Voting Members has been made as provided in this Section, such determination shall apply to any adjournment thereof.

4.5 Quorum. Members holding at least 67% of the Voting Capital in the Company represented in person, by telephonic participation, or by proxy, shall constitute a quorum at any meeting of Voting Members. In the absence of a quorum at any such meeting, a majority of the Voting Members so represented may adjourn the meeting from time to time for a period not to exceed sixty days without further notice. However, if the adjournment is for more than sixty days, or if after the adjournment a new record date is fixed for another meeting, a notice of the adjourned meeting shall be given to each Voting Member. The Voting Members present at a duly organized meeting may continue to transact business only as previously provided on the agenda until adjournment, notwithstanding the withdrawal during such meeting of that number of Voting Members whose absence would cause less than a quorum.

4.6 Voting. If a quorum is present, a unanimous vote of the Voting Members so represented shall be the act of the Members or Managers, unless the vote of a lesser proportion or number is otherwise required by the Act, by the Certificate or by this Agreement.

ARTICLE V

ALLOCATIONS AND DISTRIBUTIONS

5.1 Allocations of Profits and Losses. Profits and Losses, after deducting Guaranteed Payments, shall be allocated among the Members in proportion to their Percentage Ownership Interests. Any special allocations necessary to comply with the requirements set forth in Internal Revenue Code Section 704 and the corresponding Regulations, including, without limitation, the qualified income offset and minimum gain chargeback provisions contained therein, shall be made if the Voting Members deem these actions to be appropriate.

5.2 Distributions. Subject to applicable law and any limitations elsewhere in this Agreement, the Voting Members shall determine the amount and timing of all distributions of cash, or other assets, by the Company. Except as otherwise provided in this Agreement, all distributions shall be made to all of the Members, in proportion to their Percentage Ownership Interests. Except as otherwise provided in this Agreement, the decision as to whether to make distributions shall be within the sole discretion of the Voting Members.

All such distributions shall be made only to the Members who, according to the books and records of the Company, are the holders of record on the actual date of distribution. The Voting Members may base a determination that a distribution of cash may be made on a balance sheet, profit and loss statement, cash flow statement of the Company or other relevant information. Neither the Company nor the Members shall incur any liability for making distributions.

5.3 Form of Distribution. No Member has the right to demand and receive any distribution from the Company in any form other than money. No Member may be compelled to accept from the Company a distribution of any asset in kind in lieu of a proportionate distribution of money being made to other Members except on the dissolution and winding up of the Company.

ARTICLE VI

TRANSFER AND ASSIGNMENT OF INTERESTS

6.1 Resignation of Membership and Return of Capital. For a period of one (1) year after the Articles of Organization for the Company are filed ("the filing"), no Member may voluntarily resign his membership in the Company, and no Member shall be entitled to any return of capital from the company, except upon the written consent of all of the other Voting Members. During the second year after the filing, a Member may voluntarily resign his membership, but such Member shall be entitled to receive from the Company only the book value of his Ownership Interest, adjusted for profits and losses to the date of resignation, unless otherwise agreed by written consent of all of the other Voting Members. Subsequent to the second year after filing, a Member may voluntarily resign his membership and shall be entitled to receive from the Company the fair market value of his Ownership Interest, adjusted for profits and losses to the date of resignation. Fair market value may be determined informally by unanimous agreement of all of the Voting Members, including the resigning Member. In the absence of an informal agreement as to fair market value, the Voting Members shall hire an appraiser to determine fair market value. The cost of any appraisal shall be deducted from the fair market value to which the resigning Member is entitled. The other Voting Members may elect, by written notice that is provided to the resigning Member within thirty (30) days after the resignation date, for the Company to purchase the resigning Member's Interest (whether the interest is being purchased at book value or fair market value) in four (4) equal annual installments, with the first installment being due sixty (60) days after the Member's resignation.

6.2 Death of a Member. Upon the death of a Member, the Member's estate or beneficiary or beneficiaries, as the case may be, shall be entitled to receive from the Company, in exchange for all of the deceased Member's Ownership Interest, the fair market value of the deceased Member's Ownership Interest, adjusted for profits and losses to the date of death. Fair market value may be determined informally by a unanimous good-faith agreement of all of the Voting Members. In the absence of an informal agreement as to fair market value, the Voting Members shall hire an appraiser to determine fair market value. The cost of any appraisal shall be deducted from the fair market value to which the deceased Member's estate or beneficiary or beneficiaries is or are entitled. The Voting Members may elect, by written notice that is provided to the deceased Member's estate or beneficiary or beneficiaries, within thirty (30) days after the Member's death, to purchase the deceased Member's Ownership Interest over a one-year (1 year) period, in four (4) equal installments, with the first installment being due sixty (60) days after the Member's date of death. Unless otherwise agreed unanimously by the Voting Members, prior to the completion of such purchase, the Member's estate or beneficiary or beneficiaries, shall have no right to become a Member or to participate in the management of the business and affairs of the Company as a Member or Manager, and shall only have the rights of an Assignee and be entitled only to receive the share of profits and the return of capital to which the deceased Member would otherwise have been entitled. The Company, or the other Voting Members, in its or their discretion, may purchase insurance on the lives of any of the Members, with the company or the purchasing Member named as the beneficiary, as the purchaser may decide, and use all or any of the proceeds from such insurance as a source of proceeds from which the deceased Member's Membership Ownership Interest may be purchased by the Company.

6.3 Restrictions on Transfer. Except (i) as otherwise provided in this Article or (ii) upon the unanimous consent of all of the other Voting Members, no Member shall sell, hypothecate, pledge, assign or otherwise transfer, with or without consideration, any part or all of his Ownership Interest in the Company to any other person or entity (a "Transferee"), without first offering (the "Offer") that portion of his or her Ownership Interest in the Company subject to the contemplated transfer (the "Offered Interest") first to the Company, and secondly, to the other Voting Members, at the purchase price (hereinafter referred to as the "Transfer Purchase Price") and in the manner as prescribed in the Offer.

The Offering Member shall make the Offer first to the Company by written notice (hereinafter referred to as the "Offering Notice"). Within twenty (20) days (the "Company Offer Period") after receipt by the Company of the Offering Notice, the Company shall notify the Offering Member in writing (the "Company Notice"), whether or not the Company shall accept the Offer and shall purchase all but not less than all of the Offered Interest. If the Company accepts the Offer to purchase the Offered Interest, the Company Notice shall fix a closing date not more than twenty-five (25) days (the "Company Closing Date") after the expiration of the Company Offer Period.

In the event the Company decides not to accept the Offer, the Offering Member or the Company, at his or her or its election, shall, by written notice (the "Remaining Member Notice") given within that period (the "Member Offer Period") terminating ten (10) days after the expiration of the Company Offer Period, make the Offer of the Offered Interest to the other Voting Members, each of whom shall then have a period of twenty-five (25) days (the "Member Acceptance Period") after the expiration of the Member Offer Period within which to notify in writing the Offering Member whether or not he or she intends to purchase all but not less than all of the Offered Interest. If two (2) or more Voting Members of the Company desire to accept the Offer to purchase the Offered Interest, then, in the absence of an agreement between them, such Voting Members shall have the right to purchase the Offered Interest in proportion to their respective Percentage Voting Interests. If the other Voting Members intend to accept the Offer and to purchase the Offered Interest, the written notice required to be given by them shall fix a closing date not more than sixty (60) days after the expiration of the Member Acceptance Period (hereinafter referred to as the "Member Closing Date").

The aggregate dollar amount of the Transfer Purchase Price shall be payable in cash on the Company Closing Date or on the Member Closing Date, as the case may be, unless the Company or the purchasing Voting Members shall elect by written notice that is delivered to the Offering Member, prior to or on the Company Closing Date or the Member Closing Date, as the case may be, to purchase such Offered Interest in four (4) equal annual installments, with the first installment being due on the Closing Date.

If the Company or the other Voting Members fail to accept the Offer or, if the Offer is accepted by the Company or the other Voting Members and the Company or the other Voting Members fail to purchase all of the Offered Interest at the Transfer Purchase Price within the time and in the manner specified, then the Offering Member shall be free, for a period (hereinafter referred to as the "Free Transfer Period") of sixty (60) days from the occurrence of such failure, to transfer the Offered Interest to a Transferee; provided, however, that if all of the other Voting Members other than the Offering Member do not approve of the proposed transfer by unanimous written consent, the Transferee of the Offered Interest shall have no right to become a Member or to participate in the management of the business and affairs of the Company as a Member or Manager, and shall only have the rights of an Assignee and be entitled to receive the share of profits and the return of capital to which the Offering Member would otherwise have been entitled. A Transferee shall be admitted as a Member of the Company , and as a result of which he or she shall become a substituted Member, with the rights that are consistent with the Membership Interest that was transferred, only if such new Member (i) is approved unanimously by the Voting Members; (ii) delivers to the Company his required capital contribution; (iii) agrees in writing to be bound by the terms of this Agreement by becoming a party hereto.

If the Offering Member shall not transfer the Offered Interest within the Free Transfer Period, his or her right to transfer the Offered Interest free of the foregoing restrictions shall thereupon cease and terminate.

6.4 Involuntary Transfer of a Membership Interest. A creditor's charging order or lien on a Member's Membership Interest, bankruptcy of a Member, or other involuntary transfer of Member's Membership Interest, shall constitute a material breach of this Agreement by such Member. The creditor, transferee or other claimant, shall only have the rights of an Assignee, and shall have no right to become a Member, or to participate in the management of the business and affairs of the Company as a Member or Manager under any circumstances, and shall be entitled only to receive the share of profits and losses, and the return of capital, to which the Member would otherwise have been entitled. The Voting Members, including a Voting Member whose interest is the subject of the charging order, lien, bankruptcy, or involuntary transfer, may unanimously elect, by written notice that is provided to the creditor, transferee or other claimant, at any time, to purchase all or any part of Membership Interest that was the subject of the creditor's charging order, lien, bankruptcy, or other involuntary transfer, at a price that is equal to one-half (1/2) of the book value of such interest, adjusted for profits and losses to the date of purchase. The Members agree that such valuation is a good-faith attempt at fixing the value of the interest, after taking into account that the interest does not include all of the rights of a Member or Manager, and after deducting damages that are due to the material breach of this Agreement.

ARTICLE VII

ACCOUNTING, RECORDS AND REPORTING

7.1 Books and Records. The Company shall maintain complete and accurate accounts in proper books of all transactions of or on behalf of the Company and shall enter or cause to be entered therein a full and accurate account of all transactions on behalf of the Company. The Company's books and accounting records shall be kept in accordance with such accounting principles (which shall be consistently applied throughout each accounting period) as the Voting Members may determine to be convenient and advisable. The Company shall maintain at its principal office all of the following:

A current list of the full name and last known business or residence address of each Member in the Company set forth in alphabetical order, together with, for each Member, the Class A Voting Capital account and Class B Nonvoting Capital account, including entries to these accounts for contributions and distributions; the Ownership Interest, Percentage Ownership and Voting Interests; a copy of the Certificate and any and all amendments thereto together with executed copies of any powers of attorney pursuant to which the Certificate or any amendments thereto have been executed; copies of the Company's federal, state and local income tax or information returns and reports, if any, for the six most recent taxable years; a copy of this Agreement and any and all amendments hereto together with executed copies of any powers of attorney pursuant to which this Agreement or any amendments thereto have been executed; copies of the financial statements of the Company, if any, for the six most recent Fiscal Years; the Company's books and records as they relate to the internal affairs of the Company for at least the current and past four Fiscal Years; true and full information regarding the status of the business and financial condition of the Company; and true and full information regarding the amount of cash and a description and statement of the agreed value of any other property or services contributed by each Member and which each Member has agreed to contribute in the future, and the date on which each became a Member.

7.2 Each Member has the right, on reasonable request for purposes reasonably related to the interest of the person as a Member or a Manager, to: (a) inspect and copy during normal business hours any of the Company's records described in Section 7.1; and (b) obtain from the Company promptly after their becoming available a copy of the Company's federal, state and local income tax or information returns for each Fiscal Year.

7.3 Accountings. As soon as is reasonably practicable after the close of each Fiscal Year, the Voting Members shall make or cause to be made a full and accurate accounting of the affairs of the Company as of the close of that Fiscal Year and shall prepare or cause to be prepared a balance sheet as of the end of such Fiscal Year, a profit and loss statement for that Fiscal Year and a statement of Members' equity showing the respective Capital Accounts of the Members as of the close of such Fiscal Year and the distributions, if any, to Members during such Fiscal Year, and any other statements and information necessary for a complete and fair presentation of the financial condition of the Company, all of which the Manager shall furnish to each Member. In addition, the Company shall furnish to each Member information regarding the Company necessary for such Member to complete such Member's federal and state income tax returns. The Company shall also furnish a copy of the Company's tax returns to any Member requesting the same. On such accounting being made, profits and losses during such Fiscal Year shall be ascertained and credited or debited, as the case may be, in the books of account of the Company to the respective Members as herein provided.

7.4 Filings. The Voting Members, at Company expense, shall cause the income tax returns for the Company to be prepared and timely filed with the appropriate authorities. The Voting Members, at Company expense, shall also cause to be prepared and timely filed with appropriate federal and state regulatory and administrative bodies amendments to, or restatements of, the Certificate and all reports required to be filed by the Company with those entities under the Act or other then current applicable laws, rules, and regulations. If the Company is required by the Act to execute or file any document and fails, after demand, to do so within a reasonable period of time or refuses to do so, any Member may prepare, execute and file that document with the Delaware Secretary of State.

7.5 Bank Accounts. The Company shall maintain its funds in one or more separate bank accounts in the name of the Company, and shall not permit the funds of the Company to be co-mingled in any fashion with the funds of any other Person.

7.6 Tax Matters Partner. The Voting Members may, in their exclusive discretion, appoint, remove and replace a Tax Matters Partner at any time or times. The Voting Members shall from time to time cause the Company to make such tax elections as they deem to be in the interests of the Company and the Members generally. The Tax Matters Partner, as defined in Internal Revenue Code Section 6231, shall represent the Company (at the Company's expense) in connection with all examinations of the Company's affairs by tax authorities, including resulting judicial and administrative proceedings, and shall expend the Company funds for professional services and costs associated therewith.

ARTICLE VIII

DISSOLUTION AND WINDING UP

8.1 Dissolution. The Company shall be dissolved, its assets shall be disposed of, and its affairs wound up on the first to occur of: the entry of a decree of judicial dissolution pursuant to the Act; or the unanimous approval of the Voting Members.

8.2 Winding Up. On the occurrence of an event specified in Section 8.1, the Company shall continue solely for the purpose of winding up its affairs in an orderly manner, liquidating its assets and satisfying the claims of its creditors. The Voting Members shall be responsible for overseeing the winding up and liquidation of Company, shall take full account of the assets and liabilities of Company, shall cause such assets to be sold or distributed, and shall cause the proceeds therefrom, to the extent sufficient therefor, to be applied and distributed as provided in Section 9.4. The Voting Members shall give written notice of the commencement of winding up by mail to all known creditors and claimants whose addresses appear on the records of the Company. The Members shall be entitled to reasonable compensation for such services.

8.3 Distributions in Kind. Any noncash assets distributed to the Members shall first be valued at their fair market value to determine the profit or loss that would have resulted if such assets were sold for such value. Such profit or loss shall then be allocated pursuant to this Agreement, and the Members' Capital Accounts shall be adjusted to reflect such allocations. The amount distributed and charged against the Capital Account of each Member receiving an interest in a distributed asset shall be the fair market value of such interest (net of any liability secured by such asset that such Member assumes or takes subject to). The fair market value of such asset shall be determined by the Voting Members, or if any Voting Member objects, by an independent appraiser (and any such appraiser must be recognized as an expert in valuing the type of asset involved) selected by a Majority of the Voting Members.

8.4 Order of Payment of Liabilities on Dissolution. After a determination that all known debts and liabilities of the Company in the process of winding up, including, without limitation, debts and liabilities to Members who are creditors of the Company, have been paid or adequately provided for, the remaining assets shall be distributed to the Members in proportion to their positive Capital Account balances, after taking into account profit and loss allocations for the Company's taxable year during which liquidation occurs.

8.5 Adequacy of Payment. The payment of a debt or liability, whether the whereabouts of the creditor is known or unknown, shall have been adequately provided for if payment thereof shall have been assumed or guaranteed in good faith by one or more financially responsible Persons or by the United States government or any agency thereof, and the provision, including the financial responsibility of the Person, was determined in good faith and with reasonable care by the Members to be adequate at the time of any distribution of the assets pursuant to this Section. This Section shall not prescribe the exclusive means of making adequate provision for debts and liabilities.

8.6 Compliance with Regulations. All payments to the Members on the winding up and dissolution of Company shall be strictly in accordance with the positive capital account balance limitation and other requirements of Regulations Section 1.704-1(b)(2)(ii)(d), as the voting Members deem appropriate.

8.7 Limitations on Payments Made in Dissolution. Except as otherwise specifically provided in this Agreement, each Member shall only be entitled to look solely to the assets of the Company for the return of such Member's positive Capital Account balance and shall have no recourse for such Member's Capital Contribution or share of profits (on dissolution or otherwise) against any other Member.

8.8 Certificate of Cancellation. The Voting Members conducting the winding up of the affairs of the Company shall cause to be filed in the office of, and on a form prescribed by the Delaware Secretary of State, a certificate of cancellation of the Certificate on the completion of the winding up of the affairs of the Company.

ARTICLE IX

EXCULPATION AND INDEMNIFICATION

9.1 Exculpation of Members. No Member shall be liable to the Company or to the other Members for damages or otherwise with respect to any actions taken or not taken in good faith and reasonably believed by such Member to be in or not opposed to the best interests of the Company, except to the extent any related loss results from fraud, gross negligence or willful or wanton misconduct on the part of such Member or the material breach of any obligation under this Agreement or of the fiduciary duties owed to the Company or the other Members by such Member.

9.2 Indemnification by Company. The Company shall indemnify, hold harmless and defend the Members, in their capacity as Members, Managers or Officers, from and against any loss, expense, damage or injury suffered or sustained by them by reason of any acts or omissions arising out of their activities on behalf of the Company or in furtherance of the interests of the Company, including but not limited to any judgment, award, settlement, reasonable attorneys' fees and other costs or expenses incurred in connection with the defense of any actual or threatened action, proceeding or claim, if the acts or omissions were not performed or omitted fraudulently or as a result of gross negligence or willful misconduct by the indemnified party. Reasonable expenses incurred by the indemnified party in connection with any such proceeding relating to the foregoing matters may be paid or reimbursed by the Company in advance of the final disposition of such proceeding upon receipt by the Company of (i) written affirmation by the Person requesting indemnification of its good-faith belief that it has met the standard of conduct necessary for indemnification by the Company and (ii) a written undertaking by or on behalf of such Person to repay such amount if it shall ultimately be determined by a court of competent jurisdiction that such Person has not met such standard of conduct, which undertaking shall be an unlimited general obligation of the indemnified party but need not be secured.

9.3 Insurance. The Company shall have the power to purchase and maintain insurance on behalf of any Person who is or was a Member or an agent of the Company against any liability asserted against such Person and incurred by such Person in any such capacity, or arising out of such Person's status as a Member or an agent of the Company, whether or not the Company would have the power to indemnify such Person against such liability under Section 10.1 or under applicable law.

ARTICLE X

MISCELLANEOUS

10.1 Authority. This Agreement constitutes a legal, valid and binding agreement of the Member, enforceable against the Member in accordance with its terms. The Member is empowered and duly authorized to enter into this Agreement (including the power of attorney herein) under every applicable governing document, partnership agreement, trust instrument, pension plan, charter, certificate of incorporation, bylaw provision or the like. The Person, if any, signing this Agreement on behalf of the Member is empowered and duly authorized to do so by the governing document or trust instrument, pension plan, charter, certificate of incorporation, bylaw provision, board of directors or stockholder resolution or the like.

10.2 Indemnification by the Members. Each Member hereby agrees to indemnify and defend the Company, the other Members and each of their respective employees, agents, partners, members, shareholders, officers and directors and hold them harmless from and against any and all claims, liabilities, damages, costs and expenses (including, without limitation, court costs and attorneys' fees and expenses) suffered or incurred on account of or arising out of any breach of this Agreement by that Member.

ARTICLE XI

DISPUTE RESOLUTION

11.1 Disputes Among Members. The Members agree that in the event of any dispute or disagreement solely between or among any of them arising out of, relating to or in connection with this Agreement or the Company or its organization, formation, business or management ("Member Dispute"), the Members shall use their best efforts to resolve any dispute arising out of or in connection with this Agreement by good-faith negotiation and mutual agreement. The Members shall meet at a mutually convenient time and place to attempt to resolve any such dispute.

However, in the event that the Members are unable to resolve any Member Dispute, such parties shall first attempt to settle such dispute through a non-binding mediation proceeding. In the event any party to such mediation proceeding is not satisfied with the results thereof, then any unresolved disputes shall be finally settled in accordance with an arbitration proceeding. In no event shall the results of any mediation proceeding be admissible in any arbitration or judicial proceeding.

11.2 Mediation. Mediation proceedings shall be conducted in accordance with the Commercial Mediation Rules of the American Arbitration Association (the "AAA") in effect on the date the notice of mediation was served, other than as specifically modified herein, and shall be non-binding on the parties thereto.

Any Member may commence a mediation proceeding by serving written notice thereof to the other Members, by mail or otherwise, designating the issue(s) to be mediated and the specific provisions of this Agreement under which such issue(s) and dispute arose. The initiating party shall simultaneously file two copies of the notice with the AAA, along with a copy of this Agreement. A Member may withdraw from the Member Dispute by signing an agreement to be bound by the results of the mediation, to the extent the mediation results are accepted by the other Members as provided herein. A Member who withdraws shall have no further right to participate in the Member Dispute.

The Members shall select one neutral third party AAA mediator (the "Mediator") with expertise in the area that is in dispute. If a Mediator has not been selected within five (5) business days thereafter, then a Mediator shall be selected by the AAA in accordance with the Commercial Mediation Rules of the AAA.

The Mediator shall schedule sessions, as necessary, for the presentation by all Members of their respective positions, which, at the option of the Mediator, may be heard by the Mediator jointly or in private, without any other members present. The mediation proceeding shall be held in the city that is the company's principal place of business or such other place as agreed by the Mediator and all of the Members. The Members may submit to the Mediator, no later than ten (10) business days prior to the first scheduled session, a brief memorandum in support of their position.

The Mediator shall make written recommendations for settlement in respect of the dispute, including apportionment of the mediator's fee, within ten (10) business days of the last scheduled session. If any Member involved is not satisfied with the recommendation for settlement, he may commence an arbitration proceeding.

11.3 Arbitration. Arbitration proceedings shall be conducted under the Rules of Commercial Arbitration of the AAA (the "Rules"). A Member may withdraw from the Member Dispute by signing an agreement to be bound by the results of the arbitration. A Member who withdraws shall have no further right to participate in the Member Dispute.

The arbitration panel shall consist of one arbitrator. The Members shall select one neutral third party AAA arbitrator (the "Arbitrator") with expertise in the area that is in dispute. If an Arbitrator has not been selected within five (5) business days thereafter, then an Arbitrator shall be selected by the AAA in accordance with the Commercial Arbitration Rules of the AAA. The arbitration proceeding shall be held in the city that is the company's principal place of business or such other place as agreed by the Arbitrator and all of the Members. Any arbitrator who is selected shall disclose promptly to the AAA and to both parties any financial or personal interest the arbitrator may have in the result of the arbitration and/or any other prior or current relationship, or expected or discussed future relationship, with the Members or their representatives. The arbitrator shall promptly conduct proceedings to resolve the dispute in question pursuant to the then existing Rules. To the extent any provisions of the Rules conflict with any provision of this Section, the provisions of this Section shall control.

In any final award and/or order, the arbitrator shall apportion all the costs (other than attorney's fees which shall be borne by the party incurring such fees) incurred in conducting the arbitration in accordance with what the arbitrator deems just and equitable under the circumstances.

Discovery shall not be permitted in such arbitration except as allowed by the rules of arbitration, or as otherwise agreed to by all the parties of the Member Dispute. Notwithstanding, the Members agree to make available to one another and to the arbitrator, for inspection and photocopying, all documents, books and records, if determined by the arbitration panel to be relevant to the dispute, and by making available to one another and to the arbitration panel personnel directly or indirectly under their control, for testimony during hearings if determined by the arbitration panel to be relevant to the dispute. The Members agree, unless undue hardship exists, to conduct arbitration hearings to the greatest extent possible on consecutive business days and to strictly observe time periods established by the Rules or by the arbitrator for the submission of evidence and of briefs. Unless otherwise agreed to by the Members, a stenographic record of the arbitration proceedings shall be made and a transcript thereof shall be ordered for each Member, with each party paying an equal portion of the total cost of such recording and transcription.

The arbitrator shall have all powers of law and equity, which it can lawfully assume, necessary to resolve the issues in dispute including, without limiting the generality of the foregoing, making awards of compensatory damages, issuing both prohibitory and mandatory orders in the nature of injunctions and compelling the production of documents and witnesses for presentation at the arbitration hearings on the merits of the case. The arbitration panel shall neither have nor exercise any power to act as amicable compositeur or ex aequo et bono; or to award special, indirect, consequential or punitive damages. The decision of the arbitration panel shall be in written form and state the reasons upon which it is based. The statutory, case law and common law of the State of Delaware shall govern in interpreting their respective rights, obligations and liabilities arising out of or related to the transactions provided for or contemplated by this Agreement, including without limitation, the validity, construction and performance of all or any portion of this Agreement, and the applicable remedy for any liability established thereunder, and the amount or method of computation of damages which may be awarded, but such governing law shall not include the law pertaining to conflicts or choice of laws of Delaware; provided however, that should the parties refer a dispute arising out of or in connection with an ancillary agreement or an agreement between some or all of the Members which specifically references this Article, then the statutory, case law and common law of the State whose law governs such agreement (except the law pertaining to conflicts or choice of law) shall govern in interpreting the respective rights, obligations and liabilities of the parties arising out of or related to the transactions provided for or contemplated by such agreement, including, without limitation, the validity, construction and performance of all or any portion of such agreement, and the applicable remedy for any liability established thereunder, and the amount or method of computation of damages which may be awarded.

Any action or proceeding subsequent to any Award rendered by the arbitrator in the Member Dispute, including, but not limited to, any action to confirm, vacate, modify, challenge or enforce the arbitrator's decision or award shall be filed in a court of competent jurisdiction in the same county where the arbitration of the Member Dispute was conducted, and Delaware law shall apply in any such subsequent action or proceeding.

ARTICLE XII

MISCELLANEOUS

12.1 Notices. Except as otherwise expressly provided herein, any notice, consent, authorization or other communication to be given hereunder shall be in writing and shall be deemed duly given and received when delivered personally, when transmitted by facsimile if receipt is acknowledged by the addressee, one business day after being deposited for next-day delivery with a nationally recognized overnight delivery service, or three business days after being mailed by first class mail, charges and postage prepaid, properly addressed to the party to receive such notice at the address set forth in the Company's records.

12.2 Severability. If any provision of this Agreement, or the application of such provision to any Person or circumstance, shall be held by a court of competent jurisdiction to be invalid or unenforceable, the remainder of this Agreement, or the application of such provision to Persons or circumstances other than those to which it is held to be invalid or unenforceable, shall not be affected thereby.

12.3 Binding Effect. Subject to Article VII, this Agreement shall bind and inure to the benefit of the parties and their respective Successors.

12.4 Counterparts. This Agreement may be executed in one or more counterparts, each of which shall be deemed an original, but all of which together shall constitute one and the same instrument.

12.5 Entire Agreement. This Agreement contains the entire agreement of the parties and supersedes all prior or contemporaneous written or oral negotiations, correspondence, understandings and agreements between or among the parties, regarding the subject matter hereof.

12.6 Further Assurances. Each Member shall provide such further information with respect to the Member as the Company may reasonably request, and shall execute such other and further certificates, instruments and other documents, as may be necessary and proper to implement, complete and perfect the transactions contemplated by this Agreement.

12.7 Headings; Gender; Number; References. The headings of the Sections hereof are solely for convenience of reference and are not part of this Agreement. As used herein, each gender includes each other gender, the singular includes the plural and vice versa, as the context may require. All references to Sections and subsections are intended to refer to Sections and subsections of this Agreement, except as otherwise indicated.

12.8 Parties in Interest. Except as expressly provided in the Act, nothing in this Agreement shall confer any rights or remedies under or by reason of this Agreement on any Persons other than the Members and their respective Successors nor shall anything in this Agreement relieve or discharge the obligation or liability of any third Person to any party to this Agreement, nor shall any provision give any third Person any right of subrogation or action over or against any party to this Agreement.

12.9 Amendments. All amendments to this Agreement shall be in writing and signed by all of the Members to the agreement at the time of the amendment.

12.10 Attorneys' Fees. In any dispute between or among the Company and one or more of the Members, including, but not limited to, any Member Dispute, the prevailing party or parties in such dispute shall be entitled to recover from the non-prevailing party or parties all reasonable fees, costs and expenses including, without limitation, attorneys' fees, costs and expenses, all of which shall be deemed to have accrued on the commencement of such action, proceeding or arbitration. Attorneys' fees shall include, without limitation, fees incurred in any post-award or post-judgment motions or proceedings, contempt proceedings, garnishment, levy, and debtor and third party examinations, discovery, and bankruptcy litigation, and prevailing party shall mean the party that is determined in the arbitration, action or proceeding to have prevailed or who prevails by dismissal, default or otherwise.

12.11 Remedies Cumulative. Subject to Article XI, remedies under this Agreement are cumulative and shall not exclude any other remedies to which any Member may be lawfully entitled.

12.12 Jurisdiction and Venue/Equitable Remedies. The Company and each Member hereby expressly agrees that if, under any circumstances, any dispute or controversy arising out of or relating to or in any way connected with this Agreement shall, notwithstanding Article XI, be the subject of any court action at law or in equity, such action shall be filed exclusively in the courts of the State of _____ or of the United States of America located in the counties of _____ or _____, as selected by the Member that is the plaintiff in the action, or that initiates the proceeding or arbitration. Each Member agrees not to commence any action, suit or other proceeding arising from, relating to, or in connection with this Agreement except in such a court and each Member irrevocably and unconditionally consents and submits to the personal and exclusive jurisdiction of such courts for the purposes of litigating any such action, and hereby grants jurisdiction to such courts and to any appellate courts having jurisdiction over appeals from such courts or review of such proceedings. Because the breach of the provisions of this Section would cause irreparable harm and significant injury to the Company and the other Members, which would be difficult to ascertain and which may not be compensable by damages alone, each Member agrees that the Company and the other Members will have the right to enforce the provisions of this Section by injunction, specific performance or other equitable relief in addition to any and all other remedies available to such party or parties without showing or proving any actual damage to such parties. Members will be entitled to recover all reasonable costs and expenses, including but not limited to all reasonable attorneys' fees, expert and consultants' fees, incurred in connection with the enforcement of this Section.

IN WITNESS WHEREOF, this Limited Liability Company Operating Agreement has been duly executed by or on behalf of the parties hereto as of the date first above written.

_____   _____

_____   _____

_____   _____

_____   _____

_____   _____

Appendix E

Sample Funding and Withdrawal Forms

In this appendix, we reproduce a number of contracts and forms that are useful in forming and operating a business with a maximum level of asset protection. From the earliest agreement to start a company to ways to remove valuable assets from a growing business, these forms cover the most popular strategies and gives clues as to how best to structure your operation. Equipment leases and various financing arrangements are also covered, allowing you the greatest protections under the law.

Warning

Some of these forms contain technical language and create significant legal obligations. Do not use any form without first having an attorney review the form and determine that it is suitable for the purpose for which you intend it.

The following form might be used when two or more individuals decide to form a business entity together. Sometimes, parties will not follow-through on their promises, and thus fail to contribute anything toward the cost of forming the entity, or fail to contribute any capital to the entity. Without the sharing of costs, or additional capital that was expected, formation or operation of the business may not be feasible.

While this agreement is relatively simple, it may make someone reconsider such a decision, or give the other party recourse in the event that this is the outcome. An operating agreement still should be executed after the entity is formed.

Sample Agreement To Form Business Entity

The undersigned parties hereby agree to form a _____ (specify type of business entity), in the state of _____, primarily for the following purposes: _____

The principal place of business is planned to be in _____

Upon formation of said entity, each of the parties intends to make the following amount and type of contribution, in exchange for the type of interest that is identified:

Name_____ Type and Value of Contribution. Specify Equity (Voting Capital or Nonvoting Capital) Interest or Debt Interest; and a description of the assets or services to be contributed, and the agreed value, for each type of interest: _____

Name_____ Type and Value of Contribution. Specify Equity (Voting Capital or Nonvoting Capital) Interest or Debt Interest; and a description of the assets or services to be contributed, and the agreed value, for each type of interest: _____

Name_____ Type and Value of Contribution. Specify Equity (Voting Capital or Nonvoting Capital) Interest or Debt Interest; and a description of the assets or services to be contributed, and the agreed value, for each type of interest: _____

Name_____ Type and Value of Contribution. Specify Equity (Voting Capital or Nonvoting Capital) Interest or Debt Interest; and a description of the assets or services to be contributed, and the agreed value, for each type of interest: _____

The costs of forming said entity, including, but not limited to, attorney's fees, fees paid to the state of formation, and initial foreign registration and fictitious name fees, shall be apportioned among the undersigned parties in the following manner, irrespective as to whether the entity is actually formed: _____

Each of the parties agrees to pay his proportional share of said costs. Each party shall be entitled to be reimbursed by the business entity for such payment, after the entity is formed.

Additional understandings among the parties (describe): _____

_____

Each of the parties acknowledges that the parties are relying on the reciprocal promises made herein in deciding to form the above-described business entity. A party who breaches this agreement shall be liable for the costs the non-breaching parties incur in enforcing this Agreement, including, but not limited to, attorney's fees and court costs, in addition to any other form of damages.

_____

_____

_____

_____

Printed Names and Signatures   Date

Every action by a business entity should be properly authorized and documented. This simple form can accomplish these purposes. It is especially appropriate for use with the Sample Operating Agreement for a Delaware LLC that appears in Appendix D.

Sample Action by Voting Members/Managers

The undersigned, being all of the Voting Members and Managers of _____
do hereby take the following action:

_____

_____

_____

_____

_____

_____

_____

_____

_____

_____

Printed Names and Signatures   *Date*

The following Sample Security Agreement can be used to accomplish one of the strategies advocated in this book—funding the business entity (the operating entity) partly with debt, and encumbering the entity's assets with liens that secure the debt and run to the holding entity or to the owner personally. In this way, even the owner's equity interest may be protected. To accomplish these purposes, the owner personally (or his holding entity) would be the secured party, and the operating entity would be the borrower. The agreement is very broad, applying to *all existing and future extensions of credit, in any form.*

This form might be first executed in conjunction with the Sample Open-Ended Promissory Note, which also follows, but this is not necessary. If a promissory note was not executed because the form first secured some other obligation (e.g., unpaid salary), the reference to a "Promissory Note" in paragraph 1 should be deleted, and a description of the other obligation should be substituted in its place. (Of course, a promissory note might be used to accrue interest on an obligation such as unpaid salary).

This Sample Security Agreement normally should be perfected by the execution and filing of the Sample UCC1 Financing Statement, which follows this form. Note that each state has its own version of the

UCC1 financing statement. Some states will accept a generic form, but charge extra for this, while other states accept only their prescribed form. It is recommended that the particular state's actual UCC1 financing statement form be used. This form can be obtained through the appropriate state's secretary of state's office, where the form also usually is filed.

Sample Open-Ended Security Agreement

THIS OPEN-ENDED SECURITY AGREEMENT ("Agreement") is made and effective this _____, by and between _____ ("Borrower"), and _____ ("Secured Party").

Borrower hereby grants to the Secured Party a security interest in certain property ("Collateral") of Borrower to secure such obligations as now are owed, and such obligations as in the future may be owed, by Borrower to the Secured Party. The Borrower and the Secured Party expressly agree that this Agreement shall automatically govern all existing obligations that the Borrower owes to the Secured Party, and all future obligations, in any form, from the Secured Party to the Borrower, without further action by either party, and without express reference to such obligations in this Agreement or in such obligations.

Secured Party and Borrower further agree as follows:

1. The following described property, together with all additions and substitutions to such property, and all proceeds therefrom, shall constitute the Collateral for this Agreement:

all inventory, equipment, appliances, furnishings, and fixtures now or hereafter placed upon the premises known as _____, located at _____, _____ (the "Premises") or used in connection therewith and in which Borrower now has or hereafter acquires any right. As additional collateral, Borrower assigns to Secured Party, a security interest in all of its right, title, and interest to any trademarks, trade names, contract rights, and leasehold interests which it now has or hereafter acquires. The Security Interest shall secure the payment and performance of Borrower's promissory note of even date herewith in the principal amount of _____ ($_____) Dollars and the payment and performance of all other liabilities and obligations of Borrower to Secured Party of every kind and description, direct or indirect, absolute or contingent, due or to become due now existing or hereafter arising.

2. Borrower shall keep and maintain, at its expense, complete records of the Collateral. Secured Party shall have the right at any time and from time to time, without notice, to call at Borrower's place of business during normal business hours to inspect the Collateral and to inspect the correspondence, books, and records of Borrower relating to the Collateral.

3. Borrower represents and warrants to Secured Party that, with respect to the Collateral, Borrower possesses and shall possess at all times while this Security Agreement is in effect, full, complete and unencumbered title to such goods, subject only to Secured Party's security interest hereunder, and liens, if any, for current taxes, assessments and other governmental charges are not delinquent; that the Collateral shall be kept at _____, and Borrower shall not change the location of the Collateral without the prior written consent of Secured Party; that Borrower shall not at any time cause or suffer any part of the Collateral, or any interest in any of Collateral to be subject to any Security Interest other than that of Secured Party, except upon the written consent of the Secured Party; that Borrower shall defend the Collateral against the claims and demands of all persons other than Secured Party; that Borrower shall at all times promptly pay and discharge, at Borrower's expense, all taxes, assessments and other governmental charges which constitute or may become liens on the Collateral; that, at the request of Secured Party, at any time, Borrower shall execute such financing statements and other documents, pay such filing, recording and other fees, and do or cause to be done such other acts or things as Secured Party deems reasonably necessary to establish, perfect, and continue its security interest hereunder; and that Borrower shall pay all costs, expenses, charges and other obligations, including, without limitation, reasonable attorneys' fees, suffered or incurred by Secured Party to protect, preserve, maintain and obtain possession of or title to the Collateral, to perfect, protect, preserve and maintain the security interest granted by this Security Agreement, and to enforce or assert any one or more of its rights, powers, remedies and defenses under this Security Agreement.

4. Borrower shall be in default under this Security Agreement if Borrower fails timely to observe and perform any covenants, conditions or agreements required to be observed or performed by Borrower under this Security Agreement, or if Borrower defaults upon any material promise in the obligation. At any time upon or following the occurrence of one or more of the events of default, Secured Party may, at its option, assert or avail itself of any one or more of the rights, powers, remedies and defenses conferred upon Secured Party under the Uniform Commercial Code and other laws of the State of _____, which laws shall generally govern the construction and interpretation of this Agreement, or assert or avail itself of any one or more of the rights, powers, remedies and defenses conferred upon Secured Party under any other appropriate law or regulation, whether federal or state. Any and all proceeds resulting from the disposition of all or any part of the Collateral following the occurrence of one or more events of default shall be applied to pay and provide for the Obligations of Borrower to Secured Party, with any balance remaining to be paid to Borrower or its successors and assigns, as their respective interests may appear.

5. The invalidity or unenforceability of any provision in this Agreement shall not cause any other provision to be invalid or unenforceable.

6. This Agreement constitutes the final agreement and understanding between the parties on the subject matter hereof and supersedes all prior understandings or agreements whether oral or written. This Agreement may be modified only by a further writing that is duly executed by both parties.

Borrower and Secured Party have executed this Security Agreement on the date first above written.

Borrower _____

By: _____ *Name/Title*

Secured Party _____

*When recorded/filed, return to:*_____

_____

Sample Uniform Commercial Code Financing Statement

1. Name of Debtor: _____

Address of Debtor: _____

_____

2. Name of Secured Party: _____

Address of Secured Party: _____

_____

3. This Financing Statement covers the following types (or items) of property:

(Describe) _____

_____

4. Check here ____ if collateral is crops. The above described crops are growing or are to be grown on (Describe real estate): _____.

5. (Check here ____ if collateral is goods which are or are to become fixtures, timber to cut, or minerals or the like (including oil and gas) or accounts to be financed at the wellhead or minehead of the well or mine). The legal description of the real estate is: _____

_____

and this Financing Statement is to be filed in the office where a mortgage on the real estate would be recorded. If the debtor does not have an interest of record, the name of the record owner is: _____.

6. Proceeds and products of collateral are also covered.

_____

Signature of Secured Party

_____

Signature of Debtor

The following form should be used when the owner (or his holding entity) lends money, or otherwise extends credit (e.g., unpaid salary), to the operating entity. It also can be used whenever the owner or his holding entity *extends any type of credit* to the operating entity *in the future,* if the extension of credit specifically incorporates the note.

Sample Open-Ended Promissory Note

The undersigned (the "Borrower") promises to pay to the order of _____ (the "Lender") the sum of _____ ($)
Dollars, together with interest thereon at the rate of _____ % per annum on the unpaid balance.

This Note is executed in return for the following extension of credit from the Lender to the Borrower:

The Borrower and Lender agree that this Note shall automatically govern any future extension of credit, in any form, from the Lender to the Borrower, if such future extension of credit expressly states that it is subject to this Note.

The principal and interest shall be payable as follows (state whether payment is On Demand, or state payment terms):

All payments shall be first applied to interest and late charges, and the balance to principal. This note may be prepaid, at any time, in whole or in part, without penalty. This note shall be at the option of any holder thereof immediately due and payable upon the occurrence of any of the following: Failure to make any payment due hereunder within on or before its due date; breach of any condition of any security interest, mortgage, loan agreement, pledge agreement or guarantee granted as collateral security for this note; breach of any condition of any loan agreement, security agreement or mortgage, if any, having a priority over any loan agreement, security agreement or mortgage on collateral granted, in whole or in part, as collateral security for this note; upon the death, incapacity, dissolution or liquidation of any of the undersigned, or any endorser, guarantor or surety hereto; upon the filing by any of the undersigned of an assignment for the benefit of creditors, bankruptcy or other form of insolvency, or by suffering an involuntary petition in bankruptcy or receivership not vacated within thirty (30) days.

In the event this note shall not be in default and placed for collection, then the undersigned agree to pay all reasonable attorney fees and costs of collection. Payments not made within five (5) days of the due date shall be subject to a late charge of _____ % of said payment. All payments hereunder shall be made to such address as may from time to time be designated by any holder.

The undersigned and all other parties to this note, whether as endorsers, guarantors or sureties, agree to remain fully bound until this note shall be fully paid and waive demand, presentment and protest and all notices hereto and further agree to remain bound notwithstanding any extension, modification, waiver, or other indulgence or discharge or release of any obligor hereunder or exchange, substitution, or release of any collateral granted as security for this note. No modification or indulgence by any holder hereof shall be binding unless in writing; and any indulgence on any one occasion shall not be an indulgence for any other or future occasion. Any modification or change in terms, hereunder granted by any holder hereof, shall be valid and binding upon each of the undersigned, notwithstanding the acknowledgment of any of the undersigned, and each of the undersigned does hereby irrevocably grant to each of the others a power of attorney to enter into any such modification on their behalf. The rights of any holder hereof shall be cumulative and not necessarily successive. This note shall take effect as a sealed instrument and shall be construed, governed and enforced in accordance with the laws of the State of _____.

The Borrower may prepay this Note in whole or in part without penalty. In the event any payment due hereunder is not paid when due, the entire balance shall be immediately due and payable upon demand of the holder. Upon default, the undersigned shall pay all reasonable attorney fees and costs necessary for the collection of this Note.

Signed under seal this _____ day of _____, 20___.

_____

By:_____

Name/Title

The following form might be used when the business owner seeks to personally own "tools of the trade" and lease the same to the operating entity to preserve an exemption; or when the intent is for the holding entity to own the assets, and lease the same to the operating entity, to reduce the exposure to liability.

Sample Equipment Lease

THIS EQUIPMENT LEASE ("Lease") is made and effective _____, by and between _____ (the "Lessor") and _____(the "Lessee").

1. Lessor hereby leases to Lessee, and Lessee hereby leases from Lessor, the following described equipment (the "Equipment"): _____

_____

2. The term of this Lease shall commence on _____ and shall expire on _____.

3. The monthly rent for the Equipment shall be paid in advance in installments of _____ ($) dollars each month, beginning on _____, and on the first day of each succeeding month throughout the term hereof, at _____, or at such other place as Lessor may designate from time to time. Any installment payment not made by the tenth (10th) day of the month shall be considered overdue and in addition to Lessor's other remedies, Lessor may levy a late payment charge equal to one percent (1%) per month on any overdue amount. Rent for any partial month shall be prorated.

4. Lessee shall pay a security deposit in the following amount prior to taking possession of the Equipment: _____ ($) dollars . The security deposit will be refunded to Lessee promptly following Lessee's performance of all obligations in this Lease.

5. Lessee shall use the Equipment in a careful and proper manner and shall comply with and conform to all national, state, municipal, police and other laws, ordinances and regulations in any way relating to the possession, use or maintenance of the Equipment.

6.   Lessor disclaims any and all other warranties, express or implied, including but not limited to implied warranties of merchantability and fitness for a particular purpose, except that lessor warrants that lessor has the right to lease the equipment, as provided in this lease.

7. Lessee, at its own cost and expense, shall keep the Equipment in good repair, condition and working order and shall furnish any and all parts, mechanisms and devices required to keep the Equipment in good mechanical working order.

8. Lessee hereby assumes and shall bear the entire risk of loss and damage to the Equipment from any and every cause whatsoever. No loss or damage to the Equipment or any part thereof shall impair any obligation of Lessee under this Lease, which shall continue in full force and effect through the term of the Lease. In the event of loss or damage of any kind whatever to the Equipment, Lessee shall, at Lessor's option: Place the same in good repair, condition and working order; or replace the same with like equipment in good repair, condition and working order; or pay to Lessor the replacement cost of the Equipment.

9. Upon the expiration or earlier termination of this Lease, Lessee shall return the Equipment to Lessor in good repair, condition and working order, ordinary wear and tear resulting from proper use thereof alone excepted, by delivering the Equipment at Lessee's cost and expense to such place as Lessor shall specify within the city or county in which the same was delivered to Lessee.

10. Lessee shall procure and continuously maintain and pay for all risk insurance against loss of and damage to the Equipment for not less than the full replacement value of the Equipment, naming Lessor as loss payee, and combined public liability and property damage insurance with limits as approved by Lessor, naming Lessor as additionally named insured and a loss payee. The insurance shall be in such form and with such company or companies as shall be reasonably acceptable to Lessor, shall provide at least thirty (30) days advance written notice to Lessor of any cancellation, change or modification, and shall provide primary coverage for the protection of Lessee and Lessor without regard to any other coverage carried by Lessee or Lessor protecting against similar risks. Lessee shall provide Lessor with an original policy or certificate evidencing such insurance. Lessee hereby appoints Lessor as Lessee's attorney in fact with power and authority to do all things, including, but not limited to, making claims, receiving payments and endorsing documents, checks or drafts necessary or advisable to secure payments due under any policy of insurance required under this Agreement.

11. Lessee shall keep the Equipment free and clear of all levies, liens and encumbrances. Lessee, or Lessor at Lessee's expense, shall report, pay and discharge when due all license and registration fees, assessments, sales, use and property taxes, gross receipts, taxes arising out of receipts from use or operation of the Equipment, and other taxes, fees and governmental charges similar or dissimilar to the foregoing, together with any penalties or interest thereon, imposed by any state, federal or local government or any agency, or department thereof, upon the Equipment or the purchase, use, operation or leasing of the Equipment or otherwise in any manner with respect thereto and whether or not the same shall be assessed against or in the name of Lessor or Lessee. However, Lessee shall not be required to pay or discharge any such tax or assessment so long as it shall, in good faith and by appropriate legal proceedings, contest the validity thereof in any reasonable manner which will not affect or endanger the title and interest of Lessor to the Equipment; provided, Lessee shall reimburse Lessor for any damages or expenses resulting from such failure to pay or discharge.

12. In case of failure of Lessee to procure or maintain said insurance or to pay fees, assessments, charges and taxes, all as specified in this Lease, Lessor shall have the right, but shall not be obligated, to effect such insurance, or pay said fees, assignments, charges and taxes, as the case may be. In that event, the cost thereof shall be repayable to Lessor with the next installment of rent, and failure to repay the same shall carry with it the same consequences, including interest at ten percent (10%) per annum, as failure to pay any installment of rent.

13. Lessee shall indemnify Lessor against, and hold Lessor harmless from, any and all claims, actions, suits, proceedings, costs, expenses, damages and liabilities, including reasonable attorney's fees and costs, arising out of, connected with, or resulting from Lessee's use of the Equipment, including without limitation the manufacture, selection, delivery, possession, use, operation, or return of the Equipment.

14. If Lessee fails to pay any rent or other amount herein provided within ten (10) days after the same is due and payable, or if Lessee fails to observe, keep or perform any other provision of this Lease required to be observed, kept or performed by Lessee, Lessor shall have the right to exercise any one or more of the following remedies: To declare the entire amount of rent hereunder immediately due and payable without notice or demand to Lessee; to sue for and recover all rents, and other payments, then accrued or thereafter accruing; to take possession of the Equipment, without demand or notice, wherever same may be located, without any court order or other process of law; to terminate this Lease; to pursue any other remedy at law or in equity.

Lessee hereby waives any and all damages occasioned by such taking of possession. Notwithstanding any repossession or any other action which Lessor may take, Lessee shall be and remain liable for the full performance of all obligations on the part of the Lessee to be performed under this Lease. All of Lessor's remedies are cumulative, and may be exercised concurrently or separately.

15. Neither this Lease nor any interest therein is assignable or transferable by operation of law. If any proceeding under the Bankruptcy Act, as amended, is commenced by or against the Lessee, or if the Lessee is adjudged insolvent, or if Lessee makes any assignment for the benefit of his creditors, or if a writ of attachment or execution is levied on the Equipment and is not released or satisfied within ten (10) days thereafter, or if a receiver is appointed in any proceeding or action to which the Lessee is a party with authority to take possession or control of the Equipment, Lessor shall have and may exercise any one or more of the remedies set forth in Section 14 hereof; and this Lease shall, at the option of the Lessor, without notice, immediately terminate and shall not be treated as an asset of Lessee after the exercise of said option.

16. The Equipment is, and shall at all times be and remain, the sole and exclusive property of Lessor; and the Lessee shall have no right, title or interest therein or thereto except as expressly set forth in this Lease.

17. If Lessor shall so request, Lessee shall execute and deliver to Lessor such documents as Lessor shall deem necessary or desirable for purposes of recording or filing to protect the interest of Lessor in the Equipment including, but not limited to a UCC financing statement.

18. Lessee shall not assign this Lease or its interest in the Equipment without the prior written consent of Lessor.

19. The invalidity or unenforceability of any provision in this Agreement shall not cause any other provision to be invalid or unenforceable.

20. This Lease shall be construed and enforced according to laws of the State of _____. This instrument constitutes the entire agreement between the parties on the subject matter hereof and it shall not be amended, altered or changed except by a further writing signed by the parties hereto.

The parties hereto have executed this Lease as of the day and year first above written.

Lessee _____

By: _____

    Name/Title

Lessor _____

This form can be used to quickly remove valuable receivables from the operating entity. Cash paid to the operating entity for the receivables is then quickly withdrawn as payments to the owner (or the holding entity) as salary, rents, loan payments, etc.

Sample Assignment of Accounts Receivable with Recourse

For the sum of _____ ($ ____) dollars, _____ (the "Assignor") hereby sells and transfers all right, title and interest in and to the accounts receivable that are identified in the attached schedule to _____ (the "Assignee").

The Assignor warrants that said accounts are just and due and the Assignor has not received payment for same or any part thereof; and that if any said account does not make full payment within _____ (____) days, said accounts may be re-transferred to the Assignor and the Assignor shall re-purchase same for the balance then owing on said accounts.

Date: _____

Assignor _____

By: _____

    Name/Title

Assignee _____

Index

. . . *Formulating and Writing an Effective Business Plan?*

Business Plans That Work for Your Small Business now in its second edition- clearly translates complicated marketing and financial concepts into down-to-earth practical advice, explains all the essential elements and formulas, and offers concrete examples throughout. Five newly developed sample plans from real small businesses provide readers with the blueprints for their own plans, as well as a wealth of detailed information about how a successful small business should operate.

This book will appeal not only to budding entrepreneurs who are planning a new venture on paper to see whether it will fly, but also to new or existing business owners who need a business plan document as part of a business loan application, and to established owners who want to create a plan for internal use.

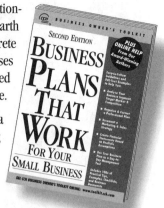

304 pages / Book No. 0-5246-200   **$19.⁹⁵***

$19.95*

. . . *Making the Government Your Best Customer?*

All government contracts under $100,000 are targeted to small businesses.
Win Government Contracts for Your Small Business—now fully updated in its second edition—will show you how to get in on the action in just 10 easy-to-understand steps. By following our practical advice, you'll be accurately listed in the federal procurement system, allowing you to start receiving bids right away.

In this book you'll learn the simple most important step to take before you start bidding, where to find government buyers, the best source of bid leads for you and your company, how to write a winning proposal, listings of essential web sites, and how to use the Internet to your advantage. All together, this is the only book that covers, step-by-step and in detail, how to successfully compete for government contracts— and make more money for your small business.

$19.⁹⁵*   *506 pages / Book No. 0-5352-300*

. . . *Securing the Necessary Financing for Your Business?*

Small Business Financing: How and Where To Get It, now in its newly revised second edition, thoroughly but simply discusses each source of debt and equity capital, whether public or private—from bookstrapping and IPOs to commercial loans and SBA- guaranteed programs, and everything in between. This book covers methods for determining the amount of capital needed, choosing an appropriate source and type of financing, selecting a business form, and planning successful applications or presentations.

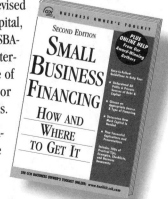

Sample forms are integrated into the text to facilitate learning the details and the data-gathering skills needed for the financing process. A handy glossary is included to take the mystery out of dealing with bankers and other financial professionals.

224 pages / Book No. 0-5142-200   **$17.⁹⁵***

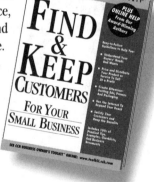